READINGS IN

SOCIAL PSYCHOLOGY

READINGS IN

SOCIAL PSYCHOLOGY

Alfred R. Lindesmith
Indiana University

Anselm L. Strauss
University of California
San Francisco

HOLT, RINEHART AND WINSTON
New York   Chicago   San Francisco   Atlanta   Dallas
Montreal   Toronto   London   Sydney

Copyright © 1969 by Holt Rinehart and Winston, Inc.
All rights reserved
Library of Congress Catalog Card Number: 76–81179
SBN: 03–081400–6
Printed in the United States of America
0123 17 98765432

PREFACE

THIS BOOK OF SELECTED READINGS is designed primarily for use in conjunction with our textbook, *Social Psychology*, as a means of broadening and enriching the perspective of beginning students in the field of social psychology. We have keyed the selections to specific chapters in the text to increase their usefulness as supplementary materials and to facilitate the work of teachers introducing social psychology to their students. For the students themselves, these readings will provide a challenge and stimulus to further study through a deeper appreciation of the promise and problems of social psychology as developed in the text and as they exist throughout the entire field.

The field of social psychology, dealing as it does with the most complex forms of human behavior and interaction, admittedly is far from satisfactorily integrated into a cohesive body of knowledge: it is characterized by fragmentary theories, conflicting ideologies, changing intellectual fashions and fads, and eclecticism. In this situation, our choice has been to present as systematically and persuasively as possible a single view of the nature of human social behavior—one that appeals to us and to many other social psychologists, and appears to do the greatest justice to the subtlety and complexity of human conduct. This general orientation—known as "symbolic interactionism" or, more simply, "interactionism"—does justice also to the complex relationships that exist between social structure on the one hand, and the behavior and interactions of individuals on the other.

In selecting the readings presented in this volume, we have extended our conviction, as expressed in the theme of *Social Psychology*, that the basic

challenge of social psychology is to understand how countless fluid and changing relationships among individuals with unique personalities and backgrounds
can fit together in a complex but nevertheless structured and orderly society.

Alfred R. Lindesmith
Bloomington, Indiana

Anselm L. Strauss
San Francisco, California

July 1969

CONTENTS

INTRODUCTION

A BASIC IDEA IN THE INTERACTIONIST ORIENTATION is that man is the only language-manipulating animal; this fact is of decisive and central importance in the analysis of those forms of human behavior that are unique to man and that set him apart from other animals. Language is considered as the basic human institution, which is at once a product and a precondition of complex group life; it is both a part of the social heritage and the means by which this heritage is transmitted. The influence of language permeates and makes possible the great cultural achievements of man, represented in his intellectual, artistic, political, scientific, technological, philosophic, and religious creations. The basic argument might be said to be that the invention of language has elevated man to his troubled eminence in the animal world. The basic scientific problem is to trace the far-reaching consequences of this potent invention in the day-to-day lives of people, in the activities of social groups, and in the workings of organizations and institutions.

We prefer not to think of this intellectual position as a "school of thought," founded primarily on the work of George Herbert Mead and other founding fathers and propagated now by a dedicated band of disciples. This attitude seems both stultifying and inappropriate: it tends to focus attention on the past rather than on the present and the future; it encourages exegesis rather than creative research and useful theory. We would therefore ask our readers not to consider the symbolic interaction position as a school of thought but as a loosely structured cluster of fundamental ideas—a general image of man not confined to a single discipline and not limited by geographical boundaries.

Symbolic interactionism is an open system that is in process of change, not a set of dogmas inherited from sages of the past. The challenge is not that of determining whether the inherited ideas are right or wrong, but rather of applying and using them in new and creative ways, qualifying or discarding them as the evidence requires. It is true, of course, that any general theory of social psychology must stand or fall on the evidence produced by research that it suggests or stimulates. From this standpoint there is no established general theory of human behavior. To develop it is one of the great challenges facing our contemporaries and successors.

In consequence, we have selected articles for inclusion in this book on the basis of the ideas they present and the relevance of those ideas to our position. As always in preparing books of this kind, there was far too much material for the available space; therefore, we were compelled to make hard choices and arbitrary decisions when making our selections. The final product is thus only a sampling of a larger universe. Many authors represented here are sociologists. While some undoubtedly have been influenced by the Meadian tradition, probably very few if any can be adequately or correctly characterized as disciples of Mead. The selections represent a considerable number of other disciplines, including general, comparative and child psychology, linguistics, anthropology, philosophy, psychiatry, and neurology. Since undergraduate students probably are (and should be) more effectively motivated by interesting ideas than by methodological brilliance, we have not included any selections solely to illustrate research techniques. Their study belongs to a phase of concentration that should come later in the careers of students who decide to do advanced work in social psychology. However, there is no dearth of research materials among these readings: a substantial portion consists either of research reports or of general statements of positions derived from an author's research—in some cases from a lifetime of research. A small number of the selections are valuable exploratory studies, or are concerned with the analysis or elucidation of significant concepts.

We hope and believe that our system of selection, as opposed to one that might have concentrated more exclusively on the writings of sociologists in the Meadian tradition, will result in more stimulating reading for both students and instructors, and will serve as an antidote to any tendency of this tradition to become crystallized into a body of doctrine. Some readers may be encouraged, we would hope, to follow some of the leads suggested by the materials, even if their paths should take them into new and unfamiliar areas currently exploited by disciplines other than sociology. Surely it is vital to any theoretical scheme that it should remain open and ready to assimilate relevant contributions from fields other than those to which it seems usually to pertain.

The contributions by Soviet writers included in this volume deserve special comment, and may be of particular interest to those who are familiar with the work of Pavlov and his influence on American psychologists. Pavlov, of course, is known primarily for his elaboration of the idea of conditioned reflexes and for his experimental work with dogs. During his later years, however, he devoted some attention to the study of human subjects and developed the idea of the "second signalling system," which consists of language behavior. This system he contrasted with the "first signalling system," which consists simply of sensory stimulation. He suggested that lower animals operate solely within this first system while the second signalling system is the unique possession of man—basic to all of his specifically human attributes. This idea of Pavlov's has not been picked up by American psychologists, but did receive attention from a considerable number of Soviet psychologists who have produced a body of research publication that closely relates to the viewpoint reflected in our text and in the present book. Two outstanding representatives of this Soviet tradition are Luria and Vygotsky, both of whom are becoming increasingly well known to American psychologists. As far as we know, these Soviet scholars make no reference to, and were evidently uninfluenced by, American writing that derived from Mead or John Dewey. It is of interest that the Soviet researchers, like the Meadian social psychologists in the United States, also have been intrigued by and paid close attention to the work of the Swiss psychologist Jean Piaget. The latter's work is now enjoying widespread and increased attention in this country. We gave considerable attention to his writings in the first edition of our textbook, published approximately twenty years ago.

It may seem curious to some readers that there should be included in this book of readings an article by a neurologist, Henry Head, author of a classical study on aphasia. However, a reading of this article, and those by Luria as well, will indicate that aphasia is a research area of extraordinary interest and relevance to those social psychologists who are concerned with brain mechanisms and functions, which are preconditions of the higher mental activities of human beings. Aphasia is not only an area of extraordinary intrinsic interest but also provides striking evidence of the complex and pervasive influences of language mechanisms on almost all of the activities in which humans engage. Most social psychologists, not being in a position to do their own research on this subject, must of necessity rely for their knowledge of it on the work of scholars from other disciplines.

Another subject, which seems to us to be of great intrinsic interest and to present an unusual challenge to behavioral scientists in general, is that of hypnotism. This phenomenon definitely exists, even though one gathers from the writings of some authors that they almost wish it did not. The subject has been tarnished by charlatans and exploited by entertainers, and it has proved to be extremely recalcitrant to theoretical explanation, as Eysenck, a psychologist, makes very clear in one of the selections in this volume. The phenomenon of hypnotism, like that of aphasia, provides a fertile and not fully explored possibility for a more profound understanding of the nature of human behavior and of the role of language in shaping and controlling it. Here again the student is invited to use this volume as a point of departure for a more thorough and inclusive examination of a phenomenon.

One of the most difficult problems of the social psychologist is to work out ways and means for dealing with the individual's world of inner experience, with how he thinks of himself and his body, and how he interprets sensations and occurrences that originate or take place inside of himself. To illustrate how this kind of inner experience has been handled, we have included two articles that pertain to a subject of intense current interest—the effects of drugs—authored by sociologists Becker and Lindesmith. Both men have published studies of drug users that are frequently referred to, but, as far as we know, no sociologist has identified either study as belonging within the symbolic interaction tradition. The articles are included here not only for their interest and for their relevance to inner experience but to correct this oversight, which probably springs from too narrow a conception of the symbolic interactionist position: equating the position only with two basic concepts, those of self and role.

Other substantive areas that are represented in the readings and are worthy of special comment are the following: medical sociology as dealt with in papers by Glaser, Davis, Schatzman and Bucher, and Strauss; and sociolinguistics as represented by materials from Fishman and Bernstein. These are areas that have received increasing attention from sociologists in recent years, and from which significant contributions are being made to the literature and theory of social psychology. The popular subject of deviance is represented by three articles authored by Wilkins, Tannebaum, and Davis; and mass communications by articles written by Klapp and by Horton and Wohl. Another topic of special interest to sociologists is interaction: several research papers pertain to interaction, including ones by Goffman, Davis, and Schatzman and Bucher. The three related areas of disorganization, conflict, and change are represented by excerpts from the writings of Schaw and of Lifton.

Numerous other subjects and authors come to our minds as worthy candidates for inclusion in this volume. Limitations of space and our own restricted objectives made it necessary to exclude some of them, and to content ourselves with a sampling of both subjects and authors that would effectively serve the use to which we expect the volume to be put; namely, the teaching of undergraduate students. Since we have concerned ourselves with the presentation of one general orientation toward social psychology that is current primarily among sociologically trained social psychologists, we anticipate these readings will be used mainly in courses taught by sociologists. By the same token, we have not included articles to represent different and competing theoretical positions, of which there are many. To do justice to all of these positions would have been impossible. (Freudian theory alone, in its many versions and ramifications, would have required at least a volume of its own.) Indeed, we are inclined to feel somewhat uneasy about whether we have done full justice to the single theoretical perspective to which we confined ourselves. Others faced with this same task no doubt would have made very different selections. We are, however, convinced of the general usefulness and interest of this array of readings.

In general, they parallel the major parts in the textbook rather than the individual chapters themselves. The parts are five in number: Statement of Position; Symbolic Processes: Nature and Setting; Differentiation and Internalization; Socialization and Interaction; and Deviance. Each is briefly introduced in this volume at appropriate places. Not all materials touched on in the text are given equal coverage here, but we have chosen with some deliberation so as to suggest the main thrust of each section in the text. Readers who wish to know how each selection is keyed to the text should refer to the source footnote of each selection. (A few of these readings have been extensively discussed in the text.) If appetites are whetted by these materials, readers will also find suggestions for further reading in the bibliographies printed in the text.

PART I

STATEMENT OF POSITION

SOCIAL PSYCHOLOGY IS CONCERNED with the behavior and psychological processes of individuals
who occupy positions in social structures, organizations, and groups. On the one hand, social
psychology is focused upon explaining the behavior of individuals as it is controlled, influenced,
or limited by the social environment. On the
other hand, it is concerned with the manner in
which the behavior of individuals reacts upon,
shapes, and alters social structures and enters into
the functioning of groups.

There are three rather separate approaches to
social psychology as reflected in the actual work
of sociologists, psychologists, and anthropologists.
To sociologists, social psychology has meant a
field directed toward several problems that are
central to sociology. "Socialization" is one such
problem: the processes by means of which both
children and adults are incorporated into groups
of all types and by means of which the norms,
perspectives, and values of such groups are acquired by the individual. Another central problem
in sociology is interaction. In its broadest sense
this term refers to the way people act toward or
communicate with each other as individuals or
groups within social contexts. The study of interaction is essential for understanding how groups,
institutions, or social structures manage to function; how they maintain their existence and control internal dissension and conflict; how they

change but manage to persist; and how they may disintegrate and disappear as functioning units.

The general position taken in this Reader is known as "symbolic interactionism." Symbolic interactionism emphasizes the symbolic or communicative aspects of human behavior plus the importance of social structure. The distinctive attributes of human behavior, which grow from man's participation in varying types of social structures, depend in turn upon the existence of language behavior or the creation and manipulation of high-order signs. Interaction between and among humans is viewed as a symbolic interaction. In its most obvious aspects it involves spoken or written language, but even in its nonverbal forms the interaction involves levels of meaning that could not exist without complex symbols. The specific forms, directions, and outcomes of interaction depend very much on who the interactants happen to be. Their membership in given social groups or structures makes them carriers of sets of symbols—otherwise known as beliefs, attitudes, perspectives, and so on. Their membership has also made them who they are in terms of their personal commitments and allegiances. In interaction they may act self-consciously as representatives of given groups, institutions, or organizations; even action at its most personal is symbolic, as it is grounded in social memberships.

Whether a sociologist studies particular plans of an individual or concerted action of an organization and its division of labor, his analysis necessarily makes central the symbolic structures and processes that guide and coordinate action. He is interested in aspects of social structure that enter into the observed interaction—that enter not as crude determinants of that action but as elements that profoundly affect its form, direction, and outcome.

Both social structure and symbolic interaction are necessarily in continual transformation. Interaction at the symbolic level is a creative process in which new meanings and unforeseen contingencies are constantly created by new situations and by the endless permutations and enormous flexibility of the symbolic processes themselves. The social psychologist must thus be simultaneously concerned with (1) stability and change, (2) established forms and norms and the emergence of new ones, (3) conformity and deviance, and (4) social structure and personal freedom.

The readings in the section illustrate these themes. Mead, Glaser and Strauss, and Klapp write in the symbolic interaction tradition. Dewey, like Mead, was a pragmatist—a philosophical position with which symbolic interactionism was closely allied in its earliest years. Luria is a Soviet psychologist whose work on high-order signs brings post-Pavlovian research into close conjunction with certain aspects of symbolic interactionism.

1

MIND, SELF, AND SOCIETY

George H. Mead

IN THE STUDY OF THE EXPERIENCE AND BEHAVIOR of the individual organism or self in its dependence upon the social group to which it belongs, we find a definition of the field of social psychology.

While minds and selves are essentially social products, products or phenomena of the social side of human experience, the physiological mechanism underlying experience is far from irrelevant—indeed is indispensable—to their genesis and existence; for individual experience and behavior is, of course, physiologically basic to social experience and behavior: the processes and mechanisms of the latter (including those which are essential to the origin and existence of minds and selves) are dependent physiologically upon the processes and mechanisms of the former and upon the social functioning of these. Individual psychology, nevertheless, definitely abstracts certain factors from the situation with which social psychology deals more nearly in its concrete totality. We shall approach this latter field from a behavioristic point of view.

There is no necessary or inevitable reason why social institutions should be oppressive or rigidly conservative, or why they should not rather be, as many are, flexible and progressive, fostering individuality rather than discouraging it. In any case, without social institutions of some sort, without the organized social attitudes and activities by which social institutions are constituted, there could be no fully mature individual selves or personalities at all; for the individuals involved in the general social life-process of which social institutions are organized, manifestations can develop and possess fully mature selves or personalities only insofar as each one of them reflects or prehends in his individual experience these organized attitudes and activities which social institutions embody or represent. Social institutions, like individual selves, are developments within, or particular and formalized manifestations of, the social life-process at its human evolutionary level. As such, they are not necessarily subversive of individuality in the individual members; and they do not necessarily represent or uphold narrow definitions of certain fixed and specific patterns of acting which in any given circumstances should characterize the behavior of all intelligent and socially responsible individuals (in opposition to such unintelligent and socially irresponsible individuals as morons and imbeciles) as members of the given community or social group. On the contrary, they need to define the social, or socially responsible, patterns of individual conduct in only a very broad and general sense, affording plenty of scope for originality, flexibility, and variety of such conduct; and as the main formalized functional aspects or phases of the whole organized structure of the social life-process at its human level, they properly partake of the dynamic and progressive character of that process.

A highly developed and organized human society is one in which the individual members are interrelated in a multiplicity of different intricate and complicated ways whereby they all share a number of common social interests—interests in, or for the betterment of, the society—and yet, on the other hand, are more or less in conflict relative to numerous other interests which they possess only individually or else share with one another only in small and limited groups. Conflicts among individuals in a highly developed and organized human society are not mere conflicts among their respective primitive impulses but are conflicts among their respective selves or personalities, each with its definite social structure—highly complex and organized and unified—and each with a number of different social facets or aspects, a number of different sets of social attitudes constituting it. Thus, within such a society, conflicts arise between different aspects or phases of the same individual self (conflicts leading to cases of split personality when they are extreme or violent enough to be psychopathological), as well as between different individual selves. And both these types of individual conflict are settled or terminated by reconstructions of the particular social situations and modifications of the given framework of social relationships wherein they arise or occur in the general human social life-process. These reconstructions and modifications are performed, as we have said, by the minds of the individuals in whose experience or between whose selves these conflicts take place.

The changes that we make in the social order in which we are implicated necessarily involve our also making changes in ourselves.[1] The social conflicts among the individual members of a given organized human society, which, for their removal, necessitate conscious or intelligent reconstructions and modifications of that society by those individuals, also and equally necessitate such reconstructions or modifications by those individuals of their own selves or personalities. Thus the relations between social reconstruction and self or personality reconstruction are reciprocal and internal or organic; social reconstruction by the individual members of any organized human society entails self or personality reconstruction in some degree or other by each of these individuals, and vice versa; for, since their selves or personalities are constituted by their organized social relations to one another, they cannot reconstruct those selves or personalities without also reconstructing, to some extent, the given social order, which is, of course, likewise constituted by their organized social relations to one another. In both types of reconstruction the same fundamental material of organized social relations among human individuals is involved and is simply treated in different ways, or from different angles or points of view, in the two cases, respectively; or in short, social reconstruction and self or personality reconstruction are the two sides of a single process—the process of human social evolution. Human social progress involves the use by human individuals of their socially derived mechanism of self-consciousness, both in the effecting of such progressive social changes, and also in the development of their individual selves or personalities in such a way as adaptively to keep pace with such social reconstruction.

Ultimately and fundamentally societies develop in complexity of organization only by means of the progressive achievement of greater and greater degrees of functional, behavioristic differentiation among the individuals who constitute them; these functional, behavioristic differentiations among the individual members implying or presupposing initial oppositions among them of individual needs and ends, oppositions which in terms of social organization, however, are or have been transformed into these differentiations or into mere specializations of socially functional individual behavior.

[1] The reflexive character of self-consciousness enables the individual to contemplate himself as a whole; his ability to take the social attitudes of other individuals and also of the generalized other toward himself, within the given organized society of which he is a member, makes possible his bringing himself, as an objective whole, within his own experiential purview; and thus he can consciously integrate and unify the various aspects of his self, to form a single consistent and coherent and organized personality. Moreover, by the same means, he can undertake and effect intelligent reconstructions of that self or personality in terms of its relations to the given social order, whenever the exigencies of adaptation to his social environment demand such reconstructions.

2

SOCIAL ORDER
AND THE ANALYSIS
OF INTERACTION

Barney G. Glaser

Anselm L. Strauss

OTHER SOCIOLOGISTS HAVE DULY TAKEN INTO ACCOUNT [the] phenomenon of problematic identity, or assumed its existence, but few of them have analyzed awareness of identity and interaction in detail. Some theorists (Simmel, Cooley, Mead, Icheiser, Goffman, and Davis) have written in detail about awareness and consequent interaction, but generally there has been little theoretical cognizance of either the structural context within which types of awareness occur, or the structure of the awareness context itself. As a result, they have tended to restrict their range in considering the problem of awareness. Their characteristic theoretical perspectives and concerns may have led them to focus on one or two types of awareness: George Mead's concern with the implications of mutual understanding is a good example. Or a writer's ideas may be directly affected by the particular kinds of data with which he has worked.

Our own approach to the problem of interaction is much affected by a set of convictions about the maintenance of social order. Concerning social order, Norton Long, a political scientist, recently wrote that there is a sociology of John Locke and a sociology of Thomas Hobbes: the one emphasizes a realm of stable unquestioned values underlying the social order, and the other, the highly problematic character of social order.[1] George Mead earlier re-

Reprinted from *Awareness of Dying* (Chicago: Aldine Publishing Company, 1965), pp. 13–15; copyright © 1965 by Barney G. Glaser and Anselm L. Strauss. (Text, Chapter 1)

[1] "The Political Act as an Act of Will," *American Journal of Sociology,* 69 (July 1963), pp. 1–6.

phrased the Hobbesian view by noting that social changes occur constantly; he argued that the human task is "to bring those changes about in an orderly fashion," to direct change so that it is not chaotic, or in Hobbes' language, anarchistic.[2] Our version, which combines both views of this overdrawn dichotomy, is that the bases of social order must be reconstituted continually, must be "worked at," both according to established values and with the purpose of establishing values to preserve order.[3] The maintenance of social order, whether in society, organizations, groups or interaction, we believe, turns about handling relatively unforeseen consequences in this twofold manner.

Our assumptions about social order have naturally led us to explore the developmental possibilities of interaction, though our assumptions need not be accepted to legitimate this aim as of immense sociological importance. In his recent *Behavior in Public Places,* Erving Goffman analyzed interaction in terms of the social regulations that subtly govern it and make it the genuine embodiment of social order;[4] in contrast, we are cognizant of rules but are principally interested in analyzing interaction in terms of its open-ended and problematic character. Rather than focusing on interactional *stability,* we shall be preoccupied in this book with *changes* that may occur during the course of interaction. However, relatively stable or purely repetitive interaction also demands analysis beyond detailing the governing regulations: that is, one must also consider the tactics sustaining that stasis which constantly is subjected to change and unforeseen consequences; one must combine both the rule and the "working at" basis of social order. Thus, in our account of the interaction that centers around dying patients, we shall be interested not only in the social regulations and other structural conditions entering into the interaction, but also in the tendency for interaction to move out of regulated social bounds and into new interactional modes.

[2] "The Problem of Society—How We Become Selves," *Movements of Thought in the Nineteenth Century* (Chicago: University of Chicago Press, 1936), pp. 360–61. See also Herbert Blumer, "Society as Symbolic Interaction," in Arnold Rose (ed.), *Human Behavior and Social Processes* (Boston: Houghton-Mifflin, 1962), pp. 179–192.

[3] For an analysis of "working at" social order, see Anselm Strauss, Leonard Schatzman, Rue Bucher, Danuta Ehrlich, and Melvin Sabshin, "The Hospital and Its Negotiated Order," in Eliot Freidson (ed.), *The Hospital in Modern Society* (New York: Free Press of Glencoe, 1964), pp. 147–169; also by Strauss *et al., Psychiatric Ideologies and Institutions* (New York: Free Press of Glencoe, 1964), pp. 292–315.

[4] Erving Goffman, *Behavior in Public Places* (New York: Free Press of Glencoe, 1963). For our contrasting view, see Anselm Strauss, *Mirrors and Masks* (Chicago: Free Press of Glencoe, 1959), especially the section on "Self-appraisals and the Course of Âction," and "Interaction," pp. 31–88.

3

PUBLIC DRAMA
AND CHANGING SOCIETY

Orrin E. Klapp

IT IS UNAVOIDABLE that, where drama supervenes, "reality" is not what the hard-headed man would like it to be; nor do events always follow his prediction. For from the moment drama begins we start to project and interpret roles, and there is an important nexus between what a thing "is" and what the audience sees that is, at the same time, the reality and the magic of drama. The "magic" is an outcome that matter-of-fact analysis could not predict—a "sentimental," "frivolous," "romantic" change of status. Thus public drama defeats material or economic determinism, for we cannot predict the dramas of a society or their outcomes from our knowledge of objective and material forces.

Every society, of course, has a dramatic dimension. From ancient China to Chinatown, from Australian aboriginal dance to color TV, this dimension is preserved in religion, dance, legend, storytelling, song, ritual drama, theater, and fiction. The function of the dramatic dimension in any society has always been to burst through the routines of life into the wonderful and mysterious.

TV, movies, and modern news-reporting may not have brought more magic to life than they have displaced, but I do not think one can truly say that there is less magic. It is nonetheless a different kind of drama that is involved; its audiences are different and its implications for the modern society are different. For example, audiences relatively less often form within institutional

Reprinted from Orrin E. Klapp, *Symbolic Leaders* (Chicago: Aldine Publishing Company, 1964), pp. 250–257, 259–260, copyright © 1964 by Orrin E. Klapp. (Text, Chapter 1)

settings, such as temples, and tradition no longer sets effective limits to the content of dramas. We are oriented more toward what a live man does on a screen than toward what a dead man did. In short, there has been a movement of the dramatic dimension from tradition and local events (community audiences) to that range of things conventionally called news, entertainment, and reading, which are presented before shifting, transitory, and boundless audiences. This I call the "public drama."

Two points may help to explain why the public drama is unsettling to the social order. One is the size and extent of audiences. The dramas themselves are larger, simply in terms of audience if nothing else. The smallest event may become a matter of concern to the whole world, and it is almost impossible to anticipate the alignments and shifting audiences that will be created.

The other point is in the range of things that can become dramatic. Though modern man may have lost something in his own personal drama and be more submerged in the anonymity of audiences and though there are fewer community dramas in daily life, the range of events that can become dramatic and the amount of the world's territory that can be involved is enormously larger than it used to be. This increase in range is linked with the inherent transcending power of drama; through its experience people are refocused away from the ordinary structural facts of daily life. They are lifted out of their families, jobs, institutions, political parties, classes, nations, and so on.

A central fact about all drama, as opposed to daily life, is that the role one gets is not part of his regular routine and structure. It may be part of the repertoire of roles available in the society (as when a Hopi plays "mudhead" or an American father plays Santa), but it still takes the actor out of his regular roles of church, work, and so on. Likewise, from the very nature of drama it follows that while it obtains, you are not "you" but the part you take; there is an identity-transcending character that goes hand in hand with structure transcendence. The transcending power of drama works even when the drama itself is part of social structure (as in a ritual) and has its own social structure (for example, the frontier-town setting for a "horse opera").

Along with this structure transcendence is the fact that things are happening to persons—our symbolic leaders—that could not be predicted from the facts of their social status. Looking at the mass today and their organizational leaders, one cannot tell who the stars of tomorrow will be or from what stratum they will come. What, then, allows us to predict them? The answer given in this book is in terms of dramatic factors. To whom can a drama happen? The answer is: to anybody. And who can be the audience or following? The answer is, again, and with the help of mass communication: anybody. And if dramas move people, where can they be moved? In this already mobile and rootless world, the answer is: anywhere.

Whereas drama can be subservient to organization—as shown by Goffman, Hughes, Van Gennep, and any number of other studies familiar to sociologists[1]—it is also plainly capable of being its enemy. This is because drama has no indigenous relationship to a particular social structure; it does not "belong" to a certain context of class, politics, or ethnicity. Drama is concerned no more with democracy than with oligarchy, whites than Negroes, Catholics than Protestants, order than anarchy. Audiences can form that unite very different kinds of people from all parts of the structure, and from other structures, in the same perspective, at least for a moment. Thus drama is inherently a solvent in its effect on structure.

The universality of drama is based not so much on intellectual perception of general truths as on the ease with which humans identify with roles other than their own and persons different from themselves.[2] It is safer to emphasize than underestimate this ability. Charles H. Cooley held that sympathy and drama are facts of human nature and are therefore basically cross-cultural, in spite of their limitations, because we have a common stock of sentiments to draw upon and because we can learn to sympathize. Indeed, our mental health and maturity are measured by our breadth of sympathy.[3] A dramatic crisis is a turning point, a moment of unpredictability and emergence. The "hero" is the one to whom we turn as a vehicle to carry us through the crisis. So by our power of identification we have great freedom to choose heroes, from various times, places, races, and statuses.

By stressing this freedom of drama, I am not denying that people often fail to identify with dramas from other cultures or social positions than their own. Yet I think our tendency today is perhaps to overemphasize ethnocentrism, reference groups, and other such limitations of audiences rather than see the potentialities of these audiences and their actual range of identifications that may transcend group barriers. It is not so much that they cannot identify outside their "interests" as that they do not because the right conjuncture of dramatic elements has not been found.

We are only beginning the study of audiences to find out what they actually

[1] Erving Goffman, *The Presentation of Self in Everyday Life* (Garden City, N.Y.: Doubleday, 1959); Everett C. Hughes, "Work and the Self," in J. H. Rohrer and Muzafer Sherif (eds.), *Social Psychology at the Crossroads* (New York: Harper, 1951); Arnold Van Gennep, *Les Rites de Passage* (Paris, 1909; London: Routledge and Kegan Paul, 1960).

[2] Including a wide range of animals. Franz Kafka succeeded in making a story hero of an animal as unattractive as a cockroach, as did Don Marquis (though in a much different vein!). I was convinced of this ability of men to identify with unattractive characters by an experience I once had while shaving. A rather alarming insect flew into the bathroom and landed in the tub. No insect-lover, I reached down to scoop it out. At this moment it assumed what seemed to be a bravely defiant posture, with its "arms" outspread. I felt an immediate sympathy for this little bug, making his stand "alone against the world." I was the giant; he was the hero; and my feeling was much the same as when reading about Roland standing off the charge of the Saracens.

[3] "One's range of sympathy is a measure of his personality, indicating how much or how little of a man he is." (*Human Nature and the Social Order* [New York: Scribner, 1922], p. 140.)

do see and can identify with. Let us concede the obvious, that audiences are different on account of their cultures and places in the social structure. Symbols—language, music, dance, and so on—must be understood for drama to be effective. But these cultural and structural elements are not the essence of drama; they may be instruments and, for the same reasons, may be obstacles to drama. In explaining lack of universality, we can say that drama is deformed by these various biases, contents, and symbols.

The transcending tendency of drama has a creative power to make and break statuses, to give and take prestige, to generate enthusiasm, to involve and mobilize masses in new directions, and to create new identities. Within the framework of an orderly society we have a turbulent, almost chaotic, process in which statuses are made and mass attention and alignments are shifted drastically from one subject to another.

This book deals with a process of vast importance and scope that is almost impossible to reduce to structural terms, a process that occurs within structures, using the props, settings, and symbols provided by particular institutions and cultures, but that is essentially fluid and not attached to these structures. It flows through them like water through a net. Our subject then, invokes the "process" view of modern society by its focus on the flowing stream of drama, with its structure-transcending tendencies, within the "order" of society. Governments and classes fall, but the public drama goes on. It does not require a given social structure to maintain it because its sources are in human nature.

We have in the study of emergent symbolic leaders a way of seeing how society finds and serves needs by choosing people who best symbolize something that others want or want to do. But this function is performed within a structure no more definite than an audience, though formal fan clubs, political parties, and organized movements may come out of the audience. It would be stretching a point to call a mere audience the "informal structure" of leadership. The public drama is working much of the time without building any structures at all. Moreover, it is often at war with structures, whether it generates "escapist" tendencies or a movement to change a structure. The public drama is actually working to keep society relatively structureless by its function of satisfying audiences in ever-shifting alignments, occasionally arousing movements that disturb the status quo. The paradox is that even when a public drama uses a traditional pattern (poor boy makes good, Cinderella, delivering hero), it may bring in a leader who does something quite new.

On the other hand, drama does have a structure or pattern of its own. There is surely something for structuralists in the notion of "laws" and configurations of drama, which confine and limit an actor as much as do considerations like income, schooling, and civil service rating. It is the pattern of this process, working largely as a solvent within the more formal, obvious, and static structures, that the study of the public drama helps the student of society —traditional or modern—to see.

4

THE EXISTENTIAL MATRIX
OF INQUIRY: CULTURAL

John Dewey

THE ENVIRONMENT IN WHICH HUMAN BEINGS live, act, and inquire, is not simply physical. It is cultural as well. Problems which induce inquiry grow out of the relations of fellow beings to one another, and the organs for dealing with these relations are not only the eye and ear, but the meanings which have developed in the course of living, together with the ways of forming and transmitting culture with all its constituents of tools, arts, institutions, traditions and customary beliefs.

I. To a very large extent the ways in which human beings respond even to physical conditions are influenced by their cultural environment. Light and fire are physical facts. But the occasions in which a human being responds to things as merely physical in purely physical ways are comparatively rare. Such occasions are the act of jumping when a sudden noise is heard, withdrawing the hand when something hot is touched, blinking in the presence of a sudden increase of light, animal-like basking in sunshine, etc. Such reactions are on the biological plane. But the typical cases of human behavior are not represented by such examples. The *use* of sound in speech and listening to speech, making and enjoying music; the kindling and tending of fire to cook and to keep warm; the production of light to carry on and regulate occupations and social enjoyments:—these things are representative of distinctively human activity.

To indicate the full scope of cultural determination of the conduct of living one would have to follow the behavior of an individual throughout at least a day; whether that of a day laborer, of a professional man, artist or scientist, and whether the individual be a growing child or a parent. For the result would show how thoroughly saturated behavior is with conditions and factors that are of cultural origin and import. Of distinctively human behavior it may be said that the strictly physical environment is so incorporated in a cultural environment that our interactions with the former, the problems that arise with reference to it, and our ways of dealing with these problems, are profoundly affected by incorporation of the physical environment in the cultural.

Man, as Aristotle remarked, is a *social* animal. This fact introduces him into situations and originates problems and ways of solving them that have no precedent upon the organic biological level. For man is social in another sense than the bee and ant, since his activities are encompassed in an environment that is culturally transmitted, so that what man does and how he acts, is determined not by organic structure and physical heredity alone but by the influence of cultural heredity, embedded in traditions, institutions, customs and the purposes and beliefs they both carry and inspire. Even the neuromuscular structures of individuals are modified through the influence of the cultural environment upon the activities performed. The acquisition and understanding of language with proficiency in the arts (that are foreign to other animals than men) represent an incorporation within the physical structure of human beings of the effects of cultural conditions, an interpenetration so profound that resulting activities are as direct and seemingly "natural" as are the first reactions of an infant. To speak, to read, to exercise any art, industrial, fine or political, are instances of modifications wrought *within* the biological organism by the cultural environment.

This modification of organic behavior in and by the cultural environment accounts for, or rather is, the transformation of purely organic behavior into behavior marked by intellectual properties with which the present discussion is concerned. Intellectual operations are foreshadowed in behavior of the biological kind, and the latter prepares the way for the former. But to foreshadow is not to exemplify and to prepare is not to fulfil. Any theory that rests upon a naturalistic postulate must face the problem of the extraordinary differences that mark off the activities and achievements of human beings from those of other biological forms. It is these differences that have led to the idea that man is completely separated from other animals by properties that come from a non-natural source. The conception to be developed in the present chapter is that the development of language (in its widest sense) out of prior biological activities is, in its connection with wider cultural forces, the key to this transformation. The problem, so viewed, is not the problem of the transition of organic behavior into something wholly discontinuous with it—as is the case when, for example, Reason, Intuition and the *A priori* are appealed to for explanation of the difference. It is a special form of the general problem of continuity of change and the emergence of new modes of activity—the problem of development at any level.

Viewing the problem from this angle, its constituents may be reduced to certain heads, three of which will be noted. Organic behavior is centered in *particular* organisms. This statement applies to inferring and reasoning as existential activities. But if inferences made and conclusions reached are to be valid, the subject-matter dealt with and the operations employed must be such as to yield identical results for all who infer and reason. If the same evidence leads different persons to different conclusions, then either the evidence is only speciously the same, or one conclusion (or both) is wrong. The *special* constitution of an individual organism which plays such a role in biological behavior is so irrelevant in controlled inquiry that it has to be discounted and mastered.

Another phase of the problem is brought out by the part played in human judgments by emotion and desire. These *personal* traits cook the evidence and determine the result that is reached. That is, upon the level of organic factors (which are the actively determining forces in the type of cases just mentioned), the individual with his individual peculiarities, whether native or acquired, is an active participant in producing ideas and beliefs, and yet the latter are logically grounded only when such peculiarities are deliberately precluded from taking effect. This point restates what was said in connection with the first point, but it indicates another phase of the matter. If, using accepted terminology, we say that the first difference is that between the singular and the general, the present point may be formulated as the difference between the subjective and the objective. To be intellectually "objective" is to discount and eliminate merely personal factors in the operations by which a conclusion is reached.

Organic behavior is a strictly temporal affair. But when behavior is *intellectually* formulated, in respect both to general ways of behavior and the special environing conditions in which they operate, propositions result and the terms of a proposition do not sustain a temporal relation to one another. It was a temporal event when someone landed on Robinson Crusoe's island. It was a temporal event when Crusoe found the footprint on the sands. It was a temporal event when Crusoe inferred the presence of a possibly dangerous stranger. But while the proposition was *about* something temporal, the *relation* of the observed fact as evidential to the inference drawn from it is non-temporal. The same holds of every logical relation in and of propositions.

In the following discussion it is maintained that the solution of the problem just stated in some of its phases, is intimately and directly connected with cultural subject-matter. Transformation from organic behavior to intellectual behavior, marked by logical properties, is a product of the fact that individuals live in a cultural environment. Such living compels them to assume in their behavior the standpoint of customs, beliefs, institutions, meanings and beliefs which are at least relatively general and objective.

II. Language occupies a peculiarly significant place and exercises a peculiarly significant function in the complex that forms the cultural environment. It is itself a cultural institution, and, from one point of view, is but one among many such institutions. But it is (1) the agency by which other institutions and acquired habits are *transmitted,* and (2) it *permeates* both the forms and the contents of all other cultural activities. Moreover, (3) it has its own distinctive structure which is capable of abstraction as a *form.* This structure, when abstracted as a form, had a decisive influence historically upon the formulation of logical theory; the symbols which are appropriate to the form of language as an agency of inquiry (as distinct from its original function as a medium of communication) are still peculiarly relevant to logical theory. Consequently, further discussion will take the wider cultural environment for granted and confine itself to the especial function of language in effecting the transformation of the biological into the intellectual and the potentially logical.

In this further discussion, language is taken in its widest sense, a sense wider than oral and written speech. It includes the latter. But it includes also not only gestures but rites, ceremonies, monuments and the products of industrial and fine arts. A tool or machine, for example, is not simply a simple or complex physical object having its own physical properties and effects, but is also a mode of language. For it *says* something, to those who understand it, about operations of use and their consequences. To the members of a primitive community a loom operated by steam or electricity says nothing. It is composed in a foreign language, and so with most of the mechanical devices of modern civilization. In the present cultural setting, these objects are so intimately bound up with interests, occupations, and purposes that they have an eloquent voice.

The importance of language as the necessary, and, in the end, sufficient condition of the existence and transmission of non-purely organic activities and their consequences lies in the fact that, on one side, it is a strictly biological mode of behavior, emerging in natural continuity from earlier organic activities, while, on the other hand, it compels one individual to take the standpoint of other individuals and to see and inquire from a standpoint that is not strictly personal but is common to them as participants or "parties" in a conjoint undertaking. It may be directed by and towards some physical existence. But it first has reference to some other person or persons with whom it institutes *communication*—the making of something common. Hence, to that extent its reference becomes general and "objective."

Language is made up of physical existences; sounds, or marks on paper, or a temple, statue, or loom. But these do not *operate* or function as mere physical things when they are media of communication. They operate in virtue of their *representative* capacity or *meaning.* The particular physical existence which has meaning is, in the case of speech, a conventional matter. But the convention or common consent which sets it apart as a means of recording and communicating meaning is that of agreement in *action;* of shared modes of responsive behavior and participation in their consequences. The physical sound or mark gets its meaning in and by conjoint community of functional use, not by any explicit convening in a "convention" or by passing resolutions that a certain sound or mark shall have a specified meaning. Even when the meaning of certain legal words is determined by a court, it is not the agreement of the judges which is finally decisive. For such assent does not finish the matter. It occurs for the sake of determining future agreements in associated *behavior,* and it is this subsequent behavior which finally settles the actual meaning of the words in question. Agreement in the proposition arrived at is significant only through this function in promoting agreement in action.

The reason for mentioning these considerations is that they prove that the meaning which a conventional symbol has is not itself conventional. For the meaning is established by agreements of different persons in existential activities having reference to existential consequences. The particular existential sound or mark that stands for *dog* or *justice* in different cultures is arbitrary or conventional in the sense that although it has *causes* there are no *reasons* for it. But *in so far* as it is a medium of communication, its meaning is common, because it is constituted by existential conditions. If a word varies in meaning in intercommunication between different cultural groups, then to that degree communication is blocked and misunderstanding results. Indeed, there ceases to be communication until variations of understanding can be translated, through the meaning of words, into a meaning that is the same to both parties. Whenever communication is blocked, and yet is supposed to exist, misunderstanding, not merely absence of understanding, is the result. It is an error to suppose that the misunderstanding is about the meaning of the *word* in isolation, just as it is fallacious to suppose that because two persons accept the same dictionary meaning of a word they have therefore come to agreement and understanding. For agreement and disagreement are determined by the consequences of conjoint activities. Harmony or the opposite exists in the effects produced by the several activities that are occasioned by the words used.

III. Reference to concord of consequences as the determinant of the meaning of any sound used as a medium of communication shows that there is no such thing as a *mere* word or *mere* symbol. The physical existence that is the vehicle of meaning may as a particular be called *mere;* the recitation of a number of such sounds or the stringing together of such marks may be called *mere* language. But in fact there is no word in the first case and no language in the second. The activities that occur and the consequences that result which are not determined by meaning, are, by description, only physical. A sound or mark of any physical existence is a part of *language* only in virtue of its *operational* force; that is, as it functions as a means of evoking different activities performed by different persons so as to produce consequences that are shared by all the participants in the conjoint undertaking. This fact is evident and direct in oral communication. It is indirect and disguised in written communication. Where written literature and literacy abound, the conception of language is likely to be framed upon their model. The intrinsic connection of language with community of action is then forgotten. Language is then supposed to be simply a means of expressing or communicating "thoughts"— a means of conveying ideas or meanings that are complete in themselves apart from communal operational force.

Much literature is read, moreover, simply for enjoyment, for esthetic purposes. In this case, language is a means of action only as it leads the reader to build up pictures and scenes to be enjoyed by himself. There ceases to be immediate inherent reference to conjoint activity and to consequences mutually participated in. Such is not the case, however, in reading to get at the meaning of the author; that is, in reading that is emphatically intellectual in distinction from esthetic. In the mere reading of a scientific treatise there is, indeed, no direct overt participation in action with another to produce consequences that are *common* in the sense of being immediately and personally shared. But there must be imaginative construction of the materials and operations which led the author to certain conclusions, and there must be agreement or disagreement with his conclusions as a consequence of following through conditions and operations that are imaginatively reinstated.

Connection with overt activities is in such a case indirect or mediated. But so far as definite grounded agreement or disagreement is reached, an attitude is formed which is a preparatory readiness to act in a responsive way when the conditions in question or others similar to them actually present themselves. The connection with action in question is, in other words, with *possible* ways of operation rather than with those found to be *actually* and immediately required.[1] But preparation for *possible* action in situations not as yet existent in actuality is an essential condition of, and factor in, all intelligent behavior. When persons meet together in conference to plan in advance of actual occasions and emergencies what shall later be done, or when an individual deliberates in advance regarding his possible behavior in a possible future contingency, something occurs, but more directly, the same sort as happens in understanding intellectually the meaning of a scientific treatise.

I turn now to the positive implication of the fact that no sound, mark, product of art, is a word or part of language in isolation. Any word or phrase has the meaning which it has only as a member of a constellation of related meanings. Words as representatives are part of an inclusive code. The code may be public or private. A public code is illustrated in any language that is current in a given cultural group. A private code is one agreed upon by members of special groups so as to be unintelligible to those who have not been initiated. Between these two come argots of special groups in a community, and the technical codes invented for a restricted special purpose, like the one used by ships at sea. But in every case, a particular word has its meaning only in relation to the code of which it is one constituent. The distinction just drawn

---

[1] Literature and literary habits are a strong force in building up the conception of separation of ideas and theories from practical activity.

between meanings that are determined respectively in fairly direct connection with action in situations that are present or near at hand, and meanings determined for possible use in remote and contingent situations, provides the basis upon which language codes as systems may be differentiated into two main kinds.

While all language or symbol-meanings are what they are as parts of a system, it does not follow that they have been determined on the basis of their fitness to be such members of a system; much less on the basis of their membership in a comprehensive system. The system may be simply the language in common use. Its meanings hang together not in virtue of their examined relationship to one another, but because they are current in the same set of group habits and expectations. They hang together because of group activities, group interests, customs and institutions. Scientific language, on the other hand, is subject to a test over and above this criterion. Each meaning that enters into the language is expressly determined in its relation to other members of the language system. In all reasoning or ordered discourse this criterion takes precedence over that instituted by connection with cultural habits.

The resulting difference in the two types of language-meanings fundamentally fixes the difference between what is called common sense and what is called science. In the former cases, the customs, the *ethos* and spirit of a group is the decisive factor in determining the system of meanings in use. The system is one in a practical and institutional sense rather than in an intellectual sense. Meanings that are formed on this basis are sure to contain much that is irrelevant and to exclude much that is required for intelligent control of activity. The meanings are coarse, and many of them are inconsistent with each other from a logical point of view. One meaning is appropriate to action under certain institutional group conditions; another, in some other situation, and there is no attempt to relate the different situations to one another in a coherent scheme. In an intellectual sense, there are many languages, though in a social sense there is but one. This multiplicity of language-meaning constellations is also a mark of our existing culture. A word means one thing in relation to a religious institution, still another thing in business, a third thing in law, and so on. This fact is the real Babel of communication. There is an attempt now making to propagate the idea that education which indoctrinates individuals into some special tradition provides the way out of this confusion. Aside from the fact that there are in fact a considerable number of traditions and that selection of some one of them, even though that one be internally consistent and extensively accepted, is arbitrary, the attempt reverses the *theoretical* state of the case. Genuine community of language or symbols can be achieved only through efforts that bring about community of activities under existing conditions. The ideal of scientific-language is construction of a system in which meanings are related to one another in inference and discourse and where the symbols are such as to indicate the relation.

I shall now introduce the word "symbol" giving it its signification as a synonym for a word *as* a word, that is, as a meaning carried by language in a system, whether the system be of the loose or the intellectual rigorous kind.[2] The especial point in the introduction of the word "symbol" is to institute the means by which discrimination between what is designated by it and what is now often designated by *sign* may be instituted. What I have called symbols are often called "artificial signs" in distinction from what are called *natural signs.*

IV. It is by agreement in conjoint action of the kind already described, that the *word* "smoke" stands in the English language for an object of certain qualities. In some other language the same vocable and mark may stand for something different, and an entirely different sound stand for "smoke." To such cases of representation the word *"artificial signs"* applies. When it is said that smoke as an actual existence points to, is evidence of, an existential fire, smoke is said to be a *natural* sign of fire. Similarly, heavy clouds of given qualities are a natural sign of probable rain, and so on. The representative capacity in question is attributed to *things in their connection with one another,* not to marks whose meaning depends upon agreement in social use. There is no doubt of the existence and the importance of the distinction designated by the words "natural" and "artificial" signs. But the fundamentally important difference is not brought out by these words. For reasons now to be given, I prefer to mark the difference by confining the application of *sign* to so-called "natural signs"—employing *symbol* to designate "artificial signs."

The difference just stated is actual. But it fails to note the distinctive intellectual property of what I call symbols. It is, so to speak, an incidental and external fact, logically speaking, that certain things are given representative function by social agreement. The fact becomes logically relevant only because of the possibility of free and independent development of meanings in discourse which arises when once symbols are instituted. A "natural sign," by description, is something that exists in an actual spatial-temporal context. Smoke, as a thing having certain observed qualities, is a sign of fire only when the thing exists and is observed. Its representative capacity, taken by itself, is highly restricted, for it exists only under limited conditions. The situation is very different when the *meaning* "smoke" is embodied in an existence, like a sound or a mark on paper. The actual quality found in existence is then subordinate to a representative office. Not only can the sound be produced practically at will, so that we do not have to wait for the occurrence of the object; but, what is more important, the meaning when embodied in an indifferent or neutral existence is *liberated* with respect to its representative

---

[2] This signification is narrower than the popular usage, according to which anything is a symbol that has representative *emotional* force even if that force be independent of its intellectual representational force. In this wider sense, a national flag, a crucifix, a mourning garb, etc., are symbols. The definition of the text is in so far arbitrary. But there is nothing arbitrary about the *subject-matters* to which the limited signification applies.

function. It is no longer tied down. It can be related to other meanings in the language-system; not only to that of fire but to such apparently unrelated meanings as friction, changes of temperature, oxygen, molecular constitution, and, by intervening meaning-symbols, to the laws of thermodynamics.

I shall, accordingly, in what follows, connect *sign* and *significance, symbol* and *meaning,* respectively, with each other, in order to have terms to designate two different kinds of representative capacity. Linguistically, the choice of terms is more or less arbitrary, although sign and significance have a common verbal root. This consideration is of no importance, however, compared with the necessity of having some words by which to designate the two kinds of representative function. For purposes of theory the important consideration is that existent things, as signs, are *evidence* of the existence of something else, this something being at the time *inferred* rather than observed.

But words, or symbols, provide no *evidence* of any existence. Yet what they lack in this capacity they make up for in creation of another dimension. They make possible ordered discourse or reasoning. For this may be carried on without any of the existences to which symbols apply being actually present: without, indeed, assurance that objects to which they apply anywhere actually exist, and, as in the case of mathematical discourse, without direct reference to existence at all.

Ideas as ideas, hypotheses as hypotheses, would not exist were it not for symbols and meanings as distinct from signs and significances. The greater capacity of symbols for manipulation is of practical importance. But it pales in comparison with the fact that symbols introduce into inquiry a dimension different from that of existence. Clouds of certain shapes, size and color may signify to us the probability of rain; they portend rain. But the *word* cloud when it is brought into connection with other words of a symbol-constellation enable us to relate the meaning of being a cloud with such different matters as differences of temperature and pressures, the rotation of the earth, the laws of motion, and so on.

The difference between sign-significance and symbol-meaning (in the sense defined) is brought out in the following incident.[3] A visitor in a savage tribe wanted on one occasion "the word for Table. There were five or six boys standing around, and tapping the table with my forefinger I asked 'What is this?' One boy said it was *dodela,* another that it was an *etanda,* a third stated that it was *bokali,* a fourth that it was *elamba,* and the fifth said it was *meza.*" After congratulating himself on the richness of the vocabulary of the language the visitor found later "that one boy had thought he wanted the word for tapping; another understood we were seeking the word for the material of which the table was made; another had the idea that we required the word for hardness; another thought we wished the name for that which covered the table; and the last . . . gave us the word *meza,* table."

This story might have been quoted earlier as an illustration of the fact that

---

[3] Quoted by and from Ogden and Richards, *The Meaning of Meaning,* p. 174.

there is not possible any such thing as a direct one-to-one correspondence of names with existential objects; that words mean what they mean in connection with conjoint activities that effect a common, or mutually participated in, consequence. The word sought for was involved in conjoint activities looking to a common end. The act of tapping in the illustration was isolated from any such situation. It was, in consequence, wholly indeterminate in reference; it was no part of *communication,* by which alone acts get significance and accompanying words acquire meaning.[4] For the point in hand, the anecdote illustrates the lack of any evidential status in relation to existence of the symbols or representative values that have been given the name "meanings." Without the intervention of a specific kind of existential operation they cannot indicate or discriminate the *objects* to which they refer. Reasoning or ordered discourse, which is defined by development of symbol-meanings in relation to one another, may (and should) provide a basis for performing these operations, but of itself it determines no existence. This statement holds no matter how comprehensive the meaning-system and no matter how rigorous and cogent the relations of meanings to one another. On the other hand, the story illustrates how, in case the right word had been discovered, the meaning symbolized would have been capable of entering into relations with any number of other meanings independently of the actual presence at any given time of the object *table.* Just as the sign-significance relation defines *inference,* so the relation of meanings that constitutes propositions defines *implication* in discourse, if it satisfies the intellectual conditions for which it is instituted. Unless there are words which mark off the two kinds of relations in their distinctive capacities and offices, with reference to existence, there is danger that two things as logically unlike as inference and implication will be confused. As a matter of fact, the confusion, when inference is treated as identical with implication, has been a powerful agency in creating the doctrinal conception that logic is purely formal—for, as has been said, the relation of meanings (carried by symbols) to one another is, *as such,* independent of existential reference.[5]

V. So far the word "relation" has been rather indiscriminately employed. The discussion has now reached a point where it is necessary to deal with the ambiguity of the word as it is used not merely in ordinary speech but in logical texts. The word "relation" is used to cover three very different matters which in the interest of a coherent logical doctrine must be discriminated. (1) Symbols are "related" directly to one another; (2) they are "related" to existence by the mediating intervention of existential operations; (3) existences are "related" to one another in the evidential sign-signified function. That these three modes of "relation" are different from one another and that the use of

---

[4] Another aspect of the same general principle, not directly connected with language, is brought out in consideration of the meaning of any demonstrated object in relation to *"this."*

[5] A further important logical aspect of this matter is dealt with in the necessity of distinguishing *judgment* from propositions, and *involvement* from *implication.*

one and the same word tends to cover up the difference and thereby create doctrinal confusion, is evident.

In order to avoid, negatively, the disastrous doctrinal confusion that arises from the ambiguity of the word *relation,* and in order to possess, positively, linguistic means of making clear the logical nature of the different subject-matters under discussion, I shall reserve the word *relation* to designate the kind of "relation" which symbol-meanings bear to one another *as* symbol-meanings. I shall use the term *reference* to designate the kind of relation they sustain to existence; and the words *connection* (and *involvement*) to designate that kind of relation sustained by *things* to one another in virtue of which *inference* is possible.

The differences, when once pointed out, should be so obvious as hardly to require illustration. Consider, however, propositions of mathematical physics. (1) As propositions they form a system of *related* symbol-meanings that may be considered and developed as such. (2) But as propositions of *physics,* not of mere mathematics, they have *reference* to existence; a reference which is realized in operations of *application.* (3) The final test of *valid* reference or applicability resides in the *connections* that exist among things. Existential involvement of things with one another alone warrants inference so as to enable further connections among things themselves to be discovered.

The question may be raised whether meaning-relations in discourse arise before or after significance-connections in existence. Did we first infer and then use the results to engage in discourse? Or did relations of meanings, instituted in discourse, enable us to detect the connections in things in virtue of which some things are evidential of other things? The question is rhetorical in that the question of historical priority cannot be settled. The question is asked, however, in order to indicate that in any case ability to treat things as signs would not go far did not symbols enable us to mark and retain just the qualities of things which are the ground of inference. Without, for example, words or symbols that discriminate and hold on to the experienced qualities of sight and smell that constitute a thing "smoke," thereby enabling it to serve as a sign of fire, we might react to the qualities in question in animal-like fashion and perform activities appropriate to them. But no inference could be made that was not blind and blundering. Moreover, since *what* is inferred, namely fire, is not present in observation, any anticipation that could be formed of it would be vague and indefinite, even supposing an anticipation could occur at all. If we compare and contrast the range and the depth of the signifying capacity of existential objects and events in a savage and a civilized group and the corresponding power of inference, we find a close correlation between it and the scope and the intimacy of the relations that obtain between symbol-meanings in discourse. Upon the whole, then, it is language, originating as a medium of communication in order to bring about deliberate cooperation and competition in conjoint activities, that has conferred upon existential things their signifying or evidential power.

VI. We are thus brought back to the original problem: namely, transformation of animal activities into intelligent behavior having the properties which, when formulated, are *logical* in nature. Associated behavior is characteristic not only of plants and animals, but of electrons, atoms and molecules; as far as we know of everything that exists in nature. Language did not originate association, but when it supervened, as a natural emergence from previous forms of animal activity, it reacted to transform prior forms and modes of assoicated behavior in such a way as to give experience a new dimension.

1. "Culture" and all that culture involves, as distinguished from "nature," is both a condition and a product of language. Since language is the only means of retaining and transmitting to subsequent generations *acquired* skills, acquired information and acquired habits, it is the latter. Since, however, meanings and the significance of events differ in different cultural groups, it is also the former.

2. Animal activities, such as eating and drinking, searching for food, copulation, etc., acquire new properties. Eating food becomes a group festival and celebration; procuring food, the art of agriculture and exchange; copulation passes into the institution of the family.

3. Apart from the existence of symbol-meanings the results of prior experience are retained only through strictly organic modifications. Moreover, these modifications once made, tend to become so fixed as to retard, if not to prevent, the occurrence of further modifications. The existence of symbols makes possible deliberate recollection and expectation, and thereby the institution of new combinations of selected elements of experiences having an intellectual dimension.

4. Organic biological activities end in overt actions, whose comsequences are irretrievable. When an activity and its consequences can be rehearsed by representation in symbolic terms, there is no such final commitment. If the representation of the final consequence is of unwelcome quality, overt activity may be foregone, or the way of acting be replanned in such a way as to avoid the undesired outcome.[6]

These transformations and others which they suggest, are not of themselves equivalent to accrual of logical properties to behavior. But they provide requisite conditions for it. The use of meaning-symbols for institution of purposes or ends-in-view, for deliberation, as a rehearsal through such symbols of the activities by which the ends may be brought into being, is at least a rudimentary form of reasoning in connection with solution of problems. The habit of reasoning once instituted is capable of indefinite development on its own account. The ordered development of meanings in their relations to one another may become an engrossing interest. When this happens, im-

---

[6] Generalizing beyond the strict requirements of the position outlined, I would say that I am not aware of any so-called merely "mental" activity or result that cannot be described in the objective terms of an organic activity modified and directed by symbols-meaning, or language, in its broad sense.

plicit logical conditions are made explicit and then logical theory of some sort is born. It may be imperfect; it will be imperfect from the standpoint of the inquiries and symbol-meanings that later develop. But the first step, the one that costs and counts, was taken when some one began to reflect upon language, upon *logos,* in its syntactical structure and its wealth of meaning contents. Hypostization of *Logos* was the first result, and it held back for centuries the development of inquiries of a kind that are competent to deal with the problems of the existent world. But the hypostization was, nevertheless, a tribute to the power of language to generate reasoning and, through application of the meanings contained in it, to confer fuller and more ordered significance upon existence.

In later chapters we shall consider in some detail how a logic of ordered discourse, a logic that gathered in a system the relations which hold meanings consistently together in discourse, was taken to be the final model of logic and thereby obstructed the development of effective modes of inquiry into existence, preventing the necessary reconstruction and expansion of the very meanings that were used in discourse. For when these meanings in their ordered relations to one another were taken to be final in and of themselves, they were directly superimposed upon nature. The necessity of existential operations for application of meanings to natural existence was ignored. This failure reacted into the system of meanings as meanings. The result was the belief that the requirements of rational discourse constitute the measure of natural existence, the criterion of complete Being. It is true that logic emerged as the Greeks became aware of language as Logos with the attendant implication that a system of ordered meanings is involved.

This perception marked an enormous advance. But it suffered from two serious defects. Because of the superior status assigned to forms of rational discourse, they were isolated from the operations by means of which meanings originate, function and are tested. This isolation was equivalent to the hypositization of Reason. In the second place, the meanings that were recognized were ordered in a gradation derived from and controlled by a class-structure of Greek society. The means, procedures and kinds of organization that arose from active or "practical" participation in natural processes were given a low rank in the hierarchy of Being and Knowing. The scheme of knowledge and of Nature became, without conscious intent, a mirror of a social order in which craftsmen, mechanics, artisans generally, held a low position in comparison with a leisure class. Citizens as citizens were also occupied with doing, a doing instigated by need or lack. While possessed of a freedom denied to the artisan class, they were also taken to fail in completely self-contained and self-sufficient activity. The latter was exemplified only in the exercise of Pure Reason untainted by need for anything outside itself and hence independent of all operations of doing and making. The historic result was to give philosophic, even supposedly ontological, sanction to the cultural conditions which prevented the utilization of the immense potentialities for attainment of knowledge that were resident in the activities of the arts—resident in them because they involve operations of active modification of existing conditions which contain the procedures constituting the experimental method when once they are employed for the sake of obtaining knowledge, instead of being subordinated to a scheme of uses and enjoyments controlled by given socio-cultural conditions.

5

THE SOCIAL NATURE
OF HIGHER
MENTAL PROCESSES

A. R. Luria

THE MERE FACT THAT WE RECOGNIZE the reflex character of all mental processes and can relate psychology to the physiological theories of higher nervous
activity does not in itself reveal the specific features distinguishing human
higher mental functions.

From the point of view of modern psychology, the higher human mental
functions are complex reflex processes, social in origin, mediate in structure,
and conscious and voluntary in mode of function. We must pause here to
consider this definition in more detail.

Modern materialistic psychology considers that the higher forms of human
mental activity are sociohistorical in origin. In contrast to the animal, man
is born and lives in a world of objects created by the work of society and in
a world of people with whom he forms certain relationships. From the very
beginning, this milieu influences his mental processes. The natural reflexes of
the child (sucking, grasping, etc.) are radically reorganized as a result of
the handling of objects. New motor patterns are formed, creating what is
virtually a "mold" of these objects, so that the movements begin to match
the properties of the objects. The same applies to human perception, formed
under the direct influence of the objective world of things, themselves of
social origin and the product of what Marx broadly called "industry."

All these conditions lead to the formation of the highly complex systems of

From *Higher Cortical Functions in Man* by A. R. Luria, translated by Basil Haigh,
pp. 32–34, © 1966 Consultants Bureau Enterprises, Inc., and Basic Books, Inc., Publishers, New York. (Text, Chapter 1)

reflex connections, which reflect the objective world of products created by the practical efforts of society; these connections require the combined working of many receptors and the formation of new functional systems.

However, the child does not live entirely in a world of ready-made objects, produced by the work of society. From the very beginning of his life he must always be in contact with other people, and, in so doing, he must objectively master the existing language system and, with its aid, profit from the experience of other generations. This contact becomes the decisive factor in his future mental development, the decisive condition for the formation of the higher mental functions distinguishing man from animals.

Janet (1928) pointed out that the roots of processes such as voluntary memorizing, in daily use by everybody, are quite irrationally sought in the natural, distinctive features of the human brain; rather, in order to discover the origin of these complex forms of conscious mental activity it is necessary to turn to social history. The development of the higher forms of mental activity in the course of ontogenesis was studied by Vygotskii (1956, 1960), who showed that social contact between the child and adults always lies at the root of such forms of activity as paying attention or voluntary movement. By initially carrying out the adult's verbal command—pointing out a certain object or aspect of an object, suggesting a certain movement, etc.—and then reproducing the activity suggested by this verbal instruction and initiating it himself, the child gradually forms a new voluntary action that, in time, becomes a part of his individual behavior. Vygotskii's supposition that an action intially shared by two people later becomes an element of individual behavior has, as a corollary, the social origin of the higher mental functions and points to the social nature of those psychological phenomena that have usually been regarded as purely individualistic. The historical approach to the higher mental processes, revealing their social nature, thus eliminates both the spiritualistic and the naturalistic interpretations of these processes.

The social genesis of the higher mental functions—their formation in the process of objective activity and social communication—determines the second fundamental characteristic of these functions, *their mediate structure.* Vygotskii (1960) repeatedly declared that mental faculties do not evolve along "pure" lines, i.e., a particular property gradually perfecting itself, but, rather, develop along "mixed" lines, i.e., the creation of new, intermediate structures of mental processes and new "interfunctional" relationships directed toward the performance of previous tasks by new methods. The concept of "pure" and "mixed" evolution was introduced by the Russian psychologist, Vagner (1928), who conducted important research in the field of comparative psychology.

As examples of the mediate structure of higher mental functions, we may use any performance of a practical task by means of tools or solution of an internal, psychological problem by means of an auxiliary sign in order to organize the mental processes. When a person ties a knot in his handkerchief or makes a note in order to remember something, he carries out an operation apparently quite unrelated to the task in hand. In this way, however, the person masters his faculty of memory; by changing the structure of the memorizing process and giving it a mediate character, he thereby broadens its natural capacity. Mediate memorizing illustrates the structural principles of the higher mental functions. A closer analysis shows that this mediate structure is a characteristic feature of all higher mental processes.

Speech plays a decisive role in the mediation of mental processes. By being given a name, an object or its property is distinguished from its surroundings and is related to other objects or signs. The fact that "every word is a generalization" (Lenin) is vitally important to the systematic reflection of the outside world, to the transition from sensation to thinking, and to the creation of new functional systems. Speech not only gives names to the objects of the outside world; it also distinguishes among their essential properties and includes them in a system of relationships to other objects. As a result of language, man can evoke an image of a particular object and use it in the absence of the original. At the same time, speech, differentiating among the essential signs and generalizing on the objects or phenomena denoted, facilitates deeper penetration of the environment. Human mental processes are thereby elevated to a new level and are given new powers of organization, and man is enabled to direct his mental processes.

The reorganization of mental activity by means of speech and the incorporation of the system of speech connections into a large number of processes, hitherto direct in character, are among the more important factors in the formation of the higher mental functions, whereby man, as distinct from animals, acquires consciousness and volition.

The fact that the speech system is a factor in the formation of the higher mental functions is their most important feature. Because of this, Pavlov was justified in considering the "second signal system," which is based on speech, not only "an extraordinary addition, introducing a new principle of nervous activity," but also "the highest regulator of human behavior" (*Complete Collected Works,* Vol. 3, pp. 476, 490, 568–569, 577).

It would be wrong to suppose that the mediate structure of the higher mental functions, formed with the intimate participation of speech, is characteristic only of such forms of activity as memorizing, voluntary attention, or logical thinking. Recently reported investigations showed that even such mental processes as high-tone hearing, which have always been considered relatively elementary and apparently unrelated to the features described, are, in fact, formed under the influence of the prevalent social conditions and, above all, of language. The research of Leont'ev (1959, 1961) showed that high-tone hearing is one of the "systematic functions" formed in man with the close participation of language, the specific features of which cannot be understood without knowledge of the characteristic signs of the language in whose system human speech is formed. These investigations are not merely of great special interest, but are also of decisive general importance, for they demonstrate the social nature and systematic structure not only of complex, but also of relatively simple, human mental processes. Consequently, when considering the cerebral organization of higher mental functions, we must always take into account the factors just enumerated.

II

SYMBOLIC PROCESSES: NATURE AND SETTING

SOCIAL PSYCHOLOGISTS are interested in language only secondarily as a phenomenon per se, and primarily because of its relationships to behavior. A basic characteristic of human groups is that they exist because of and through communication. Language is always a group product, and it is both an intrinsic part of the social heritage and the mechanism by means of which this heritage is transmitted from one generation to the next. Psychological activity is essentially sign behavior, and ranges in complexity from the simple direct responses of lower animals to the higher thought processes of human beings. Signs are often classified as "natural" and "conventional," the latter being called "symbols." The basic type of human symbolic activity is the process of conversing. The meanings of symbols arise in interaction and are thus a group contribution: symbolic behavior is shared behavior from which common goals and understandings arise.

The reactions of human beings to their surroundings are mediated ones. They are not based on "reality" as such, but rather on ideas of that reality expressed mainly by means of symbols. The names, concepts, and categories—in short the cognitions—by means of which people seek to understand the world and in terms of which they act are social products. Our understanding of how men think and of their symbolic environments are, then, of critical significance in explaining what they do and how they act.

Cognitive structures and symbolic environments imply that many human motivations have little or no discernible biological bases. Numerous motivations arise from the social structures within which individuals are reared. Desire for fame or wealth are among such motivations. Another type of motivation is associated with, and seems to arise within, the communication process itself. An instance is the need to understand one's world—that is, to grasp it and to represent it in cognitive or symbolic schemes. The very existence of linguistic patterns creates the possibility of becoming concerned with the relationships among symbols themselves (for example, when one becomes aware of logical contradictions between two statements). The motivations of scientific theorizing are, in large part, of this nature. In any event, new cognitions produce new motivations, and as one's cognitive world becomes more complex, so do one's motives.

Men are to some extent, therefore, different from other animals. Observation of the cooperative behavior of certain species of animals has made it clear to some researchers that the idea that evolution leads only to changes in degree—and not in kind—of behavior should be rejected. Instead, the evolutionary process leads both to quantitative change and to the gradual emergence of genuinely new forms and properties of behavior. The study of lower animals helps the social psychologist to understand man by revealing the simpler forms of behavior and communication from which the complex symbolic and cultural behavior of modern man evolved.

The lack or loss of language has serious behavioral consequences. The isolated child and the blind deaf who do not learn a language fail to become socialized human beings; they exhibit types of behavioral (including motivational) disabilities. Even temporary isolation can bring about temporary disabilities. Investigations of aphasia

and schizophrenia (despite the complexity of
the disorders and the controversies over research
results) seem also to confirm the importance of
language as the integrative agent in human behavior.

6

SIGNS AND COMMUNICATION SYSTEMS

George A. Miller

INTERMEDIATE BETWEEN THE STIMULATING SITUATION and the response to it is always the activity of receptor cells and sensory nerves. As far as the brain is concerned the activity of the sensory nerves stands for, or represents, the stimuli. The representation is adequate for most behavioral adaptations; it is nonetheless a highly schematic and inaccurate picture of the world. Thus physics tells us the thing we perceive to be a table is mostly open space and is held together by fields of force in a way entirely foreign to our general knowledge of tables.

It is common to begin a discussion of communication by pointing out that words are *signs* that conveniently replace the objects or ideas they represent. It would be misleading to imply, however, that this representative character of words distinguishes them sharply from all other stimuli to which we respond. The word "chair" is clearly not the chair itself, but a symbol for the chair. Similarly, the light reflected from the object is not the chair itself. In either case the response is made to something that represents the chair. The something may be light rays reflected from the chair, or it may be sound waves arbitrarily associated with the chair. But it is not the chair.

In short, listeners respond to spoken words in the same way they respond to other energies that impinge upon their receptor organs.

Words cannot be distinguished from other stimuli on the basis of their representative role or their organization into patterns. What, then, is the distinguishing mark of a verbal stimulus? One possible distinction is that words have an *arbitrary* significance. Words signify only what we have learned that they signify. The fact that we say "chair" and not *"Stuhl"* is a matter of social coincidence. In contrast, the association between the light rays reflected from a chair and the chair itself is not arbitrary. Verbal signs that are organized into linguistic systems are usually called verbal *symbols.*

The arbitrary nature of a verbal stimulus is clear when we consider the role of learning. In general we learn to repeat those acts which are rewarded. If bumping into a chair is never rewarded, we soon stop behaving that way and start walking around it. In such cases the nature of the physical situation ensures that our responses develop in a certain way. Our response to the word "chair," however, develops differently. In order that we learn to respond correctly to the word "chair," *it is necessary for another organism to intervene and reward us each time we respond correctly.* Since the intervening organism can reward a range of possible responses, the choice of the sound pattern "chair" is quite arbitrary.

Once a society has adopted a set of symbols and rules for combining them, the conventions are no longer arbitrary. If everyone agrees to call a horse a horse, then we are no longer free to call horses by any symbol that occurs to us. Selecting new words arbitrarily isolates us from the rest of the language community. The arbitrary decision was made centuries ago, and many people abide by it. The point is that other decisions might have been made.

We have said that we must study behavior, that verbalization is a special and important kind of behavior, that behavior must be guided by stimulation, and that the association between stimulation and action may be quite arbitrary. A general introduction would not be complete, however, if it did not stress the importance of order, of pattern, in verbal behavior.

Speech sounds do not occur as isolated bits. They are interwoven in elaborate designs. It is instructive to imagine a language that makes no use of the pattern of its individual sounds. "Ah" might stand for "How do you do" and "ee" for "Please help me," and so on. There would be very few things such a language could talk about, for men can make and distinguish less than 100 different speech sounds. If we produce only some 50 different sounds and we want to use them to talk about millions of different things, we must use combinations of sounds. If, for example, we use all the possible pairs of 50 sounds, we can make 2500 different statements. If the 2500 statements are not enough, we can go on to use patterns of three or four or even a thousand sounds. There are many more patterns than there are individual sounds. The ability to use such patterns, however, is uniquely human.

A language is of little value if its elements cannot be arranged and rearranged in a variety of sequences. We must know, for example, how a child learns the word "bear" and the word "eats," but we must also study how the child learns to distinguish "the bear eats" from "eats the bear" and "bear the eats." To step on a man's toe and then to apologize is not the same as to apologize first and then step on his toe. The order of events is often more significant than the events themselves.

As soon as we begin to consider all the possible patterns of speech elements, we discover that the vast majority of these possible patterns is never used. Some patterns sound too much alike, some patterns are too hard to pronounce, some are prohibited by grammar or by common sense. Our choice of symbol sequences for the purposes of communication is restricted by rules. The job is to discover what the rules are and what advantages or disadvantages they create.

Every communication must have a *source* and a *destination* for the information that is transferred, and these must be distinct in space or time. Between the source and the destination there must be some link that spans the intervening space or time, and this link is called a communication *channel*. In order that the information can pass over the channel, it is necessary to operate on it in such a way that it is suitable for transmission, and the component that performs this operation is a *transmitter*. At the destination there must be a *receiver* that converts the transmitted information into its original form. These five components—source, transmitter, channel, receiver, and destination—comprise the idealized communication system. In one form or another these five components are present in every kind of communication.

In most communication systems the source of the information is a human being. From his past experience and present needs and perceptions this source has information to pass along to others. The transmitter discussed most thoroughly in the following pages is the human speech machinery. This machinery operates upon the information and changes it into a pattern of sound waves that is carried through the air. The channel of principal interest to us will be the air medium that connects the talker's speech machinery with the listener's ears. The ear is a receiver that operates upon the acoustic waves to convert them into nervous activity at their destination, the nervous system of the listener. This particular system is called the vocal communication system.

Many other examples of communication systems can be described. When a person writes himself a note on his memorandum pad, the writer at one time is the source, the process of writing is the transmitter, the permanence of the pad is the channel that spans intervening time, the reader's eyes are the receiver, and the same person at a later time is the destination. A telegraph system is a simple example: the source supplies a sequence of letters that is converted by the transmitter into dots, dashes, and spaces, the receiver reconverts the signal into letters, and the message is passed along to its destination.

The operation of the transmitter is often referred to as *encoding*. The code is the pattern of energies that can travel over the connecting link. The receiver reverses the operation of the transmitter and reconverts the coded message into a more usable form. Thus the operation of the receiver is referred to as *decoding*. We usually think of codes in terms of secrets and international intrigue, but here we shall speak of codes in a much more general sense. Any system of symbols that, by prior agreement between the source and destination, is used to represent and convey information will be called a code. Thus, in the sense we use the word here, the French language is one code and the German language another. Spoken English is the code that will interest us primarily, but similar considerations apply for all codes.

One additional factor must be considered before the idealized communication system is complete. This factor concerns the possibility of error. Mistakes may occur in encoding or decoding the messages or may be introduced while the signal is in transit over the channel. If the people communicating are unfamiliar with the code, or if they are unable to distinguish the differences among the symbols, errors become likely. If there is a disturbance in the channel that changes the individual symbols or permutes their order, errors in communication result. It is sometimes convenient to lump all these sources of error together under a single name, *noise*. When we say that a communication system is noisy, we mean that there is a good chance for error to occur. If the chance of error is very great, we say that the noise level is high. If errors are very unlikely, we say the noise level is low.

7

A CLUE
TO THE NATURE
OF MAN:
THE SYMBOL

Ernst Cassirer

IN THE HUMAN WORLD we find a new characteristic which appears to be the distinctive mark of human life. The functional circle of man is not only quantitatively enlarged; it has also undergone a qualitative change. Man has, as it were, discovered a new method of adapting himself to his environment. Between the receptor system and the effector system, which are to be found in all animal species, we find in man a third link which we may describe as the *symbolic system*. This new acquisition transforms the whole of human life. As compared with the other animals man lives not merely in a broader reality; he lives, so to speak, in a new *dimension* of reality. There is an unmistakable difference between organic reactions and human responses. In the first case a direct and immediate answer is given to an outward stimulus; in the second case the answer is delayed. It is interrupted and retarded by a slow and complicated process of thought. At first sight such a delay may appear to be a very questionable gain. Many philosophers have warned man against this pretended progress. "L'homme qui médite," says Rousseau, "est un animal dépravé": it is not an improvement but a deterioration of human nature to exceed the boundaries of organic life.

Yet there is no remedy against this reversal of the natural order. Man cannot escape from his own achievement. He cannot but adopt the conditions of his own life. No longer in a merely physical universe, man lives in a symbolic universe. Language, myth, art, and religion are parts of this universe.

From Ernst Cassirer, *An Essay on Man,* pp. 42–44. Copyright © 1944 by Yale University Press. (Text, Chapter 3)

They are the varied threads which weave the symbolic net, the tangled web of human experience. All human progress in thought and experience refines upon and strengthens this net. No longer can man confront reality immediately; he cannot see it, as it were, face to face. Physical reality seems to recede in proportion as man's symbolic activity advances. Instead of dealing with the things themselves man is in a sense constantly conversing with himself. He has so enveloped himself in linguistic forms, in artistic images, in mythical symbols or religious rites that he cannot see or know anything except by the interposition of this artificial medium. His situation is the same in the theoretical as in the practical sphere. Even here man does not live in a world of hard facts, or according to his immediate needs and desires. He lives rather in the midst of imaginary emotions, in hopes and fears, in illusions and disillusions, in his fantasies and dreams. "What disturbs and alarms man," said Epictetus, "are not the things, but his opinions and fancies about the things."

From the point of view at which we have just arrived we may correct and enlarge the classical definition of man. In spite of all the efforts of modern irrationalism this definition of man as an *animal rationale* has not lost its force. Rationality is indeed an inherent feature of all human activities. Mythology itself is not simply a crude mass of superstitions or gross delusions. It is not merely chaotic, for it possesses a systematic or conceptual form.[1] But, on the other hand, it would be impossible to characterize the structure of myth as rational. Language has often been identified with reason, or with the very source of reason. But it is easy to see that this definition fails to cover the whole field. It is a *pars pro toto;* it offers us a part for the whole. For side by side with conceptual language there is an emotional language; side by side with logical or scientific language there is a language of poetic imagination. Primarily language does not express thoughts or ideas, but feelings and affections. And even a religion "within the limits of pure reason" as conceived and worked out by Kant is no more than a mere abstraction. It conveys only the ideal shape, only the shadow, of what a genuine and concrete religious life is. The great thinkers who have defined man as an *animal rationale* were not empiricists, nor did they ever intend to give an empirical account of human nature. By this definition they were expressing rather a fundamental moral imperative. Reason is a very inadequate term with which to comprehend the forms of man's cultural life in all their richness and variety. But all these forms are symbolic forms. Hence, instead of defining man as an *animal rationale,* we should define him as an *animal symbolicum.* By so doing we can designate his specific difference, and we can understand the new way open to man—the way to civilization.

[1] See Cassirer, *Die Begriffsform im mythischen Denken* (Leipzig, 1921).

8
INTELLIGENCE
AND SOCIETY

Jean Piaget

THE HUMAN BEING IS IMMERSED right from birth in a social environment which affects him just as much as his physical environment. Society, even more, in a sense, than the physical environment, changes the very structure of the individual, because it not only compels him to recognize facts, but also provides him with a ready-made system of signs, which modify his thought; it presents him with new values and it imposes on him an infinite series of obligations. It is therefore quite evident that social life affects intelligence through the three media of language (signs), the content of interaction (intellectual values) and rules imposed on thought (collective logical or pre-logical norms).

Certainly, it is necessary for sociology to envisage society as a whole, even though this whole, which is quite distinct from the sum of the individuals composing it, is only the totality of relations or interaction between these individuals. Every relation between individuals (from two onwards) literally modifies them and therefore immediately constitutes a whole, so that the whole formed by society is not so much a thing, a being or a cause as a system of relations. But these relations are extremely numerous and complex since, in fact, they constitute just as much a continuous plot in history, through the action of successive generations on each other, as a synchronous system of equilibrium at each moment of history. It is therefore legitimate to

From Jean Piaget, *The Psychology of Intelligence* (New York: Humanities Press, 1950), pp. 156–159. Reprinted by permission of Humanities Press, Inc., and Routledge & Kegan Paul Ltd. (Text, Chapter 3)

adopt statistical language and to speak of "society" as a coherent whole (in the same way as a *Gestalt* is the resultant of a statistical system of relations). But it is essential to remember the statistical nature of statements in sociological language, since to forget this would be to attribute a mythological sense to the words. In the sociology of thought it might even be asked whether it would not be better to replace the usual global language by an enumeration of the types of relation involved (types which, needless to say, are likewise statistical).

When we are concerned with psychology, on the other hand, i.e., when the unit of reference is the individual modified by social relations, rather than the complex or complexes of relations as such, it becomes quite wrong to content oneself with statistical terms, since these are too general. The "effect of social life" is a concept which is just as vague as that of "the effect of the physical environment" if it is not described in detail. From birth to adult life, the human being is subject, as nobody denies, to social pressures, but these pressures are of extremely varied types and are subject to a certain order of development. Just as the physical environment is not imposed on developing intelligence all at once or as a single entity, but in such a way that acquisitions can be followed step by step as a function of experience, and especially as a function of the kinds of assimilation or accommodation— varying greatly according to mental level—that govern these acquisitions, so the social environment gives rise to interactions between the developing individual and his fellow, interactions that differ greatly from one another and succeed one another according to definite laws. These types of interaction and these laws of succession are what the psychologist must carefully establish, lest he simplify the task to the extent of giving it up in favour of the problems of sociology. Now there is no longer any reason for conflict between this science and psychology once one recognises the extent to which the structure of the individual is modified by these interactions; both of these two disciplines, therefore, stand to gain by an investigation that goes beyond a global analysis and undertakes to analyse relations.

THE SOCIALIZATION OF
INDIVIDUAL INTELLIGENCE

The interaction with his social environment in which the individual indulges varies widely in nature according to his level of development, and consequently in its turn it modifies the individual's mental structure in an equally varied manner.

During the sensori-motor period the infant is, of course, already subject to manifold social influences; people afford him the greatest pleasures known to his limited experience—from food to the warmth of the affection which surrounds him—people gather round him, smile at him, amuse him, calm him; they inculcate habits and regular courses of conduct linked to signals and words; some behaviour is already forbidden and he is scolded. In short, seen from without, the infant is in the midst of a multitude of relations which fore-run the signs, values and rules of subsequent social life. But from the point of view of the subject himself, the social environment is still not essentially distinct from the physical environment, at least up to the fifth of the stages of sensori-motor intelligence that we have distinguished (Chap. IV). The signs that are used to affect him are, as far as he is concerned, only indices or signals. The rules imposed on him are not yet obligations of conscience and he confuses them with the regularity characteristic of habit. As for peo-ple, they are seen as pictures like all the pictures which constitute reality, but they are particularly active, unpredictable and the source of the most intense feelings. The infant reacts to them in the same way as to objects, namely with gestures that happen to cause them to continue interesting actions, and with various cries, but there is still as yet no interchange of thought, since at this level the child does not know thought; nor, consequently, is there any pro-found modification of intellectual structures by the social life surrounding him.[1]

With the acquisition of language, however, i.e. with the advent of the sym-bolic and intuitive periods, new social relations appear which enrich and transform the individual's thought. But in this context three points should be noted.

In the first place, the system of collective signs does not create the symbolic function, but naturally develops it to a degree that the individual by himself would never know. Nevertheless, the sign as such, conventional (arbitrary) and ready-made, is not an adequate medium of expression for the young child's thought; he is not satisfied with speaking, he must needs "play out" what he thinks and symbolize his ideas by means of gestures or objects, and represent things by imitation, drawing and construction. In short, from the point of view of expression itself, the child at the outset is still midway be-tween the use of the collective sign and that of the individual symbol, both still being necessary, no doubt, but the second being much more so in the child than in the adult.

In the second place, language conveys to the individual an already pre-pared system of ideas, classifications, relations—in short, an inexhaustible stock of concepts which are reconstructed in each individual after the age-old pattern which previously moulded earlier generations. But it goes without saying that the child begins by borrowing from this collection only as much as suits him, remaining disdainfully ignorant of everything that exceeds his mental level. And again, that which is borrowed is assimilated in accordance with his intellectual structure; a word intended to carry a general concept at first engenders only a half-individual, half-socialised pre-concept (the word "bird" thus evokes the familiar canary, etc.).

---

[1] From the affective point of view, it is no doubt only at the stage at which the notion of an object is formed that there is a projection of affectivity on to people conceived as similar centres of independent action.

There remain, in the third place, the actual relations that the subject maintains with his fellow beings, i.e. "synchronous" relations, as opposed to the "diachronic" processes that influence the child's acquisition of language and the modes of thought that are associated with it. Now these synchronous relations are at first essential; when conversing with his family, the child will at every moment see his thoughts approved or contradicted, and he will discover a vast world of thought external to himself, which will instruct or impress him in various ways. From the point of view of intelligence (which is all that concerns us here), he will therefore be led to an ever more intensive exchange of intellectual values and will be forced to accept an ever-increasing number of obligatory truths (ready-made ideas and true norms of reasoning).

9
THE STUDY OF
PRIMATE BEHAVIOR

Sherwood L. Washburn

David A. Hamburg

ANIMAL BEHAVIOR MAY BE INVESTIGATED in the laboratory, in artificial colonies, or under natural conditions. The kinds of knowledge gained from these different approaches supplement each other, and all are necessary if the complex roots of behavior are to be understood.

The study of the clinging reflex offers an example of this interrelationship of approaches. Harlow has shown that a baby monkey will cling to a piece of cloth; if the monkey is placed on a smooth surface it will attempt to stand, but if the cloth touches the monkey it will cling instead of trying to stand. The clinging reflex thus takes precedence over the righting reflex. This isolated fact has little meaning in the laboratory, but when free-ranging monkeys are observed the infants are seen to cling to their mothers when the group moves. In all the kinds of monkeys studied so far the clinging reflex is present at birth, and the infant monkey's survival depends on this ability to cling while its mother feeds, walks, and runs. The existence of the reflex and the infant's response to various textures can be investigated only in the laboratory, but the adaptive significance of the behavior can be appreciated only in the field. Mammals have adapted to meet the problem of the care of the newborn in many different ways: by the construction of nests, burrows, and lairs in which the young may stay; by rapid maturation so the young may keep up; by births taking place in protected locations. Most primates have adapted by the ability of the young to cling.

This behavior adaptation, reflex clinging, is essential for the survival of the species, and it must be observed to be appreciated. A newborn gibbon does not cling to a calm and sitting mother, but to one which feeds at the ends of branches that are swaying in the wind. Far above the ground, the mother may suddenly run along a branch, drop below it, taking a few violent swings, and then plunge out into the air, dropping many feet to a lower branch in a neighboring tree, landing on swaying branches or with more swings. The infant clings through these violent acrobatics, and in the flight of gibbons through giant trees the infant-mother problem is shown to be very different from the way it appears in a small cage. The strength of the clinging is essential to survival, for the mother cannot be inactive and live. The mother's hands and feet are completely involved in locomotion, and in her swings and leaps she cannot help the infant and survive herself.

The behavior of mother and infant gibbon is an adaptation to the arboreal way of life. It depends on the behavior of both mother and infant, on the grasping hands and feet of the infant, on reflexes, and, probably, on behavior the adult female has learned. Monkeys brought up in isolation do not know how to take care of their infants (Harlow 1962; Mason, Chap. 15, this volume). Here again the interrelation of the field and the laboratory are shown. The field study shows the nature and importance of the infant's and the mother's behavior, but which parts of the behavior are reflex and which learned cannot be told from the field work any more than the actual problems and hazards of the relation of mother and infant can be seen in the laboratory.

The natural situation may be further complicated because the mother may be helped by other members of the group. For example, a mother baboon was seen with a newborn infant, probably only a few hours old. The infant still could not cling adequately, and its mother repeatedly helped it with one hand. The three-legged walking was difficult for the mother and she lagged behind the main body of the group of baboons and sat down every few yards. Right beside her walked an adult male. When she sat, he sat; when she started up, he started up. His actions were timed to hers, and she was never left without protection during this awkward period.

Mothers with young are centers of interest for other females, adult males, and juvenile females. It is not just the mother-infant relation that is important; this essential diadic relation is imbedded in a matrix of social interaction. The infant monkey is born into an intensely social group, and the survival of the infant depends on the adaptation and survival of the whole group. The size and composition of this group depend on the species of primate. Its patterned behavior differs depending on the structure, physiology, and ecology of the particular species and group, but in all the monkeys and apes adaptation is by group life, and survival is only possible for a member of a group.

In nature the observer sees evidence of this vital sociability in the functioning of the group, and in the laboratory Butler (1954) has shown that monkeys will work hard when the only reward is the sight of another monkey.

The behavior of the mother and of the infant monkey, and the associated behavior of the other monkeys in the group, make possible the survival of the species. Reproduction depends on breeding seasons, mating patterns, developmental physiology, and on the social structures of the group. The young are conceived, carried and born, and reared only through the coordination of a wide range of structural, physiological, and behavioral mechanisms. Behavior is an essential part of the adaptive mechanisms as seen in field studies, but much of the important adaptive behavior does not appear under normal laboratory conditions. Field studies are particularly important in discovering the actual way the adaptive behavior functions.

The relations of structure and function and behavior are so important in understanding the importance of field studies that two further examples will be given here.

1. Sleep is a major behavioral problem. Old-World monkeys sleep at night, frequently on small limbs high off the ground. By sleeping at night in positions of difficult access, the monkeys avoid most of the carnivores, since the latter are active only after dark. But since the monkeys are social, large numbers of animals must sleep in small numbers of trees, and preferably away from the trunk and large limbs where carnivores can easily climb. The monkeys have evolved specialized sitting pads, ischial callosities, that permit them to sleep sitting upright in comfort. This is the usual position in the trees, but monkeys will nap lying on their sides if comfortable protected places are available. In a zoo the same monkey that slept sitting up in the wild will sleep on its side. The structure of callosities and their distribution in the primates had been studied, but it was only in the field studies that their importance became apparent. Among the apes, the gibbons have callosities and probably sleep in a sitting position (more study is needed here). The great apes have lost their callosities and only traces are left in some individuals (Miller 1945; Schultz 1956). But they build nests and sleep in them, the nests performing the same function as the callosities, both are structures letting the animals sleep in trees. It has been shown that nest building is learned (Bernstein 1962) so a learned behavior pattern has replaced the function of the ischial callosity and has led to its evolutionary loss.

2. Fear provides a second example of structure-function. Structure need not be hard and obvious like callosities; emotional responses also are rooted in the animal's physiology and are essential adaptations. Such responses will be considered particularly in the last chapter in their relation to human evolution, but they are important in the context of structure-function as well. The primate actors in their social groups are highly emotional, and no deep understanding of primate social life is possible unless the emotions are considered. For example, it has been shown in conditioning experiments with several mammalian species that fear is hard to extinguish; fear lingers on

while learned responses of a rewarding nature drop out more readily, when the responses are no longer rewarded. This experimental finding becomes particularly interesting in relation to some recent field observations.

In Nairobi Park DeVore had begun to study a large group of more than 80 baboons, which could easily be approached in a car. A local parasitologist shot two of these baboons with a .22 rifle, and eight months later this group was still "wild" and could not be approached, even though the animal must have seen cars almost daily in the interval. The adaptive function of such behavior is striking: danger is learned in one trial and this kind of learning will not extinguish for a long time. It takes many, many neutral experiences, probably over years, to extinguish one violent experience. It should be especially noted in the baboon incident described above that it is very unlikely all the animals in the group saw the shooting; the experience of some of the animals became part of the whole group's adaptive behavior. In contrast to this, it has been found by the Japanese, who not only have provisioned monkeys but also have deliberately introduced new foods and studied their adoption, that it may take months for a new, pleasant food habit to spread to all the members of the group. In the case of fear, survival is at stake and a minimum experience produces a maximum result. In the case of a new eating habit, it is probably even advantageous that a new food be tried slowly. Adaptation under natural conditions shows clearly why it is essential for fear to be quickly learned and hard to extinguish.

The social group itself is an adaptation of supreme importance. For instance, as the preceding example of the baboon group illustrates, the members of a group do not necessarily learn fearful response to a particular situation from their individual experiences. Among baboons, when dominant animals give a warning cry and run, the others flee without looking for the source of the danger. As will be described repeatedly in later chapters reporting field observations, the majority of primates live their whole lives in close association with others. The social group occupies a range, shares knowledge of local foods, paths, and dangers, and offers opportunity for play, grooming, and close association. In the group the young and females are protected, and dominance gives an order to society. For monkeys the reproductive success that is necessary for evolutionary success occurs only within the group. Field studies are particularly important to these findings because it is only under natural conditions that the functioning group may be observed.

Under natural conditions an individual animal often cannot respond promptly to motivational pressures, even when basic physiological needs are involved. For example, a thirsty baboon cannot safely leave the group and go away seeking water. When baboons are living in country where water is restricted, the whole group moves to water, and the individual can satisfy its needs only as the whole pattern of the group's activity makes this possible.

If baboons are drinking water from many small sources (such as the puddles from the spray at Victoria Falls), any animal can drink when it wants to and drinking is frequent. But the same animals when drinking from the

Zambesi River, where there are crocodiles, monitor lizards, and pythons, drink rapidly and with extreme care. At the end of the dry season a group approaching a water hole moves with caution, frequently pausing and watching other animals to assess the safety of the area. Thirst is satisfied within the complex patterned activity of the group, and the nature of this activity shows that the animals of the group know the local problems and are prepared to meet crises.

Neither individual monkeys nor the social group can wait until confronted by needs and situations (danger, thirst, hunger, sex) to respond to them; the social system must be *adapted to anticipate* both daily needs and occasional crises. A system that could meet only day-to-day problems would not survive for long, and evolution, through natural selection, builds a substantial margin of safety into the individual animals and into their way of life. The group moves more, is more exploratory, is more playful than there is any need for on the average day, but by so doing it is preparing for crises. The individual animals appear stronger and more intelligent than is necessary for normal activity, but survival requires coping with the rare event.

In field studies the primary data are the observations of the behavior of the animals. Daily activities are recorded, and, with time and luck, encounters with carnivores, diseased animals, injuries, fights, and other crises are observed. The size of a range or the number of individuals in a group may be objectively recorded, but the comparison and interpretation of the data necessarily involve subjective evaluations. Is the number of individuals in a group determined by species-specific biology, ecological factors, social factors, or by a combination of all of these? When data on the behavior of nonhuman primates are presented, the question arises whether the behavior is instinctive or learned. Behavior may, of course, be recorded without regard to this question, but it cannot be interpreted without consideration of this issue. Recent experimental work (Mason, Chap. 15, this volume) has shown that learning is far more important in the development of social behavior than anyone had imagined; monkeys reared in isolation even fail to mate normally, an activity that many thought to be purely instinctive. Actually the relative roles of inherited and environmental factors may be very different for different items of behavior. Infant clinging may be an almost purely inbuilt reflex, and adequate sexual performance may require only a minimum of childhood play, whereas food habits may be largely learned. There is much room for further experimentation and field work.

In summary, from an evolutionary point of view selection is for successful behavior. Structure, physiology, social life, all these are the result of selection, and the structure-physiology-behavior of populations of primates are adapted to each other and to a way of life. Parts of this complex are almost entirely the result of heredity with a minimum dependence on environment, whereas others are heavily influenced by learning. It is advantageous for behavior to be adaptable, to adjust to a wide variety of circumstances. What is inherited is ease of learning, rather than fixed instinctive patterns. The species easily, almost inevitably, learns the essential behaviors for its survival. So, although it is true that monkeys learn to be social, they are so constructed that under normal circumstances this learning always takes place. Similarly, human beings learn to talk, but they inherit structures that make this inevitable, except under the most peculiar circumstances. Although great efforts have been expended, chimpanzees simply do not learn to communicate verbally. The genetically determined neural substrate is not sufficient to support speech behavior.

10

SPEECH AND
THE HUMAN REVOLUTION[1]

Charles F. Hockett

Robert Ascher

THIS ESSAY ATTEMPTS TO SET FORTH the story of the emergence of the first humans from their prehuman ancestors. A special feature is that we have tried to incorporate the various steps and stages of the evolution of language into the total picture.[2]

From Hockett, Charles F., and Robert Ascher, 1964. "The Human Revolution," in *Current Anthropology,* Vol. 5, No. 3, 135–147, 166–168. By permission of the authors and *Current Anthropology.* (Text, Chapter 4)

[1] Earlier versions of this paper were read: Wednesday, 27 February 1963, at The University of Toronto, as the last of the 1962–63 Lecture Series of the Presidential Committee on Linguistics (under the title "Language and Man: The Contribution of Linguistics to our Understanding of Human Behaviour"); Saturday, 30 March 1963, at The Northeast Anthropological Conference held in Ithaca, New York; Saturday, 27 April 1963, at The Buffalo English Linguistics Project, University of Buffalo; and Friday, 10 May 1963, at a Supper Conference of The Wenner-Gren Foundation for Anthropological Research, in New York City. Many comments from members of these audiences have been incorporated into the present version. We wish especially to acknowledge valuable suggestions from David Stout of The University of Buffalo and from Allan R. Holmberg of Cornell University.

[2] Most paleoanthropologists have either ignored language or have tried to infer from a fossil skull or jaw that its owner could, or could not, have had "articulate speech." Childe (1936; 1951 edition: 29) fell into this error, as has Keleman (1948); for a brief discussion, see Hockett (1956). Other examples are cited in Coon (1962:259 fn. 1, 299 fn. 5), where Coon shows his own healthy skepticism of such inferences. The basis of the trouble is that "articulate speech" does not mean anything. Bryan (1963) falls into the same trap.

We dedicate this essay to the memory of Paul Fejos, whose encouragement, over a number of years, played an important part in bringing the work to fruition.

The inquiry into human origins is a collective task to which hundreds of investigators have contributed. Virtually none of the proposals in the present paper are our own. Even for the ways of thinking about the evidence that seem to be fruitful, we are completely indebted to our predecessors. We do accept responsibility for the particular way in which we have chosen among alternative theories, and for the way in which we have tied them together. We believe that the time is ripe for a synthesis of this sort, if only as a clear point of departure for the further investigation of both method and detail.

The term "revolution" in our title is not intended to be flamboyant. A revolution is a relatively sudden set of changes that yield a state of affairs from which a return to the situation just before the revolution is virtually impossible. This seems to be the sense of the word intended by V. Gordon Childe (1936) when he speaks of the "Neolithic Revolution" and of the "Urban Revolution." But these two revolutions were experienced by our fully human ancestors. The second could not have occurred had it not been for the first. The first could not have taken place had it not been for an even earlier extremely drastic set of changes that turned nonhumans into humans. These drastic changes, as we shall see, may have required a good many millions of years; yet they can validly be regarded as "sudden" in view of the tens of millions of years of mammalian history that preceded them.

For the reconstruction of human evolution we have evidence of two sorts, plus certain firm and many tentative principles of interpretation.

One kind of evidence is the archeological, fossil, and geological record. The fossil record of our own ancestry is still disappointingly sparse for the bulk of the Miocene and Pliocene. It seems unlikely that such records can ever be as complete as we might wish. But techniques of interpretation improve, and we suspect that the archeological record, in particular, holds an as yet unrealized potential.

The second kind of evidence is the directly observable physical structure and ways of life of ourselves and of our nearest nonhuman cousins, the other hominoids of today. Chimpanzees, gorillas, orangutans, gibbons, siamangs,

---

Some recent discussions (e.g., Critchley 1960) try to deal with the emergence of language merely in terms of the contrast between "sign" and "symbol"; intentionally or not, these treatments give the impression that our ancestors acquired language in a single enormous leap. Anyone aware of the intricacy of design of every human language knows that such a leap was impossible; there had to be steps and stages. The contrast between "sign" and "symbol," first carefully discussed by Langer (1942), then adopted and developed by White (e.g., 1949, 1959), is too gross to serve. In White's version, the definition of the distinction is ultimately circular. A more elaborate itemization of design features found in human and animal communication will be found in Hockett (1959, 1960a, 1960b, 1963a). Stuart A. Altmann, of the Department of Zoology, University of Alberta, is currently engaged in making even more subtle discriminations in this area.

and humans have ultimately a common ancestry not shared with any other living species. We shall refer to their most recent common ancestors as the *proto-hominoids*. Since all the hominoids of today constitute continuations of the proto-hominoids, we can attempt to reconstruct something of the physical structure and of the lifeways of the common ancestors by comparing those of the descendants. Such an effort at reconstruction must at the same time propose realistic courses of development from the ancestral group down to each of the directly observable descendant groups, and must make proper provision for those strains known only through fossils or archeological remains.

The method is very much like the comparative method in historical linguistics—and, as a matter of fact, it was first devised in the latter context, only subsequently transferred to the domain of biological evolution.[3] The term "comparative" appears also in "comparative morphology" (or "comparative anatomy"); we must therefore emphasize that the method of which we are speaking applies not only to gross anatomy but also to the fine-scale phenomena dealt with in biochemistry, and not only to structure but also to behavior.

In any domain of application, a comparative method shares with all other historical methods the fact that it can yield reliable results only insofar as one can be sure of certain key *irreversible* processes. Given information about stages A and B in the history of a single system, we can posit that stage A preceded stage B if and only if the change from A to B is the sort that happens, while a change from B to A is impossible or highly improbable. In historical linguistics, the requisite irreversibility is afforded by sound change. The philologists of the late 19th century were correct when they characterized sound change as slow, constant, inexorable, and beyond conscious control; for, as we shall see later, it is a necessary by-product of a crucial design feature of all human language, and could not be eliminated save by altering language into something unrecognizable. Whenever sound change leads to the repatterning of the phonological system of a language—and this has happened about 100 times in English between King Alfred's day and our own (Hockett 1958:457)[4]—the consequences ramify through every part of the language; soon the results are so scattered, so subtle, and from the point of view of effectiveness of communication so *trivial,* that a return to the state of affairs before the repatterning has, in effect, probability zero.

The situation in biological evolution is much more complicated, with no

---

[3] The first comparative grammar was published in 1799 (Bloomfield 1933: ch. 1; see also Pederson 1931). The mutual stimulation of biologists and linguists at the time of Darwin is briefly discussed by Greenberg (1959). In the literature of the last few decades we fail to find any discussion of the comparative method that properly highlights the necessary differences in its applications to language, to human lifeways other than language, and in genetics and phylogeny. The authors are attempting to fill this hiatus in a forthcoming article; the remarks in the next few paragraphs of the present paper are only suggestive.

[4] For the nature of sound change see Hockett (1958: chs. 52–54) and Bloomfield (1933: chs. 20–21).

simple analogue for sound change. Is a particular organ in a particular species (living or fossil) vestigial or incipient? Is the swimming bladder of current teleosts a former lung, or is the lung of lungfishes a one-time swimming bladder? Evolutionists are plagued by such questions. The answers are often obtainable, but not through any simple formula. A new fossil does not automatically resolve the dispute, since one's opinions as to lines and directions of development will affect one's notions as to how the new fossil is to be fitted into the picture.

For the *mechanisms* of change we are in less trouble. We have now a good understanding of genetics, and also of the traditional transmission of lifeways. The latter was once believed to be exclusively human, but this is not so. At least for land mammals and for birds, genetics and tradition work in a constant dialectic complementation, neither being wholly responsible for anything (Hochbaum 1955; Dobzhansky 1956; 1962). We are also clearer about a point that used to be quite obscure: the domain (so to speak) within which these two mechanisms operate is not the individual but the community, which has a gene pool, a distribution of phenotypes, and a repository of lifeways, and which, as a functioning unit, faces the problems of survival (Simpson 1958).

The greatest pitfall in evolutionary thinking stems from the keenness of hindsight.[5] For example, we know that long ago, over a long period of time, our own ancestors abandoned the trees for the ground and developed effective machinery for bipedal locomotion. This seems beyond dispute, because the prehominoid primates were arboreal and we ourselves are bipedal ground walkers. But when we ask *why* this change, we must remember that our ancestors of the time were not striving to become human. They were doing what all animals do: trying to stay alive.

Thus, in searching for causes of the change we must look to conditions pertaining at the time. There are only two possibilities. The conditions at that time may have been such that minor variations in gait and posture had no bearing on survival. We should then class the change that actually did take place as fortuitous. Or, the conditions of life at the time may have positively favored selection for bipedal locomotion and upright posture. If this is what happened, then the change was adaptive. By definition, a change that

---

[5] When it comes to human evolution there is another dangerous pitfall: that of anthropomorphizing the rest of nature or (equally dangerous) of interpreting the difference between ourselves and the rest of nature in physically and biologically impossible terms. In the discussion of man's place in nature there is no place for mentalism or vitalism. The only valid assumption is that of *physicalism:* life is part of the inorganic world and subject to all the laws of physics; man is an animal and subject to all the laws of biology (Bloomfield 1936; Hockett 1948). Anthropologists still fall constantly into the error of contrasting the "cultural" and the "biological"; even Dobzhansky (1962) chooses the unfortunate terms "organic" and "superorganic" (though what he says with these terms is good). It is equally misleading to speak of "natural" versus "artificial" selection. Such pairings of terms are survivals of the mind-body dualism of an earlier day in the intellectual history of the West; they should be extirpated.

was neither adaptive nor fortuitous would lead to the extinction of the strain that underwent it, and in the present instance we know that that did not happen.[6]

The most powerful antidote for the improper use of keen hindsight is a principle that we shall call "Romer's Rule," after the paleontologist A. S. Romer who has applied it so effectively—without giving it any name—in his own work. We phrase this rule as follows:

The initial survival value of a favorable innovation is conservative, in that it renders possible the maintenance of a traditional way of life in the face of changed circumstances.

Later on, of course, the innovation may allow the exploration of some ecological niche not available to the species before the change; but this is a consequence, not a cause.

One of Romer's examples concerns the evolution of Devonian lungfishes into the earliest amphibians (1959:93–94; 1958 *passim*). The invasion of the land was feasible only with strong fins (which in due time became legs). But strong fins were not developed "in order to" invade the land. The climate of the epoch was tempestuous; the water level of the pools in which the lungfishes lived was subject to sudden recessions. There was thus selection for those strains of lungfishes which, when stranded by such a recession, had strong enough fins to *get back to the water*. Only much later did some of their descendants come to stay ashore most of the time.

It is worthy of note that Romer's Rule is not antiteleological. We are permitted to speak in terms of purposeful behavior whenever we are dealing with a system that incorporates negative feedback.[7] Individual organisms, and certain groupings of organisms (the kinds we call "communities"), are such systems. There is nothing wrong in asserting that a stranded Devonian lungfish tried his best to get back to the water. We are forced, however, to distinguish carefully between purposes and *consequences,* and we are not allowed to ascribe "purposefulness" to any such vague and long-continuing process as "evolution."

No principle, no matter how universal, answers all questions. Romer's Rule cuts as keenly as any razor ever devised by Occam to expose, excise, and discard unworkable pseudo-explanations. Yet it is applicable, in a sense, only

[6] By "extinction" we mean exclusively what Coon (1962:31) calls "utter extinction without issue"; the use of the same word for "extinction through successive evolution" is misleading, stemming from and lending support to an almost word-magical handling of the term "species."

[7] Especially since Wiener (1948), it has come to be recognized that purposeful behavior can be described as the behavior of mechanisms with certain physical properties, and that organisms are such mechanisms. On the basic assumption of physicalism (see fn. 5), we are required to speak of "purpose" only when we know, or can reasonably assume, that we are dealing with a system with the requisite physical structure. The teleological proposals in evolutionary theory, dealt with and disposed of so well by Simpson (1949: 1951 paperback edition ch. 2), do not meet these requirements.

after the fact. For example, in this paper we follow majority opinion and trace man's ancestry back to a point of separation from the ancestors of the great apes, the gibbons, and the siamangs. Having assumed this, we elaborate one of Romer's own suggestions as to how some of the early developments may have come about. Suppose, however, that new fossil finds should convince us that man is actually more closely related to some other group of surviving primates (Coon 1962: ch. 5). We should then be confronted by a different set of putative historical facts requiring explanation; but we should evoke the same Rule as we sought that explanation. The Rule does not tell us which line of descent to postulate.

THE PROTO-HOMINOIDS

From the location, date, and morphology of the fossil dryopithecine *Proconsul* we infer that the proto-hominoids lived in East Africa in the Middle or Lower Miocene or, at the earliest, in the Upper Oligocene (Oakley 1962).[8] This does not mean that *Proconsul* himself—in any of the strains or species so far identified—was a proto-hominoid; indeed, he is not a good candidate as an ancestor of the gibbons and siamangs, to whom, by definition, the proto-hominoids were ancestral. But *Proconsul* was clearly an *early* hominoid, and at the moment he is the best fossil evidence available for the date and provenience we seek.

The proto-hominoids inherited certain crucial capacities from their totally tree-dwelling ancestors.[9] It is the arboreal pattern that developed the keen accommodative vision characteristic of the higher primates, de-emphasized the sense of smell, turned forelimbs into freely movable arms with manipulative hands, and built brains somewhat larger than the average for land mammals.

The balance of the characterization we are about to give—what Count (1958) would call a "biogram" of the proto-hominoids—derives mainly from the comparative method applied to what we know of the hominoids of today (Schultz 1961 is a superb review; Sahlins 1959; Hediger 1961; Chance 1961; Spuhler 1959; Altmann 1962; Bartholomew and Birdsell 1953; Coon 1962). We shall not give all the evidence in detail. Furthermore, for the sake of vividness we shall allow some interpolations of a degree of precision that may be unwarranted. The proportion of guesswork in each statement will, we think, be fairly obvious.

Like most of their descendants, the proto-hominoids were hairy. Like all of them, they were tailless. They were smaller than we are, though not so small as present-day gibbons, whose size has decreased as an adaptation to brachiation. They had mobile facial muscles; they had neither mental eminence

[8] *Propliopithecus,* from the Fayum Oligocene, looks like a possible ancestral gibbon rather than a pre-proto-hominoid; if so, then the proto-hominoids had to be earlier than *Proconsul* (Coon 1962:196).

[9] Apparently this suggestion was first made by Smith (1913).

nor simian shelf (nor mastoid processes); they had large interlocking canines, and could chew only up and down; their tooth pattern was $\dfrac{2:1:2:3}{2:1:2:3}$. It seems likely that there was little sexual dimorphism, although on this the comparative evidence is conflicting. The chromosome count was somewhere in the forties.

They lived in bands of from ten to thirty, consisting typically of one or a very few adult males plus females and offspring. They had a roughly defined nucleated territoriality: that is, the territory within which the members of a band moved about had only roughly demarcated boundaries, but centered on the specific arboreal sites in which they built their nests.[10] The total population was probably never very great, nor very dense, from the proto-hominoids all the way down to the first true humans.[11]

They were expert climbers and spent much of their lives in the trees of the tropical or subtropical forests which were their habitat, certainly building their nests in the trees and sleeping there. Like rodents, they climbed up a tree head first; unlike rodents, they climbed down stern first. They slept at night, from dusk to dawn, which in the tropics means nearer to one-half of each twenty-four-hour period than to the one-third characteristic of ourselves in recent times. They were active during the day. Some activities, particularly the constant search for food, led them not only among the trees—in which they may have brachiated, but with no great expertness—but also quite regularly to the ground below. On the ground, they could stand with a semi-upright posture (erect enough to raise their heads above shoulder-high grass to look about), and they could sit with arms free for manipulative motions; they could walk on all fours and could run on their feet, but bipedal walking was infrequent and awkward.

Occasionally they would pick up a stick or stone and use it as a tool. Judging from modern chimpanzees,[12] they may have reshaped such tools slightly, using nothing but their hands and teeth to do so, and may have carried a tool for a short distance for immediate use, thereafter discarding it. They carried other things too, in mouth or hands or both, in connection with

[10] Students of primate behavior use the terms "band" and "troop" in technically distinct ways. Without prejudice for the subtle distinctions thus indicated, we have found it more convenient to use the term "band" throughout in a generic sense. The kind of territoriality described here is coming to be distinguished from other varieties (for instance, from the perimeter-defending territorial behavior of many birds) by the use of the term "core area." On nests: Nissen (1931); Bingham (1932); Bolwig (1959); Carpenter (1938); Hooton (1942:14–15, 155, 78–80, 124–25).

[11] This is important because of the Sewall Wright effect. If the population size range is correct, random genetic drift was operative. The development of similar but independent gene pools, and the occasional gene flow across population lines, worked in favor of the selection of those mutations important for the survival of the entire population. Such circumstances favor more rapid adaptive change.

[12] Crucial recent observations by Jane Goodall were reported to us orally by L. S. B. Leakey (see fn. 17).

nest-building; and at least the females, perhaps on occasion the males, carried infants.

Their diet was largely vegetarian, supplemented by worms and grubs, and sometimes by small mammals or birds that were injured or sick and thus unable to escape. (We might call this *"very* slow game.") They scavenged the remains of the kills of carnivores whenever they could. Unlike all other mammals except the Dalmatian coach hound, their bodies produced no uricase; hence uric acid was not converted into allantoin before secretion in the urine, and had a chance to accumulate in the bloodstream. The structural formula of uric acid is something like that of caffein and, like the latter, it seems to be a mild brain stimulant. Since this type of purine metabolism is shared by all the hominoids, it can hardly explain our own unusual brilliance; but it may help to account for the generally high level of hominoid intelligence as compared with other primates and other mammals (Coon 1962:172 and references cited).

The males had the pendulous penis typical of the primates. Copulation was effected exclusively with the dorsal approach common to land mammals in general. Gestation required about thirty weeks. The uterus was single-chambered, and twinning was as rare as it is for us today. The placenta was of the single-disc type. The young required and received maternal care for many months. Mammary glands were pectoral; nursing females held infants to the breast in their arms, though doubtless the infant clung to the mother's fur also. The eruption of permanent teeth began perhaps at two and one-half or three. Menarche was at eight or nine years; general growth stopped for both sexes at nine or ten. The females showed a year-round menstrual cycle rather than a rutting season. Inbreeding within the band was the rule. The life-span was potentially about thirty years, but death was largely from accident, disease, or predation, or a combination of these, rather than old age. Corpses were abandoned, as were members of the band too sick, injured, or feeble to keep up with the rest, and were disposed of by predators or scavengers. Adult males were sexually interested in females and "paternally" interested in infants, but without any permanent family bond, and without any jealousy when they were themselves sexually satisfied.

Relations with adjacent bands were normally hostile to neutral, rarely if ever friendly; yet there was surely enough contact to provide for some exchange of genes. Social differentiation within the band turned largely on age and sex, secondarily on physical strength. In case of conflict of interest within the band, the huskiest adult males normally got their way. Collective activities required intragroup coordination, effected by various forms of communication—patterns of body motion, pushing and prodding, changes of body odor, and vocal signals. The conventions of these forms of communication were transmitted in part genetically, but in some part by tradition, acquired by the young through guided participation in the ways of the group. This implies also a certain capacity to learn from experience, and to pass on any new skills thus acquired to other members of the band by teaching and learning, rather than merely by slow genetic selection. But we may assume that usually there was very little new in any one lifetime thus to be learned or passed on.

A kind of activity called *play* is widespread among land mammals, and obviously intensified among primates; we can be sure that the proto-hominoids indulged in it, at least before maturity (Kroeber 1948:27–30; Altmann 1962 and references cited). It is very hard to characterize play precisely, beyond saying that it resembles one or another serious activity without being serious. Play at fighting, observable for example among dogs, goes through much the same gross motions as true fighting but the participants receive no injury. Sexual play has the general contours of courtship, but ends short of coitus or with mock coitus. We suspect that play is *fun,* for any species that manifests it, and that that is the immediate motive for indulging in it. But play is also genuinely pedagogical, in that the young thereby get needed practice in certain patterns of behavior that are biologically important for adult life.

The proto-hominoids did not have the power of speech. The most that we can validly ascribe to them in this respect is a call system similar to that of modern gibbons. Even this ascription may be stretching the comparative evidence somewhat. It is not hard to assume that a line of continuity from the proto-hominoids to the gibbons should have maintained such a call system essentially unchanged. It is also quite reasonable, as we shall see, to explain the evolution of a call system into language among our ancestors. The difficulty is to account for the apparently less highly developed vocal-auditory signaling of the great apes. Our hypothesis for the proto-hominoids suggests that the communicative behavior of the great apes may be somewhat more subtle and complex than has yet been realized. Be this as it may, we posit a call system for the proto-hominoids because we know no other way to proceed.[13]

---

[13] Although we draw largely on Carpenter's account of gibbon calls (1940), vocal-auditory signaling of the sort that qualifies as a call system is widespread among land mammals; e.g., among prairiedogs, whose system has been partly described (King 1955). Hediger (1961) writes—using nontechnical terms that require to be properly interpreted: "Five elements of speech that by purely theoretical reasoning have been found to be the most essential are in fact contained in all animal systems of communication investigated up to date and receive added differentiation in the course of evolution, in accordance with the requirements imposed by the respective living conditions. These are the five sounds or signals: (a) warning signal (enemy), (b) mating and territorial possession, (c) mother-and-child contact, (d) social contact, (e) announcement of food." And Schultz (1961): "Without the hearing of sounds, produced by their own kind, monkeys and apes would never have become the intensely social animals that they are. Sounds of a surprising variety serve continually for the contact between the members of a group, for orientation of mother and young, for the information of the entire group about possible danger, and, last but not least, for scaring enemies of different or the same species and even for warning rival groups away from the territories already occupied. . . . The orgies of noise, indulged in especially by howlers, guerezas, gibbons, siamangs, and chimpanzees, seemingly so repetitious and meaningless, are probably at least as informative to the respective species as most after-dinner speaking is to *Homo sapiens*."

The essential design features of a call system are simple. There is a repertory of a half-dozen or so distinct signals, each the appropriate vocal response —or the vocal segment of a more inclusive response—to a recurrent and biologically important type of situation. Among gibbons, one such situation is the discovery of food; another is the detection of danger; a third is friendly interest and the desire for company. A fourth gibbon call apparently does nothing but indicate the whereabouts of the gibbon that emits it: this call keeps the band from spreading out too thin as it moves through the trees. One can guess at other possible situations appropriate for a special call: sexual interest; need for maternal care; pain. Band-to-band differences in calls may help to distinguish friend from alien.

A single call may be varied in intensity, duration, or number of repetitions, to correlate with and give information about the strength of the stimulus which is eliciting it. However, the signals of a call system are *mutually exclusive* in the following sense: the animal, finding himself in a situation, can only respond by one or another of the calls or by silence. He cannot, in principle, emit a signal that has some of the features of one call and some of another. If, for example, he encounters food and danger at the same time, one of these will take precedence: he is constrained to emit either the food call or the danger call, not some mixture of the two.

The technical description of this mutual exclusiveness is to say that the system is *closed*. Language, in sharp contrast, is *open* or *productive:* we freely emit utterances that we have never said nor heard before, and are usually understood, neither speaker nor hearer being aware of the novelty.

A call system differs from language in two other ways, and perhaps in a third.[14] (1) Gibbons do not emit, say, the food call unless they have found food (or, perhaps, are responding to the food call from another gibbon, as they approach for their share of it). Furthermore, the gibbon that finds food does not go back to headquarters and report; he stays by the food as he emits the call. A call system does not have *displacement*. Language does: we speak freely of things that are out of sight or are in the past or future—or even nonexistent. (2) The utterances of a language consist wholly of arrangements of elementary signaling units called *phonemes* (or *phonological components,* to be exact), which in themselves have no meanings but merely serve to keep meaningful utterances apart. Thus, an utterance has both a structure in terms of these meaningless but differentiating elements, and also a structure in terms of the minimum meaningful elements. This design feature is *duality of patterning*. A call system lacks it, the differences between any two calls being global. (3) Finally, the detailed conventions of any one language are trans-

---

14 Of the thirteen design features described in Hockett (1960*b*), the following are shared by gibbon calls and language, hence presumably also by the call system of the proto-hominoids: vocal-auditory channel; broadcast transmission and directional reception; rapid fading (combatted by repetition in the case of gibbon calls); interchangeability; total feedback; specialization; semanticity; arbitrariness; discreteness. Hence we need not deal with any of these properties in the sequel.

mitted wholly by the traditional mechanism, though, of course, the capacity to learn a language, and probably the drive to do so, are genetic. On this score we are still in ignorance about the gibbons. Regional differences in gibbon calls have been noted, but various balances between tradition and genetics can yield that. We believe it safer to assume that proto-hominoid call systems were passed down from generation to generation largely through the genes, tradition playing a minor role.[15] This assumption is the conservative one—it gives us more to try to explain in later developments than would any alternative.

This completes our characterization of the proto-hominoids, which can now serve as point of departure for the story of our own evolution.

OUT OF THE TREES

Some of the descendants of the proto-hominoids moved out of the trees and became erect bipeds. Romer's description (1959:327) of how this may have begun affords another example of the application of the Rule we ascribe to him.[16]

Geological evidence suggests that at one or more times during the East African Miocene a climatic change gradually thinned out the vegetation, converting continuous tropical forest into open savannah with scattered clumps of trees. As the trees retreated, some bands of hominoids retreated with them, never abandoning their classical arboreal existence; their descendants of today are the gibbons and siamangs. Other bands were caught in isolated groves of slowly diminishing extent. In due time, those bands whose physique made it possible for their members to traverse open country to another grove survived; those that could not do this became extinct. Thus, for those bands, the survival value of the perquisites for safe ground travel was not at all that they could therefore begin a new way of life out of the trees, but that, when necessary, they could make their way to a place where the traditional arboreal way of life could be continued. The hominoids that were successful at this included those ancestral to the great apes and to ourselves.

Sometimes the band forced to try to emigrate from a grove would be the total population of that grove. More typically, we suspect, population pressure within a diminishing grove would force bands into competition over its resources, and the less powerful bands would be displaced. Also, when a migrating band managed to reach another grove, it would often happen that

---

[15] It is exceedingly difficult to phrase a statement of this kind in such a way as to avoid misunderstanding. We are *not* sorting out various features of structure and behavior and saying: genes are responsible for these, tradition is responsible for those. Both mechanisms of transmission contribute to everything—but with great variation in the balance and the precise nature of the interplay between the two. The best discussion we know of this is Dobzhansky (1956).

[16] We elaborate Romer's brief suggestion considerably. See also Oakley (1961).

the new grove was already occupied, and once again there would be competition. Thus, in the long run, the trees would be held by the more powerful, while the less powerful would repeatedly have to get along as best they could in the fringes of the forest or in open country. Here is a double selective process. The trees went to the more powerful, provided only that they maintained a minimum ability to traverse open country when necessary: some of these successful ones were ancestral to the great apes of today. Our own ancestors were the failures. We did not abandon the trees because we wanted to, but because we were pushed out.

We are speaking here of displacements and movements of whole bands, not of individual animals. There is one thing that surely accompanied any band whenever it moved: the essential geometry of its territoriality. At any halt, no matter how temporary, whether in the trees, under the trees, or in open country, some specific site became, for the nonce, "home base"—a GHQ, a center, a focus, relative to which each member of the band oriented himself as he moved about. Headquarters was the safest place to be, if for no other reason than the safety of numbers. In a later epoch—though doubtless earlier than will ever be directly attested by archeology—headquarters among our own ancestors came to be crudely fortified, as by a piled ring of stones;[17] it became the place where things were kept or stored; in due time it became house, village, fort, city. But earliest of all it was *home*. The tradition for this sort of territoriality is much older than the proto-hominoids, and has continued unbroken to the present day.

It is at this point in our story that we must stop referring to our ancestors as "hominoids" and start calling them "hominids." Of course, all hominids are hominoids; but we have now seen the sorting-out of the pre-apes from the pre-humans, and when we wish to speak exclusively of the latter the appropriate term is "hominid."

CARRYING

It is no joke to be thrown out of one's ancestral home. If the next grove is only a few miles away, in sight, then one has something to aim for; but sooner or later movements must have taken place without any such visible target. Treeless country holds discomforts and dangers. There may not be much food, at least not of a familiar sort. There may be little available water, for the trees tend to cluster where the water is more abundant. And there are fleet four-footed predators, as well as herbivorous quadrupeds big and strong enough to be dangerous at close quarters. One cannot avoid these other animals altogether, since their presence often signals the location of water, or

[17] In a lecture at Cornell University, Wednesday, 26 March, 1963, L. S. B. Leakey showed a slide of a ring of stones unearthed at a very early East African site; in conversation, he scoffed at the traditional notion that our ancestors had no homes until they moved into caves.

of food fit also for hominid consumption. The quest for food must be carried on constantly, no matter how pressing may be the drive to find a new grove of trees in which to settle. It is a wonder that any of the waifs of the Miocene savannah survived at all. Enormous numbers of them must have died out.

The trick that made survival possible for some of them was the trick of *carrying.* The proto-hominoids, as we have seen, probably carried twigs and brush to make nests, and certainly carried infants. Also, they had fine arms and hands usable for carrying as well as for climbing, grasping, and manipulating; and the comparative evidence suggests that they occasionally picked up sticks or stones to use as tools. These are the raw-materials for the kind of carrying to which we now refer. But it takes something else to blend them into the new pattern. In the trees, hands are largely occupied with climbing. The infant-in-arms grabs onto the mother when the latter needs her hands for locomotion. The twig being taken to the nest is transferred to the mouth when the hand cannot at the same time hold it and grasp a tree branch. One puts down one's ad-hoc tool when one has to move.

The conditions for carrying are no better on the ground than in the trees if the hand must revert to the status of a foot. But if bipedal locomotion is at all possible, then the hand is freed for carrying; and the survival value of carrying certain things in turn serves to promote a physical structure adapted to bipedal locomotion.

Two sorts of ground carrying in the hands may have been extremely early; there seems to be no way of determining which came first. One is the carrying of crude weapons; the other is the transportation of scavenged food.[18]

The earliest ground-carrying of weapons may well have been a sort of accident. Imagine an early hominid—perhaps even a prehominid hominoid—sitting on the ground and pounding something (a nut, say) with a handy stone. A predator approaches. Our hero jumps up and runs away as best he can on two legs—there are no trees nearby to escape into—but keeps his grasp on the stone for no better reason than that he does not need his hand for anything else. Cornered, he turns, and either strikes out at the predator with the hand that holds the stone, or else throws it. The predator falls or runs off, and whatever in our hero's genes or life experience, or both, has contributed to his behavior stands a chance of being passed on to others.

The first carrying of scavenged food back to headquarters (instead of consuming it on the spot) may also have been a sort of accident. A scavenging hominoid is eating the remains of a predator's kill where he has found it, and is surprised by the predator who is coming back to make another meal from the same kill. The hominoid runs off towards headquarters, still holding a piece of meat in his hand. In due time, he or his successors develop the habit of carrying the spoils off without waiting for the predator to turn up.

As described, these two early kinds of hand-carrying involve movements of a single animal *within* the band's territory. The carrying-along of things as

---

[18] On the latter, Hewes (1961) is particularly convincing.

the whole band moves is another matter, and probably a later development. Surely the earliest carrying of this latter sort was of unshaped weapons of defense. Yet other things might have been taken along. Extra food would be a great rarity, but if some were taken along because no one happened to be hungry as a movement began, it would be important if the band reached a particularly barren region. Water-carrying would have been extremely valuable—primates in general have to drink at least once a day, in contrast to some mammalian species which can store up several days' supply. Short hauls of small quantities of water cupped in the large leaves of tropical plants may have been quite early; large-scale water transport as a whole band moves must have been a great deal later, since it requires technologically advanced containers.

The side-effects of carrying things in the hands are of incalculable importance. We have already seen that its immediate practical value helped to promote bipedal walking, which in turn selected both for carrying and for an upright posture that renders bipedal walking mechanically more efficient. A less obvious consequence is that carrying made for a kind of behavior that has all the outward earmarks of what we call "memory" and "foresight": one lugs around a heavy stick or stone despite the absence of any immediate need for it, as though one were remembering past experiences in which having it available was important and were planning for possible future encounters of the same kind. Taking scavenged meat back to headquarters without waiting for the predator to return to his kill also looks like foresight. We do not mean to deny the validity of the terms "memory" and "foresight." The point is that the outward earmarks surely came first, and only over a long period of time *produced* the psychological characteristics to which these terms refer.[19]

A third consequence of carrying and of wandering was a change in dietary balance. The first tools to be carried were defensive weapons. Often enough, no doubt, the use of these weapons against a predator, even if successful, would only scare him off. But sometimes the predator would be killed. Why waste the meat? We can also suppose that the wandering Miocene or Pliocene hominids occasionally found themselves in open country where no suitable plant food was available. Herbivorous animals could eat the grass; quadruped predators could eat the grazers; and the hominids, if they were lucky, could eat the grazers or the predators, or else starve. Thus the hunted became the hunters, and weapons of defense became weapons of offense.[20]

[19] This interpretation insists on the correctness of what has been called the "exogenic" rather than the "endogenic" theory as to the basic (though not the only) direction of causal connections in evolution (Hewes 1961:689). Our treatment is in general accord with Washburn's recent proposals (1959; 1960), which are also exogenic.

[20] It has often been proposed that the first non-scavenged meat was "slow game" (Coon 1962:80). We agree on the importance of slow game, except in one respect: the adventures that served as crucial impetus making for the carrying of weapons must have been adventures with fast and dangerous creatures, not slow and harmless ones. Once weapon-carrying was established, the weapons would obviously be used on slow game too—perhaps even predominantly so.

The gradual increase of meat in the diet had important consequences of its own, to which we will turn after noting one further direct consequence of hand-carrying.

The use of the hands for carrying implied that the mouth and teeth, classically used for this by land mammals, birds, and even reptiles, were freed for other activities. It can quite safely be asserted that if primate and hominid evolution had not transferred from mouth to hand first the grasping and manipulating function and then the carrying function, human language as we know it would never have evolved. What were the hominids to do with their mouths, rendered thus relatively idle except when they were eating? The answer is: they chattered.[21]

Remember that the proto-hominoids are assumed in this account to have had a call system, and that that system would not have been lost by the stage we have now reached. The hunting of dangerous animals is a challenge even with advanced weapons. With primitive weapons there is a great advantage if it can be done collaboratively. But this calls for coordination of the acts of the participants. Their hands hold weapons and are thus unavailable for any complicated semaphor. Their visual attention must be divided between the motions of the quarry and those of the other participants. All this favors an increase in flexibility of vocal-auditory communication.

Other factors also favor such an increase. Meat is a highly efficient and compactly packaged food, as compared with uncultivated plants. A small kill may not go very far, but with collective hunting larger quarry were caught. After such a large kill, there is often more food than can be consumed even by all the direct participants in the hunt. Sharing the food among all the members of the band comes about almost automatically, in that when the hunters themselves are sated they no longer care if the rest take the leavings. Thus the sharing of meat makes for the survival of the whole band. Collective hunting, general food-sharing, and the carrying of an increasing variety of things all press towards a more complex social organization, which is only possible with more flexible communication. These same factors also promote what we vaguely call the "socialization" of the members of the band.[22]

Another development bearing on the quality, if not the degree, of hominid

---

One other factor promoting meat in the diet should be mentioned. Oakley (1961:190) points out that a desiccating climate (of the sort that would thin out the forest) may have induced a change in intestinal flora and fauna, rendering the utilization of certain vegetable foods less efficient and thus increasing the hunger for protein.

[21] Some of our guesses at the lifeways of the proto-hominoids are based on observations of modern baboons (Washburn and DeVore 1961), whose conditions of life seem to be somewhat similar. But in at least one respect there is a sharp difference: the baboons carry on their affairs in a strikingly silent way. Their vocal sounds are rare.

[22] We do not imply that there was no sharing of food or "socialization" before collective hunting. The suckling of the young is a kind of food-sharing; a food call is indicative of food-sharing; scavenged meat hauled back to headquarters, perhaps long before any use of weapons for hunting, may have been shared. The developments outlined in the text are a matter of intensification and elaboration.

socialization must have taken place during this same period. At some point during the slow morphological shift to efficient upright posture, the frontal approach for copulation must have first become anatomically possible, and it was doubtless immediately exploited. It may even be imagined that, for certain strains of the hominids at certain times, the expansion of the gluteus maximus rendered the dorsal approach so awkward that the invention of the frontal approach had the conservative value required by Romer's Rule. Humans have never shown much tendency to confine themselves to this position for intercourse, but it does seem to be universally known, and is almost exclusively human.[23] Just how this change may have affected hominid lifeways is not clear. Our guess is that it changed, for the adult female, the relative roles of the adult male and of the infant, since after the innovation there is a much closer similarity for her between her reception of an infant and of a lover. This may have helped to spread the "tender emotions" of mammalian mother-infant relations to other interpersonal relationships within the band, ultimately with such further consequences as the Oedipus complex.

OPENING OF
THE CALL SYSTEM

We have seen a changing pattern of life that would be well served by a vocal-auditory communicative system of greater complexity and subtlety. Now a call system can become more flexible, within limits, through the development of totally new calls to fit additional types of recurrent situation. But it cannot take the first step towards language as we know it unless something else happens: through a process about to be described, the closed system becomes open.

Let us illustrate the way in which this can come about by describing what may occasionally happen among the gibbons of today—although, to be sure, such an occurrence has never been observed. Suppose a gibbon finds himself in a situation characterized by both the presence of food and the imminence of danger. The factors are closely balanced. Instead of emitting either the clear food call or the unmistakable danger call, he utters a cry that has some of the characteristics of each. Among gibbons such an event is doubtless so rare and unusual that the other members of the band have no way of interpreting it; thus, the consequences are negligible. But if we suppose that the early weapon-carrying hominids had a somewhat richer call system (though still closed), functioning in a somewhat more complex social order, then we may also assume that this type of event happened occasionally, and that sooner or later the other members of a band responded appropriately, there-

---

[23] The pygmy chimpanzee, the porcupine, the hamster, and the two-toed sloth are variously known or reputed to share the human habit (Coon 1962:161). Hewes also comments on it (1961:696). The guess given here as to its consequences among the hominids is, as far as we know, our own.

fore handling an unusually complex situation more efficiently than otherwise. Thus reinforced, the habit of *blending* two old calls to produce a new one would gain ground.

Indeed, we really have to believe that this is what happened, because the phenomenon of blending is the only logically possible way in which a closed system can develop toward an open one.[24] Let us represent the acoustic contours of one inherited call arbitrarily with the sequence of letters *ABCD* and those of another with *EFGH*. All we mean by either of these representations is that each call possesses two or more acoustic properties on which primate ears could focus attention; it does not matter just how many such acoustic properties are involved nor just what they are. Suppose that *ABCD* means "food here," while *EFGH* means "danger coming." Finding both food and danger, the hominid comes out with *ABGH*. If this new call becomes established, then the 2 old calls and the new one are all henceforth, *composite*, instead of unanalyzable unitary signals. For, in *ABCD*, the part *AB* now means "food" and the part *CD* means "no danger"; in *EFGH*, *EF* now means "no food" and *GH* means "danger"; while *ABGH* means "food and danger" because *AB* and *GH* have acquired the meanings just mentioned. One might eventually even get *EFCD*, obviously meaning "no food and no danger."

It must be asked whether this mechanism of blending can really turn a closed system into an open one. The answer is that it can start the transformation (while no other known mechanism can), but that further developments must follow. Consider the matter for a moment in a purely abstract way. Suppose the initial closed system has exactly ten calls, and that each is blended with each of the others. After the blending, there are exactly 100 calls. From one point of view, a repertory of 100 calls—or of 1,000, or of ten million— is just as closed as is a system of 10 calls. A second point of view is more important. Each of the hundred possible calls now consists of 2 parts, and each part recurs in other whole calls. One has the basis for the habit of *building* composite signals out of meaningful parts, whether or not those parts occur alone as whole signals. It is this habit that lies at the center of the openness of human languages. English allows only a finite (though quite large) number of sentences only two words long. But it allows an unlimited number of different sentences because there is no fixed limit on how long a sentence may be.

Surely the opening-up of the closed call system of our ancestors required literally thousands of years, just as all the other developments on which we have touched came about at an extremely leisurely pace. It is irrelevant that the production of a single blend, or the momentary accidental carrying of a

[24] This is not quite true. Continuously variable features of a single call—say pitch, or volume, or duration—could become associated with continuously variable features of a type-situation, so that, in time, a specific uttering of the danger call could quite precisely specify "danger of degree seventeen, due north, three hundred yards away." The openness of a system that had developed in this way would be logically like that of bee dances (von Frisch 1950; Lindauer 1963), which is quite unlike that of human language.

stick or stone in the hand, is a brief episode. A potentially crucial type of event can recur numberless times with no visible effect, or with effect on a band that later becomes extinct for unrelated reasons, for every one occurrence that has minuscule but viable consequences. When the opening-up of the formerly closed call system was finally achieved, the revolutionary impact on subsequent developments was as great as that of hand-carrying.

For one thing, the detailed conventions of an open system cannot be transmitted wholly through genes. The young may emit some of the calls instinctively. But they are also exposed to various more or less complex composite calls from their elders, and are obliged to infer the meanings of the parts, and the patterns by which the parts are put together to form the whole signals, from the acoustic resemblances among the calls they hear and from the behavioral contexts in which they are uttered. (To this day, that is how human infants learn their native language.) Thus, the development of an open system puts a premium on any capacity for learning and teaching that a species may have, and selects for an increase in the genetic basis for that capacity.

If the conventions of a system have largely to be learned before the system can be efficiently used, then much of that learning will eventually be carried on away from the contexts in which the utterances being practiced would be immediately relevant. We recall the general mammalian phenomenon of play. The development of an open, largely traditionally transmitted, vocal-auditory communicative system means that *verbal play* is added to play at fighting, sexual play, and any other older categories. But this, in turn, means that situations are being talked about when they do not exist—that is, it means the addition of displacement to the design features already at hand. Speaking of things which are out of sight or in the past or future is very much like carrying a weapon when there is no immediate need for it. Each of these habits thus reinforces the other.

What was formerly a closed call system has now evolved into an open system, with details transmitted largely by tradition rather than through the genes, and with the property of displacement. Let us call such a system *pre-language*. It was still not true language, because it lacked the duality of patterning of true language. Nothing like pre-language is known for sure in the world today.[25] Any hominid strain that developed its vocal-auditory communication only to this stage has become extinct. If we could hear the pre-language of our forerunners, it would probably not sound like human speech. It would sound much more like animal calls, and only very careful analysis would reveal its language-like properties.

The development of openness, with the various conquences already men-

---

[25] But many animal communicative systems have not yet been adequately studied. There is some hint that the song systems of certain passerine birds may prove to have just the array of design features that characterized pre-language (Lanyon 1960). Of course, this would not necessarily mean that the birds in question are on their way towards the development of true language.

tioned, either accompanied or paved the way for some radical developments in tool habits. We imagine that tool *manufacture*—as over against the using and carrying of tools—received its single greatest impetus from this source. If carrying a weapon selects for foresight, shaping a rough weapon into a better one indicates even greater foresight. The manufacturing of a generalized tool—one designed to be carried around for a variety of possible uses—and the development of tools specialized for use in the making of other tools, certainly followed the inception of pre-language. Weapon-making and tool-shaping are further activities at which the young can play, as they learn their communicative system and other adult ways by playing with them.

We must suppose that the detail conventions of pre-language underwent changes, and became differentiated from one band to another, much more rapidly than had the earlier call system from which it sprang (though perhaps much more slowly than languages change today). Both of these points are implied by the increased relative role of tradition as over against genetics. New blends were not uncommon. They introduced new patterns for combining elements into whole signals, and old patterns became obsolete. Any such innovation of detail spread naturally to all members of the band in which it occurred, but not readily, if at all, from one band to another. If a band fissioned into two bands—this must have happened repeatedly throughout hominoid and hominid history—the "daughter" bands started their independent existence with a single inherited pre-language, but innovations thereafter were independent, so that in course of time the two daughter bands came to have two "mutually unintelligible" pre-languages. This is exactly—except for rate of change—what has happened to true human languages in recent millennia; we must assume that the phenomena of change and of divergence are as old as the emergence of pre-language.

THE INCEPTION
OF DUALITY

Something else had been happening during prehominid and hominid evolution up to this point. In apes, the glottis lies very close to the velum, and articulatory motions anything like those involved in human language are structurally awkward. The development of upright posture, with the completion of the migration of the face from the end to the ventral side of the head, turns the axis of the oral cavity to a position approximately at right angles to the pharynx, and introduces a marked separation of glottis from velum (Spuhler 1959; DuBrul 1958). Hundreds of generations of chattering, first in a call system and then in pre-language, increases the innervation of the vocal tract and enriches the cortical representation of that region. The stage is set for the development of the kinds of articulatory motions familiar today.

Now, neither of these changes leads directly and inevitably to duality of patterning. Indeed, the first change is in no sense logically required if duality is to develop; in a way, it was fortuitous, since it was a by-product of changes taking place for a totally different set of selective reasons. In another species with a different earlier history, duality might use some other apparatus. If early primate history had for some reason promoted precision of control of the sphincter, and of the accumulation and discharge of intestinal gas, speech sounds today might be anal spirants. Everything else about the logical design of human language could be exactly as it actually is. The failure to distinguish in this way between the logically possible and the historically actual has led many investigators astray: they infer, for example, that our ancestors could not have had language until the articulatory apparatus had evolved to what it is now. They then interpret fossil jaws in invalid ways—and offer inadequate explanations of why the speech parts should have changed their morphology as they actually have during the Pleistocene.[26]

However, the two changes described above did set the stage in a certain way. The hominids were in a state in which, if duality did develop, the machinery used for it was in all probability going to be the kind of articulatory motions we still use.

We can envisage the development of duality as follows. Pre-language became increasingly complex and flexible, among the successful strains of hominids, because of its many advantages for survival. The constant rubbing-together of whole utterances (by the blending mechanism described earlier) generated an increasingly large stock of minimum meaningful signal elements —the "pre-morphemes" of pre-language. Lacking duality, however, these pre-morphemes had to be holistically different from one another in their acoustic contours. But the available articulatory-acoustic space became more and more densely packed; some pre-morphemes became so similar to others that keeping them apart, either in production or in detection, was too great a challenge for hominid mouths, ears, and brains. Something had to happen, or the system would collapse of its own weight. Doubtless many overloaded systems did collapse, their users thereafter becoming extinct. In at least one case, there was a brilliantly successful "mutation": pre-morphemes began to be listened to and identified not in terms of their acoustic gestalts but in terms of smaller features of sound that occurred in them in varying arrangements. In pace with this shift in the technique of detection, articulatory motions came to be directed not towards the generation of a suitable acoustic gestalt but towards the sufficiently precise production of the relevant smaller features of sound that identified one pre-morpheme as over against others.

With this change, pre-morphemes became true morphemes, the features of sound involved became phonological components, and pre-language had become true language.

Although brilliant and crucial, this innovation need not have been either as sudden or as difficult as our description may seem to imply. With openness,

[26]See references cited in the first paragraph of fn. 2.

but as yet without duality, the hearer is already required to pay attention to acoustic detail, rather than merely to one or another convenient symptom of a whole acoustic gestalt, if he is to recognize the constituent pre-morphemes of a composite call and thus react appropriately to the whole call. In a pure call system, the beginning of a call may be distinctive enough to identify the whole call; the rest does not have to be heard. In pre-language, one cannot predict from the beginning of a call how it will continue and end. This clearly paves the way for duality. It is then, in one sense, but a small step to stop regarding acoustic details as *constituting* morphemes and start interpreting them as *identifying* or *representing* morphemes.[27]

Here, as for all the other developments we have mentioned, we must remember Romer's Rule. The ultimate consequences of the inception of duality have been enormous. But the immediate value of the innovation was conservative. It rendered possible the continued use of a thoroughly familiar type of communicative system in a thoroughly familiar way, in the face of a gradual but potentially embarrassing increase in the complexity of the system.

The emergence of true language from a closed call system, by the steps and stages we have described, should properly be thought of not as a replacement of one sort of communicative system by another, but rather as the growth of a new system within the matrix of the old one. Certain features of the proto-hominoid call system are still found in human vocal-auditory behavior, but as accompaniments to the use of language rather than as part of language. The proto-hominoids could vary the intensity, the pitch, and the duration of a single call. We still do this as we speak sentences in a language: we speak sometimes more loudly, sometimes more softly, sometimes in a higher register and sometimes in a lower, and so on. Also, we use certain grunts and cries (*uh-huh, huh-uh, ow!*) that are not words or morphemes and not part of language. These various *paralinguistic* phenomena, as they are called (Trager 1958; Pittinger, Hockett, and Danchy 1960), have been reworked and modified in many ways by the conditions of life of speaking humans, but their pedigree, like that of communicative body motion, is older than that of language itself.

The phenomenon of sound change, mentioned briefly at the outset of this paper, began immediately upon the transition from pre-language to true language, continues now, and will continue in the future unless our vocal-

---

[27] In recorded human history a somewhat similar transformation is observable in the evolution of Chinese characters. The earliest characters were holistically different from one another to the eye—any visual resemblances between constituent parts of different characters were unsystematic and accidental. But as the system developed, and a larger and larger number of characters had to be devised, it became impossible to keep on inventing completely different new shapes; instead, new characters came to be built by putting together pieces drawn from old ones. But this incipient "duality," as an economy measure, never developed as far as it has in languages (i.e., spoken languages). Thousands of characters in use today are built out of hundreds of recurrent parts; the tens of thousands of morphemes in any language are built out of a mere double handful of phonological components, used with amazing efficiency.

auditory communication crosses some currently unforeseeable Rubicon. The phonological system of a language has almost as its sole function that of keeping meaningful utterances apart. But a phonological system is a delicately balanced affair, constantly being thrown into slight disbalance by careless articulation or channel noise and constantly repatterning itself in a slightly altered way. It is perfectly possible, in the course of time, for two phonemes to fall together—that is, for the articulatory-acoustic difference between them to disappear. Obviously, this changes the machinery with which morphemes and utterances are distinguished. The interest this holds for us is that it affords an example of the workings of Romer's Rule in a purely cultural context instead of a largely genetic one.

What happens seems to be about as follows. A particular phonemic difference is slowly eaten away by sound change, to the point that it is no longer reliable as a way of keeping utterances apart.[28] This is the "changed circumstances" of Romer's Rule. The speakers of the language develop, by analogy, a way of paraphrasing any utterance that would be potentially ambiguous if uttered in the traditional way. The paraphrase is the "innovation" of the Rule. The value of the paraphrase is that the speakers can thereby continue to speak in largely the same way they learned from their predecessors. The innovation is minor and trivial, but effective in that if the phonemic contrast disappears entirely, ease of communication is in no way impaired. The inevitable and continuous process of sound change never reduces the machinery of a language to zero. A compensation of some sort is developed for every loss of contrast.

CHRONOLOGY

We have now outlined a plausible evolutionary sequence leading from the proto-hominoids to our earliest truly human ancestors. For we assert that as soon as the hominids had achieved upright posture, bipedal gait, the use of hands for manipulating, for carrying, and for manufacturing generalized tools, and language, they had become men. The human revolution was over. Two important questions remain. How long did the changes take? How long ago were they completed?

It is certain that the changes we have talked about did not begin before the time of the proto-hominoids. But at present we have no way of knowing how much later than that was their inception. Conceivably the hominids of the Middle or Upper Pliocene, though already separated from the pongids, were very little more like modern man than were the photo-hominoids.

On the other hand, we are convinced that all the crucial developments of

---

28 A possible example in current American English is medial posttonic *t* versus *d: matter* and *madder,* or *petal* and *pedal,* or *atom* and *Adam,* are acoustically very close in the speech of many people, and absolutely identical for some. When this leads to misunderstanding, the speaker repeats with clearer articulation, or paraphrases.

which we have spoken had been achieved by about one million years ago—that is, by the beginning of the Pleistocene.

The most important evidence for the date just presented is the *subsequent* growth of the brain, attested by the fossil record. The brain of *Australopithecus* is scarcely larger than that of a gorilla. But from about three-quarters of a million years ago to about forty thousand years ago, the brain grew steadily. Part of this increase reflects an overall increase in body size (Spuhler 1959; Washburn 1959:27; Coon 1962: Table 37). Allowing for this, there is still something to be explained. Was the increase in relative size fortuitous or adaptive?

It is utterly out of the question that the growth was fortuitous. A large brain is biologically too expensive. It demands a high percentage of the blood supply—12% in modern man, though the brain accounts for only about 2% of the body's volume (Coon 1962:77–78)—and all that blood, in an upright biped, must be pumped uphill. It requires an enlarged skull, which makes for difficulty during parturition, particularly since the development of upright posture resculptures the pelvis very badly for childbirth. This cost cannot be borne unless there are compensations.

We must therefore assume that if a species has actually developed a bigger and more convoluted brain, with a particularly sharp increase in the forebrain, there was survival value in the change. For our ancestors of a million years ago the survival value of bigger brains is obvious if and only if they had *already* achieved the essence of language and culture. Continued growth would then be advantageous up to a certain maximum, but thereafter unprofitable because it made for excessive difficulties in other respects but yielded no further usable gain in brain-power.

The archeological and fossil record supports our date, or even suggests that we have been too conservative. Until recently, the earliest obviously shaped tools that had been dug up were not quite so ancient, but they implied an earlier period of development that was not directly attested. Now, however, we have the direct evidence of at least crudely shaped stone tools in association with hominid fossils from Bed I at Olduvai, for which a maximum date of one and three-quarters million years ago is seriously proposed (Leakey, Curtis, and Evernden 1962). What is more, the Australopithecines show the typically human reduction in the size of the canine teeth, formerly used for cutting and tearing; and this reduction could not have been tolerated had the hominids not developed tools with which to perform such operations.

It might be suggested that, although all other crucial innovations of the human revolution were as early as we have proposed, the inception of duality may have been later. There are two reasons why we think that duality is just as old as the rest.

One side-effect of brain growth is that the top of the head is pushed forward to form a forehead. We do not see why this should in itself entail a recession of the lower part of the face, to yield the essentially flat perpendicular human physiognomy which, with minor variations, now prevails. In terms of the balancing of the head above an upright body, perhaps the recession of the snout and the decrease in its massiveness are useful. If cooking is a sufficiently old art, then perhaps this external predigestion of food at least rendered possible the reduction in size of teeth and jaws. But it seems to us that these factors still leave room for a further influence: that of the habit of talking, in a true language that uses the kinds of articulatory motions that are now universal, requiring precise motions of lips, jaw, tongue, velum, glottis, and pulmonary musculature. If true language can be assumed for our ancestors of a million years ago, then it is old enough to have played a role in the genetically monitored evolutionary changes in what we now call the "organs of speech." And if this is correct, then "organs of speech" is no metaphor but a biologically correct description.

Our other reason for believing that duality of patterning, and the modern type of sound-producing articulatory motions, are very old, turns on time, space, and degrees of uniformity and diversity. The fossil record shows that the human diaspora from East Africa cannot be much more recent than the Middle Pleistocene. This means that several hundred thousand years have been available for a genetic adaptation to a wide variety of climates and topographies. Yet man shows an amazingly small amount of racial diversity— far less, for example, than that of dogs, which has come about in a much shorter span of time. (Of course, the difference in generation span between men and dogs must be taken into account; but when one allows liberally for this the comparison, though less striking, still seems valid.)

There is this same striking lack of diversity in certain features of language. Though we have no fossils, our observations of the languages of today, and of those few attested by written records during the past few millenia, have some relevance. Almost every type of articulation known to function in any language anywhere recurs in various other languages, with no significant pattern of geographical distribution.[29] Phonological systems—as over against individual speech sounds—show much less variety than could easily be invented by any linguist working with pencil and paper (Hockett 1963; Ferguson 1963). This uniformity precludes the independent invention of duality of patterning, and of modern articulatory motions, in two or more parts of the world. The crucial developments must have taken place once, and then spread. The innovations could have been either recent or ancient, except for an additional fact: in every language, the phonological raw materials are used with remarkable efficiency (see footnote 27). This speaks for great antiquity, since we cannot imagine that such efficiency was an instant result of the appearance of the first trace of duality.

True diversity is found in more superficial aspects of language, and in all those other phases of human life where tradition, rather than genetics, is clearly the major mechanism of change and of adaptation. We are thus led

---

[29] Coarticulated stops are commonest in west Africa, but recur in New Guinea. Clicks seen to be the least widespread: they are found only in south and east Africa, largely in languages known to be related to one another.

to a familiar conclusion. The human revolution, completed before the diaspora, established a state of affairs in which further change and adaptation could be effected, within broad limits, by tradition rather than genetics. That is why human racial diversity is so slight, and it is why the languages and cultures of all communities, no matter how diverse, are elaborations of a single inherited "common denominator."

**ADDITIONAL
PLEISTOCENE CHANGES**

The further consequences of the human revolution include, in the end, everything that we have done since. Only a few of the more striking (and earlier) of these subsequent developments need to be mentioned here.

Language and culture, as we have seen, selected for bigger brains. Bigger brains mean bigger heads. Bigger heads mean greater difficulty in parturition. Even today, the head is the chief troublemaker in childbirth. This difficulty can be combatted to some extent by expelling the fetus relatively earlier in its development. There was therefore a selection for such earlier expulsion. But this, in turn, makes for a longer period of helpless infancy—which is, at the same time, a period of maximum plasticity, during which the child can acquire the complex extra-genetic heritage of its community. The helplessness of infants demands longer and more elaborate child care, and it becomes highly convenient for the adult males to help the mothers. Some of the skills that the young males must learn can only be learned from the adult males. All this makes for the domestication of fathers. This, together with the habit of paying attention to past experiences and future contingencies (which we have seen arising in the context of play, of tool-carrying, of the displacement of pre-language, and of tool-making), promotes male jealousy. The seeds of this may have been earlier, but it now becomes eminently reasonable for a male to reserve a female, even when he is not sexually hungry, that she may be available when the need arises.

In the developments just outlined we can also see contributing sources for the complex restrictions and rituals with which human sexual relations are hedged about. These include not only all the rules of exogamy and endogamy and the varying principles controlling premarital and extramarital relations, but also the whole matter of taste—some individuals of the opposite sex are attractive, others unattractive, according to criteria learned from one's community. Any male past puberty, and any female between menarche and menopause, can, in a matter of seconds, stand a good chance of launching a new human. But child care requires time and energy thereby unavailable for other important activities. From this stem such varied modern institutions as celibate orders and beauty contests.

Among the proto-hominoids the band leaders were the strongest adult males. Language, in particular, changes this. The oldest members of the band, strong or feeble, are valued because they have had time to learn more. They are repositories of information on which the community can call as it is needed (Sahlins 1959). This use of the elderly as encyclopedias perhaps helps to select for a greater life span, though the pedomorphism discussed earlier may also have played a part in bringing about this result. Certainly the increased social utility of the elderly promotes a protection of the old and feeble by the young and strong; it may contribute to doing something positive about the disposal of the dead.

As soon as the hominids had achieved a reasonably effective bipedal *walking* gait—not running, which is useful only for fast covering of short distances[30]—they had the basic wherewithal for migrating slowly throughout all the continental territory to which they could adapt their lifeways. For the invasion of some climatic zones, protection against the cold is necessary. There are various physiological ways of doing this (Coon 1962:62–68), but the hominids developed an additional device: clothing.

The Chinese variety of *Pithecanthropus*[31] used fire for warmth. By his epoch, then, the hominid invasion of cold climates had begun. But we suspect that clothing was a much earlier invention, already available when it was first needed for warmth.

Clothing serves roughly three functions: protection, as against the cold; modesty and vanity; and *carrying*. The last of these functions was, we suggest, the one of earliest relevance. If one's way of life rests on hand-carrying, and if the number and variety of things to be carried is increasing to the point of awkwardness, then the invention of a device that helps one carry things has the conservative survival value required by Romer's Rule. The first clothing-as-harness may have been nothing more than a piece of vine pulled from the trees and draped over the shoulder or around the waist. Later, when the hominids were regularly killing small animals, the hides—useless as food —might have been put to this use. A hide cannot be eaten, but if one is hungry enough there is some nourishment to be obtained by chewing at it. Almost as early as the first use of hides as harness, it may have been discovered that a hide that has been chewed is more flexible and comfortable to wear than one that has not. This way of processing hides was still widespread only yesterday.

It is unlikely that any direct archeological evidence of these posited early clothing developments will ever turn up. But if clothing of sorts is actually that ancient, then it was already available, with only minor modifications, when it was first needed to help explore ecological niches characterized by cold. It may even be old enough to have played a part in permitting the development of the relative hairlessness characteristic of all strains of *Homo sapiens* today.

[30] A point emphasized by Washburn in a talk at the Wenner-Gren Foundation for Anthropological Research, Spring 1960.
[31] Here and throughout we have used the taxonomic terms of Simpson (1945) and LeGros Clark (1955).

REFERENCES

Altmann, Stuart A. 1962. "Social behavior of anthropoid primates: Analysis of recent concepts," in *Roots of Behavior*. Edited by E. L. Bliss, pp. 277–85. New York: Harper and Brothers.

Andrew, R. J. 1963. The origin and evolution of the calls and facial expressions of the primates. *Behavior* 20:1–109.

Arieti, Silvano. 1956. Some basic problems common to anthropology and modern psychiatry. *American Anthropologist* 58:26–39.

Baerends, G. P. 1958. Comparative methods and the concept of homology in the study of behavior. *Archives néerlandaises de zoologie* 13:401–17.

Bartholomew, George A., Jr., and Joseph B. Birdsell. 1953. Ecology and the protohominids. *American Anthropologist* 55:481–98.

Bingham, H. C. 1932. *Gorillas in a native habitat*. Carnegie Institute of Washington Publ. No. 426

Bloomfield, Leonard. 1933. *Language*. New York: Henry Holt and Company.
———. 1936. Language or ideas? *Language* 12:89–95.

Bolwig, N. A. 1959. A study of nests built by mountain gorilla and chimpanzee. *South African Journal of Science* 55:286–91.

Brace, C. Loring. 1962. "Cultural factors in the evolution of human dentition," in *Culture and the Evolution of Man*. Edited by M. F. Ashley Montagu, pp. 343–354. New York: Oxford University Press.

Bryan, Alan L. 1963. The essential morphological basis for human culture. *Current Anthropology* 4:297–306.

Buettner-Janusch, J., ed. 1962. The relatives of man: modern studies of the relation of the evolution of nonhuman primates to human evolution. *Annals of the New York Academy of Sciences* 102:181–514.

Calhoun, John B. 1962. The ecology of violence. Paper presented to the Annual Meeting of the American Association for the Advancement of Science, Philadelphia, Penna., Dec. 29.

Cappanari, Stephen. 1962. The origin of speech. Paper presented to the Annual Meeting of the American Anthropological Association, Chicago.

Carpenter, C. R. 1938. Netherlands Committee for International Nature Protection, Communication No. 12:1034.
———. 1940. A field study of the behavior and social relations of the gibbon. *Comparative Psychology Monographs* 16, No. 5.

Chance, M. R. A. 1961. "The nature and special features of the instinctive social bond of primates," in *Social Life of Early Man*. Edited by S. L. Washburn, pp. 17–33. Chicago: Aldine Publishing Company.

Childe, V. Gordon. 1936. *Man makes himself*. London: C. A. Watts & Co. (Reprinted 1951. New York: New American Library of World Literature).

Chomsky, N. 1959. Review of *Verbal behavior*, by B. F. Skinner. *Language* 35:26–58.

Clark, J. Desmond. 1963. The evolution of culture in Africa. *The American Naturalist* 97:15–28.

Coon, Carleton S. 1962. *The origin of races*. New York: Alfred A. Knopf.

Count, Earl W. 1958. The biological basis of human sociality. *American Anthropologist* 60:1049–85.

Critchley, Macdonald. 1960. "The evolution of man's capacity for language," in *Evolution after Darwin, Volume II, The Evolution of Man: Man, Culture, and Society*. Edited by Sol Tax, pp. 289–308. Chicago: University of Chicago Press.

Dobzhansky, Th. 1956. *The biological basis of human freedom*. New York: Columbia University Press.
———. 1962. *Mankind evolving*. New York and London: Yale University Press.

DuBrul, E. L. 1958. *Evolution of the speech apparatus*. Springfield: Charles C. Thomas.

Eisley, Loren. 1955. "Fossil man and human evolution," in *Yearbook of anthropology—1955*, pp. 61–78. New York: Wenner-Gren Foundation for Anthropological Research.

Ferguson, Charles A. 1963. "Assumptions about nasals: A sample study in phonological universals," in *Universals of Language*. Edited by Joseph H. Greenberg, pp. 42–47. Cambridge, Mass.: The M.I.T. Press.

Ford, C. S. and F. A. Beach. 1951. *Patterns of sexual behavior*. New York: Hoeber.

Goodall, Jane, and Hugo van Lawick. 1963. My life among wild chimpanzees. *National Geographic Magazine* 124:272–308.

Greenberg, Joseph H. 1959. "Language and evolution," in *Evolution and Anthropology: A Centennial Appraisal*. Edited by B. J. Meggars, pp. 61–75. The Anthropological Society of Washington, Washington, D.C.

Haldane, J. B. S. 1943. 2d edition. *Animal biology*. New York and London: Oxford University Press.

Harlow, H. F. 1962. "The development of learning in the Rhesus monkey," in *Science in progress: 12th Series*. Edited by W. R. Brode, pp. 239–69. New Haven: Yale University Press.

Harlow, H. F., and R. R. Zimmermann. 1959. Affectional responses in the infant monkey. *Science* 130:421–32.

Hebb, D. O. 1949. *The organization of behavior: A neuropsychological theory*. New York: John Wiley & Sons, Inc.

Hediger, Heini. 1961. "The evolution of territorial behavior," in *Social Life of Early Man*. Edited by S. L. Washburn, pp. 34–37. Chicago: Aldine Publishing Company.

Hess, E. H. 1962. "Ethnology: an approach toward the complete analysis of behavior," in *New directions in psychology*. R. Brown, *et al.*, pp. 157–266. New York: Holt, Rinehart and Winston.

Hewes, Gordon W. 1961. Food transport and the origin of Hominid bipedalism. *American Anthropologist* 63:687–710.

Hinde, R. A., and N. Tinbergen. 1958. "The comparative study of species-specific behavior," in *Behavior and evolution*. Edited by A. Roe and G. E. Simpson, pp. 251–68. New Haven: Yale University Press.

Hoagland, Hudson. 1963. Toward a redefinition of culture. Proceedings of the Conference of the American Academy of Arts and Sciences, May 10–11.

———. n.d. personal communication.

Hochbaum, H. Albert. 1955. *Travels and traditions of waterfowl*. Minneapolis: University of Minnesota Press.

Hockett, Charles F. 1948. Biophysics, linguistics, and the unity of science. *American Scientist* 36:558–72.

———. 1956. Review. *Language* 32:46–49.

———. 1958. *A course in modern linguistics*. New York: The Macmillan Company.

———. 1959. "Animal 'languages' and human language," in *The Evolution of Man's Capacity for Culture*. Edited by J. N. Spuhler, pp. 32–39. Detroit: Wayne State University Press.

———. 1960*a*. The origin of speech. *Scientific American* 203:88–96.

———. 1960*b*. "Logical considerations in the study of animal communication," in *Animal Sounds and Communication*. Edited by W. E. Lanyon, and W. N. Tavolga, pp. 392–430. American Institute of Biological Sciences, Publ. No. 7. Washington, D.C.

———. 1963*a*. "The problem of universals in language," in *Universals of Language*. Edited by Joseph H. Greenberg, pp. 1–22. Cambridge, Mass.: The M.I.T. Press.

———. 1963*b*. Comment on "The essential morphological basis for human culture," by Alan Lyle Bryan. *Current Anthropology* 4:303–4.

Hoenigswald, H. M. 1963. The history of the comparative method. *Anthropological Linguistics* 5:1–11.

Hooton, E. 1942. *Man's poor relations.* New York: Doubleday, Doran and Company, Inc.

———. 1946. *Up from the ape.* New York: Macmillan.

Huxley, Thomas H. and Julian S. Huxley. 1947. *Touchstone for ethics.* New York: Harper.

Imanishi, Kinji. 1960. Social organization of subhuman primates in their natural habitat. *Current Anthropology* 1:393–407.

Itani, Junichiro. 1958. On the acquisition and propagation of a new food habit in the natural group of the Japanese monkey at Takasaki-Yama. *Primates* 1:84–98.

Kelemen, G. 1948. The anatomical basis of phonation in the chimpanzee. *Journal of morphology* 82:229–46. (Reprinted in 1949, *Yearbook of Physical Anthropology,* 4:153–80).

King, John A. 1955. *Social behavior, social organization, and population dynamics in a black-tailed prairiedog town in the Black Hills of South Dakota.* University of Michigan Contribution from the Laboratory of Vertebrate Biology, No. 67.

Kortlandt, Adriaan. 1962. Chimpanzees in the wild. *Scientific American* 206:128–34, 137–38.

Kroeber, A. L. 1948. *Anthropology.* New York: Harcourt Brace and Company.

LaBarre, Weston. 1954. *The human animal.* Chicago: University of Chicago Press.

Langer, Susanne K. 1942. *Philosophy in a new key.* Cambridge, Mass.: Harvard University Press. (Reprinted 1948. New York: The New American Library of World Literature.)

Lanyon, W. E. 1960. "The ontogeny of vocalization in birds," in *Animal Sounds and Communication.* Edited by W. E. Lanyon and W. N. Tavolga, pp. 321–47. American Institute of Biological Sciences, Publ. 7. Washington, D.C.

Leakey, L. S. B. 1959. A new fossil skull from Olduvai. *Nature* 184:491–93.

Leakey, L. S. B., G. H. Curtis, and J. F. Evernden. 1962. Age of basalt underlying Bed I, Olduvai. *Nature* 194:610–12.

LeGros Clark, W. E. 1955. *The fossil evidence for human evolution.* Chicago: The University of Chicago Press.

Leibnitz, Gottfried Wilhelm von. 1890. *Works.* Translated by G. M. Duncan. New Haven, Conn., U.S.A.: Tuttle, Morehouse and Taylor.

Lenneberg, E. H. 1960*a.* "Language, evolution, and purposive behavior," in *Culture in history: Essays in honor of Paul Radin.* Edited by S. Diamond, pp. 869–93. New York: Columbia University Press.

———. 1960*b.* Review of *Speech and brain mechanisms,* by W. Penfield and L. Robert. *Language* 36:97–112.

Leroi-Gourhan, André. 1955. *L'équilibre mécanique des cranes des vertebrés terrestres.* D.Sc. dissertation, University of Paris.

———. 1963. "Les origines de la civilisation technique," in *Histoire générale des techniques, Tome I.* Published under the direction of Maurice Daumas. Paris: Presses Universitaires de France.

Lévi-Strauss, Claude. 1949. *Les structures élémentaires de la parenté.* Paris: Presses Universitaires de France.

Lindauer, Martin. 1963. *Communication among Social Bees.* Cambridge: Harvard University Press.

Lorenz, K. Z. 1960. Prinzipien der vergleichenden Verhaltensforschung. *Fortschritte der Zoologie* 12:265–94.

Malinowski, Bronislav. 1927. *Sex and repression in savage society.* New York: Harcourt, Brace. Reprinted 1960. New York: World Publishing Company.

Mead, Margaret. 1949. *Male and female.* New York: Morrow. Reprinted 1955. New York: New American Library.

———. 1952. "Some relationships between social anthropology and psychiatry," in *Dynamic psychiatry.* Edited by Franz Alexander and Helen Ross, pp. 401–48. Chicago: University of Chicago Press.

———. 1961. "Cultural determinants of sexual behavior," in *Sex and internal secretions,* 3d. edition. Edited by William C. Young, pp. 1433–79. Baltimore: Williams and Wilkins.

———. 1963a. "Some general considerations," in *Expression of the emotions in man*. Edited by Peter H. Knapp, pp. 318–27. New York: International Universities Press.

———. 1963b. "Violence in the perspective of culture history," in *Violence and war with clinical studies*. Edited by Jules H. Masserman, pp. 92–106. New York, London: Grune and Stratton.

———. 1963c. *Totem and taboo* reconsidered with respect. *Bulletin of the Menninger Clinic* 27:185–99.

———. 1964. *Continuities in cultural evolution*. *The Terry lectures*. New Haven, London: Yale University Press (in press).

Mead, Margaret, and Theodore Schwartz. 1960. "The cult as a condensed social process," in *Group processes, Transactions of the 5th Conference, 1958*. Edited by Bertram Schaffner, pp. 85–187. New York: Josiah Macy, Jr. Foundation.

Milne, Lorus J. and Marjorie. 1962. *The senses of animals and men*. New York: Atheneum.

Montagu, Ashley M. F. 1944. On the relation between body size, waking activity, and the origin of social life in the primates. *American Anthropologist* 46:141–45.

———. 1951. *An introduction to physical anthropology*. Springfield, Ill.: C. C. Thomas.

———. 1957. *The reproductive development of the female*. New York: Julian Press.

———. 1964. *The human revolution*. Cleveland and New York: World Publishing Company (in press).

Morris, Charles. 1946. *Signs, language, and behavior*. Englewood Cliffs, N.J., U.S.A.: Prentice-Hall.

Napier, John. 1962. The evolution of the hand. *Scientific American* 207:56–62.

Nissen, H. W. 1931. A field study of the chimpanzee. *Comparative Psychology Monographs* 8, No. 1.

Oakley, Kenneth P. 1961. "On man's use of fire, with comments on toolmaking and hunting," in *Social Life of Early Man*. Edited by S. L. Washburn, pp. 176–93. Chicago: Aldine Publishing Company.

———. 1962. Dating the emergence of man. *The Advancement of Science* 18:415–26.

Pederson, Holger. 1931. *Linguistic science in the nineteenth century*. Cambridge: Harvard University Press.

Penfield, W., and L. Roberts. 1959. *Speech and brain mechanisms*. Princeton: Princeton University Press.

Pittenger, R. E., C. F. Hockett, and J. Danehy. 1960. *The first five minutes: An example of microscopic interview analysis*. Ithaca: Paul Martineau.

Prosser, C. L. 1959. "Comparative neuropsychology," in *Evolution of nervous control from primitive organisms to man*. Edited by B. B. Brodie and A. D. Bass. American Association for the Advancement of Science, Publication No. 52.

Romer, A. S. 1958. "Phylogeny and behavior with special reference to vertebrate evolution," in *Behavior and Evolution*. Edited by Anne Roe and G. G. Simpson, pp. 48–75. New Haven: Yale University Press.

———. 1959. *The vertebrate story*. Chicago: University of Chicago Press.

Sade, Donald. 1963. Grooming patterns and the family in a group of free ranging rhesus monkeys. Paper presented to the Annual Meeting of the American Anthropological Association, San Francisco, November 21.

Sahlins, Marshall D. 1959. "The social life of monkeys, apes, and primitive man," in *The Evolution of Man's Capacity for Culture*. Edited by J. N. Spuhler, pp. 54–73. Detroit: Wayne State University Press.

Schaller, George B. 1963. *The mountain gorilla: ecology and behavior*. Chicago: University of Chicago Press.

Schultz, Adolph H. 1954. Bemerkungen zur Variabilität und Systematik der Schimpansen. *Säugetierkundliche Mitteilungen* 2:159–63.

———. 1961. "Some factors influencing the social life of primates in general and early man in particular," in *Social Life of Early Man*. Edited by S. L. Washburn, pp. 58–90. Chicago: Aldine Publishing Company.

———. 1963*a*. "Die rezenten Hominoidea," in *Ein Jahrhundert menschlicher Abstammungslehre*. Edited by G. Heberer, pp. 56–102. Stuttgart, Germany: Gustav Fischer Verlag (in press).

———. 1963*b*. "Age changes, sex differences, and variability as factors in the classification of primates," in *Classification and Human Evolution*. Edited by S. L. Washburn, pp. 85–115. Chicago: Aldine Publishing Company.

Simons, Elwyn L. 1963. Some fallacies in the study of hominid phylogeny. *Science* 141:879–889.

Simpson, George G. 1945. The principles of classification and a classification of mammals. The Ameircan Museum of Natural History, Bulletin 85, New York.

———. 1949. *The meaning of evolution*. New Haven: Yale University Press. (Reprinted 1951. New York: The New American Library of World Literature.)

———. 1958. "The study of evolution: Methods and present status of theory," in *Behavior and Evolution*. Edited by Anne Roe and G. G. Simpson, pp. 7–26. New Haven: Yale University Press.

Smith, Eliot. 1913. "The evolution of man," in *Smithsonian Report for 1912*, pp. 553–72. The Smithsonian Institution, Washington, D.C.

Southwick, Charles H. 1955. The population dynamics of confined house mice supplied with unlimited food. *Ecology* 36:212–25.

Spuhler, J. N. 1959. "Somatic paths to culture," in *The Evolution of Man's Capacity for Culture*. Edited by J. N. Spuhler, pp. 1–13. Detroit: Wayne State University Press.

———. Ed. 1959. *The Evolution of Man's Capacity for Culture*. Detroit: Wayne State University Press.

Strecker, Robert L., and John T. Emlen, Jr. 1953. Regulatory mechanisms in house-mouse populations: The effect of limited food supply on a confined population. *Ecology* 34:375–85.

Swadesh, Morris. 1960. *Tras la huella linguistica de la prehistoria*. Supplementos del Seminario de Problemas Cientificos y Filosoficos, Segunda Serie, No. 26. Mexico, D.F.: Universidad Nacional de México.

Tanner, James M. 1955. *Growth at adolescence*. Springfield, Ill.: Thomas. Reprinted 1962.

Trager, George L. 1958. Paralanguage: A first approximation. *Studies in Linguistics* 13:1–12.

———. 1959. "Language," in *Encyclopaedia Brittanica*, Vol. 13, pp. 695–702. Chicago: William Benton.

———. 1963. *Linguistics is linguistics*. Studies in Linguistics, Occasional Papers, No. 10.

von Frisch, Karl. 1950. *Bees, their vision, chemical senses, and language*. Ithaca: Cornell University Press.

Waddington, C. H. 1961. *The ethical animal*. New York: Atheneum.

Washburn, S. L. 1959. "Speculation on the interrelations of the history of tools and biological evolution," in *The Evolution of Man's Capacity for Culture*. Edited by J. N. Spuhler, pp. 21–31. Detroit: Wayne State University Press.

———. 1960. Tools and human evolution. *Scientific American* 203:63–75.

———. Ed. 1961. *Social life of early man*. Chicago: Aldine Publishing Company.

Washburn, S. L., and Irven DeVore. 1961. "Social behavior of baboons and early man," in *Social Life of Early Man*. Edited by S. L. Washburn, pp. 91–105. Chicago: Aldine Publishing Company.

White, Leslie A. 1949. *The science of culture*. New York: Farrar, Straus & Co. (Reprinted 1958. New York: Grove Press.)

———. 1959. "Summary review," in *The Evolution of Man's Capacity for Culture*. Edited by J. N. Spuhler, pp. 74–79. Detroit: Wayne State University Press.

Wiener, Alexander S., and J. Moor-Jankowski. 1963. Blood groups in anthropoid apes and baboons. *Science* 142:67–68.

Wiener, Norbert. 1948. *Cybernetics.* New York: The Technology Press and John Wiley & Sons.

Weinert, Hans. 1932. *Ursprung der Menschheit.* Stuttgart, Germany: Ferdinand Enke Verlag.

Wittgenstein, Ludwig. 1953. *Philosophical Investigations.* New York: Macmillan.

11

A CASE OF
EXTREME ISOLATION

Kingsley Davis

EARLY IN 1940 THERE APPEARED in this *Journal* an account of a girl called Anna.[1] She had been deprived of normal contact and had received a minimum of human care for almost the whole of her first six years of life. At that time observations were not complete and the report had a tentative character. Now, however, the girl is dead, and, with more information available,[2] it is possible to give a fuller and more definitive description of the case from a sociological point of view.

Anna's death, caused by hemorrhagic jaundice, occurred on August 6, 1942. Having been born on March 1 or 6,[3] 1932, she was approximately ten and a half years of age when she died. The previous report covered her development up to the age of almost eight years; the present one recapitulates the earlier period on the basis of new evidence and then covers the last two and a half years of her life.

Reprinted from "Final Note on a Case of Extreme Isolation" by Kingsley Davis, in *American Journal of Sociology* 52 (1947), 432–437, by permission of The University of Chicago Press. Copyright 1947 by The University of Chicago Press. (Text, Chapter 5)

[1] Kingsley Davis, "Extreme Social Isolation of a Child," *American Journal of Sociology,* XLV (January 1940), 554–65.
[2] Sincere appreciation is due to the officials in the Department of Welfare, Commonwealth of Pennsylvania, for their kind co-operation in making available the records concerning Anna and discussing the case frankly with the writer. Helen C. Hubbell, Florentine Hackbusch, and Eleanor Meckelnburg were particularly helpful, as was Fanny L. Matchette. Without their aid neither of the reports on Anna could have been written.
[3] The records are not clear as to which day.

EARLY HISTORY

The first few few days and weeks of Anna's life were complicated by frequent changes of domicile. It will be recalled that she was an illegitimate child, the second such child born to her mother, and that her grandfather, a widowed farmer in whose house her mother lived, strongly disapproved of this new evidence of the mother's indiscretion. This fact led to the baby's being shifted about.

Two weeks after being born in a nurse's private home, Anna was brought to the family farm, but the grandfather's antagonism was so great that she was shortly taken to the house of one of her mother's friends. At this time a local minister became interested in her and took her to his house with an idea of possible adoption. He decided against adoption, however, when he discovered that she had vaginitis. The infant was then taken to a children's home in the nearest large city. This agency found that at the age of only three weeks she was already in a miserable condition, being "terribly galled and otherwise in very bad shape." It did not regard her as a likely subject for adoption but took her in for a while anyway, hoping to benefit her. After Anna had spent nearly eight weeks in this place, the agency notified her mother to come to get her. The mother responded by sending a man and his wife to the children's home with a view to their adopting Anna, but they made such a poor impression on the agency that permission was refused. Later the mother came herself and took the child out of the home and then gave her to this couple. It was in the home of this pair that a social worker found the girl a short time thereafter. The social worker went to the mother's home and pleaded with Anna's grandfather to allow the mother to bring the child home. In spite of threats, he refused. The child, by then more than four months old, was next taken to another children's home in a near-by town. A medical examination at this time revealed that she had impetigo, vaginitis, umbilical hernia, and a skin rash.

Anna remained in this second children's home for nearly three weeks, at the end of which time she was transferred to a private foster-home. Since, however, the grandfather would not, and the mother could not, pay for the child's care, she was finally taken back as a last resort to the grandfather's house (at the age of five and a half months). There she remained, kept on the second floor in an attic-like room because her mother hesitated to incur the grandfather's wrath by bringing her downstairs.

The mother, a sturdy woman weighing about 180 pounds, did a man's work on the farm. She engaged in heavy work such as milking cows and tending hogs and had little time for her children. Sometimes she went out at night, in which case Anna was left entirely without attention. Ordinarily, it seems, Anna received only enough care to keep her barely alive. She appears to have been seldom moved from one position to another. Her clothing and bedding were filthy. She apparently had no instruction, no friendly attention.

It is little wonder that, when finally found and removed from the room in the grandfather's house at the age of nearly six years, the child could not talk, walk, or do anything that showed intelligence. She was in an extremely emaciated and undernourished condition, with skeleton-like legs and a bloated abdomen. She had been fed on virtually nothing except cow's milk during the years under her mother's care.

Anna's condition when found, and her subsequent improvement, have been described in the previous report. It now remains to say what happened to her after that.

LATER HISTORY

In 1939, nearly two years after being discovered, Anna had progressed, as previously reported, to the point where she could walk, understand simple commands, feed herself, achieve some neatness, remember people, etc. But she still did not speak, and, though she was much more like a normal infant of something over one year of age in mentality, she was far from normal for her age.

On August 30, 1939, she was taken to a private home for retarded children, leaving the county home where she had been for more than a year and a half. In her new setting she made some further progress, but not a great deal. In a report of an examination made November 6 of the same year, the head of the institution pictured the child as follows:

> Anna walks about aimlessly, makes periodic rhythmic motions of her hands, and, at intervals, makes guttural and sucking noises. She regards her hands as if she had seen them for the first time. It was impossible to hold her attention for more than a few seconds at a time—not because of distraction due to external stimuli but because of her inability to concentrate. She ignored the task in hand to gaze vacantly about the room. Speech is entirely lacking. Numerous unsuccessful attempts have been made with her in the hope of developing initial sounds. I do not believe that this failure is due to negativism or deafness but that she is not sufficiently developed to accept speech at this time. . . . The prognosis is not favorable. . . .

More than five months later, on April 25, 1940, a clinical psychologist, the late Professor Francis N. Maxfield, examined Anna and reported the following: large for her age; hearing "entirely normal"; vision apparently normal; able to climb stairs; speech in the "babbling stage" and "promise for developing intelligible speech later seems to be good." He said further that "on the Merrill-Palmer scale she made a mental score of 19 months. On the Vineland social maturity scale she made a score of 23 months."[4]

Professor Maxfield very sensibly pointed out that prognosis is difficult in such cases of isolation. "It is very difficult to take scores on tests standardized under the average conditions of environment and experience," he wrote, "and

---

[4] Letter to one of the state officials in charge of the case.

interpret them in a case where environment and experience have been so unusual." With this warning he gave it as his opinion at that time that Anna would eventually "attain an adult mental level of six or seven years."[5]

The school for retarded children, on July 1, 1941, reported that Anna had reached 46 inches in height and weighed 60 pounds. She could bounce and catch a ball and was said to conform to group socialization, though as a follower rather than a leader. Toilet habits were firmly established. Food habits were normal, except that she still used a spoon as her sole implement. She could dress herself except for fastening her clothes. Most remarkable of all, she had finally begun to develop speech. She was characterized as being at about the two-year level in this regard. She could call attendants by name and bring in one when she was asked to. She had a few complete sentences to express her wants. The report concluded that there was nothing peculiar about her, except that she was feeble-minded—"probably congenital in type."[6]

A final report from the school, made on June 22, 1942, and evidently the last report before the girl's death, pictured only a slight advance over that given above. It said that Anna could follow directions, string beads, identify a few colors, build with blocks, and differentiate between attractive and unattractive pictures. She had a good sense of rhythm and loved a doll. She talked mainly in phrases but would repeat words and try to carry on a conversation. She was clean about clothing. She habitually washed her hands and brushed her teeth. She would try to help other children. She walked well and could run fairly well, though clumsily. Although easily excited, she had a pleasant disposition.

INTERPRETATION

Such was Anna's condition just before her death. It may seem as if she had not made much progress, but one must remember the condition in which she had been found. One must recall that she had no glimmering of speech, absolutely no ability to walk, no sense of gesture, not the least capacity to feed herself even when the food was put in front of her, and no comprehension of cleanliness. She was so apathetic that it was hard to tell whether or not she could hear. And all this at the age of nearly ten years. Compared with this condition, her capacities at the time of her death seem striking indeed, though they do not amount to much more than a two-and-a-half-year mental level. One conclusion therefore seems safe, namely, that her isolation prevented a considerable amount of mental development that was undoubtedly part of her capacity. Just what her original capacity was, of course, is hard to say; but her development after her period of confinement (including the

---

[5] *Ibid.*
[6] Progress report of the school.

ability to walk and run, to play, dress, fit into a social situation, and, above all, to speak) shows that she had at least this much capacity—capacity that never could have been realized in her original condition of isolation.

A further question is this: What would she have been like if she had received a normal upbringing from the moment of birth? A definitive answer would have been impossible in any case, but even an approximate answer is made difficult by her early death. If one assumes, as was tentatively surmised in the previous report, that it is "almost impossible for any child to learn to speak, think, and act like a normal person after a long period of early isolation," it seems likely that Anna might have had a normal or near-normal capacity, genetically speaking. On the other hand, it was pointed out that Anna represented "a marginal case, [because] she was discovered before she had reached six years of age," an age "young enough to allow for some plasticity."[7] While admitting, then, that Anna's isolation *may* have been the major cause (and was certainly a minor cause) of her lack of rapid mental progress during the four and a half years following her rescue from neglect, it is necessary to entertain the hypothesis that she was congenitally deficient.

In connection with this hypothesis, one suggestive though by no means conclusive circumstance needs consideration, namely, the mentality of Anna's forebears. Information on this subject is easier to obtain, as one might guess, on the mother's than on the father's side. Anna's maternal grandmother, for example, is said to have been college educated and wished to have her children receive a good education, but her husband, Anna's stern grandfather, apparently a shrewd, hard-driving, calculating farmowner, was so penurious that her ambitions in this direction were thwarted. Under the circumstances her daughter (Anna's mother) managed, despite having to do hard work on the farm, to complete the eighth grade in a country school. Even so, however, the daughter was evidently not very smart. "A schoolmate [of Anna's mother] stated that she was retarded in school work; was very gullible at this age; and that her morals even at this time were discussed by other students." Two tests administered to her on March 4, 1938, when she was thirty-two years of age, showed that she was mentally deficient. On the Stanford Revision of the Binet-Simon Scale her performance was equivalent to that of a child of eight years, giving her an I.Q. of 50 and indicating mental deficiency of "middle-grade moron type."[8]

As to the identity of Anna's father, the most persistent theory holds that he was an old man about seventy-four years of age at the time of the girl's birth. If he was the one, there is no indication of mental or other biological deficiency, whatever one may think of his morals. However, someone else may actually have been the father.

---

[7] Davis, *op. cit.*, p. 564.

[8] The facts set forth here as to Anna's ancestry are taken chiefly from a report of mental tests administered to Anna's mother by psychologists at a state hospital where she was taken for this purpose after the discovery of Anna's seclusion. This excellent report was not available to the writer when the previous paper on Anna was published.

To sum up: Anna's heredity is the kind that *might* have given rise to innate mental deficiency, though not necessarily.

COMPARISON WITH
ANOTHER CASE

Perhaps more to the point than speculations about Anna's ancestry would be a case for comparison. If a child could be discovered who had been isolated about the same length of time as Anna but had achieved a much quicker recovery and a greater mental development, it would be a stronger indication that Anna was deficient to start with.

Such a case does exist. It is the case of a girl found at about the same time as Anna and under strikingly similar circumstances. A full description of the details of this case has not been published, but, in addition to newspaper reports, an excellent preliminary account by a speech specialist, Dr. Marie K. Mason, who played an important role in the handling of the child, has appeared.[9] Also the late Dr. Francis N. Maxfield, clinical psychologist at Ohio State University, as was Dr. Mason, has written an as yet unpublished but penetrating analysis of the case.[10] Some of his observations have been included in Professor Zingg's book on feral man.[11] The following discussion is drawn mainly from these enlightening materials. The writer, through the kindness of Professors Mason and Maxfield, did have a chance to observe the girl in April, 1940, and to discuss the features of her case with them.

Born apparently one month later than Anna, the girl in question, who has been given the pseudonym Isabelle, was discovered in November, 1938, nine months after the discovery of Anna. At the time she was found she was approximately six and a half years of age. Like Anna, she was an illegitimate child and had been kept in seclusion for that reason. Her mother was a deaf-mute, having become so at the age of two, and it appears that she and Isabelle had spent most of their time together in a dark room shut off from the rest of the mother's family. As a result Isabelle had no chance to develop speech; when she communicated with her mother, it was by means of gestures. Lack of sunshine and inadequacy of diet had caused Isabelle to become rachitic. Her legs in particular were affected; they "were so bowed that as she stood erect the sole of her shoes came nearly flat together, and she got about with a skittering gait."[12] Her behavior toward strangers, especially men, was

---

[9] Marie K. Mason, "Learning To Speak after Six and One-Half Years of Silence," *Journal of Speech Disorders,* VII (1942), 295–304.

[10] Francis N. Maxfield, "What Happens When the Social Environment of a Child Approaches Zero." The writer is greatly indebted to Mrs. Maxfield and to Professor Horace B. English, a colleague of Professor Maxfield, for the privilege of seeing this manuscript and other materials collected on isolated and feral individuals.

[11] J. A. L. Singh and Robert M. Zingg, *Wolf-Children and Feral Man* (New York: Harper & Bros., 1941), pp. 248–51.

[12] Maxfield, unpublished manuscript cited above.

almost that of a wild animal, manifesting much fear and hostility. In lieu of speech she made only a strange croaking sound. In many ways she acted like an infant. "She was apparently utterly unaware of relationships of any kind. When presented with a ball for the first time, she held it in the palm of her hand, then reached out and stroked my face with it. Such behavior is comparable to that of a child of six months."[13] At first it was even hard to tell whether or not she could hear, so unused were her senses. Many of her actions resembled those of deaf children.

It is small wonder that, once it was established that she could hear, specialists working with her believed her to be feeble-minded. Even on nonverbal tests her performance was so low as to promise little for the future. Her first score on the Stanford-Binet was 19 months, practically at the zero point of the scale. On the Vineland social maturity scale her first score was 39, representing an age level of two and a half years.[14] "The general impression was that she was wholly uneducable and that any attempt to teach her to speak, after so long a period of silence, would meet with failure."[15]

In spite of this interpretation, the individuals in charge of Isabelle launched a systematic and skilful program of training. It seemed hopeless at first. The approach had to be through pantomime and dramatization, suitable to an infant. It required one week of intensive effort before she even made her first attempt at vocalization. Gradually she began to respond, however, and, after the first hurdles had at last been overcome, a curious thing happened. She went through the usual stages of learning characteristic of the years from one to six, not only in proper succession but far more rapidly than normal. In a little over two months after her first vocalization she was putting sentences together. Nine months after that she could identify words and sentences on the printed page, could write well, could add to ten, and could retell a story after hearing it. Seven months beyond this point she had a vocabulary of 1,500–2,000 words and was asking complicated questions. Starting from an educational level of between one and three years (depending on what aspect one considers), she had reached a normal level by the time she was eight and a half years old. In short, she covered in two years the stages of learning that ordinarily require six.[16] Or, to put it another way, her I.Q. trebled in a year and a half.[17] The speed with which she reached the normal level of mental development seems analogous to the recovery of body weight in a growing child after an illness, the recovery being achieved by an extra fast rate of growth for a period after the illness until normal weight for the given age is again attained.

When the writer saw Isabelle a year and a half after her discovery, she gave him the impression of being a very bright, cheerful, energetic little girl.

[13] Mason, *op. cit.*, p. 299.
[14] Maxfield, unpublished manuscript.
[15] Mason, *op. cit.*, p. 299.
[16] *Ibid.*, pp. 300–304.
[17] Maxfield, unpublished manuscript.

She spoke well, walked and ran without trouble, and sang with gusto and accuracy. Today she is over fourteen years old and has passed the sixth grade in a public school. Her teachers say that she participates in all school activities as normally as other children. Though older than her classmates, she has fortunately not physically matured too far beyond their level.[18]

Clearly the history of Isabelle's development is different from that of Anna's. In both cases there was an exceedingly low, rather blank, intellectual level to begin with. In both cases it seemed that the girl might be congenitally feeble-minded. In both a considerably higher level was reached later on. But the Ohio girl achieved a normal mentality within two years, whereas Anna was still marked inadequate at the end of four and a half years. This difference in achievement may suggest that Anna had less initial capacity. But an alternative hypothesis is possible.

One should remember that Anna never received the prolonged and expert attention that Isabelle received. The result of such attention, in the case of the Ohio girl, was to give her speech at an early stage, and her subsequent rapid development seems to have been a consequence of that. "Until Isabelle's speech and language development, she had all the characteristics of a feeble-minded child." Had Anna, who, from the standpoint of psychometric tests and early history, closely resembled this girl at the start, been given a mastery of speech at an earlier point by intensive training, her subsequent development might have been much more rapid.[19]

The hypothesis that Anna began with a sharply inferior mental capacity is therefore not established. Even if she were deficient to start with, we have no way of knowing how much so. Under ordinary conditions she might have been a dull normal or, like her mother, a moron. Even after the blight of her isolation, if she had lived to maturity, she might have finally reached virtually the full level of her capacity, whatever it may have been. That her isolation did have a profound effect upon her mentality, there can be no doubt. This is proved by the substantial degree of change during the four and a half years following her rescue.

Consideration of Isabelle's case serves to show, as Anna's case does not clearly show, that isolation up to the age of six, with failure to acquire any form of speech and hence failure to grasp nearly the whole world of cultural meaning, does not preclude the subsequent acquisition of these. Indeed, there seems to be a process of accelerated recovery in which the child goes through the mental stages at a more rapid rate than would be the case in normal development. Just what would be the maximum age at which a person could remain isolated and still retain the capacity for full cultural acquisition is hard to say. Almost certainly it would not be as high as age fifteen; it might possibly be as low as age ten. Undoubtedly various individuals would differ considerably as to the exact age.

[18] Based on a personal letter from Dr. Mason to the writer, May 13, 1946.
[19] This point is suggested in a personal letter from Dr. Mason to the writer, October 22, 1946.

Anna's is not an ideal case for showing the effects of extreme isolation, partly because she was possibly deficient to begin with, partly because she did not receive the best training available, and partly because she did not live long enough. Nevertheless, her case is instructive when placed in the record with numerous other cases of extreme isolation. This and the previous article about her are meant to place her in the record. It is to be hoped that other cases will be described in the scientific literature as they are discovered (as unfortunately they will be), for only in these rare cases of extreme isolation is it possible "to observe *concretely separated* two factors in the development of human personality which are always otherwise only analytically separated, the biogenic and the sociogenic factors."[20]

[20] Singh and Zingg, *op. cit.*, pp. xxi–xxii, in a foreword by the writer.

12
LANGUAGE
AND THINKING

Henry Head

ACTS OF
DIRECT REFERENCE

WHEN WE ARE FACED WITH A PROBLEM demanding an active response, we mobilise all the powers we possess for its solution. Thought presupposes the existence of language, but exceeds it widely in range, and there are many forms of behaviour, the result of thinking, which do not require the intervention of a symbol. Percepts and emotions alone may determine the form of the response. We often act without thinking of ourselves as acting, or formulating beforehand the exact nature of the reply to the conditions of the moment. Many actions in a game such as lawn-tennis or in piloting an aeroplane belong to this order. Some fresh situation is dealt with successfully with extreme rapidity; the manipulator is conscious only of the result and he may be unable to recall the movements he has actually performed.

The tests which I have employed in this research comprise a certain number of intellectual operations, based on correspondences of a sensory order or on similarity and difference of perceptions. Such acts are not directly disturbed in aphasia and kindred disorders of speech. All those on the contrary which imply more complex adaptation, the recognition of signs, logical symbols or diagrams, suffer more or less severely.

From *Aphasia and Kindred Disorders of Speech,* Vol. I (New York: Macmillan, 1926), pp. 513–532. By permission of Cambridge University Press. (Text, Chapter 5)

Acts of direct reference do not form a sign-situation and are not affected even in severe examples of disorders of speech, provided the patient can be made to understand exactly what he is expected to do. He can choose a familiar object or a colour from amongst those before him, which exactly corresponds to the one he was shown. Here the act of matching depends on reaction to similarity in successive visual impressions.[1]

But suppose some article such as a knife, or even a geometrical figure, is placed in his hand out of sight. The patient has no difficulty in selecting its duplicate, provided no words are employed. Moreover, if he has been given a pyramid cut out of a block of wood, he can match it with any pyramidal object, however greatly the two may differ in relative size and structure. He deduces from the multifarious sensations yielded by his hand certain characteristics, which are also possessed by the object within sight, and ignores the many differences. In both percepts he reacts to a common quality, the pyramidal factor, although the one is the result of tactile the other of visual impressions.

So long as the act to be performed is one of direct matching it can usually be executed in spite of the defective use of language. But as soon as a symbol intervenes between the initiation and performance of any task, the patient is liable to fail to carry it out correctly. Suppose, for instance, he has succeeded in matching a single object shown to him with the one on the table which resembles it. If he is then given two objects at a time, he may fail to select the two corresponding duplicates, because he attempts to register what he has seen in words and to make his choice accordingly. A symbolic formula has been interjected and the act is no longer one of direct matching.

To place the hands of a clock into the exact position of those on one set by the observer is in most cases an act of pure imitation. But should the patient have any difficulty in appreciating the relative significance of the two hands, even this simple task may be badly executed. He confuses the hour and minute hand, or fails to comprehend exactly what he is expected to do.

Certain forms of behaviour, which at first sight appear to be purely imitative, in reality require the intervention of some verbal symbol or formula. If I am seated face to face with a patient and touch an eye or an ear with one or other hand, he may fail to imitate my movements because he cannot bear in mind that our actions are apparently reversed. To carry out this test successfully he is compelled to formulate to himself that my right hand is opposite to his left and that the same is true for eye or ear. In some instances he attempts to express this fact silently in words by saying to himself, "It is the opposite," or even, "His right is my left."

But as soon as I stand behind him and my movements are reflected in a mirror, all necessity for such formulation disappears; the act becomes in

---

[1] Gelb and Goldstein have shown however that the same patient may fail to sort the various shades of the Holmgren wools correctly. (Vide Part I, p. 132.)

most instances one of pure imitation. Many patients express this by saying, "It is easy because I don't have to think." When, however, the disorder assumes a semantic form the essential nature and intention of the movements to be performed become a matter of doubt; the patient grows confused in his attempts to reason out what he is required to do and fails to execute even this simple act of imitation. Any task that leads to "thinking," or the intervention of certain symbols, tends to be badly performed. Thus, even if the patient imitates with ease and certainty my movements reflected in a mirror, he cannot write them down, not because he is unable to form the necessary words in writing, but because a verbal formula intervenes between this mode of expression and what he sees.

To copy capital letters line by line is an act of imitative drawing; it can be executed by a child before he has learnt to write. But to translate them into their small cursive equivalents demands symbolic formulation and is difficult or impossible in many cases of aphasia. This does not depend on any peculiar inherent difficulty in cursive script; for if the letters to be copied are set out in this form, they can be reproduced correctly by the same patient who was unable to translate capitals into common handwriting. All transliteration demands the intervention of a certain degree of logical thinking however slight, and consequently tends to suffer in many cases of aphasia.

In most instances the patient can draw from a simple model and can even reproduce his drawing from memory. Should he fail, however, to appreciate the intention or aim of the action he is expected to perform, he may be unable even to draw from a model; yet he can produce a fair representation of some object that has risen to his mind as a spontaneous image or idea. It is not the mechanical act of drawing which is affected, even in semantic aphasia, but the power to formulate a conception of how to undertake the solution of the problem.

There are certain other acts, which can be performed correctly in spite of these disorders by a process of direct reference, but not by a formal statement of symbolic relations. A patient who cannot state how many sixpences make up half-a-crown, when they are placed before him, can pile up a heap of coins of the exact value of either piece of money. He may be unable to state the price he pays for his tobacco; yet he knows that, when he asks for two ounces and tenders two shillings, he receives threepence in change. Capt. C. (No. 2) was fully aware that his railway journey cost him five shillings minus twopence halfpenny and this sum he expected to receive together with his ticket. Such patients can register an event and act upon it, although they cannot state a formal relation either to themselves or others.

During the period when No. 2 was unable to tell the time from a clock face shown to him, he was punctual for his engagements. Moreover, if the hands pointed to half-past one, he said "That's when we have dinner," which was correct. He still possessed some appreciation of the passage of time by means of which he regulated his actions, although he could not state the hour formally either aloud or to himself.

In the same way, in spite of the confusion between right and left, he was conscious that the traffic of the streets kept to the left in England, but not in other countries, and could indicate this fact to me by suitable gestures.

Thus, amongst the multifarious processes comprised in unrestricted thinking, some can still lead to the desired result in spite of the existence of aphasia and kindred disorders of speech. These are brought to a successful conclusion mainly by direct reference; but the same tasks may be rendered impossible if an act of symbolic formulation or expression is interposed between their initiation and completion.

IMAGES
AND THINKING

Images play a double part in unrestrained thinking and may or may not suffer according to the manner in which they are employed. We know very little of the behaviour of auditory images in aphasia; but the direct reproduction of melody and the recognition of time and tune are not affected, apart from the difficulty of forming the words of a song, or reading the notes of music. Careful interrogation failed to reveal in any of my cases that the patient was in the habit before his injury of hearing the words of his internal speech without moving his vocal organs; nor could I obtain satisfactory evidence of direct auditory reproduction of phrases previously heard or arising spontaneously to the mind.

But I have been able to gather a good deal of information concerning visual imagery from the highly intelligent and educated patients with whom I have been brought into contact. In persons with a strong visual memory all the processes of thinking are accompanied by and at times essentially composed of more or less vivid and detailed imagery. If I think of a horse, it is not the word in any form which springs into my mind, but a picture of a horse. This image assumes a familiar general character, which usually represents a horse to me; it is in reality a nominal symbol or visual noun. If it has been aroused by something I have heard or read, the figure is suitably varied in colour, form or posture in accordance with the descriptive details, and in this way reproduces adjectival meaning. Such images stand in place of words and as such tend to be affected in aphasia.

On the other hand, during spontaneous thinking visual images may appear in a sequence suggested by association, or corresponding to the order in which the objects were originally perceived. Such images form perceptual data, which may remain unaffected in disorders of speech. For instance, No. 10 was able to recall spontaneously the shape and colour of his hives and to see the bees arriving at the entrance laden with yellow pollen.

But visual images are fragmentary and uncertain; each one of them may be vivid and full of detail, but the connecting links with those which accompany or follow it are too weak to lead unaided to a definite intellectual conclusion. Yet they may amply suffice for purely descriptive purposes.

Thus, when No. 2 attempted to give an account of a famous prize fight, he failed grossly so long as he relied on recalling what he had read. But my question "Can you see it?" evoked so lively a series of visual images that he was able to describe many more details correctly; finally, springing out of bed, he assumed the exact attitude of the triumphant Carpentier gazing down on his vanquished opponent.

Even a vivid and accurate series of visual images is insufficient alone for constructive and logical thought. In many cases of aphasia they can be employed for direct reference, but the links between them are too tenuous to insure reproduction of a sequence of events without some kind of verbal formulation. Visual images form isolated points in the complicated mechanism of thought, unless they are connected by symbolic processes adequate to express the relational aspects of constructive thinking. Such links are of the nature of the general or universal, and therefore suffer in aphasia and kindred disorders of speech. When No. 2 was asked to describe how he would walk from the hospital to the War Office, he said he could see the big stores, Westminster Abbey and other buildings he would meet on his way. Each appeared as an isolated event; he could not connect them together and pass with ease from one to the other, in consequence of his want of names. He explained that it was "all in bits," and that he had to "jump from one thing to the other" because he "had no names." For, normally, as each image arises it is fixed by its name or some other appropriate formula, and the final conclusion is recorded as a conceptual statement. Images are less easily manipulated than words; they appear and disappear without being strictly connected in logical sequence. Without some verbal form of symbolic substitution it is impossible to express their essential likeness and difference or their significant relations in time and space.

However vivid and detailed these visual images may be, they are elusive and fleeting; the patient complains, "They seem to go faint and I can't get them when I want to." Once aroused, they recur insistently in no obvious connection with the train of thought, or they disappear before the task is completed. One image not infrequently ousts its predecessor, instead of being added to it. Suppose, for instance, the words "The dog and the cat" are presented orally or in print, the patient may obtain a clear picture of the dog, which is obliterated by the subsequent appearance of the visual image of the cat; the two are not present in consciousness together, but the second displaces the first. Conversely, the word dog may evoke an image so vivid and dominant that the word cat produces no effect. These abnormalities and the want of control over imagery lead to uncertainty in choice, even when two percepts are employed in acts of direct relation.

Such images cannot be freely evoked at will. The greater the effort expended by the patient, the more difficult it is to "get into touch" with those he requires even for non-verbal processes of thinking. Still less can they be recalled with certainty in response to external commands given in the form of spoken or written words, phrases, or a consecutive narration. This inability of a word to evoke an image in persons with a strong visual memory is one of the most obvious signs that it has lost more or less of its meaning as a verbal symbol.

In spite of these defects, visual images can frequently be translated into some form of expression, such as drawing, provided the image and its representation stand in direct relation to one another and no verbal or logical formula intervenes. Thus, No. 2 drew an excellent picture of a camel, when he was attempting to describe the means of transport in the East; yet he was totally unable to draw an elephant to command. No. 23 produced spontaneously a detailed drawing of the house in which he lived, indicating by dark shading the window which had been blocked up and no longer admitted the light.

But images of objects that can be drawn in elevation cannot be transferred to a ground-plan. This demands a higher degree of symbolic representation. The patient may recognise the position relatively to himself of the salient features in some familiar room; he asserts that he sees them clearly. Yet he cannot indicate them on a ground-plan; he tends to represent the various pieces of furniture more or less in elevation, a method which approximates more closely to the form assumed by his visual images. All such acts of translation suffer in accordance with the degree of difficulty of the symbolic formulation demanded.

Under normal conditions, a visual image may be so vivid that it replaces the name we are seeking. I can see a mental picture of an acquaintance with such clearness that I am unable to recall his name. So closely does this visual symbol satisfy the internal situation that I cannot discover its verbal equivalent for the purposes of external expression. Again, an image may produce a false or misleading association; for instance, if I am thinking of Capt. C. and, instead of visualising him as a whole, see mainly the huge opening in his skull, I go off at a tangent and cannot concentrate on his general behaviour and mode of speech. Finally, an image may produce an affective state which interrupts a train of logical thought; grief at the loss of a dead friend may inhibit my comprehension of the meaning of a passage in a book which recalls him to my mind. All these processes, recognisable in normal persons with strong visual imagery, operate even more powerfully in many aphasics.

Thus, visual images suffer or escape in aphasia according to the part they play in the processes of language and thinking. They can frequently be evoked spontaneously and used for direct reference; but they are employed with difficulty as symbols or substitution signs. Moreover, the closer the disorder approaches want of power to appreciate either the detailed significance or the general meaning of a situation, the less easily can a visual image be summoned at will or to command.

THE USE OF
SYMBOLS IN THINKING

When man learnt to speak and to understand spoken words, he acquired the power of registering relations. Action was no longer determined by perception or unformulated emotional responses. He not only drew near to a fire to experience its heat, but was able to state, either for his own information or that of his fellows, that "a fire makes me warm." The use of symbols materially shortened the processes and extended his powers of thinking.

Now we have already seen that, although all substitute signs may rightly be treated as language, some only function as expressions of thought. True symbolic reference postulates subsequent behaviour, or the assumption of an attitude, in consequence of the intervention of a symbol, and it is this aspect of thinking which suffers most profoundly in these disorders of speech. The greater the difficulty of the task from this point of view, the more likely is it to be affected. Under normal conditions statement of a problem in symbolic terms increases the ease and certainty of its solution, whilst in aphasia exactly the opposite is true. Even acts which can be performed spontaneously may be imitated with difficulty if they necessitate the use of a symbol. Thus the patient is unable to repeat to command a word or phrase he can utter unprompted, and, although he can copy my movements reflected in a mirror, he may be unable to do so when we sit face to face; for in this case some kind of linguistic formula is required between perception of my actions and their exact imitation.

In the same way, when an aphasic is shown a common object, he can pick out its duplicate from amongst those on the table by relating the two similar perceptions. But, if two familiar objects are presented to him at the same time and he then attempts to choose those which correspond to them, he is liable to fail because he attempts to register what he has seen in some form of words. When, for instance, a normal person is shown a knife and a key, he tends to record the fact by saying the names to himself in order to reinforce his memory, whilst he searches for the two objects amongst those on the table. It is here that the aphasic tends to fail; for he cannot find or retain the suitable words he requires for this dual operation.

The first method by which the use of symbols aids thinking and facilitates action is by obviating the necessity of trying several alternatives. It is no longer necessary to adopt the lengthy process of trial and error. Given a bottle and a number of corks, we may try them one by one until we find that which fits the opening. Or, if we have become expert by practice, we reject the majority of them as too large or too small, setting aside a few for systematic trial. But if we know the diameter of the neck of the bottle and each cork is marked with a number on the same scale of measurement, all necessity for trial is avoided and we at once select the cork which satisfies the situation.

In the same way, if I am told to take the second turning to the right, I am precluded from choosing any one on my left hand and also the first on the right. But many aphasics, unable to comprehend or retain the exact terms of a command, fall back on the method of trial and error. Having taken a false turning, they look around to discover that the objects actually in sight do not correspond with those they expected. They then cast back and explore other ways until, catching sight of some familiar landmark, they walk on confidently towards their goal.

This return to a more primitive method is particularly evident during the tests with the alphabet. Given the twenty-six letters on separate blocks, the normal man looks them over and selects without trial the one which is required to make a direct sequence; A leads to the choice of B, B to C, and so on. Having placed a letter, for example M, in position, he formulates some symbol, verbal or visual, for N and fixes his attention on finding it; or his procedure may be even more direct. But the aphasic tries the most unlikely combinations one after the other until he discovers the particular letter which fits the sequence.

Symbolic formulation also assures and amplifies the processes of thinking by enabling us to record the likeness or dissimilarity of two percepts and all forms of identity or difference. When we are shown a pyramid, we recognise at once that it resembles an object of similar shape on the table and that it differs fundamentally from a cone. Most aphasics can carry out this test correctly because it is based on direct perceptual relations; no verbal symbol is required. But if, when shown a pyramid, the patient attempts in vain to name it before making his choice, he may subsequently be unable to select the object of the same shape from amongst those placed before him. Direct perception of the likeness of the two figures has now been complicated by failure to record their similarity by means of a name. On the other hand, in normal persons the power of recording likeness and difference by means of a symbol enormously extends the power of conceptual thinking and underlies all scientific classification.

Words and other symbols knit together and give permanence to non-verbal processes of thought, which would otherwise be fleeting. This is particularly evident in the case of visual images. Should an aphasic possess this kind of memory in a strongly developed form, images may still arise spontaneously and play a considerable part in his mental processes. But he cannot evoke them at will or to command; nor can he unite them to a coherent logical sequence without the help of verbal symbols. They are episodic, fleeting and transient; they arise and perish without leaving behind them any permanent or certain addition to thought. Without names we cannot record their relation in time or space, nor their essential likeness or difference.

Logical thinking holds in check and diminishes affective and intuitive responses. An animal, or even man under certain conditions, tends to react directly to the perceptual or emotional aspects of a situation; but symbolic formulation enables us to subject it to analysis and to regulate our behaviour accordingly. We thereby gain the power of breaking up a situation for the purpose of selective action; but many aphasics are compelled by reason of their disability to fall back on more primitive methods of solving a problem.

When an article of familiar use is presented to our senses, we formulate certain of the more characteristic impressions which it makes upon us and designate them "qualities." These aspects of the event we attribute to something outside ourselves, which we call the "object"; we speak of them as the "elements" out of which the "object" is composed, whereas they are in reality the formulated results of selection from the total reaction to a situation.

The form assumed by this selection depends on the use we are about to make of our knowledge. Choice is regulated in each instance by our attitude of mind. When we "recognise an object," the use to which we intend to put it determines the name it receives. A treasury note is paper currency, a sovereign, twenty shillings, four and a half dollars, an interesting sociological document, or a printed slip of peculiar colour and design, according to the manner in which it is employed. The inexhaustibleness of Nature is due to the fact that we can never come to the end of such possibilities of selection; however rigorous and exacting the analysis, there is always something over, when we have completed a categorical examination.

Such systematic analysis would be impossible without symbolic formulation, of which the commonest manifestation is the power of naming. Now a name is a descriptive label employed to designate some aspect of an event, selected for special attention with a view to subsequent behaviour. We speak of a name as concrete, when it covers a small group of "objects," whilst a more abstract designation is applicable to a wider range of events. Thus the word "knife" is more concrete than the word "red." For the former can be applied to a small group of things only, which have many characters in common, whilst the latter expresses a "quality" to be discovered in articles of profoundly different use, shape and texture. A concrete name or description is attached strongly to the thing it designates, whilst an abstract term is more mobile and of wider application.

Thus to find a name for a colour is a categorical act of higher intellectual order and is liable to suffer more severely than the power of naming articles of familiar use, especially if the defects of speech assume a nominal form. But with verbal aphasia, this is not the case; for here the main difficulty is to discover the correct verbal form, and in this respect all names, abstract or concrete, are equally words.

When abstraction is carried still further and the task set to the patient demands expression of the formal relations between two or more abstract terms, he is still more likely to fail to execute it correctly. Should capacity to carry out the required operation be a comparatively recent acquisition, the loss of response is liable to assume an extreme form; this is particularly the case with tests based on arithmetic or a knowledge of foreign languages.

On the other hand, when an aphasic cannot employ more abstract terms, he can often use descriptive phrases, similes and metaphorical expressions in an appropriate manner. They are less definite and are more closely allied to the use and manipulation of the object; they place before the hearer a wide range of points of attachment, whilst an abstract term tends to hit or miss the mark.

It is common knowledge that such descriptive designations are frequently employed by aphasics; unable to discover the name of an object, they fall back on the easier method of describing its use or composition. Given a pair of scissors they either perform the act of cutting or reply, "Something to cut with"; they may even approach more closely to a name with the words, "The tweezers you cut with," or, like one of Jackson's patients, call a kitten, "A little fur-child."

Similarly both No. 2 and No. 22 were unable to name colours correctly; but the former succeeded in designating them by using similes such as "What you do for the dead" to indicate black, and the latter, who was a house painter, described to me exactly how he would compose each colour from the materials used in his trade.

We are accustomed to think of an object as possessing "qualities," such as colour, which can be considered apart from the remaining impressions it makes upon us. My observations seem to show that, in these disorders of speech, capacity to formulate the relations of objects to one another in space may be affected in association with want of power to select any one of them in response to a command given orally or in print.

When the patient is shown a familiar object or colour and is asked to indicate the one he has seen, he not only makes a correct choice, but rapidly learns the order in which the duplicates lie on the table before him. If the screen, which hides them from his sight, is not removed with sufficient rapidity, he may place his finger exactly over the position of the one he is seeking to indicate. So long as the act consists of matching one percept with another he has no difficulty in moving at once to the right spot. But as soon as the selection depends on the name presented to him orally or in print, his finger wanders up and down the set of objects or colours on the table until he finds the one he wants.

This relative position in a series is as much part of the characteristic features of an object as its shape or colour. So long as an aphasic is not required to formulate these characters and makes his choice directly as an act of matching, he behaves as if he knew its position. But whenever he has difficulty in recognising the meaning of a verbal symbol, he loses the power to formulate the relative position of the object to which it corresponds. He is not only uncertain about such qualities as its shape and colour, but also with regard to its spacial relationships.

These relational factors are a part of perceptual data and, as far as symbolic formulation and expression are concerned, behave like other characters of this order. So long as the act to be performed can be carried out by matching two percepts, the response is prompt and accurate. But, whenever it requires the intervention of some symbolic formula, the patient may be unable to execute the task correctly and with ease.

Right and left, up and down and similar designations for relative positions in space are the formal expression of direct perceptions. With nominal aphasia power to appreciate their exact meaning and to apply them correctly suffers in the same way as other names, such as those for form or colour. This difficulty in expressing spacial relations leads to some confusion in action; but the patient is not fundamentally disorientated. He still possesses a general conception of right and left and can communicate it by gestures, although he cannot employ the appropriate terms. He may be unable to remember whether he should take a turning to the right or to the left; yet, if he chooses the wrong one, he stops and turns back, because he does not perceive the landmarks he expected. He possesses a sense of direction and can guide himself by recognising the familiar objects on his course. But he lacks the power of employing spacial nomenclature both for his own use and that of others.

On the other hand, the patient with semantic aphasia has lost the power of appreciating or formulating general space data. He cannot think out a route beforehand and does not guide himself by recognisable landmarks. He forgets in which direction he was walking, becoming helplessly confused should he take a wrong turning. He may even lose himself in the hospital, unable to find his room, or the bed he occupies in the general ward. His disorientation is general and comprises more than loss of power to formulate detailed spacial relations and to express them in symbolic terms.

With the progress of mental development and education we gain increasing capacity to generalise with the help of abstract terms or symbols. This reaches its highest development in certain mathematical procedures. But as soon as symbolic formulation and expression are affected, the patient reverts to more primitive methods of solving the problem. In many instances he succeeds in bringing out a correct answer, but the means he employs are clumsy, uncertain and difficult. For example, instead of adding 6 and 3 he counts on his fingers, "Six, seven, eight, nine"; or told to multiply 5 by 3, he replies, "Five and five is ten and five is fifteen." When a penny and a shilling are laid before him and he is asked how many of the former go into the latter, he answers, "Eleven"; he states the number it would be necessary to add instead of the multiple.

Again, when reading we snatch the sense of phrases or even long sentences without actually formulating the words of which they are composed. The aphasic is compelled to adopt a more childish method, deciphering each word as an isolated task and spelling out the more difficult ones letter by letter. This mode of reading is less likely to convey a complete impression of the meaning than a more rapid generalisation. Even a normal reader, compelled, when correcting proof for the press, to pay attention to the structure of the words, fails to appreciate their full significance.

The primitive methods adopted by the patient may be insufficient to furnish an answer in the form demanded, although the essential fact can be expressed in some less abstract manner. He may be unable to state the relation of two pieces of money and yet he can pile up a number of coins exactly equal to either of them in value. He remembers the situation of the salient objects in some familiar room with regard to the position he usually occupied in it, but cannot formulate their relation to one another. The first act is less categorical and therefore easier, whilst the latter requires a higher degree of symbolic aptitude.

Symbolic formulation enables us not only to analyse a situation, but to combine a series of diverse events into a coherent and logical conception. When we look at a picture, we receive and register a general idea of its meaning; should it contain many details, we consider them one by one and reinforce or correct the first impression. It may be that a printed legend is necessary for complete comprehension of the picture; if so we combine what we gather from the words with the pictorial details into a general formula for the benefit of ourselves or others. Should the picture convey a command, the full significance of its various parts must be appreciated as a whole before the order can be executed.

It is this power of synthesising detail so as to produce a general conception of its meaning for the purposes of thought or action that is so gravely affected in cases of semantic aphasia. An intelligent man, who has constructed the pieces of a cupboard or the sides of a wooden beehive, cannot fix them together. Miss S. built up a model out of blocks on a scale of an inch to the foot, but had no conception of its general dimensions. These patients cannot lay the table for a meal and are puzzled how to fit the various utensils into a general scheme. They cannot play billiards, because they are unable to foresee the effect of striking the ball on one side or the other and the results that will follow a rebound from the cushion. They have lost the power of exhibiting that "togetherness of things" which is their general significance.

It is not necessary that this should be expressed in actual verbal symbols. My observations seem to show that an organic lesion can disturb the power of formulating without words the general aim or intention of an act to be performed in response to spontaneous suggestion or to command.

The existence of pre-linguistic formulation has been hotly disputed and affirmed. Pick attempted to divide the processes of speech into a sequence consisting of intuitive thought, the proposition, the grammatical schema and the explicit verbal statement. Van Woerkom has also erected four stages: massive conception of the idea, a psychical process of analysis and synthesis in time and space, schematic conception of the phrase without verbal symbols, and the choice of words.

Such detailed analysis seems to me to fail because an act of speech does not come into being and run its course in this diagrammatic manner. The processes which occur between the genesis of an idea and its expression in words, or conversely between verbal recognition and consequent assumption of a mental attitude, comprise a total alteration in psychical conditions. These changes are not composed of stages strictly and uniformly sequent in time; they consist of a state of mind which develops out of one set of dispositions and merges inseparably into another.

But pathologically the total act can be disturbed in such a way that non-linguistic formulation is more particularly affected. The patient has plenty of words and names, but he cannot summon up and manipulate with ease those general symbolic conceptions which are necessary for all consecutive action or logical thought. Such defects form the principal manifestations of semantic aphasia which is more particularly distinguished by inability to appreciate or formulate the total meaning of a situation.

Even in normal persons words, phrases and other symbolic modes of expression assume a form determined by the attitude of the speaker to his hearer and to the matter in hand. This becomes particularly evident in aphasia. The ease or difficulty with which a desired meaning can be conveyed has a profound effect on the means employed for its expression; the patient adopts that style of utterance which enables him to transmit to his auditor at any rate something of what he wants to say. Thus, a verbal aphasic employs single words or short syncopated phrases with a simple grammatical structure, helped out by gestures; a man with nominal defects perpetually attempts to clarify his meaning by uttering one more or less appropriate name after the other and by the use of descriptive or metaphorical appellations. The syntactical aphasic, on the other hand, rushes on in the hope that his volubility may convey something to his hearer.

Both the power and mode of expression are profoundly affected by the relation of the patient to his auditor. One person can help an aphasic, whilst another produces an inhibitory effect, even on his capacity to think. We all adopt a different method of expressing ourselves to an adult or a child, and we watch the effect of our words, prepared to repeat them in some other form, if they do not lead to the desired response. So the intelligent aphasic adapts his defective speech to the necessities of the moment, although his power to execute such variations is greatly diminished. I was able to carry on lengthy conversations with one of my patients, aided by maps, pictures and his use of a pencil, although his wife reduced him to incomprehensible jargon and insisted that he was out of his mind. Sometimes the patient does not trouble to correct his faults and confesses, "I just let myself go and hope it will be understood"; if he finds that this is the case, his pleasure greatly increases his power of subsequent expression. On the other hand, disappointment or anger may profoundly affect both the character and ease of utterance. If he is encouraged to write freely and carelessly and is then allowed to correct and copy his manuscript, he may be able to produce a coherent and intelligible document; yet, when he pays meticulous attention to the structure of each word, he cannot produce a single perfect sentence and gives up the attempt in disgust.

Conversely, when an aphasic attempts to understand what he has heard or read, his powers of comprehension depend not only on the inherent difficulty of the task, but also on his intellectual attitude as a whole. Much that is said by an educated person is incomprehensible to one on a lower grade of education; he accepts just enough to enable him to execute a given command, hoping that what he has understood may be sufficiently accurate for practical purposes. Now an aphasic of high intelligence may be reduced to this level; recognising his defects, he jumps to a conclusion without the usual logical steps. He no longer possesses the normal means of certain comprehension and his responses are sometimes right and at others wrong. Moreover, he is compelled to adopt childish methods of arriving at an answer, such as spelling out the words letter by letter as he reads, or counting on his fingers during the solution of arithmetical problems.

Nothing is more puzzling to the intelligent aphasic than the diffuse and tentative modes of expression so common in ordinary conversation. On the other hand, a short well-turned phrase frequently conveys its meaning at once in spite of its apparent complexity. Thus No. 2 explained that he understood "clever people," because they expressed what they wanted to say in a few words, whereas he was puzzled by the diffuseness of others.

The attitude of the patient towards the nature of the task in hand is of fundamental importance for the formulation and comprehension of symbolic signs. Interest in the subject has a profound effect on the ease and rapidity both of expression and understanding. Miss S. laid particular emphasis on the importance of arousing this attitude of mind towards the task in hand. She confessed, "Just as one word . . . turned me off the whole thing, so one word or sentence bearing upon something of interest will jog my attention in the same way and cause me to read a passage or a page over and over again, until I get its full meaning. But this has to be done, and, if the interest is not there to 'jog,' the effort is not made because one is unconscious that an effort is needed."

Thus the employment of substitute signs facilitates and secures consecutive thinking; in fact logical thought would be impossible without them. The statement of a problem in symbolic terms increases the ease and certainty of its solution. For their use gives permanence to perceptual and other non-verbal methods of thinking, records similarity and difference of all kinds and avoids the cumbrous procedure of trial and error. It enables us to subject a situation to analysis or to synthesise details into a coherent whole and so permits of the widest categorical distinctions and generalisations.

When the power of symbolic formulation and expression is disturbed, all these activities suffer more or less severely. The patient is compelled to revert to more primitive methods of thinking, not only because they are the way by which he acquired his power of using language, but because under pathological conditions they are easier of fulfillment and present a simpler intellectual task.

III

DIFFERENTIATION
AND INTERNALIZATION

IN THE COURSE OF ACQUIRING A LANGUAGE it becomes internalized by the individual. In the process it is progressively differentiated into a variety of forms, linked with more and more aspects of behavior, and used in increasingly discriminating ways. The internalization of language ultimately creates what are called the higher mental functions. Since language has a structure and is a group or social product, it is plausible and expectable that the thinking activities of persons, permeated as they are by the influence of language, will be influenced by its structure and by the social environment that nurtures it. The thinking and reasoning of individuals reflects the nature of their group associations and is generally oriented toward them.

Such complex mental functions as perceiving and remembering are examples of complex sign behavior. Memory is response to signs representing the past; perception is response to signs representing the present environment. Skill in interpretation of and response to signs on any level is intelligent behavior. Perceiving, remembering, and reasoning arise in connection with social experience and with involvement in a complex network of communication.

People also react to their own bodies, and the processes that occur in them, on the basis of sensory cues that are assimilated in conceptual schemes. These schemes include ideas of the nature of the body and its functions and malfunctions. Like cognitions of the external world, these ideas are socially derived and vary from one society and community to another. The experiences induced by drugs, such as marijuana, LSD, and the opiates, are examples of how internal processes are brought into the social sphere by being named, explained, and talked about. Subjective experiences that cannot be shared or communicated are, in fact, felt to be "uncanny" and are often interpreted by self and others as evidence of insanity, or as religious or mystic experiences.

The internal environment, then, ordinarily is categorized, perceived, and brought into relation with the outside world. Since action is predicated in those terms it is only a short step to asking an important general question: How is an individual's control of his own actions related to societal control of his actions? Another question is: How can an individual's action be controlled by another person or persons? Because humans live in symbolic environments and by virtue of their internalized language, they have voluntary control over some of their actions. Voluntary behavior depends upon ability to initiate responses from oneself, which, in turn, inhibit or facilitate other responses. These controlling responses are verbal in nature or are derived from verbal behavior. The phenomenon of hypnosis provides striking examples of symbolic control over a wide range of human behavior. The hypnotized subject may be viewed as someone who, in a peculiar sense, is relatively lacking in self-control, because behavior (ordinarily evoked by the person himself) is evoked by the hypnotist. The loss of self-control under hypnosis indicates the extensive role of language mechanisms in voluntary behavior. Behavior under hypnosis is only a more extreme form of the type of influence constantly exerted by people over each other in ordinary social intercourse. Since social control also implies control of behavior by symbol manipulation, it is closely related to self-control. In certain institutionalized situations, such as when a person is hospitalized, it is expected that others will take over the control of some or much of one's activities. The processes of religious conversion, "brainwashing," and other kinds of coercive persuasion may be considered as other instances of the partial loss of personal autonomy to outside forces, persons, or groups.

13

SPEECH AND
THOUGHT PROCESSES

A. R. Luria

SOCIAL ORIGINS OF
PSYCHOLOGICAL PROCESSES

THE SUGGESTION THAT PSYCHOLOGICAL ACTIVITY is reflex in nature, made
for the first time by Sechenov, demands that we approach the problem from
the same principles that were formulated above, firmly refusing to make any
attempt to understand it as a manifestation of primary "faculties" or "properties," embodied in mental life, and that we interpret its cerebral basis not
as stable centers, in which these properties are localized, but as a systematic
apparatus, responsible for performing this highly complex type of reflex
activity.

In one respect, however, human mental activity differs radically from the
reflex activity of the animal. This refers to its *social-historical origin and its
structural organization.*

Among the more important achievements of Soviet psychology, as may be
found in the writings of many authors (Vygotsky, 1956, 1960; Leont'ev,
1959, 1961) are the introduction of the historical method into psychology
and the confirmation of Marx's statement that the human mind is the result
of the social form of life and that the formation of the five external senses
is the work of basic processes of world history (K. Marx and F. Engels,

Abridged from pp. 21–24, 294–295, 354–357, *Human Brain and Psychological Processes* by A. R. Luria. Copyright © 1966 by Harper & Row, Publishers, Incorporated.
Reprinted by permission of the publishers. (Text, Chapter 6)

Early Works, Moscow, 1956, pp. 593–594). This fundamental principle has received concrete application in the work of Soviet psychologists and of a number of Western scholars (Wallon, 1942, etc.), and it has provided a completely new approach to human psychological processes which is completely different from that advocated by contemporary positivism.

The behavior of an animal, however complex, is the result of two factors: inborn tendencies, on the one hand, and direct, individual experience, formed in the course of conditioned-reflex activity, on the other. In contrast to this, the conditions in which human behavior is formed include yet a third factor, beginning to play a decisive role in the development of human faculties: the assimilation of the experience of mankind in general, which is incorporated in objective activity, in language, in the products of work, and in the forms of social life of human beings.

This social experience not only forms the methods of human work and operations with objects in the external environment but it also creates complex and plastic methods of controlling the individual's own behavior and the wide range of generalized images and ideas composing human consciousness.

We know that animals retain traces of their previous experience arising during reflex activity. Only man, however, can make deliberate changes in his environment in order to create methods of influencing his own memory. Tying a knot in his handkerchief, cutting a notch, or marking the item to be memorized by a certain sign, he lifts his memory to the level of controllable processes. As the investigations of L. S. Vygotsky (1956, 1960), A. N. Leont'ev (1959), P. Ya. Gal'perin (1959) and A. V. Zaporozhets (1960) have shown, all complex forms of voluntary attention and logical memory, conceptual perception and abstract intellectual activity are the result of the assimilation of socially-formulated activity and have a similar, complex structure. These types of mental processes cannot, therefore, by any stretch of imagination be understood as direct properties of the mind or as natural functions of the brain incapable of further analysis; all these processes must be interpreted as products of social life, passing through a complex period of historical evolution, organized at different levels and carried out by means of highly involved forms of reflex activity, and all established within the conditions of existence of human society.

Soviet psychologists have convincingly shown that the assimilation of social experience, leading to the development of complex forms of mental activity, cannot be regarded as a simple process of acquiring something which is already in existence, but that it is a specifically human form of mental development. This development of mental processes passes through several stages, and only after its historical evolution can it lead to the formation of complex behavioral functions in the form in which we know them from observations of the mental activity of the human adult. The investigations of A. N. Leont'ev (1931, 1960), for instance, showed that voluntary memorizing is actually based on the use of a series of external devices, a process which the child carries out step by step, and only later are these devices apparently put aside, so that the process acquires the features of an internal act of memory. The investigations of P. Ya. Gal'perin (1957, 1959) showed that an equally complicated path of development is traced by abstract ideas and mental actions, behind which lie discarded forms of material activity resting on an objective system of language, using expanded forms of speech and only gradually becoming converted into succinct and apparently simple mental acts. The investigations of L. S. Vygotsky (1956, 1960), A. V. Zaporozhets (1960), A. R. Luria (1956a and b, 1958b, 1961), and their collaborators have confirmed that voluntary movements develop along the same lines and have shown that behind an apparently simple and direct effort of will lies a complex story which starts when the child for the first time obeys the spoken instructions of an adult, and then begins to model his behavior by his own speech, which is gradually pushed into the background. The stage in which every detail is spoken aloud is replaced by one of internal speech and, in some cases, it seems that speech disappears completely (A. N. Sokolov, 1959).

All these facts show that the higher mental functions which, at a first approximation, may appear direct, simple, and indivisible properties of mental life or direct functions of circumscribed areas of brain tissue, in fact, are the result of historical development and are social in origin and complex in psychological structure. This was well expressed by L. S. Vygotsky (1960), who stated that: *"a function which initially was shared by two people and bore the character of communication between them gradually crystallized and became a means of organization of the mental life of man himself."* This historical genesis and complex structure are essential features of the higher mental functions of man.

It would be incorrect, however, to suppose that a social-historical genesis and a complex structure are peculiar to the higher mental functions such as voluntary attention, logical memory, or abstract intellectual activity.

Recent investigations by A. N. Leont'ev and co-workers (1959, 1961) have shown that such an apparently simple and natural function as tonal hearing is social in nature in man and must be formed during life. The complex structure of tonal hearing in man is also illustrated by the fact that in many people the accurate discrimination between tonal relationships is complicated by the participation of a more powerful system, also social in nature, the phonematic structure of language. Because of this, the formation of accurate tonal hearing demands the use of special methods enabling the person to escape from the influence of this factor and to incorporate his hearing function into another system—the system of musical relationships.

We shall not dwell in greater detail on these important principles of Soviet psychological science for they are adequately discussed in the Soviet psychological literature. The most important conclusion is that human psychological processes, however integral and indivisible they seem to be, are in fact products of historical development and possess a complex psychological structure. They are the result of manifold reflex activity, formerly external in character and performed step by step, but have subsequently undergone gradual contraction and have been converted into those "mental functions" which we observe when we study the complex psychological processes of the adult person. The sources of human development always include objective action and language. The latter, the basis of the second signal system, is not only a means of communication but also a powerful tool for the formation of human conscious processes. The social-historical conditions of life do not abrogate the laws of reflex processes laid down in the course of biological evolution, but enrich and reorganize these processes, converting them into more complex functional systems, formed under the influence of objective activity, and with the close participation of language.

NATURE AND FUNCTION OF
INTERNALIZED SPEECH[1]

Previous investigations, some of which are described in this book, showed that a lesion of the premotor divisions of the cortex may, in certain conditions, lead to the disintegration of complex skilled movements and may substantially change the course of intellectual processes. These investigations led to the formation of the hypothesis that the lesions described above disturb the function of internal speech, which is responsible for the contraction or abbreviation of speech activity into contracted internal schemes leading to the formation of an intellectual action, and is also responsible for the subsequent expansion of these contracted dynamic schemes into fluent narrative speech.

We must now verify this hypothesis and analyze the disturbance of internal speech in the lesions described above, determining what forms these disturbances may take.

The fact that the speech processes taking part in intellectual operations are gradually condensed and converted into contracted internal verbal schemes has been demonstrated by several investigators. The essential role played by internal speech, contracted in form and predicative in structure, in the course of various intellectual operations was demonstrated some time ago by L. S. Vygotsky (1934, 1956) and has subsequently been described from different angles by a number of investigators.

A. N. Sokolov (1919), L. A. Novikova (1955), F. V. Bassin and E. S. Bein (1957) showed that nearly every intellectual operation is accompanied by a minutely determined innervation of the organs of speech, which may be detected by means of special electromyographic recording systems, and that this innervation, which at first is of a well marked character, gradually be-

---

[1] Z. Ya. Rudenko assisted with the collection of material for this investigation.

comes contracted, and in highly automatized operations, no trace of it remains.

P. Ya. Gal'perin (1957, 1959) and his co-workers examined this process from a genetic point of view. Following L. S. Vygotsky, they showed that every complex intellectual action, taking place initially as a consecutive cycle of external, material actions, is based on expanded external speech, which gradually becomes contracted, and passes through the stage of whispered speech to internal speech, which is evidently the essential component of intellectual actions.

Finally, certain investigators (Nazarova, 1952) have demonstrated that the exclusion of external speech in phases before internal speech has become properly established, and also a restriction of the part played by internal speech in intellectual operations (Zhinkin, 1958), may lead to significant disturbances of their course. The part played by these forms of speech in processes such as writing, calculation, and memorizing was confirmed by these observations.

All this showed that the kinesthetic impulses flowing from the speech organs to the cerebral cortex create the "basal component of the second signal system" (Pavlov, 1949, chap. 3, pp. 476, 480), and represent a significant factor in the mechanisms of complex intellectual operations.

In this chapter we have given a detailed analysis of two cases in which a lesion situated predominantly in the postfrontal divisions of the left hemisphere led to a pathological state of the cerebral cortex and caused characteristic disturbances in the course of mental processes.

These disturbances consisted, first, of a loss of the smoothness of the course of motor and intellectual processes; the patients were unable to perform complex actions organized as successive series of a single "kinetic melody." Dynamic stereotypes (or higher automatisms), developed in the past, became seriously disorganized; normal, consecutively organized mental actions were disturbed, and could be performed only with the aid of extended external speech or auxiliary external actions in substitution for it.

These profound changes in the dynamic organization of mental processes suggest that the mechanisms of internal speech, which according to L. S. Vygotsky (1934, 1956) and P. Ya. Gal'perin (1957, 1959) are the main mechanism of complex mental actions, were particularly affected in these patients.

We have suggested that the fine, consecutively organized verbal kinesthesias constituting an important physiological component of internal speech are disturbed in these cases and that the exclusion (or restriction) of coarse verbal kinesthesias by fixation of the tongue has the result that all operations whose normal course is dependent on the participation of verbal kinesthesias become impossible, whereas all operations whose performance can take place without the participation of verbal kinesthesias remain relatively intact in these conditions.

The observations we made justify these suggestions. They showed that the removal of external speech in fact left some motor, mnestic and intellectual operations intact, but led to marked disturbances of others.

The first group of operations, whose performance evidently does not require the participation of verbal kinesthesias, included: reproduction of motor poses, copying of drawings, making simple geometrical shapes from a pattern, memorizing of single words, the development of simple associations in response to a suggested word. This group also included the understanding of simple and familiar sentences, provided that this understanding did not require a series of intermediate operations including the transformation of the sentence, and the successive analysis of logical relationships embodied in it.

Conversely, the second group of operations disintegrated when external speech was excluded and verbal kinesthesias restricted. This group included operations such as the retention and reproduction of long verbal (and in some cases, nonverbal) series, and writing (unless reconstructed in the course of rehabilitation). This group also included the understanding of logico-grammatical constructions requiring for their analysis operations of preliminary transformation and successive analysis of the relationships embodied in them. Finally, it also included arithmetical operations based on series of contracted auxiliary operations. All these processes disintegrated in our patients when external speech was excluded and verbal kinesthesias restricted.

An essential fact is that inability to perform these operations developed only when extended speech was excluded in the first stage of performance of the task, or in other words, at the period associated with analysis of the prevented material, digestion of the information supplied, fixation of the sequence of acts to be performed, transformation of the structure presented, and selection of auxiliary operations. If external speech was excluded in the last stage of performance of the task, when all the work listed above had been completed with the participation of verbal kinesthesias, no such disturbance of the operations took place. This fact indicates that the role of extended verbal kinesthesias is particularly important at the time when the information received is being analyzed, and its importance diminishes to zero after this analysis is complete.

Important information is also given by the qualitative analysis of the manner in which complex intellectual operations disintegrate during the exclusion (or restriction) of verbal kinesthesias. This shows that if internal speech is severely disturbed, the exclusion of external speech not only delays the performance of a given operation, but may lead to the true disintegration of those of its components which appeared on the basis of originally extended, and later contracted, speech, and compels the patient to make use of methods which can be applied without the participation of these complex components. It is a particularly interesting fact that, with the exclusion (or restriction) of verbal kinesthesias, in both patients calculation by means of tables, embodying a series of hierarchically constructed intermediate operations, showed signs of disintegration, and arithmetical operations were converted into the primitive methods of counting in ones or of elementary forms of simple addition.

These results are a signpost pointing the way to the analysis of forms of intellectual operations normally effected with the participation of internal speech and requiring for their performance "kinesthetic impulses passing from the speech apparatus to the cerebral cortex."

14

A SYSTEMATIZATION
OF THE WHORFIAN
HYPOTHESIS

Joshua A. Fishman

WHEN WHORF SAYS that "there is a precarious dependence of all we know upon linguistic tools which themselves are largely unknown or unnoticed," he hits all of us where it hurts most—at the foundations of our certainty in our scientific findings and in our everyday decisions. When he attacks the view that grammars are "merely norms of conventional and social correctness" and claims that they are, instead, the cement out of which we fashion experience, we feel that he must either be pointing at an unnoticed and potentially dangerous popular fallacy or tilting at nonexistent windmills. When he says that "we cut up nature—organize it into concepts—and ascribe significances as we do . . . largely because of the . . . absolutely obligatory . . . patterns of our [own] language," he stirs in us both our ethnocentric group-pride as well as our universalistic anti-ethnocentrism. In short, Whorf (like Freud) impugns our objectivity and rationality. It is not surprising then that recent years have seen many logical as well as not a few experimental efforts to evaluate and re-evaluate both the conceptual and the empirical grounds upon which the Whorfian hypothesis rests.

From Joshua A. Fishman, "A Systematization of the Whorfian Hypothesis," in *Behavioral Science*, Vol. 5 (1960), 323–339. Reprinted by permission of the author and *Behavioral Science*. (Text, Chapter 6)

Level 1
LINGUISTIC CODIFIABILITY AND
CULTURAL REFLECTIONS

The weakest level of the Whorfian hypothesis (in the sense of being least pretentious or least novel) is that which (provides evidence that languages differ "in the same ways" as the general cultures or surrounding environments of their speakers differ.) Evidence along these lines has long been provided by ethnologists and folklorists, and its fragmentary and belated presentation by Whorfians can hardly be considered as either a serious contribution to the social sciences generally or as a substantiation of higher levels of the Whorfian hypothesis specifically.

From the point of view of the language data presented at this first level of argumentation, it is not the grammatical structure as such that is under consideration but, rather, the lexical store or the so-called "semantic structure." Actually, that which is dealt with at this level might be referred to in present-day terms as (contrasts in *codifiability*.) Language *X* has a single term for phenomenon *x*, whereas language *Y* either has no term at all (and therefore refers to the phenomenon under consideration—if at all—only via a relative circumlocution) or it has three terms, y_1, y_2, and y_3, all within the same area of reference. As a result, it is much *easier* to refer to certain phenomena or to certain nuances of meaning in certain languages than in others. Thus, codifiability is also related to the question of translatability and to "what gets lost" in translation from one language to another.

Admittedly Whorf's examples are largely drawn from American Indian languages (and contrasted with American English), and the implication is therefore strong that we are not only dealing with groups whose languages differ markedly but whose lives and outlooks also differ greatly. Nevertheless, at *this* level of analysis, Whorf (and others even more frequently than he) does not take pains to relate linguistic factors to nonlinguistic ones, but merely (presents an enchanting catalog of codifiability differences.) English has separate words for "pilot," "fly (n.)," and "airplane," but Hopi has only one. Eskimo has many words for different kinds of "snow" but English has only two. On the other hand, Aztec has only one basic word for our separate words "cold," "ice," and "snow." We have one word for "water," whereas Hopi has two, depending on whether the water is stationary or in motion. English has such words as "speed" and "rapid," whereas Hopi has no real equivalents for them and normally renders them by "very" or "intense" plus a verb of motion. English has separate terms for "blue" and "green" but only one term for all intensities of "black" short of "gray." Navaho, on the contrary, does not have separate highly codeable terms for "blue" and "green" but does have two terms for different kinds of "black." English has the generic term "horse" but Arabic has only scores of different terms for different breeds or conditions of horses. The kinship terminology in some languages is certainly vastly different (and in certain respects both more refined and more gross) than it is in English. In all of these cases, it is not difficult to relate the codifiability differences to gross cultural differences. Obviously, Eskimos are more interested in snow, and Arabs in horses, than are most English speakers. Obvious, also, is the fact that these codifiability differences help speakers of certain languages to be more easily aware of certain aspects of their environment and to communicate more easily about them. This, essentially, was the lesson we learned from Bartlett's early work on remembering. In this sense, then, their languages structure their verbal behavior in a non-trivial way and ostensibly also structure their pre-verbal conceptualizations as well.

Level 2
LINGUISTIC CODIFIABILITY AND
BEHAVIORAL CONCOMITANTS

At the second level of analysis of the Whorfian hypothesis, we leave behind the limitations of *inference* from codifiability in language to ease of formulation or expression via language. That is to say, we leave behind the *language-language behavior* level for the level in which *language-nonlanguage behavior* becomes of paramount interest to us. That this is a necessary direction for our inquiry to take has been recognized by Carroll and Casagrande:

> In order to find evidence to support the linguistic relativity hypothesis it is not sufficient merely to point to differences between languages and to assume that users of these languages have correspondingly different mental experiences. If we are not to be guilty of circular inference, it is necessary to show some correspondence between the presence or absence of a certain linguistic phenomenon and the presence or absence of a certain kind of non-linguistic response.

Note that the above quotation merely refers to *"a certain linguistic phenomenon"* rather than restricting the *type* of linguistic phenomenon that requires attention. The hallmark of the second level is that the "predictor" variables seem once more to be of the lexical or semantic codifiability type (and in this respect similar to Level 1, discussed above), whereas the "criterion variables" are of the non-linguistic behavior type (and in this respect different from, and an advance over, those encountered at Level 1). Thus far, there have been only a very few studies which strike me as operating at this level of analysis. The earliest one by far is that of Lehmann who demonstrated that identifying a different number with each of nine different shades of gray was of substantial help in behaviorally discriminating between these shades of gray. In essence, then, the numbers functioned as verbal labels. The availability (codifiability) of such labels for some Ss resulted in much better discrimination-identification of the shades of gray than that which obtained in other Ss who had to perform the same discrimination-identification task without being provided with such labels.

Some exceptionally interesting and sophisticated work with the codifiability concept in the color area has more recently been reported by Brown and Lenneberg and by Lenneberg alone. These investigators have shown that culturally encoded colors (i.e., colors that can be named with a single word) require a shorter response latency when they need to be named than do colors that are not culturally encoded (i.e., that require a phrase—often an individually formulated phrase—in order to be described). At this point, their evidence pertains to Level 1 that we have previously discussed. In addition, these investigators have gone on to show that the more highly codified colors are more readily recognized or remembered when they must be selected from among many colors after a period of delay subsequent to their original presentation. This finding was replicated among speakers of English and speakers of Zuni, although somewhat different segments of the color spectrum were highly codeable for the two groups of *S*s. The investigators summarize their findings to this point as follows:

> It is suggested that there may be general laws relating codeable to cognitive processes. All cultures could conform to these laws although they differ among themselves in the values the variables assume in particular regions of experience.

Going on from this original statement, Lenneberg has further refined its experimental underpinnings by showing that the *learning* of color-nonsense syllable associations was predictably easier or harder as the learning task involved color categories that varied in degree from the ones that were most commonly recognized by his English-speaking *S*s. He therefore concluded that "there is good evidence that the shape of word frequency distributions over stimulus continua regulates the ease with which a person learns to use a word correctly." This conclusion should be as applicable to original language learning as it is to second and to artificial language learning, for it basically pertains not to language usage per se but to concept formation as such.

The color continuum seems to be a particularly fortunate area in which to study codifiability-cognition phenomena precisely because it is a real continuum. As such, no "objective" breaks occur in it and it is a matter of cultural or sub-cultural consensus as to just which breaks are recognized, just where on the spectrum they are located, and how much of a range they include. The demonstration that these various codifiability considerations influence recognition, recall, and learning has been most fortunately executed. Lenneberg and Brown are also alert to the fact that at this level it is perfectly acceptable to work with intralinguistic designs rather than to necessarily utilize the interlinguistic designs in terms of which the Whorfian hypothesis is most frequently approached. What is easily codifiable, and the specific range and content of easily codeable categories, does depend on the particular language under consideration. It also depends on the particular experiences of subgroups of speakers. As a result, contrasts in rate, ease or accuracy of various cognitive functions should be (and are) demonstrable both intralinguistically and interlinguistically as a function of codeable norms. Intralinguistic codifiability-cognition differentials in various natural population groupings should be of particular interest to students of social stratification.

Brown and Lenneberg have conducted their work with a conscious awareness of the Whorfian hypothesis and how it must be further specified or delimited. On the other hand, there have been other investigators who have also worked in the language-behavior domain at this level without any particular awareness of the Whorfian hypothesis as such. If the organizational framework here being advanced has been insightfully developed, it should nevertheless be possible to subsume their findings within it. In fact, it may turn out that within the context of the Whorfian hypothesis these other studies will obtain a new coherence and provocativeness.

The only study at this level that is directly inspired by the Whorfian hypothesis while utilizing an *interlinguistic* design is the one which Carroll and Casagrande refer to as "Experiment I."

Level 3
LINGUISTIC STRUCTURE AND
ITS CULTURAL CONCOMITANTS

When we turn our attention from the second to the third and fourth levels of the Whorfian hypothesis, we progress from lexical differences and so-called "semantic structure" to the more "formal" and systematized grammatical differences to which linguists have most usually pointed when considering the structure of a language or structural differences between languages. There is some evidence that although Whorf and others may, at times, have reverted to lower levels of presentation and documentation they, nevertheless, did associate linguistic relativity in its most pervasive sense with structural (i.e., grammatical) rather than merely with lexical aspects of language. This is suggested by such formulations as Sapir's that meanings are "not so much discovered in experience as imposed upon it, because of the tyrannical hold that linguistic *form* has upon our orientation to the world." Somewhat more forcefully stated is Whorf's claim that "the world is presented in a kaleidoscopic flux of impressions which has to be organized . . . largely by the linguistic *systems* in our minds." More forceful still—and there are a large number of possible quotations of this kind—is Whorf's statement that

> . . . the background linguistic system (in other words, the grammar) of each language is not merely a reproducing instrument for voicing ideas, but rather is itself the shaper of ideas, the program and guide for the individual's mental activity, for his analysis of impressions, for his synthesis of his mental stock in trade. Formulation of ideas is not an independent process, strictly rational in the old sense, but it is part of a particular grammar and differs, from slightly to greatly, between grammars.

Finally, we may offer in evidence the paraphrasings of the Whorfian hypothesis by two eminent American linguists who have been both interested in and sympathetic to this hypothesis. The first of these says simply that "It is in the attempt properly to interpret the *grammatical categories* of Hopi that Whorf best illustrates his principle of linguistic relativity." The other, as part of a more extended and systematic argument, says

> Language as a whole has structure and all of its parts and subdivisions also have structure . . . [if] the rest of cultural behavior has been conditioned by language, then there must be a relationship between the *structure* of language and the *structure* of behavior.

At the third level of analysis, we once more find ourselves in a realm of rich though ambiguous anthropological and ethnological data. As was the case with Level 1, above, the direct association or chain of reasoning between grammatical structure on the one hand and "something else" (be it *Weltanschauung* or even some less embracing segment of culture or values) on the other is not explicitly stated. Often, the "something else" is not stated at all and yet there is the general implication that grammatical oddities of the type presented cannot help but be paralleled by unique ways of looking at or thinking about or reacting to the surrounding environment. Thus, one encounters such evidence as that Chinese has no singular and plural or that it has no relative clauses (which we English speakers *do* have), whereas other languages have more levels of grammatical number (including singular, dual, tri-al, and plural forms—which we English speakers do *not* have). In this vein, the cataloging of grammatical differences can continue at great length (languages that do recognize gender of nouns and those that do not, languages that have tenses and those that do not, etc.); for both anthropologists, linguists, and a variety of nonspecialists have contributed to the fund of knowledge of phenomena of this type, always with the implication that it is clearly illogical to seriously suggest that linguistic phenomena such as these would have no relationship to life, to thought, and to values.

On the other hand, there are also several investigators that *have* attempted to indicate what the "something else" might be. In contrasting Hopi with English, Whorf has pointed to such odd grammatical features in Hopi as the absence of tenses, the classification of events by duration categories such that "events of necessarily brief duration (lightning, wave, flame, meteor, puff of smoke, pulsation) cannot be anything but verbs," the presence of grammatical forms for indicating the type of validity the speaker intends to attribute to his utterance (statement of current fact, statement of fact from memory, statement of expectation, and statement of generalization or law), etc. To Whorf all of these grammatical features seemed congruent with an outlook on life that was "timeless" and ahistorical in the sense that past, present, and future are seen as a continuity of duration, experience being cumulative and unchanging for countless generations. As a result of the "timelessness" of Hopi life, it is of greater importance for Hopi speakers to distinguish between the duration of events and their certainty than to indicate when they occurred. A similarly ingenious and sensitive analysis is followed by Hoijer in connection with the Navaho verb system in which there is no clean separation between actors, their actions, and the objects of these actions. As Hoijer sees it, the Navaho verb links the actor to actions which are defined as pertaining to classes-of-beings. Thus it would appear that people merely "participate in" or "get involved in" somehow pre-existing classes of actions rather than serve as the initiators of actions. Hoijer interprets these grammatical characteristics as being consistent with the "passivity" and "fatefulness" of Navaho life and mythology in which individuals adjust to a universe that is given. Finally, in Nootka, Whorf finds a connection between the absence of noun-verb distinctions and "a monistic view of nature."

The efforts by Whorf, Hoijer, Glenn and similar scholars merit considerable respect. They must be separated in our evaluation from pseudo-serious efforts to attribute or relate the musicalness of Italians to the light, melodious nature of the Italian language, or the stodginess of Germans to the heavy, lugubrious quality of the German language, or the warm, folksiness of Eastern European Jews to the intimate emotional quality of Yiddish, etc. Superficially, the two approaches may seem similar, but the latter approach does not even have a serious structural analysis of language to recommend it. Nevertheless, the appeal of the Whorfian hypothesis for some lies precisely in the fact that it attempts to apply modern scientific methods and disciplined thought to such "old chestnuts" as the presumed "naturalness" that Hebrew (or Greek, or Latin, or Old Church Slavonic) be the language of the Bible, given its "classic ring" and its "otherworldly purity." However, with all of our admiration for those who have had the temerity as well as the ingenuity to attempt a rigorous analysis at this level, we must also recognize the limitations which are built into this approach. As many critics have pointed out, the third level of analysis has not normally sought or supplied independent confirmation of the existence of the "something else" which their grammatical data is taken to indicate. As a result, the very same grammatical designata that are said to have brought about (or merely to reflect) a given *Weltanschauung* are also most frequently the only data advanced to prove that such a *Weltanschauung* does indeed exist. Thus, once more, we are back at a language-language level of analysis (language structure ←→ language-behavior-as-indication-of-world-view).

Verbal behavior may long continue as our major avenue of insight into values and motives. What we must be ever more dissatisfied with, however, are the self-selected lists of grammatical examples and the self-selected enumerations of cultures, cultural values or themes, and the evidence pertaining to the existence of such themes. In attempting to avoid these particular pitfalls, students of the Whorfian hypothesis have increasingly come to express a preference for a study design which investigates the relationship between grammatic structure on the one hand and *individual* non-linguistic behavior on the other. Although this is both a logical and a very promising solution to many of the above-mentioned problems, there is nevertheless no need to conclude at this point in our knowledge that it is the only one possible.

Level 4
LINGUISTIC STRUCTURE AND
ITS BEHAVIORAL CONCOMITANTS

The conceptual and methodological superiority of the fourth level of the Whorfian hypothesis is one thing. The accessibility of this level for study may well be quite another thing. It does seem that this level is in some ways the most demanding of all, for it requires detailed technical training at both the predictor and the criterion ends of the relationship to be investigated. This may be the reason why there currently appears to be only one study which might possibly be said to be an example of work at this level, although in the future we might expect it to elicit greatly increased interest among socio-linguists and social psychologists with technical linguistic training. This is the study by Carroll and Casagrande which they refer to as Experiment II. The grammatic features of interest to Carroll and Casagrande in this study are the particular verb forms required in Navaho verbs for handling materials in accord with the shape or other physical attribute (flexibility, flatness, etc.) of the object being handled. Note that Carroll and Casagrande are concerned here with distinctions in verb *forms* rather than distinctions between mere lexical absence or presence of verbs as such. Presumably it is this fact which permits us to consider Experiment II as a Level 4 study rather than as a Level 2 study. The non-linguistic data utilized by Carroll and Casagrande are the object-classifying behaviors of their *S*s when presented first with a pair of objects which differ from each other in *two* respects (e.g., color and shape) and then with a third object similar to each member of the original pair in one of the two relevant characteristics. The *S*s were asked to indicate "which member of the (original) pair went best with the (third) object shown him." If the *S*'s reaction was governed by the requirements of Navaho verbal form, he would have to select a certain one of the original set of objects.

THE DEGREE OF
LINGUISTIC RELATIVITY

The fascination of the Whorfian hypothesis is in some ways compounded of both delights and horrors. We have already speculated concerning the delights. Let us now mention the horrors. The first is the *horror of helplessness,* since all of us in most walks of life and most of us in all walks of life are helplessly trapped by the language we speak. We cannot escape from it—and, even if we could flee, where would we turn but to some other language with its own blinders and its own vice-like embrace on what we think, what we perceive, and what we say. The second horror is the *horror of hopelessness*—for what hope can there be for mankind?; what hope that one group will ever understand the other?; what hope that one nation will ever fully communicate with the other? This is not the place for a full-dressed philosophical attack on these issues. Let us merely consider them from the point of view of the kinds of evidence supplied by some of the very studies we have mentioned.

The most "reassuring" facts that derive from Levels 1 and 2, the lexical and semantic codifiability levels of the Whorfian hypothesis, are that the noted non-translatability and the selective codifiability really pertain not so much to all-or-none differences between languages as to differences in relative ease or felicity of equivalent designation. Whenever we argue that there is no English word (or expression) for ——, which means so-and-so (or approximately so-and-so, or a combination of Y and Z) in English, we are partially undercutting our own argument. In the very formulation of our argument that there is "no English word (or expression) for ——" we have gone on to give an English approximation to it. This approximation may not be a very successful one but if that becomes our concern we can go through the contortions (both intellectual and gesticulational) that are required for an inching up on or a zeroing in on the non-English word or expression that we have in mind. The amount of effort involved may, at times, be quite considerable and even the final approximation may leave us dissatisfied. However, after all is said and done, this is not so different, in terms of both process and outcome, as the communication problems that we face with one another even within our *own* speech community. We can do no better than to quote Hockett's conclusions at this point, in support of what has just been said.

> Languages differ not so much as to what *can* be said in them, but rather as to what it is *relatively easy* to say in them. The history of Western logic and science constitutes not so much the story of scholars hemmed in and misled by the nature of their specific languages, as the story of a long and fairly successful struggle *against* inherited linguistic limitations. Where everyday language would not serve, special sub-systems (mathematics, e.g.) were devised. However, even Aristotle's development of syllogistic notation carries within itself aspects of Greek language structure.
>
> The impact of inherited linguistic pattern on activities is, in general, *least* important in the most practical contexts and most important in such "purely verbal" goings-on as story-telling, religion, and philosophizing. As a result, some types of literature are extremely difficult to translate accurately, let alone appealingly.

Turning now to Levels 3 and 4, where we become concerned with the imbedded structural features of a language, it seems to be important that we realize that Whorf never proposed that *all* aspects of grammatical structure must *inevitably* have direct cognitive effects. Thus, to begin with, we are faced with the task of locating those few grammatical features which might have definable but unconscious functional correlates in our unguarded behavior.

If we look to Levels 2 and 4, these being the levels in which the behavioral concomitants of linguistic features are experimentally derived, we once more must reach the conclusion that linguistic relativity, where it does exist, is not necessarily an awesomely powerful factor in cognitive functioning. The relationships that have been encountered, though clear-cut enough, seem to be neither very great nor irreversible in magnitude. The very fact that increased infant and early childhood experience with toys and objects requiring primarily a form reaction can result in a *Navaho-like classifying preference* among monolingual English-speaking children also means that other kinds of environmental experiences might very well produce an *English-like classifying preference* among monolingual Navaho-speaking children. No one has yet directly studied the success with which behaviors predicted on the basis of linguistic relativity can be counteracted by either (a) simply making Ss aware of how their language biases affect their thinking or (b) actively training Ss to counteract these biases. It may be, after all, that this is an area in which Ss can, with relatively little effort, learn how to "fake good." Furthermore, one might suspect that the impact of language *per se* on cognition and expression ought somehow to be greater and more fundamental than the impact of one or another language feature. Thus the impact of language *determinism* upon cognition ought to be more pervasive and more difficult to counteract than that of language *relativity*.

None of the foregoing should be interpreted as implying that linguistic relativity, wherever it exists, is an unimportant factor in human experience or one that deserves no particular attention except from those who are professionally committed to unraveling the unimportant in painful detail. Quite the contrary; just because it is such a seemingly innocuous factor it is very likely to go unnoticed and, therefore, requires our particular attention in order that we may appropriately provide for it.

SUMMARY AND CONCLUSIONS

The four levels of the Whorfian hypothesis that have been presented here are essentially subsumable under a double dichotomy. As Figure 14.1 reveals, we have essentially been dealing with two factors—one pertaining to characteristics of a given language or languages and the other pertaining to behavior of the speakers of the language or languages under consideration. The first factor has been dichotomized so as to distinguish between lexical or semantic structure on the one hand (both of these being considered as codeability features) and grammatical structure on the other. The second factor has been dichotomized so as to distinguish between verbal behavior per se (frequently interpreted in terms of cultural themes or *Weltanschauungen*) and individual behavioral data which is other than verbal in nature.

In a rough way, we might say that Levels 1 and 3 are concerned with *large group phenomena* whereas Levels 2 and 4 are concerned with *individual behavior*. Whorf was aware of and interested in both kinds of data, for he held that "our linguistically determined thought world not only collaborates with our *cultural idols and ideals* but engages even our unconscious *personal reactions* in its patterns and gives them certain typical character(istic)s."

| | Data of (Cognitive) Behavior | |
Data of Language Characteristics	Language Data ("cultural themes")	Non-linguistic Data
Lexical or "Semantic" characteristics	Level 1	Level 2
Grammatical characteristics	Level 3	Level 4

Figure 14.1   Schematic systematization of the Whorfian hypothesis

In general, Whorf is not deeply concerned with "which was first, the language patterns or the cultural norms?" He is content to conclude that "in the main they have grown up together, constantly influencing each other." Nevertheless, he does state that if these two streams are to be separated from each other for the purposes of analysis he considers language to be by far the more impervious, systematic, and rigid of the two. Thus, after a long association between culture and language, innovations in the former will have but minor impact on the latter, "whereas to inventors and innovators it (i.e., language) legislates with the decree immediate." Although Whorf is leery of the term correlation it seems most likely that he considered language structure not only as interactingly reflective of "cultural thought" but as directly formative of "individual thought." With proper cautions, the four levels of the Whorfian hypothesis that have been differentiated in this review may be seen as quite consistent with this conclusion.

Some of the characteristics, difficulties, and potentials of further empirical and theoretical study at each of the four differentiated levels have been considered. All levels can make use of both interlinguistic or intralinguistic designs, although Levels 1 and 3 most commonly employ the former—if only for purposes of contrast.

Although evidence favoring the Whorfian hypothesis exists at each level, it seems likely that linguistic relativity, though affecting some of our cognitive behavior, is nevertheless only a moderately powerful factor and a counteractable one at that. Certainly much experimental evidence has accumulated that points to a large domain of contra-Whorfian universality in connection with the relationships between *certain* structures of particular languages and *certain* cognitive behaviors of their speakers. The time might, therefore, now be ripe for putting aside attempts at grossly "proving" or "disproving" the Whorfian hypothesis and, instead, focusing on attempts to delimit more sharply the types of language structures and the types of non-linguistic behaviors that do or do not show the Whorfian effect as well as the degree and the modifiability of this involvement when it does obtain.

Because of Whorf's central role in making us aware of this phenomenon so that we may now better come to grips with it, both intellectually and practically, none can deny that he richly deserves to be characterized by his own standard for what constitutes a real scientist.

> All real scientists have their eyes primarily on background phenomena in our daily lives; and yet their studies have a way of bringing out a close relation between these unsuspected realms . . . and . . . foreground activities.

15

ELABORATED AND RESTRICTED CODES: THEIR SOCIAL ORIGINS AND SOME CONSEQUENCES

Basil Bernstein

THIS PAPER REPRESENTS AN ATTEMPT to discuss some aspects of the inter-relationships between social structure, forms of speech, and the subsequent regulation of behavior. The practical context of the enquiry is the differential response to educational opportunity made by children from different social classes. It has become abundantly clear that the determinants of this response are complex and that the response encapsulates the effects of socialization. The problem requires specification of the sociological processes which control the way the developing child relates himself to his environment. It requires an understanding of how certain areas of experience are differentiated, made specific and stabilized, so that which is relevant to the functioning of the social structure becomes relevant for the child. What seems to be needed is the development of a theory of social learning which would indicate what in the environment is available for learning, the conditions of learning, the constraints on subsequent learning, and the major reinforcing process.

The behavioral implications of the physical and social environment are transmitted in some way to the child. What is the major channel for such transmissions? What are the principles which regulate such transmissions? What are the psychological consequences and how are these stabilized in the developing child? What factors are responsible for variations in the prin-

From Basil Bernstein, "Elaborated and Restricted Codes: Their Social Origins and Some Consequences" reproduced by permission of the author and the American Anthropological Association from the *American Anthropologist* 66, 6, part 2:55–69 (Dec. 1964). (Text, Chapter 7)

ciples which regulate the transmissions? The socio-linguistic approach used here is a limited attempt to provide some kind of answer to these questions.

The general framework of the argument will be given first. This will be followed by a detailed analysis of two general linguistic codes. Towards the end of the paper, some variants of the codes will be very crudely associated with social class.

In order to make a distinction between language and speech, a simple view of language has been adopted. Only two levels of language will be distinguished. The first level consists of the formal elements which may be used for the purposes of organization. These are relational elements and syntactic devices. There are rules regulating the use of such elements. This level is referred to as <u>structure</u>. Language may be looked at from this point of view, in terms of the range of structural alternatives or options which may be used for the purposes of organization. The second level consists of words which have objective reference or can be given objective reference. This level is called vocabulary. From the point of view of vocabulary, language may be considered as the totality of meanings evoked by the words which carry objective reference. Putting the two levels together, it could be said that language represents the world of the possible. On the one hand, it contains a finite set of options and the rules of their regulation at the structural level and a set of options at the level of vocabulary. Language then represents the totality of options and the attendant rules for doing things with words. It symbolizes what can be done.

Speech, on the other hand, is constrained by the circumstances of the moment, by the dictate of a local social relation and so symbolizes not what can be done, but what *is* done with different degrees of frequency. Speech indicates which options at the structural and vocabulary level are taken up. Between language in the sense defined and speech is social structure. The particular form a social relationship takes acts selectively on what is said. In terms of this approach, the form the social relationship takes regulates the options which speakers select at both the structural and vocabulary levels. Inasmuch as the social relationship does this, then it may establish for the speakers specific principles of choice: coding principles. These specific principles of choice, the canons which regulate selections, entail from the point of view of the speakers and listeners planning procedures which guide the speakers in the preparation of their speech and which guide the listeners in the reception of speech.

Changes in the form of the social relationship, it will be argued, act selectively upon principles of selection. Changes in the form of the social relationship can affect the planning procedures an individual uses in the preparation of his speech and it can affect the orientation of the listener. Different forms of social relationships may generate quite different speech systems or linguistic codes by affecting the planning procedures. These different speech systems or codes may create for their speakers different orders of significance. The experience of the speakers may then be transformed by what is made significant or relevant by the different speech systems. This is a sociological argument, because the speech system is taken as a consequence of the form of the social relationship, or, put more generally, is a quality of the social structure. The social structure becomes the independent variable. There are important psychological implications. The speech system or linguistic code, itself a function of the social structure, marks out selectively for the individual what is relevant in the environment. The experience of the individual is transformed by the learning which is generated by his own apparently voluntary acts of speech.

Summarizing the argument, the following is obtained. Different social structures may generate different speech systems or linguistic codes. The latter entail for the individual specific principles of choice which regulate the selections he makes from the totality of options represented by a given language. The principles of choice originally elicit, progressively strengthen, and finally stabilize the planning procedures an individual uses in the preparation of his speech and guide his orientation to the speech of others. What he actually says, from a developmental perspective, transforms him in the act of saying.

As the child learns his speech, or in the terms used here, learns specific codes which regulate his verbal acts, he learns the requirements of his social structure. The social structure becomes the substratum of his experience essentially through the effects of the linguistic process. The identity of the social structure, it is thought, is transmitted to the child essentially through the implications of the linguistic code which the social structure itself generates. From this point of view, every time the child speaks or listens, the social structure of which he is part is reinforced and his social identity is constrained. The social structure becomes for the developing child his psychological reality by the shaping of his acts of speech. Underlying the general pattern of the child's speech are, it is held, critical sets of choices, preferences for some alternatives rather than for others, which develop and are stabilized through time and which eventually come to play an important role in the regulation of intellectual, social and affective orientation. Children who have access to different speech systems or linguistic codes, by virtue of their position in the class structure, may adopt quite different intellectual and social procedures which may be only tenuously related to their purely psychological abilities.

ELABORATED AND
RESTRICTED LINGUISTIC CODES

A start may be made by putting the following questions, although the answers are bound to be both limited and inadequate.

1. What kinds of social relations generate what kinds of speech systems?

2. What kinds of principles or planning procedures control the speech systems?

3. What kinds of relationships in the environment do these planning procedures both give access to and stabilize?

Two general coding systems will be distinguished. These systems will be defined in terms of the kinds of options speakers take up in order to organize what they have to say. These speech systems or linguistic codes are *not* defined in terms of vocabulary. If it is difficult to predict the syntactic options or alternatives a speaker uses to organize his meanings over a representative range of speech, this system of speech will be called an elaborated code. In the case of an elaborated code, the speaker will select from a wide range of syntactic alternatives and so it will not be easy to make an accurate assessment of the organizing elements he uses at any one time. However, with a restricted code, the range of alternatives, syntactic alternatives, is considerably reduced and so it is much more likely that prediction is possible. In the case of a restricted code, the vocabulary will be drawn from a narrow range but because the vocabulary is drawn from a narrow range, this in itself is no indication that the code is a restricted one.

If a speaker is oriented towards using an elaborated code, then the code through its planning procedures will facilitate the speaker in his attempt to put into words his purposes, his discrete intent, his unique experience in a verbally explicit form. If a speaker is moving towards a restricted code, then this code, through its planning procedures, will *not* facilitate the verbal expansion of the individual's discrete intent. In the case of an elaborated code, the speech system requires a higher level of verbal planning for the preparation of speech than in the case of a restricted code. It will be argued that the general behavior elicited from speakers by these two codes is directed towards different dimensions of significance. The events in the environment which take on significance when the codes used are different, whether the events be social, intellectual, or emotional. These two codes, elaborated and restricted, it will be argued, are generated by particular forms of social relationships. They do not necessarily develop as a result of the speaker's innate intelligence. The level at which a speaker operates a particular code may well be a function of his native ability, but the *orientation* is entirely a matter of the sociological constraints acting upon the speaker.

I want first to examine some variants of a restricted code which exemplify the social characteristics of this code. These variants represent ideal cases and so they will be referred to as examples of the pure form of a restricted code. These variants all have one major common attribute: the verbal component of the message, given the social context, is highly predictable. Because the verbal component of the message is highly predictable, it necessarily follows that this must also be the case for the syntactic alternatives. Prediction refers to an ability of an observer who knows the code. In the case of the variants to be discussed, both observers and speakers share the ability to make the same level of prediction. Thus these variants can be subsumed under the general title of restricted code, as a special case of lexicon prediction.

RESTRICTED CODE
(LEXICON PREDICTION)

predictable

A distinction will be made between the verbal component of the message and the extraverbal components. The verbal channel in this paper refers only to the transmission of words. The extraverbal channels include messages transmitted through the expressive associates of the words (intonation, etc.), and messages transmitted through gesture, physical set, and facial modifications. In the first variant of the ideal case, the messages transmitted through all channels (verbal and extraverbal) approach maximal redundancy from the perspective of both transmitter and receiver. This variant will occur where the organization and selection of all signals is bound by rigid and extensive prescriptions. The social relations will be of an ascribed status form, located usually, but not always, in religious, legal, and military social structures. The status relations are such that the area of discretion available to the incumbents is severely reduced, with the consequence that few options exist through which the incumbents may signal their discrete intent. The individual is transformed into a cultural agent. In these social relations, if discrete intent is signaled, that is, if the messages depart from maximal redundancy, then such messages are likely to be evaluated by the receiver(s) as violations, as profane.

The second variant of the ideal case of a restricted code is one where there is considerably less redundancy in the messages carried through the extraverbal channels, while the verbal channel carries messages approaching maximal redundancy. Consider the case of a mother telling her child stories which both know by heart—"And little Red Riding Hood went into the woods" ritualistic pause, "and what do you think happened?" ritualistic question. . . . This is another social relationship which constrains the options available to the incumbents of the statuses for the transmission of difference, or for the transmission of discrete intent. If the mother wishes to transmit her discrete experience or her uniqueness, she is unable to do this by varying her verbal selections. She can do it only by varying the messages transmitted through the *extraverbal channels*; through changes in muscular tension if she is holding the child, changes in facial set, gesture, or intonation. The verbal component of the messages ensures that ascribed status aspects of the social relation are made salient or the saliency of ascribed status aspects of the relation generates the characteristics of the order of communication. Notice that in this variant, the code defines the channels through which new information will be transmitted. New information will be made available *through the extraverbal channels. Interpersonal* aspects of this social relation will be regulated by the encoding and decoding of messages passing through the extraverbal channels. The code symbolizes and reinforces the form of the social relation and controls the channel through which new learning is made available. The mutual intents of mother and child are transmitted through extraverbal channels, and these channels are likely to become objects of special perceptual activity.

The third variant refers to an order of communication where the verbal component approaches maximal redundancy, but where the extraverbal channels permit messages of a relatively much lower order of prediction. If this is the case, then it is very likely that the extraverbal channels will become objects of special perceptual activity, as both transmitter and receiver will signal their discrete experience through the agency of such channels. There are many examples of this variant. I shall give only one. Consider a dance hall downtown. A boy asks a girl to dance. They have never met before. Although the precise nature of their initial communications will vary, it is suggested that they will take this form from the point of view of the boy.

"Do you come here often?"
"Bit crowded-n'it?"
"S'nice floor?"
"Band's alright/dead/with it."

Clearly there are many examples of such routines. It is suggested that the exchange of social routines approaching maximal redundancy occurs in those social relationships where the participants have low predictability about each other's discrete intent. The routine establishes predictability at a high level of consensus. The consensus is obtained by making the status aspect of the social relation salient. In fact, the form of the social relation at this point is one of ascribed status, as in the other two cases previously discussed. What is said is impersonal in the sense that the verbal component comes prepacked. Interpersonal aspects of the relation will be again transmitted through the extraverbal channels, and these will again become objects of special perceptual activity. How the social relation develops will depend upon the decoding of extraverbal messages, as these will carry new information which refers to the discrete intent of the participants. Further, this variant of a restricted code affords the possibility of deferred commitment to the relation. Whether the relation will shift from one of status to an interpersonal form regulated by speech will depend upon the decoding of extraverbal messages. This variant differs from the preceding two in terms of a greater use of potential options available in the extraverbal channels. It is suggested that the preliminaries to oriental bargaining relationships also exemplify this variant of a restricted code (lexicon prediction).

In all the three variants of a restricted code (lexicon prediction), the following interrelated characteristics may be found. Clearly, the social contents and function of these variants greatly differ. Attention has been drawn only to very general characteristics of the code.

1. The status aspect of the social relation is salient.

2. New information is made available through extraverbal channels and these channels will become objects of special perceptual activity.

3. Discrete intent can only be transmitted through variations in the extraverbal signals.

4. The code reinforces the form of the social relation by restricting the verbal signaling of differences.

RESTRICTED CODE
(HIGH STRUCTURAL PREDICTION)

In this form, which is empirically the most general, only the syntactic alternatives taken up to organize meaning across a representative range of speech carry high predictability. In the case of a restricted code (lexicon prediction), it was argued that the controls on lexicon selection and syntactic organization were functions of social assumptions common to the speakers. These assumptions, translated behaviorally, refer to prescriptions inhering in the relative statuses the speakers are filling. It was noted that the speech refracted through these prescriptions did not permit the signaling of discrete intent. In the case of a restricted code (structural prediction) the options available for verbal and extraverbal messages are very much greater than in the case of a restricted code (lexicon prediction). The constraint exists essentially at the syntactic level. The range of syntactic alternatives used in this code is reduced and therefore the alternatives are relatively predictable. The lexicon, however, is likely to be drawn from a narrow range; but the fact that the lexicon is drawn from a narrow range is no criterion for deciding whether the code is restricted.

What is responsible for the simplification of the structure, the narrowing of the lexicon range, and the consequent constraint on the *verbal* elaboration of unique experience? It is suggested that the code is a function of a specific form of social relation. In the case of a restricted code (structural prediction), the speech is played out against a backdrop of assumptions common to the speakers, against a set of closely shared interests and identifications, against a system of shared expectations; in short, it presupposes a local cultural identity which reduces the need for the speakers to elaborate their intent verbally and to make it explicit. In one sentence the extent to which the intent of the other person may be taken for granted, the more likely that the structure of the speech will be simplified and the vocabulary drawn from a narrow range.

Concretely, a restricted code (structural prediction) will arise in closed communities like prisons, combat units of the armed service, criminal subcultures, and also in peer groups of children and adolescents and between married couples of long standing. In fact, the code will develop wherever the form of the social relation is based upon some extensive set of closely shared identifications, self-consciously held by the members. It is important to note that the use of specialist terms does not of itself indicate a restricted code (structural prediction). (For the sake of simplicity the term restricted code will be used for this speech system unless the context requires greater precision.)

I would like to examine in some detail the characteristics of this code. Consider a group of boys at a street corner, or a group of close friends in a bar, or a courting couple. I suggested that if one were observing these relationships, one would be struck by the following:

1. The observer would be eavesdropping on inclusive relationships, and so he would be struck by the measure of his own exclusion. He might have difficulty at first in following the speech as it would tend to be fast, fluent, relatively unpaused, and so the articulatory clues would be reduced.

2. On the other hand, if he could write down the sequences, he might be surprised to find that they would be relatively impersonal. If intent does not have to be verbalized and made explicit, if much can be assumed and taken for granted, there is no need to use a level of verbal planning which requires careful selection and fine discriminations. Consequently, he could expect that there would be a reduction in the number of qualifiers, a simple verbal stem limited to the active voice. There might be an increase in some personal pronouns like "you" and "they," and a reduction in others like the self-reference pronoun "I." He might find, over and above idiosyncratic use, a greater frequency of terminal sequences like "isn't it," "wouldn't they," "you know," "you see," etc. In other words, he might expect a reduction in the use of those elements which facilitate the verbal transmission of discrete experience and the speech would emphasize the communality of the speakers. This does not mean that there would be no differences between the speakers, only that the differences would be transmitted in a particular way. The verbal meanings would be condensed, but the amount of speech would still be considerable. The change would be in quality, not quantity.

3. He might notice the vitality of the speech and this vitality would serve an important function. The burden of changes in meaning would be carried through the extraverbal component of the communication. The "how" of the communication would be important rather than the "what." The discrete intent of the speakers, the "I" of the speakers, would be transmitted not through varying their verbal selections, but through varying the expressive features of the communication, through changes in gesture, physical set, intonation, facial modification.

4. He might also notice that the speech sequences, from his point of view, would tend to be dislocated—disjunctive. There might well be logical gaps in the flow of meaning. The speakers would not be worried because they could take much for granted. The connecting devices in the speech might not clarify the logical organization of meaning. In fact, the observer might find that the meanings were strung together rather like beads on a string rather than being logically ordered.

5. Finally, the content of the speech is likely, but not necessarily, to be concrete, narrative and descriptive, rather than analytical or abstract. If the speech moved in the direction of the abstract, it would be likely that the propositions would not be fully developed, relying on sequences like "you see," "you know," "wouldn't it" to bridge points of uncertainty.

Putting all this together, an observer might be struck by the fact that the speech in these social relationships was fast, fluent, with reduced articulatory clues, the meanings might be discontinuous, dislocated, condensed and local, but the quantity of speech might not be affected, that there would be a low level of vocabulary and syntactic selection, and that the "how" rather than the "what" of the communication would be important. *The unique meaning of the person would tend to be implicit.*

In fact, the sequence might have the same *general* form as this:

It's all according like well those youth and that if they get with
gangs and that they most
they most
have a bit of a lark around and
say it goes wrong
and that and they probably knock some off I think they do it just to be a
bit big you know
getting publicity here and there.

Verbal I.Q. average
(lower working-class)
Transcript of a tape-recorded discussion

The point I want to make is that a restricted code is available to *all* members of society as the social conditions which generate it are universal. But it may be that a considerable section of our society has access only to this code by virtue of the implications of class background. I am suggesting that there is relatively high probability of finding children limited to this code among sections of the lower working-class population. On this argument, the general form of their speech is not substandard English but is related to and shares a similar social origin with the restricted code I have just outlined. It is a special case—a case where children can use one and only one speech system. What this code makes relevant to them, the learning generated by apparently spontaneous acts of speech, is not appropriate for their formal educational experience. But only from this point of view is it inappropriate.

A restricted code (structural prediction) shares the general social characteristics of the variants of a restricted code (lexicon prediction). It is perhaps somewhat less misleading to say that it is on the same dimension but at the opposite end. It limits the verbal signaling of discrete intent; the extraverbal signals become important bearers of changes in meaning and so tend to become the objects of special perceptual activity. *The status aspect of the social relation is salient with a consequent reduction in role discretion.* The code is a facility for the transmission of global, concrete, descriptive, narrative statements in which discrete intent is unlikely to be raised to the level of elaboration and so made explicit.

ELABORATE CODES
(LOW STRUCTURAL PREDICTION)

I shall consider finally the nature of an elaborated code, its regulatory function and its social origin. Restricted codes can be considered status-oriented speech systems. The codes reinforce the form of the social relation, by limiting the verbal signaling of personal difference. The forms of an elaborated code are quantitatively and qualitatively different from the codes so far discussed. An elaborated code was defined in terms of the difficulty of predicting the syntactic alternatives taken up to organize meaning across a representative range of speech. This difficulty arises because an extensive range of syntactic alternatives is available within this code and therefore the probability of which alternatives will at any one time be taken up is low. This code, through its planning procedures, allows the speaker to elaborate verbally and to make explicit his discrete intent. An elaborated code, or at least an orientation towards this code, will develop to the extent that the discrete intent of the other person may *not* be taken for granted. Inasmuch as the other person's intent may not be taken for granted, then the speaker is forced to expand and elaborate his meanings, with the consequence that he chooses more carefully among syntactic and vocabulary options.

Now to the extent a speaker does this his sequences will carry *verbally* the elaboration of his experience. The potential discrepancy between speakers in expectations, in nuances of interests, generates in them a tension to select from their linguistic resources a verbal arrangement which closely specifies a given referent. Meanings which are discrete and local to the speaker are cut so that they are intelligible to the listener. The condition of the listener, unlike the case of a restricted code, will be taken into account in the preparation of the speech. In terms of what is transmitted *verbally* rather than what is transmitted *extraverbally,* an elaborated code encourages the speaker to focus upon the other person as an experience different from his own. An elaborated code is *person* rather than status oriented.

In the case of a restricted code, what is transmitted *verbally* refers to the other person in terms of his status or local group membership. What is *said* reflects the form of the social relation and its basis of shared assumptions. Speakers using a restricted code are dependent upon these shared assumptions. The mutually held range of identifications defines the area of common intent and so the range of the code. The dependency underpinning the social relation generating an elaborated code is not of this order. With an elaborated code, the listener is dependent upon the *verbal elaboration of meaning.* In restricted codes, to varying degrees, the extraverbal channels become objects of special perceptual activity; in elaborated codes it is the verbal channel.

It is important to consider differences in the role relations which these codes presuppose.

The form of the social relation which generates an elaborated code is such that a range of discretion must inhere in the role if it is to be produced at all. Further, the speaker's social history must have included practice and training for the role. These role relations receive less support from shared expectations. The orientation of the speaker is based upon the expectations of psychological difference—his own and that of others. Individuated speech released through an elaborated code presupposes a history of a particular role relation if it is to be both prepared *and* delivered appropriately. The range of discretion which must necessarily inhere in the role involves the speaker in a measure of social isolation. He may be differentiated from his social group as a figure is differentiated from its ground. The role relations which presuppose a restricted code are quite different. The range of discretion of the role is confined to the area of common intent and, therefore, the role receives explicit support from the status components of the relationship. Looked at from another point of view, control on the role is mediated through a restricted self-editing process as far as the *verbal* messages are concerned. Although it is going too far to argue that the role relations of a restricted code orient its speakers to seeking affirmation, confirmation, or similarity, it is likely that role strain results from persistent attempts to signal discrete intent in a verbally elaborated form. This source of role strain in restricted code relationships is precisely the role relationship appropriate for an elaborated code.

These codes are translations of different forms of social relations or even qualities of different social structures; thus, different orientations, different ranges of discretion, different forms of dependency, and different sources of strain inhere in the respective roles. Thus speakers limited to a restricted code may be unable to manage the role requirements which are necessary for the production of an elaborated code. Conversely, it is possible that an individual limited to an elaborated code cannot switch codes because of an inability to switch roles.

An elaborated code generated originally by the form of the social relation becomes a facility for transmitting individuated verbal responses. As far as any one speaker is concerned, he is not aware of a speech system or code, but the planning procedures which he is using both in the preparation of his speech and in the receiving of speech are creating one. These planning procedures promote a relatively higher level of structural organization and vocabulary selection than in the case of a restricted code. What is then made available for learning by an elaborated code is of a different order from what is made available in the case of a restricted code. The learning generated by these speech systems is quite different, whether it be social, intellectual, or affective. From a developmental perspective, an elaborated code user comes to perceive language as a set of theoretical possibilities available for the transmission of unique experience. The concept of self, unlike the concept of self of a speaker limited to a restricted code, will be verbally differentiated, so that it becomes in its own right the object of special perceptual activity. In the case of a speaker limited to a restricted code the concept of self will tend to be refracted through the implications of the status arrangements. Here there is no problem of self, *because the problem is not relevant.*

The preparation and delivery of relatively explicit meaning is the major purpose of an elaborated code. This affects the manner of delivery. The speech of a restricted code, it was argued above, would be delivered in a fast, fluent, relatively unpaused style with reduced articulatory clues. The speech controlled by an elaborated code will be punctuated by relatively frequent pauses and longer hesitations. A specific monitoring, or self-editing, system initially generates the code. The time dimension underlying the planning process producing an elaborated code tends to be longer than the time dimension underlying the planning process producing a restricted code. The delay between impulse and verbal signal is mediated through an extensive self-editing process in the case of an elaborated code. If a speaker is limited to a restricted code, then a specific planning or monitoring system develops and becomes progressively strengthened. These differences in the time dimension inhering in the planning processes of the two codes will have a number of psychological consequences, which cannot be developed here.

As a child learns an elaborated code, he learns to scan a particular syntax, to receive and transmit a particular pattern of meaning, to develop a particular planning process and *very early learns to orient towards the verbal channel.* He learns to manage the role requirements necessary for the effective production of the code. He becomes aware of a certain order of relationships (intellectual, social, and emotional) in his environment and his experience is transformed by these relations. As the code, through its planning procedures, becomes established, the developing child voluntarily through his acts of speech generates these relations. He comes to perceive language as a set of theoretical possibilities for the presentation of his discrete experience to others. An elaborated code through its regulation, induces developmentally in its speakers an expectation of separateness and difference from others. It points to the possibilities inherent in a complex conceptual hierarchy for the organization of experience.

It is possible to distinguish two modes of an elaborated code. One mode facilitates relations between *persons* and the second facilitates relations between *objects.* These two modes of an elaborated code would, in principle, differentiate different ranges of experiences and would presuppose different role relations. Although there is little time to develop this distinction, it might have some relevance to the present problems of C. P. Snow's two cultures.

A child *limited* to a restricted code will tend to develop essentially through the regulation inherent in the code. For such a child, speech does not become an object of special perceptual activity, neither does a theoretical attitude develop towards the structural possibilities of sentence organization. The speech is epitomized by a low level and limiting syntactic organization and there is little motivation or orientation toward increasing vocabulary. This code becomes a facility for transmitting and receiving concrete, global, descriptive, narrative statements involving a relatively low level of conceptualization. The planning processes which generate the speech involve a relatively short time dimension and, thus, a reduced self-editing function. Extraverbal channels tend to become the agencies through which discrete intent is signaled and so these extraverbal channels early become objects of special perceptual activity. It is a status-oriented code and elicits and progressively strengthens a relatively undifferentiated adherence to the normative arrangements of a local social structure. The verbal channel promotes the transmission of social rather than individual symbols. As the child learns a restricted code, he learns to control a particular role relation, and code switching may be hampered by the role requirements of a restricted code. Finally, an individual limited to a restricted code will tend to mediate an elaborated code through the regulation of his own. Clearly one code is not better than another; each possesses its own esthetic, its own possibilities. Society, however, may place different values on the orders of experience elicited, maintained, and progressively strengthened through the different coding systems.

The orientation towards these codes, elaborated and restricted, may be independent of the psychology of the child, independent of his native ability, although the *level* at which a code is used will undoubtedly reflect purely psychological and physiological attributes. The orientation toward these codes may be governed entirely by the form of the social relation, or more generally by the quality of the social structure. The intellectual and social procedures by which individuals relate themselves to their environment may be very much a question of their speech models within the family and the codes these speech models use.

Finally, I should like to draw attention to the relations between social class and the two coding systems. The subcultural implications of social class give rise to discrete socialization procedures. The different normative systems create different family role systems operating with different modes of social control. It is considered that the normative systems associated with the middle-class and associated strata are likely to give rise to the modes of an elaborated code while that associated with some sections of the working class is likely to create individuals limited to a restricted code. Clearly, social class is an extremely crude index for the codes, and more specific conditions for their emergence have been given in this paper. Variations in behavior found within groups who fall within a particular class (defined in terms of occupation and education) within a mobile society are often very great. It is possible to locate the two codes more precisely by considering the orientation of the family role system, the mode of social control, and the resultant verbal feedback. Variations in the orientation of the family role system can be linked to the external social network of the family and to occupational roles. It is not possible to do more than mention the possibilities of these more sensitive indices.

Very broadly, then, children socialized within middle-class and associated strata can be expected to possess *both* an elaborated and a restricted code while children socialized within some sections of the working-class strata, particularly the lower working-class, can be expected to be *limited* to a restricted code. As a child progresses through a school it becomes critical for him to possess, or at least to be oriented toward, an elaborated code if he is to succeed.

Some research specific to this thesis based upon small samples of subjects and speech does indicate that middle-class and working-class subjects aged fifteen years, male, matched for average verbal I.Q., differ in their coding orientation in the predicted direction. This research further indicates that differences in the time dimension of the planning processes inhering in the respective codes are also in the predicted direction. It is important to repeat that these results are based upon small samples. Further research has shown that middle-class and working-class subjects, male, at two age levels, matched for average verbal and average nonverbal I.Q., operated with the predicted codes in a sample of representative written work. This study also showed a relation between levels of abstraction and the use of the respective codes.

There is also firm evidence showing a relative deterioration in verbal I.Q. between the ages of eight and eleven years and between eleven and fifteen years for working-class children when compared with middle-class children between the same ages. Other research shows clearly that the verbal I.Q. scores of working-class subjects, particularly lower working-class, are likely to be severely depressed in relation to their scores at the higher ranges of a nonverbal test. This deterioration in verbal I.Q., discrepancy between verbal and nonverbal I.Q. tests and failure to profit from formal education on the part of working-class children, particularly those of lower working-class origins, is thought to be closely related to the control on types of learning induced by a restricted code. The relative backwardness of some working-class children may well be a form of culturally induced backwardness transmitted to the child through the implications of the linguistic process. The code the child brings to the school symbolizes his social identity. It relates him to his kin and to his local social relations. The code orients the child progressively to a pattern of relationships which constitute for the child his psychological reality and this reality is reinforced every time he speaks.

CONCLUSION

An attempt has been made to show how two general coding systems and their variants are elicited by the structure of social relations. The dimensions of relevance created by the different coding systems have been explored. Although the main burden of the paper has been to examine broad social class affiliations of the codes and to indicate briefly their socializing and formal educational consequences, it is tentatively thought that the theory might well have a more general application. Elaborated and restricted codes and their variants should be found in any social structure where their originating conditions exist. The definitions should, in principle, be capable of application to a range of languages although in any one case elaboration and restriction will be relative.

16

DEFINITIONS
OF TIME AND RECOVERY
IN PARALYTIC POLIO
CONVALESCENCE[1]

Fred Davis

IT IS AN OFT-REPEATED, although seldom analyzed, truism that recovery from a disease is as much a psychological process as it is a physiochemical process. The rate and extent of the recovery are presumed to be influenced significantly by optimism, the will to get well, and self-confidence in the body's recuperative process. More often than not, these traits and motivations are assumed to be inherent in the patient; he brings them, pre-formed, to the sickbed, and they serve to his recuperative advantage. Seldom does the precise role played by the hospital and its personnel in this psychological process of recovery come under scrutiny.

In the course of a long-range, longitudinal study of the psychological and social impact of paralytic poliomyelitis on children and their families, the author and his associates have examined the ways in which the hospital and its personnel structure and define the recuperative motivations and orientations of the stricken child and his parents. More concretely, we have examined the ways in which therapeutic personnel attempt to gear the child and his family to an acceptance of institutional and somewhat special definitions of the patient's paralysis and progress in recovery—definitions which, it might be added, both draw upon broad cultural values and motivational patterns and, in a number of respects, conflict with them.

Reprinted from *American Journal of Sociology* 61 (1956), 582–587, by permission of The University of Chicago Press. Copyright, 1956 by The University of Chicago Press. (Text, Chapter 8)

[1] Aided by a grant from the National Foundation for Infantile Paralysis.

Let us consider the situation of the child who is stricken with paralytic poliomyelitis. In a very real sense he is thrown into an entirely new world from the one to which he is accustomed. The paralysis affects not only his ability to manipulate his own body but also severely alters his customary motor relations with significant persons and social objects. In a great many cases he cannot walk for several months following the acute attack. He is taken away from family and playmates and set down in strange surroundings where the routine is unfamiliar and where the faces of those who minister to his needs change with great frequency. No longer is he the only child or one among several children. He is one among many. Generally, he has only the vaguest idea of what is being done to him and why it is being done. In short, the child and his parents are confronted by an unknown world which requires definition of its procedures and purposes as well as its relationship to the everyday world with which they are familiar.

This paper will consider the question of how the hospital and its personnel —especially the physiotherapist, who is most actively involved in the polio child's day-by-day treatment—go about effectuating what W. I. Thomas has called the "definition of the situation." Two aspects are singled out for discussion. These are the definition of time and the definition of progress in recovery.

Let us begin with the definition of time. When the stricken child is first admitted to the hospital in the acute stage of poliomyelitis, doctors, nurses, and other attending personnel are inevitably, and understandably, bombarded by the family with such questions as: How long will it be? When can I have my child back? etc. The children themselves, although often in a high fever and suffering from muscle spasms, at first ask incessantly when their parents will come for them and when they will be sent home. A few weeks later, upon admission to the convalescent hospital—the scene of the long-term pull toward recovery—the same questions are raised by parent and child, albeit with somewhat less persistence and a certain sense of resignation learned from what has already transpired.

Invariably, what happens to the children and families we have studied is that an initial perspective of short-time hospital confinement with associated thoughts of rapid recovery is, within a few weeks after the acute onset, replaced by a long-term perspective wherein the extent of ultimate recovery from the paralysis is viewed in a more qualified and ambiguous fashion. As a physiotherapist at one of the Baltimore convalescent hospitals has put it: "When they come in here, the children think in terms of days. Very soon they're thinking in terms of weeks and not long after that in terms of months."

How is this change in time perspective brought about? Of course, to begin with, a large part of this, obviously, is accomplished by the doctor in communicating to the parent specific facts about the nature and course of the disease, knowledge with which even a well-informed parent is only slightly familiar. But it is important to examine the situational and institutional contexts of communication between expert and layman to understand the lengthening of the time perspective.

Very significant is, of course, the discrepancy in power in the doctor-patient relationship. Little need be said on this oft-noted point, except to repeat the observation made by Parsons in his discussion of medical practice, namely, that, when the patient is placed in the hands of the doctor, he and his family relinquish, in effect, all *technical* responsibility for the patient's treatment and somatic recovery.[2] Said a father whose nine-year-old daughter was paralyzed in the lower extremities: "I've never felt so helpless in all my life. There's nothing you can do except put your trust in the doctors and hope for the best."

This in itself constitutes an important point of leverage for the doctor as he begins to redefine the time perspective of parent and child. However, although a good deal of factual knowledge regarding the course of the disease is imparted to the parent, in polio, as in so many pathological conditions, much is unknown, and the practitioner is confronted by significant areas of therapeutic uncertainty. This uncertainty is for the most part on the socially crucial questions of the rate of recovery and the ultimate extent of disability with which the patient will be left. It is thus necessary for the doctor somehow to communicate to the parents that the uncertainty stems from the nature of the disease itself and not from therapeutic incompetence or an unwillingness to speak the truth. His status as an expert generally insures that the child and his parents will believe him. That it is not always so, however, is attested to by the "shopping around" inside and outside the hospital which numerous parents in our study engage in.

"Shopping around" inside the hospital usually means that the parents direct inquiries at physiotherapists and nurses and sometimes at other parents whom they meet on visiting days and who, they feel, may be more knowledgeable than themselves. As can be expected, this rarely provides the answers they are seeking. Other parents, they soon learn, are as much in the dark as they. As subordinates of the doctor, the nurses are most averse, as a rule, to making prognosticatory statements of any kind. Beyond "handling" the parents with the customary retort that the patient "is doing fine" or "as well as can be expected," they invariably refer them to the doctor.

The physiotherapist, however, does generally possess an intimate knowledge of the child's condition; sometimes she knows more than the doctor. Early in the convalescent period she is likely to have reached certain well-founded conclusions concerning the type and degree of residual muscle damage. But, partly because the communication of prognoses is the professional responsibility of the doctor and partly because the probable in polio convalescence is by no means certain, she is careful not to speak her mind in full or go into too great detail. When pressed by the parents for definitive statements concerning the child's future, she, too, refers them to the doctor.

"Shopping around" outside the hospital typically involves consultations

---

[2] Talcott Parsons, *The Social System* (Glencoe: Free Press, 1951), chap. x.

by the parents with other doctors and talks with suddenly discovered, near or distant, neighbors whose children have had polio. The former is seldom satisfactory in that the private practitioner, on the basis of what the parents can tell him, is in less of a position to prognosticate or offer reassurance than is the doctor who is resident in the hospital. And visits with neighbors who have faced polio in their own families generally result in an exchange of experiences and beliefs which, at best, pertain to but a few cases. The cases they hear about display so much variability in onset and outcome that the parents soon come to feel that few, if any, generalizations are possible. All these frustrating encounters serve only to reinforce the doctor's initial injunction that "much is unknown and only time will tell." "Time" in this context connotes, of course, a long time.

Another important factor in the lengthening of the time perspective is the gradient approach to recovery which the hospital institutes: treatment procedures are so progressively arranged and serve so clearly to delineate the sequence of benchmarks on the road to recovery that time begins to be conceived as measured intervals in the striving toward a goal. The significance of this for the child will be discussed later. Here let us briefly consider some implications for the parent.

Parents are permitted to visit their children in the hospital only once or twice a week at regularly scheduled times. This in itself frequently imparts to their time perspective a certain attenuated periodicity. Further, in the course of these visits they soon become aware that they are able to observe only slight changes from week to week and are led to believe anew that recovery is a long, slow process. This belief is reinforced by doctor and physiotherapist, who caution the parent "not to expect too much too quickly." Optimism is not completely discouraged, however, for it is an attitude of "restrained hopefulness" which hospital personnel typically regard as most conducive to establishing a proper therapeutic environment. Thus, the physiotherapist at a polio convalescent hospital told a parent who phoned almost daily to inquire about her child's condition: "Mrs. Smith, if you call me every day, there's not much progress I can report in Harry's condition. But, if you would call me every other week, I think I'll be able to give you a good report." Such periodic reports, along with the ordered sequence of physiotherapeutic exercises and formal muscle checks taken at six-week intervals, also have the effect of directing the parents' expectations to points in the future.

Thus far we have been considering the hospital's management of time perspective chiefly with reference to the family of the paralyzed child. How does the institution manage to lengthen the child's own time perspective? Of predominant importance in this connection is the loosening of the child's affective ties with home and his immersion in the hospital's subculture of sickness. As long as the child senses his separation from parents and home acutely and unremittingly, the incorporation of hospital routine and values in his motivational system is mechanical at best. The passage of each day is keenly felt as but further forced separation from the familiar and loved. In the phraseology of the hospital personnel, this child is not "a co-operative patient."

The rapid immersion of the child in the subculture of sickness proceeds on many well-charted fronts. In general, this is accomplished by restricting parents' visits to once or twice a week; by the hospital personnel's assuming in surrogate fashion many of the functions of parents; by duplicating in the hospital many of the activities and diversions of the home (e.g., television, games, picture and comic books, group play, etc.); by a reward and punishment system, both formal and informal, which sanctions good behavior and co-operative attitudes as these are defined by the treatment personnel; and—most important of all, perhaps—by the fact of living in a milieu in which sickness is the norm rather than the deviation and which permits the child to relate in a more thorough and structured fashion to a common universe of special meanings, goals, and evaluative rankings.

This raises, in passing, the interesting problem of certain dysfunctional consequences in the very thorough assimilation of hospital definitions and values which many of the children experience during their convalescent stay. For the values of the hospital are not precisely those of the society to which the child will have to return one day. The severely paralyzed child who after long treatment is able to get out of bed and move about on crutches has, in the eyes of the physiotherapist, for example, made marked and important progress. Naturally, he and others in the hospital encourage and support him in this conviction. To outsiders—and possibly to his parents—he may just be a "poor crippled kid." Hence, a number of the children in our study, particularly those approaching adolescence, voice reluctance and strong foreboding when discharge time draws near. Growing increasingly aware of the trauma frequently attending the shift from hospital to home, some polio convalescent centers have begun to institute a policy whereby the children are allowed home for several week-end visits a month or so prior to discharge. There remains, however, the broader problem of the extent to which the values of the two worlds can be effectively reconciled without detriment to either.

Before taking up the question of how the hospital defines progress in recovery, let us consider some of the latent functions of the lengthening of the time perspective. First, it encourages the paralyzed child to shift his attention from the ultimate hope of walking, running, playing ball, etc., to such short-range goals as sitting up in bed, moving a specific muscle, and locomotion in a wheel chair. Second, for the treatment personnel—especially the doctor—it serves the purpose of blocking repetitive and incessant questioning by the family. Because recovery is defined as slow and full of uncertainty, many parents soon begin to feel that there is not much point in "pestering" the busy doctor, particularly if they will be told very little, as is generally the case. Hence the doctor can either rightly or wrongly shed some of the onerous burden of continually answering questions and devote himself more fully to what he regards as his significant duties, namely, diagnosis, prescription, and treatment. Third, from the parents' standpoint, the lengthening of the time perspective provides them sufficient time to assimilate the crisis and thereupon gradually to reorganize their attitudes in accordance with the changed circumstances of their child's life. Particularly significant is the psychological time required for the parents to accept the fact that their child, as is so often the case, will be left with a residual disability.

Customarily we think of recovery from a disease or ailment as a more or less spontaneous process. True, there are the usual medical interventions and medications, but we assume for the most part that the feeling of getting well is a subjective state which hardly requires definition. Yet closer examination reveals a whole class of pathological conditions in which this would not seem to be the case. Questions can be raised as to whether the experience of recovery from any disease or ailment is ever as subjectively spontaneous as we think, but, in particular, we refer to those conditions in which the precise course and extent of recovery are obscured by uncertainty factors and where, as a rule, the patient's state upon recovery is significantly different from what it was originally. Certain mental diseases, diabetes, numerous cardiac conditions, and paralytic poliomyelitis seem to fall in this class.

What distinguishes this class of pathology is that without the explanations provided by the therapeutic personnel, as well as the implicit cues in the treatment procedures, the patient would have little way of sensing progress and knowing that he is getting better. It has been pointed out, for example, that in mental disease an important first step around which ward-treatment procedures are structured is for the patient to recognize verbally that he is sick and to express an intention to get better. This is institutionally labeled as "achieving insight." When this occurs, the patient's course of treatment is changed accordingly.[3] In recovery from paralytic polio, signs and movement tendencies, similar in form although different in content, are also structured into the everyday treatment procedures and interaction between physiotherapist and patient. These treatment procedures, in general, involve a graduated, step-by-step approach by the patient toward what the doctor and physiotherapist calculate to be optimal muscle functioning within the limits imposed by the initial muscle damage. Very frequently, of course, this means something less than total recovery of muscle use.

Consider the example of a child with extensive muscle damage in one leg which permits him neither to stand nor to walk. Treatment may begin on a stretcher bed on which the physiotherapist bends and manipulates the paralyzed leg to the point of pain. Besides familiarizing the physiotherapist with the exact site and extent of muscle damage, this procedure serves to indicate to the child that the leg is potentially of use, something which a passive regime of bed rest would not make evident so early. Several days later the child

---

[3] Private communication with Erving Goffman, visiting sociologist, Laboratory of Socio-environmental Studies, National Institute of Mental Health, Bethesda, Md.

may be suspended for the first time in the hydrotherapy pool, where the buoyancy of the water permits him to move the damaged leg about more easily than he could on dry land. This in itself is a rewarding and pleasurable experience and serves to reinforce the sense of muscle potential. In the course of several months the child may progress from moving the leg to and fro while lying prone upon a mat on the floor of the physiotherapy room, to standing up while being held by the physiotherapist, to ambulating up and down a ramp while he supports himself on arm rails, to taking his first tentative steps with the aid of braces or crutches, or both.

As each phase of the treatment is being mastered, the child is prepared by the physiotherapist for the next phase. The progression not only defines his recovery for him but also functions as something of a reward for the efforts he has made. New movements and sensations he experiences in his leg are referred by him to the physiotherapist for definition as to whether they are "good" or "mean anything." In short, even though his disability when viewed by the layman might turn out to be marked, in his physiotherapeutic experiences he learns by word and deed that he is "getting well." In addition, particular physiotherapeutic routines become so intimately associated with particular stages of motion and ambulation that the former frequently comes to be thought of by the children as an indispensable condition for the latter. This led one perceptive twelve-year-old at a polio convalescent center to remark somewhat sarcastically: "Nobody around here walks until after they've had their second muscle check." Physiotherapists are concerned lest the polio convalescents "sneak in too many walks" prior to the appointed time. This concern certainly stems in large degree from the possible harmful effects on gait and body-muscle balance which premature ambulation can cause. At the same time, though, the "scheduling" of so critical a physical advance as ambulation suggests that factors like patient morale[4] and maintaining routinized treatment procedures are also at play.

The treatment procedures in a very real sense tap the deep and implicit faith of parents and children concerning the efficacy of "will power" in overcoming adverse circumstances. The gradient structuring of the recovery process not only gives a public demonstration of the concept of will power but, as their child moves from stage to stage, gives fresh assurances that he has successfully demonstrated this quality. Therefore, the paralytic polio treatment procedure is of the quintessence of the Protestant ideology of achievement in America—namely, slow, patient, and regularly applied effort in pursuit of a long-range goal. Moreover, the great amount of activity and application called for in the physiotherapeutic regime, as well as the elaborate technological apparatus surrounding it, leave little room for doubt that "something is being done," thereby further reassuring the child and his parents. This accords in significant respects with what Parsons has termed the "activity

---

[4] In the course of their work physiotherapists must frequently take into account how rapid progress by some children affects the morale of those who progress more slowly.

bias" of American medical practice,[5] especially as it relates to the problem of coping with uncertainty. In this connection it is interesting to report that, while many orthopedic surgeons privately doubt that physiotherapy per se contributes anything beyond that which natural recuperative processes themselves accomplish, most realize, if only unconsciously, that it fulfils important psychological functions like those touched on here.

What has been written here refers chiefly to the effect of patterned institutional schema on the stricken child and his family. This is not to say that all cases proceed alike or that significant deviations from the pattern cannot be found. Indeed, they can, and they constitute an ongoing source of strain in the functioning of the treatment system. An examination of these aspects of the treatment system must, however, await another occasion.

17

SOCIAL BASES
OF DRUG-INDUCED
EXPERIENCES

Howard S. Becker

IN 1938, ALBERT HOFFMAN DISCOVERED the peculiar effects of lysergic acid dieythlamide (LSD-25) on the mind. He synthesized the drug in 1943 and, following the end of World War II, it came into use in psychiatry, both as a method of simulating psychosis for clinical study and as a means of therapy.[1] In the early 1960's, Timothy Leary, Richard Alpert and others began using it with normal subjects as a means of "consciousness expansion." Their work received a great deal of publicity, particularly after a dispute with Harvard authorities over its potential danger. Simultaneously, LSD-25 became available on the underground market and, although no one has accurate figures, the number of people who have used or continue to use it is clearly very large.

The publicity continues and a great controversy now surrounds LSD use. At one extreme, Leary considers its use so beneficial that he has founded a new religion in which it is the major sacrament. At the other extreme, psychiatrists, police and journalists allege that LSD is extremely dangerous, that it produces psychosis, and that persons under its influence are likely to com-

From Howard S. Becker, "History Culture and Subjective Experience," from *Journal of Health & Social Behavior,* Vol. 8 (1967), 163–176. Reprinted by permission of the author and the American Sociological Association. (Text, Chapter 8)

[1] See "D-lysergic Acid Diethylamide—LSD," *Sandoz Excerpta,* 1 (1955), pp. 1–2, quoted in Sanford M. Unger, "Mescaline, LSD, Psilocybin and Personality Change," in David Solomon, editor, *LSD: The Consciousness-Expanding Drug,* New York: Berkley Publishing Corp., 1966, p. 206.

mit actions dangerous to themselves and others that they would not otherwise have committed. Opponents of the drug have persuaded the Congress and some state legislatures to classify it as a narcotic or dangerous drug and to attach penal sanctions to its sale, possession, or use.

In spite of the great interest in the drug, I think it is fair to say that the evidence of its danger is by no means decisive.[2] If the drug does prove to be the cause of a bona fide psychosis, it will be the only case in which anyone can state with authority that they have found *the* unique cause of any such phenomenon; a similar statement applies to causes of crime and suicide. Whatever the ultimate findings of pharmacologists and others now studying the drug, sociologists are unlikely to accept such an asocial and unicausal explanation of any form of complex social behavior. But if we refuse to accept the explanations of others we are obligated to provide one of our own. In what follows, I consider the reports of LSD-induced psychoses and try to relate them to what is known of the social psychology and sociology of drug use. By this means I hope to add both to our understanding of the current controversy over LSD and to our general knowledge of the social character of drug use.

In particular, I will make use of a comparison between LSD use and marihuana use, suggested by the early history of marihuana in this country. That history contains the same reports of "psychotic episodes" now current with respect to LSD. But reports of such episodes disappeared at the same time as the number of marihuana users increased greatly. This suggests the utility of considering the historical dimension of drug use.

I must add a cautionary disclaimer. I have not examined thoroughly the literature on LSD, which increases at an alarming rate.[3] What I have to say about it is necessarily speculative with respect to its effects; what I have to say about the conditions under which it is used is also speculative, but is based

---

[2] On this point, to which I return later, the major references are: Sydney Cohen, "Lysergic Acid Diethylamide: Side Effects and Complications," *Journal of Nervous and Mental Diseases,* 130 (January, 1960), pp. 30–40; Sydney Cohen and Keith S. Ditman, "Prolonged Adverse Reactions to Lysergic Acid Diethylamide," *Archives of General Psychiatry,* 8 (1963), pp. 475–480; Sydney Cohen and Keith S. Ditman, "Complications Associated with Lysergic Acid Diethylamide (LSD-25)," *Journal of the American Medical Association,* 181 (July 14, 1962), pp. 161–162; William A. Frosch, Edwin S. Robbins and Marvin Stern, "Untoward Reactions to Lysergic Acid Diethylamide (LSD) Resulting in Hospitalization," *New England Journal of Medicine,* 273 (December 2, 1965), pp. 1235–1239; A. Hoffer, "D-Lysergic Acid Diethylamide (LSD): A Review of its Present Status," *Clinical Pharmacology and Therapeutics,* 6 (March, 1965), pp. 183–255; S. H. Rosenthal, "Persistent Hallucinosis Following Repeated Administration of Hallucinogenic Drugs," *American Journal of Psychiatry,* 121 (1964), pp. 238–244; and J. Thomas Ungerleider, Duke D. Fisher and Marielle Fuller, "The Dangers of LSD: Analysis of Seven Months' Experience in a University Hospital's Psychiatric Service," *Journal of the American Medical Association,* 197 (August 8, 1966), pp. 389–392.

[3] Hoffer's recent review of this literature, for which he disclaims completeness, cites 411 references (Hoffer, *op. cit.*).

in part on interviews with a few users. I present no documented conclusions, but do hope that the perspective outlined may help orient research toward generalizations that will fit into the corpus of sociological and social psychological theory on related matters.

THE SUBJECTIVE
EFFECTS OF DRUGS

The physiological effects of drugs can be ascertained by standard techniques of physiological and pharmacological research. Scientists measure and have explanations for the actions of many drugs on such observable indices as the heart and respiratory rates, the level of various chemicals in the blood, and the secretion of enzymes and hormones. In contrast, the subjective changes produced by a drug can be ascertained only by asking the subject, in one way or another, how he feels. (To be sure, one can measure the drug's effect on certain measures of psychological functioning—the ability to perform some standardized task, such as placing pegs in a board or remembering nonsense syllables—but this does not tell us what the drug experience is like.)[4]

We take medically prescribed drugs because we believe they will cure or control a disease from which we are suffering; the subjective effects they produce are either ignored or defined as noxious side effects. But some people take some drugs precisely because they want to experience these subjective effects; they take them, to put it colloquially, because they want to get "high." These recreationally used drugs have become the focus of sociological research because the goal of an artificially induced change in consciousness seems to many immoral, and those who so believe have been able to transform their belief into law. Drug users thus come to sociological attention as lawbreakers, and the problems typically investigated have to do with explaining their lawbreaking.

Nevertheless, some sociologists, anthropologists and social psychologists have investigated the problem of drug-induced subjective experience in its own right. Taking their findings together, the following conclusions seem justified.[5] First, many drugs, including those used to produce changes in sub-

---

[4] See, for instance: New York City Mayor's Committee on Marihuana, *The Marihuana Problem in the City of New York,* Lancaster: Jacques Cattell Press, 1944, pp. 69–77; and C. Knight Aldrich, "The Effect of a Synthetic Marihuana-Like Compound on Musical Talent as Measured by the Seashore Test," *Public Health Reports,* 59 (1944), pp. 431–433.

[5] I rely largely on the following reports: Howard S. Becker, *Outsiders,* New York: The Free Press, 1963, pp. 41–58 (marihuana); Alfred R. Lindesmith, *Opiate Addiction,* Bloomington: Principia Press, 1947 (opiates); Richard Blum and associates, *Utopiates,* New York: Atherton Press, 1964 (LSD); Ralph Metzner, George Litwin and Gunther M. Weil, "The Relation of Expectation and Mood to Psilocybin Reactions: A Questionnaire Study," *Psychedelic Review,* No. 5, 1965, pp. 3–39 (psilocybin); David F. Aberle, *The Peyote Religion Among the Navaho,* Chicago: Aldine Publishing Co., 1966,

jective experience, have a great variety of effects and the user may single out many of them, one of them, or none of them as definite experiences he is undergoing. He may be totally unaware of some of the drug's effects, even when they are physiologically gross, although in general the grosser the effects the harder they are to ignore. When he does perceive the effects, he may not attribute them to drug use but dismiss them as due to some other cause, such as fatigue or a cold. Marihuana users, for example, may not even be aware of the drug's effects when they first use it, even though it is obvious to others that they are experiencing them.[6]

Second, and in consequence, the effects of the same drug may be experienced quite differently by different people or by the same people at different times. Even if physiologically observable effects are substantially the same in all members of the species, individuals can vary widely in those to which they choose to pay attention. Thus, Aberle remarks on the quite different experiences Indians and experimental subjects have with peyote[7] and Blum reports a wide variety of experiences with LSD, depending on the circumstances under which it was taken.[8]

Third, since recreational users take drugs in order to achieve some subjective state not ordinarily available to them, it follows that they will expect and be most likely to experience those effects which produce a deviation from conventional perceptions and interpretations of internal and external experience. Thus, distortions in perception of time and space and shifts in judgments of the importance and meaning of ordinary events constitute the most common reported effects.

Fourth, any of a great variety of effects may be singled out by the user as desirable or pleasurable, as the effects for which he has taken the drug. Even effects which seem to the uninitiated to be uncomfortable, unpleasant or frightening—perceptual distortions or visual and auditory hallucinations—can be defined by users as a goal to be sought.[9]

Fifth, how a person experiences the effects of a drug depends greatly on

---

pp. 5–11 (peyote); Stanley Schacter and Jerome E. Singer, "Cognitive, Social and Physiological Determinants of Emotional State," *Psychological Review,* 69 (September, 1962), pp. 379–399 (adrenalin); and Vincent Newlis and Helen H. Newlis, "The Description and Analysis of Mood," *Annals of the New York Academy of Science,* 65 (1956), pp. 345–355 (benzedrine, seconal and dramamine).

Schacter and Singer propose a similar approach to mine to the study of drug experiences, stressing the importance of the label the person attaches to the experience he is having.

[6] Becker, *op. cit.*

[7] Aberle, *op. cit.,* and Anthony F. C. Wallace, "Cultural Determinants of Response to Hallucinatory Experience," *Archives of General Psychiatry,* 1 (July, 1959), pp. 58–69 (especially Table 2 on p. 62). Wallace argues that ". . . . both the subjective feeling tone and the specific content of the hallucination are heavily influenced by . . . . the cultural milieu in which the hallucination, and particularly the voluntary hallucination, takes place." (p. 62.)

[8] Blum, *et al., op. cit.,* p. 42.

[9] See the case cited in Becker, *op. cit.,* pp. 55–56.

the way others define those effects for him.[10] The total effect of a drug is likely to be a melange of differing physical and psychological sensations. If others whom the user believes to be knowledgeable single out certain effects as characteristic and dismiss others, he is likely to notice those they single out as characteristic of his own experience. If they define certain effects as transitory, he is likely to believe that those effects will go away. All this supposes, of course, that the definition offered the user can be validated in his own experience, that something contained in the drug-induced melange of sensations corresponds to it.

Such a conception of the character of the drug experience has its roots, obviously, in Mead's theory of the self and the relation of objects to the self.[11] In that theory, objects (including the self) have meaning for the person only as he imputes that meaning to them in the course of his interaction with them. The meaning is not given in the object, but is lodged there as the person acquires a conception of the kind of action that can be taken with, toward, by and for it. Meanings arise in the course of social interaction, deriving their character from the consensus participants develop about the object in question. The findings of such research on the character of drug-induced experience are therefore predictable from Mead's theory.

DRUG PSYCHOSES

The scientific literature and, even more, the popular press frequently state that recreational drug use produces a psychosis. The nature of "psychosis" is seldom defined, as though it were intuitively clear. Writers usually seem to mean a mental disturbance of some unspecified kind, involving auditory and visual hallucinations, an inability to control one's stream of thought, and a tendency to engage in socially inappropriate behavior, either because one has lost the sense that it is inappropriate or because one cannot stop oneself. In addition, and perhaps most important, psychosis is thought to be a state that will last long beyond the specific event that provoked it. However it occurred, it is thought to mark a more-or-less permanent change in the psyche and this, after all, is why we usually think of it as such a bad thing. Overindulgence in alcohol produces many of the symptoms cited but this frightens no one because we understand that they will soon go away.

Verified reports of drug-induced psychoses are scarcer than one might think.[12] Nevertheless, let us assume that these reports have not been fabri-

---

[10] The studies cited in footnote 5, *supra,* generally make this point.

[11] See George Herbert Mead, *Mind, Self and Society,* Chicago: University of Chicago Press, 1934, and Herbert Blumer, "Sociological Implications of the Thought of George Herbert Mead," *American Journal of Sociology,* 71 (March, 1966), pp. 535–544.

[12] See the studies cited in footnote 2, *supra,* and the following reports of marihuana psychoses: Walter Bromberg, "Marihuana: A Psychiatric Study," *Journal of the American Medical Association,* 113 (July 1, 1939), pp. 4–12; Howard C. Curtis, "Psychosis

cated, but represent an interpretation by the reporter of something that really happened. In the light of the findings just cited, what kind of event can we imagine to have occurred that might have been interpreted as a "psychotic episode"? (I use the word "imagine" advisedly, for the available case reports usually do not furnish sufficient material to allow us to do more than imagine what might have happened.)

The most likely sequence of events is this. The inexperienced user has certain unusual subjective experiences, which he may or may not attribute to having taken the drug. He may find his perception of space distorted, so that he has difficulty climbing a flight of stairs. He may find his train of thought so confused that he is unable to carry on a normal conversation and hears himself making totally inappropriate remarks. He may see or hear things in a way that he suspects is quite different from the way others see and hear them.

Whether or not he attributes what is happening to the drug, the experiences are likely to be upsetting. One of the ways we know that we are normal human beings is that our perceptual world, on the evidence available to us, seems to be pretty much the same as other people's. We see and hear the same things, make the same kind of sense out of them and, where perceptions differ, can explain the difference by a difference in situation or perspective.[13] We may take for granted that the inexperienced drug user, though he wanted to get "high," did not expect an experience so radical as to call into question that common sense set of assumptions.

In any society whose culture contains notions of sanity and insanity, the person who finds his subjective state altered in the way described may think he has become insane. We learn at a young age that a person who "acts funny," "see things," "hears things," or has other bizarre and unusual experiences may have become "crazy," "nuts," "loony" or a host of other synonyms.[14] When a drug user identifies some of these untoward events occurring in his own experience, he may decide that he merits one of those titles—that he has lost his grip on reality, his control of himself, and has in fact "gone crazy." The interpretation implies the corollary that the change is irreversible or, at least, that things are not going to be changed back very easily. The drug experience, perhaps originally intended as a momentary entertainment, now looms as a momentous event which will disrupt one's life, possibly permanently. Faced with this conclusion, the person develops a full-blown anxiety attack, but it is an anxiety caused by his reaction to the drug experience

---

Following the Use of Marihuana with Report of Cases," *Journal of the Kansas Medical Society,* 40 (1939), pp. 515–517; and Marjorie Nesbitt, "Psychosis Due to Exogenous Poisons," *Illinois Medical Journal,* 77 (1940), 278–281.

[13] See Alfred Schutz, *Collected Papers,* vols. I and II, The Hague: Martinus Nijhoff, 1962 and 1964, and Harold Garfinkel, "A Conception of and Experiments with 'Trust' as a Condition of Stable Concerted Actions," in O. J. Harvey, editor, *Motivation and Social Interaction,* New York: Ronald Press Co., 1963, pp. 187–238.

[14] See Thomas J. Scheff, *Being Mentally Ill: A Sociological Theory,* Chicago: Aldine Publishing Co., 1966.

rather than a direct consequence of the drug use itself. (In this connection, it is interesting that, in the published reports of LSD psychoses, acute anxiety attacks appear as the largest category of untoward reactions.)[15]

It is perhaps easier to grasp what this must feel like if we imagine that, having taken several social drinks at a party, we were suddenly to see vari-colored snakes peering out at us from behind the furniture. We would instantly recognize this as a sign of delirium tremens, and would no doubt become severely anxious at the prospect of having developed such a serious mental illness. Some such panic is likely to grip the recreational user of drugs who interprets his experience as a sign of insanity.

Though I have put the argument with respect to the inexperienced user, long-time users of recreational drugs sometimes have similar experiences. They may experiment with a higher dosage than they are used to and experience effects unlike anything they have known before. This can easily occur when using drugs purchased in the illicit market, where quality may vary greatly, so that the user inadvertently gets more than he can handle.

The scientific literature does not report any verified cases of people acting on their distorted perceptions so as to harm themselves and others, but such cases have been reported in the press. Press reports of drug-related events are very unreliable, but it may be that users have, for instance, stepped out of a second story window, deluded by the drug into thinking it only a few feet to the ground.[16] If such cases have occurred, they too may be interpreted as examples of psychosis, but a different mechanism than the one just discussed would be involved. The person, presumably, would have failed to make the necessary correction for the drug-induced distortion, a correction, however, that experienced users assert can be made. Thus, a novice marihuana user will find it difficult to drive while "high," but experienced users have no difficulty. Similarly, novices find it difficult to manage their relations with people who are not also under the influence of drugs, but experienced users can control their thinking and actions so as to behave appropriately.[17] Although it is commonly assumed that a person under the influence of LSD

[15] See Frosch, *et al., op. cit.,* Cohen and Ditman, "Prolonged Adverse Reactions . . .," *op. cit.,* and Ungerleider, *et al., op. cit.* It is not always easy to make a judgment, due to the scanty presentation of the material, and some of the reactions I count as anxiety are placed in these sources under different headings. Bromberg, *op. cit.,* makes a good case that practically all adverse reactions to marihuana can be traced to this kind of anxiety, and I think it likely that the same reasoning could be applied to the LSD reports, so that such reactions as "hallucination," "depression" and "confused" (to use Ungerleider's categories) are probably reactions to anxiety.

[16] Although LSD is often said to provoke suicide, there is very little evidence of this. Cohen, *op. cit.,* after surveying 44 investigators who had used LSD with over 5,000 patients, says that the few cases reported all occurred among extremely disturbed patients who might have done it anyway; Hoffer, *op. cit.,* remarks that the number is so low that it might be argued that LSD actually lowers the rate among mental patients. Ungerleider reports that 10 of 70 cases were suicidal or suicide attempts, but gives no further data.

[17] See Becker, *op. cit.,* pp. 66–72.

must avoid ordinary social situations for 12 or more hours, I have been told[18] of at least one user who takes the drug and then goes to work; she explained that once you learn "how to handle it" (i.e., make the necessary corrections for distortions caused by the drug) there is no problem.

In short, the most likely interpretation we can make of the drug-induced psychoses reported is that they are either severe anxiety reactions to an event interpreted and experienced as insanity, or failures by the user to correct, in carrying out some ordinary action, for the perceptual distortions caused by the drug. If the interpretation is correct, then untoward mental effects produced by drugs depend in some part on its physiological action, but to a much larger degree find their origin in the definitions and conceptions the user applies to that action. These can vary with the individual's personal makeup, a possibility psychiatrists are most alive to, or with the groups he participates in, the trail I shall pursue here.

THE INFLUENCE OF
DRUG-USING CULTURES

While there are no reliable figures, it is obvious that a very large number of people use recreational drugs, primarily marihuana and LSD. From the previous analysis one might suppose that, therefore, a great many people would have disquieting symptoms and, given the ubiquity in our society of the concept of insanity, that many would decide they had gone crazy and thus have a drug-induced anxiety attack. But very few such reactions occur. Although there must be more than are reported in the professional literature, it is unlikely that drugs have this effect in any large number of cases. If they did there would necessarily be many more verified accounts than are presently available. Since the psychotic reaction stems from a definition of the drug-induced experience, the explanation of this paradox must lie in the availability of competing definitions of the subjective states produced by drugs.

Competing definitions come to the user from other users who, to his knowledge, have had sufficient experience with the drug to speak with authority. He knows that the drug does not produce permanent disabling damage in all cases, for he can see that these other users do not suffer from it. The question, of course, remains whether it may not produce damage in some cases and whether his is one of them, no matter how rare.

When someone experiences disturbing effects, other users typically assure him that the change in his subjective experience is neither rare nor dangerous. They have seen similar reactions before, and may even have experienced them themselves with no lasting harm. In any event, they have some folk knowledge about how to handle the problem.

They may, for instance, know of an antidote for the frightening effects;

18 By David Oppenheim.

thus, marihuana users, confronted with someone who had gotten "too high," encourage him to eat, an apparently effective countermeasure.[19] They talk reassuringly about their own experiences, "normalizing" the frightening symptom by treating it, matter-of-factly, as temporary. They maintain surveillance over the affected person, preventing any physically or socially dangerous activity. They may, for instance, keep him from driving or from making a public display that will bring him to the attention of the police or others who would disapprove of his drug use. They show him how to allow for the perceptual distortion the drug causes and teach him how to manage interaction with non-users.

They redefine the experience he is having as desirable rather than frightening, as the end for which the drug is taken.[20] What they tell him carries conviction, because he can see that it is not some idiosyncratic belief but is instead culturally shared. It is what "everyone" who uses the drug knows. In all these ways, experienced users prevent the episode from having lasting effects and reassure the novice that whatever he feels will come to a timely and harmless end.

The anxious novice thus has an alternative to defining his experience as "going crazy." He may redefine the event immediately or, having been watched over by others throughout the anxiety attack, decide that it was not so bad after all and not fear its reoccurrence. He "learns" that his original definition was "incorrect" and that the alternative offered by other users more nearly describes what he has experienced.

Available knowledge does not tell us how often this mechanism comes into play or how effective it is in preventing untoward psychological reactions; no research has been addressed to this point. In the case of marihuana, at least, the paucity of reported cases of permanent damage coupled with the undoubted increase in use suggests that it may be an effective mechanism.

For such a mechanism to operate, a number of conditions must be met. First, the drug must not produce, quite apart from the user's interpretations, permanent damage to the mind. No amount of social redefinition can undo the damage done by toxic alcohols, or the effects of a lethal dose of an opiate or barbiturate. This analysis, therefore, does not apply to drugs known to have such effects.

Second, users of the drug must share a set of understandings—a culture—which includes, in addition to material on how to obtain and ingest the drug,

---

[19] Cf. the New York City Mayor's Committee on Marihuana, *op. cit.,* p. 13: "The smoker determines for himself the point of being 'high,' and is over-conscious of preventing himself from becoming 'too high.' This fear of being 'too high' must be associated with some form of anxiety which causes the smoker, should he accidentally reach that point, immediately to institute measures so that he can 'come down.' It has been found that the use of beverages such as beer, or a sweet soda pop, is an effective measure. A cold shower will also have the effect of bringing the person 'down.' "

[20] *Ibid.,* and Becker, *op. cit.*

definitions of the typical effects, the typical course of the experience, the permanence of the effects, and a description of methods for dealing with someone who suffers an anxiety attack because of drug use or attempts to act on the basis of distorted perceptions. Users should have available to them, largely through face-to-face participation with other users but possibly in such other ways as reading as well, the definitions contained in that culture, which they can apply in place of the common-sense definitions available to the inexperienced man in the street.

Third, the drug should ordinarily be used in group settings, where other users can present the definitions of the drug-using culture to the person whose inner experience is so unusual as to provoke use of the common-sense category of insanity. Drugs for which technology and custom promote group use should produce a lower incidence of "psychotic episodes."

The last two conditions suggest, as is the case, that marihuana, surrounded by an elaborate culture and ordinarily used in group settings, should produce few "psychotic" episodes.[21] At the same time, they suggest the prediction that drugs which have not spawned a culture and are ordinarily used in private, such as barbiturates, will produce more such episodes. I suggest possible research along these lines below.

NON-USER INTERPRETATIONS

A user suffering from drug-induced anxiety may also come into contact with non-users who will offer him definitions, depending on their own perspectives and experiences, that may validate the diagnosis of "going crazy" and thus prolong the episode, possibly producing relatively permanent disability. These non-users include family members and police, but most important among them are psychiatrists and psychiatrically oriented physicians. (Remember that when we speak of reported cases of psychosis, the report is ordinarily made by a physician, though police may also use the term in reporting a case to the press.)

Medical knowledge about the recreational use of drugs is spotty. Little research has been done, and its results are not at the fingertips of physicians who do not specialize in the area. (In the case of LSD, of course, there has been a good deal of research, but its conclusions are not clear and, in any case, have not yet been spread throughout the profession.) Psychiatrists are not anxious to treat drug users, so few of them have accumulated any clinical experience with the phenomenon. Nevertheless, a user who develops severe and uncontrollable anxiety will probably be brought, if he is brought anywhere, to a physician for treatment. Most probably, he will be brought to a

[21] I discuss the evidence on this point below.

psychiatric hospital, if one is available; if not, to a hospital emergency room, where a psychiatric resident will be called once the connection with drugs is established, or to a private psychiatrist.[22]

Physicians, confronted with a case of drug-induced anxiety and lacking specific knowledge of its character or proper treatment, rely on a kind of generalized diagnosis. They reason that people probably do not use drugs unless they are suffering from a severe underlying personality disturbance; that use of the drug may allow repressed conflicts to come into the open where they will prove unmanageable; that the drug in this way provokes a true psychosis; and, therefore, that the patient confronting them is psychotic. Furthermore, even though the effects of the drug wear off, the psychosis may not, for the repressed psychological problems it has brought to the surface may not recede as it is metabolized and excreted from the body.

Given such a diagnosis, the physician knows what to do. He hospitalizes the patient for observation and prepares, where possible, for long-term therapy designed to repair the damage done to the psychic defenses or to deal with the conflict unmasked by the drug. Both hospitalization and therapy are likely to reinforce the definition of the drug experience as insanity, for in both the patient will be required to "understand" that he is mentally ill as a precondition for return to the world.[23]

The physician then, does *not* treat the anxiety attack as a localized phenomenon, to be treated in a symptomatic way, but as an outbreak of a serious disease heretofore hidden. He may thus prolong the serious effects beyond the time they might have lasted had the user instead come into contact with other users. This analysis, of course, is frankly speculative; what is required is study of the way physicians treat cases of the kind described and, especially, comparative study of the effects of treatment of drug-induced anxiety attacks by physicians and by drug users.

Another category of non-users deserves mention. Literary men and journalists publicize definitions of drug experiences, either of their own invention or those borrowed from users, psychiatrists or police. (Some members of this category use drugs themselves, so it may be a little confusing to classify them as non-users; in any case, the definitions are provided outside the ordinary channels of communication in the drug-using world.) The definitions of literary men—novelists, essayists and poets—grow out of a long professional tradition, beginning with De Quincey's *Confessions,* and are likely to be colored by that tradition. Literary descriptions dwell on the fantasy component of the experience, on its cosmic and ineffable character, and on the

---

[22] It may be that a disproportionate number of cases will be brought to certain facilities. Ungerleider, *et al., op. cit.,* say (p. 392): "A larger number of admissions, both relative and real, than in other facilities in the Los Angeles area suggests the prevalence of a rumor that 'UCLA takes care of acid heads,' as several of our patients have told us."
[23] See Thomas Szasz, *The Myth of Mental Illness,* New York: Paul B. Hoeber, Inc., 1961.

threat of madness.[24] Such widely available definitions furnish some of the substance out of which a user may develop his own definition, in the absence of definitions from the drug-using culture.

Journalists use any of a number of approaches conventional in their craft; what they write is greatly influenced by their own professional needs. They must write about "news," about events which have occurred recently and require reporting and interpretation. Furthermore, they need "sources," persons to whom authoritative statements can be attributed. Both needs dispose them to reproduce the line taken by law enforcement officials and physicians, for news is often made by the passage of a law or by a public statement in the wake of an alarming event, such as a bizarre murder or suicide. So journalistic reports frequently dwell on the theme of madness or suicide, a tendency intensified by the newsman's desire to tell a dramatic story.[25] Some journalists, of course, will take the other side in the argument, but even then, because they argue against the theme of madness, the emphasis on that theme is maintained. Public discussion of drug use thus tends to strengthen those stereotypes that would lead users who suffer disturbing effects to interpret their experience as "going crazy."

AN HISTORICAL DIMENSION

A number of variables, then, affect the character of drug-induced experiences. It remains to show that the experiences themselves are likely to vary according to when they occur in the history of use of a given drug in a society. In particular, it seems likely that the experience of acute anxiety caused by drug use will so vary.

Consider the following sequence of possible events, which may be regarded as a natural history of the assimilation of an intoxicating drug by a society. Someone in the society discovers, rediscovers or invents a drug which has the properties described earlier. The ability of the drug to alter subjective experience in desirable ways becomes known to increasing numbers of people, and the drug itself simultaneously becomes available, along with the information needed to make its use effective. Use increases, but users do not have a sufficient amount of experience with the drug to form a stable conception of it as an object. They do not know what it can do to the mind, have no firm idea of the variety of effects it can produce, and are not sure how permanent or dangerous the effects are. They do not know if the effects can

[24] For a classic in the genre, see Fitzhugh Ludlow, *The Hasheesh Eater*, New York: Harper and Brothers, 1857. A more modern example is Alan Harrington, "A Visit to Inner Space," in Solomon, *op. cit.*, pp. 72–102.

[25] Examples are J. Kobler, "Don't Fool Around with LSD," *Saturday Evening Post*, 236 (November 2, 1963), pp. 30–32, and Noah Gordon, "The Hallucinogenic Drug Cult," *The Reporter*, 29 (August 15, 1963), pp. 35–43.

be controlled or how. No drug-using culture exists, and there is thus no authoritative alternative with which to counter the possible definition, when and if it comes to mind, of the drug experience as madness. "Psychotic episodes" occur frequently.

But individuals accumulate experience with the drug and communicate their experiences to one another. Consensus develops about the drug's subjective effects, their duration, proper dosages, predictable dangers and how they may be avoided; all these points become matters of common knowledge, validated by their acceptance in a world of users. A culture exists. When a user experiences bewildering or frightening effects, he has available to him an authoritative alternative to the lay notion that he has gone mad. Every time he uses cultural conceptions to interpret drug experiences and control his response to them, he strengthens his belief that the culture is indeed a reliable source of knowledge. "Psychotic episodes" occur less frequently in proportion to the growth of the culture to cover the range of possible effects and its spread to a greater proportion of users. Novice users, to whom the effects are most unfamiliar and who therefore might be expected to suffer most from drug-induced anxiety, learn the culture from older users in casual conversation and in more serious teaching sessions and are thus protected from the dangers of "panicking" or "flipping out."

The incidence of "psychoses," then, is a function of the stage of development of a drug-using culture. Individual experience varies with historical stages and the kinds of cultural and social organization associated with them.

Is this model a useful guide to reality? The only drug for which there is sufficient evidence to attempt an evaluation is marihuana; even there the evidence is equivocal, but it is consistent with the model. On this interpretation, the early history of marihuana use in the United States should be marked by reports of marihuana-induced psychoses. In the absence of a fully formed drug-using culture, some users would experience disquieting symptoms and have no alternative to the idea that they were losing their minds. They would turn up at psychiatric facilities in acute states of anxiety and doctors, eliciting a history of marihuana use, would interpret the episode as a psychotic breakdown. When, however, the culture reached full flower and spread throughout the user population, the number of psychoses should have dropped even though (as a variety of evidence suggests) the number of users increased greatly. Using the definitions made available by the culture, users who had unexpectedly severe symptoms could interpret them in such a way as to reduce or control anxiety and would thus no longer come to the attention of those likely to report them as cases of psychosis.

Marihuana first came into use in the United States in the 1920's and early '30's, and all reports of psychosis associated with its use date from approximately that period.[26] A search of both *Psychological Abstracts* and the *Cumu-*

---

[26] Bromberg, *op. cit.,* Curtis, *op. cit.,* and Nesbitt, *op. cit.*

lative Index Medicus (and its predecessors, the *Current List of Medical Literature* and the *Quarterly Index Medicus*) revealed no cases after 1940. The disappearance of reports of psychosis thus fits the model. It is, of course, a shaky index, for it depends as much on the reporting habits of physicians as on the true incidence of cases, but it is the only thing available.

The psychoses described also fit the model, insofar as there is any clear indication of a drug-induced effect. (The murder, suicide and death in an automobile accident reported by Curtis, for instance, are equivocal in this respect; in no case is any connection with marihuana use demonstrated other than that the people involved used it.)[27] The best evidence comes from the 31 cases reported by Bromberg. Where the detail given allows judgment, it appears that all but one stemmed from the person's inability to deal with either the perceptual distortion caused by the drug or with the panic at the thought of losing one's mind it created.[28] Bromberg's own interpretation supports this:

> In occasional instances, and these are the cases which are apt to come to medical attention, the anxiety with regard to death, insanity, bodily deformity and bodily dissolution is startling. The patient is tense, nervous, frightened; a state of panic may develop. Often suicide or assaultive acts are the result [of the panic]. The anxiety state is so common . . . that it can be considered a part of the intoxication syndrome.[29]
>
> The inner relationship between cannabis [marihuana] and the onset of a functional psychotic state is not always clear. The inner reaction to somatic sensation seems vital. Such reactions consisted of panic states which disappeared as soon as the stimulus (effects of the drug) faded.[30]

Even though Bromberg distinguishes between pure panic reactions and those in which some underlying mental disturbance was present (the "functional psychotic state" he refers to), he finds, as our model leads us to expect, that the episode is provoked by the user's interpretation of the drug effects in terms other than those contained in the drug-using culture.

The evidence cited is extremely scanty. We do not know the role of elements of the drug-using culture in any of these cases or whether the decrease in incidence is a true one. But we are not likely to do any better and, in the absence of conflicting evidence, it seems justified to take the model as an accurate representation of the history of marihuana use in the United States.

The final question, then, is whether the model can be used to interpret current reports of LSD-induced psychosis. Are these episodes the consequence of an early stage in the development of an LSD-using culture? Will the number of episodes decrease while the number of users rises, as the model leads us to predict?

[27] Curtis, *op. cit.*
[28] See Table 1 in Bromberg, *op. cit.*, pp. 6–7.
[29] *Ibid.*, p. 5.
[30] *Ibid.*, pp. 7–8.

LSD

We cannot predict the history of LSD by direct analogy to the history of mari-huana, for a number of important conditions may vary. We must first ask whether the drug has, apart from the definitions users impose on their experience, any demonstrated causal relation to psychosis. There is a great deal of controversy on this point, and any reading of the evidence must be tentative. My own opinion is that LSD has essentially the same characteristics as those described in the first part of this paper; its effects may be more powerful than those of other drugs that have been studied, but they too are subject to differing interpretations by users,[31] so that the mechanisms I have described can come into play.

The cases reported in the literature are, like those reported for marihuana, mostly panic reactions to the drug experience, occasioned by the user's interpretation that he has lost his mind, or further disturbance among people already quite disturbed.[32] There are no cases of permanent derangement directly traceable to the drug, with one puzzling exception (puzzling to those who report it as well as to me). In a few cases the visual and auditory distortions produced by the drug reoccur weeks or months after it was last ingested; this sometimes produces severe upset among those who experience it. Observers are at a loss to explain the phenomenon, except for Rosenthal, who proposes that the drug may have a specific effect on the nerve pathways involved in vision; but this theory, should it prove correct, is a long way from dealing with questions of possible psychosis.[33]

The whole question is confused by the extraordinary assertions about the effects of LSD made by both proponents and opponents of its use. Both sides agree that it has a very strong effect on the mind, disagreeing only as to whether this powerful effect is benign or malignant. Leary, for example, argues that we must "go out of our minds in order to use our heads,"[34] and that this can be accomplished by using LSD. Opponents[35] agree that it can drive you out of your mind, but do not share Leary's view that this is a desirable goal. In any case, we need not accept the premise simply because both parties to the controversy do.

Let us assume then, in the absence of more definitive evidence, that the drug does not in itself produce lasting derangement, that such psychotic episodes as are now reported are largely a result of panic at the possible meaning of the experience, that users who "freak out" do so because they fear they have permanently damaged their minds. Is there an LSD-using culture? In what stage of development is it? Are the reported episodes of psychosis congruent with what our model would predict, given that stage of development?

[31] Blum, *et al., op. cit.,* p. 42.
[32] See footnote 2, *supra.*
[33] Rosenthal, *op. cit.*
[34] Timothy Leary, "Introduction" to Solomon, *op. cit.,* p. 13.
[35] Frosch, *et al., op. cit.* and Ungerleider, *et al., op. cit.*

Here again my discussion must be speculative, for no serious study of this culture is yet available.[36] It appears likely, however, that such a culture is in an early stage of development. Several conceptions of the drug and its possible effects exists, but no stable consensus has arisen. Radio, television and the popular press present a variety of interpretations, many of them contradictory. There is widespread disagreement, even among users, about possible dangers. Some certainly believe that use (or injudicious use) can lead to severe mental difficulty.

At the same time, my preliminary inquiries and observations hinted at the development (or at least the beginnings) of a culture similar to that surrounding marihuana use. Users with some experience discuss their symptoms and translate from one idiosyncratic description into another, developing a common conception of effects as they talk. The notion that a "bad trip" can be brought to a speedy conclusion by taking thorazine by mouth (or, when immediate action is required, intravenously) has spread. Users are also beginning to develop a set of safeguards against committing irrational acts while under the drug's influence. Many feel, for instance, that one should take one's "trip" in the company of experienced users who are not under the drug's influence at the time; they will be able to see you through bad times and restrain you when necessary. A conception of the appropriate dose is rapidly becoming common knowledge. Users understand that they may have to "sit up with" people who have panicked as a result of the drug's effects, and they talk of techniques that have proved useful in this enterprise.[37] All this suggests that a common conception of the drug is developing which will eventually see it defined as pleasurable and desirable, with possible untoward effects that can however be controlled.

Insofar as this emergent culture spreads so that most or all users share the belief that LSD does not cause insanity, and the other understandings just listed, the incidence of "psychoses" should drop markedly or disappear. Just as with marihuana, the interpretation of the experience as one likely to produce madness will disappear and, having other definitions available to use in coping with the experience, users will treat the experience as self-limiting and not as a cause for panic.

The technology of LSD use, however, has features which will work in the opposite direction. In the first place, it is very easily taken; one need learn no special technique (as one must with marihuana) to produce the characteristic effects, for a sugar cube can be swallowed without instruction. This

---

[36] The book by Blum, et al., op. cit., attempts this, but leaves many important questions untouched.

[37] Ungerleider, et al., deny the efficacy of these techniques (pp. 391–392): "How do we know that persons taking LSD in a relaxed friendly environment with an experienced guide or 'sitter' will have serious side effects? We have no statistical data to answer this, but our impression (from our weekly group sessions) is that bad experiences were common with or without sitters and with or without 'the right environment.' This does not minimize the importance of suggestion in the LSD experience."

means that anyone who gets hold of the drug can take it in a setting where there are no experienced users around to redefine frightening effects and "normalize" them. He may also have acquired the drug without acquiring any of the presently developing cultural understandings so that, when frightening effects occur, he is left with nothing but current lay conceptions as plausible definitions. In this connection, it is important that a large amount of the published material by journalists and literary men places heavy emphasis on the dangers of psychosis.[38] It is also important that various medical facilities have become alerted to the possibility of patients (particularly college students and teenagers) coming in with LSD-induced psychoses. All these factors will tend to increase the incidence of "psychotic episodes," perhaps sufficiently to offset the dampening effect of the developing culture.

A second feature of LSD which works in the opposite direction is that it can be administered to someone without his knowledge, since it is colorless, tasteless and odorless. (This possibility is recognized in recent state legislation which specifies *knowing* use as a crime; no such distinction has been found necessary in laws about marihuana, heroin, peyote or similar drugs.) It is reported, for instance, that LSD has been put in a party punchbowl, so that large numbers of people have suffered substantial changes in their subjective experience without even knowing they had been given a drug that might account for the change. Under such circumstances, the tendency to interpret the experience as a sudden attack of insanity might be very strong.[39] If LSD continues to be available on the underground market without much difficulty, such events are likely to continue to occur. (A few apocalyptic types speak of introducing LSD into a city water supply—not at all impossible, since a small amount will affect enormous quantities of water—and thus "turning a whole city on." This might provoke a vast number of "psychoses," should it ever happen.)

In addition to these technological features, many of the new users of LSD, unlike the users of most illicit recreational drugs, will be people who, in addition to never having used any drug to alter their subjective experience before, will have had little or nothing to do with others who have used drugs in that way. LSD, after all, was introduced into the United States under very reputable auspices and has had testimonials from many reputable and conventional persons. In addition, there has been a great deal of favorable publicity to

---

[38] For journalistic accounts, see Kobler, *op. cit.;* Gordon, *op. cit.;* R. Coughlan, "Chemical Mind-Changers," *Life,* 54 (March 15, 1963); and H. Asher, "They Split My Personality," *Saturday Review,* 46 (June 1, 1963), pp. 39–43. See also two recent novels in which LSD plays a major role: B. H. Friedman, *Yarborough,* New York: Knopf, 1964; and Alan Harrington, *The Secret Swinger,* New York: World Publishing Co., 1966.

[39] Cf. Cohen and Ditman, "Complications. . . .," *op. cit.,* p. 161: "Accidental ingestion of the drug by individuals who are unaware of its nature has already occurred. This represents a maximally stressful event because the perceptual and ideational distortions then occur without the saving knowledge that they were drug induced and temporary."

accompany the less favorable—the possibility that the drug can do good as well as harm has been spread in a fashion that never occurred with marihuana. Finally, LSD has appeared at a time when the mores governing illicit drug use among young people seem to be changing radically, so that youth no longer reject drugs out of hand. Those who try LSD may thus not even have had the preliminary instruction in being "high" that most novice marihuana users have before first using it. They will, consequently, be even less prepared for the experience they have. (This suggests the prediction that marihuana users who experiment with LSD will show fewer untoward reactions than those who have had no such experience.)[40]

These features of the drug make it difficult to predict the number of mental upsets likely to be "caused" by LSD. If use grows, the number of people exposed to the possibility will grow. As an LSD-using culture develops, the proportion of those exposed who interpret their experience as one of insanity will decrease. But people may use the drug without being indoctrinated with the new cultural definitions, either because of the ease with which the drug can be taken or because it has been given to them without their knowledge, in which case the number of episodes will rise. The actual figure will be a vector made up of these several components.

A NOTE ON
THE OPIATES

The opiate drugs present an interesting paradox. In the drugs we have been considering, the development of a drug-using culture causes a decrease in rates of morbidity associated with drug use, for greater knowledge of the true character of the drug's effects lessens the likelihood that users will respond to those effects with uncontrolled anxiety. In the case of opiates, however, the greater one's knowledge of the drug's effects, the more likely it is that one will suffer its worst effect, addiction. As Lindesmith has shown,[41] one can only be addicted when he experiences physiological withdrawal symptoms, recognizes them as due to a need for drugs, and relieves them by taking another dose. The crucial step of recognition is most likely to occur when the user participates in a culture in which the signs of withdrawal are interpreted for what they are. When a person is ignorant of the nature of withdrawal sickness, and has some other cause to which he can attribute his discomfort (such as a medical problem), he may misinterpret the symptoms and thus escape addiction, as some of Lindesmith's cases demonstrate.[42]

This example makes clear how important the actual physiology of the drug response is in the model I have developed. The culture contains interpreta-

---

[40] Negative evidence is found in Ungerleider, *et al., op. cit.* Twenty-five of their 70 cases had previously used marihuana.
[41] Lindesmith, *op. cit.*
[42] *Ibid.,* cases 3, 5 and 6 (pp. 68–69, 71, 72).

tions of the drug experience, but these must be congruent with the drug's actual effects. Where the effects are varied and ambiguous, as with marihuana and LSD, a great variety of interpretations is possible. Where the effects are clear and unmistakable, as with opiates, the culture is limited in the possible interpretations it can provide. Where the cultural interpretation is so constrained, and the effect to be interpreted leads, in its most likely interpretation, to morbidity, the spread of a drug-using culture will increase morbidity rates.

CONCLUSION

The preceding analysis, to repeat, is supported at only a few points by available research; most of what has been said is speculative. The theory, however, gains credibility in several ways. Many of its features follow directly from a Meadian social psychology and the general plausibility of that scheme lends it weight. Furthermore, it is consistent with much of what social scientists have discovered about the nature of drug-induced experiences. In addition, the theory makes sense of some commonly reported and otherwise inexplicable phenomena, such as variations in the number of "psychotic" episodes attributable to recreational drug use. Finally, and much the least important, it is in accord with my haphazard and informal observations of LSD use.

The theory also has the virtue of suggesting a number of specific lines of research. With respect to the emerging "social problem" of LSD use, it marks out the following areas for investigation: the relation between social settings of use, the definitions of the drug's effects available to the user, and the subjective experiences produced by the drug; the mechanisms by which an LSD-using culture arises and spreads; the difference in experiences of participants and non-participants in that culture; the influence of each of the several factors described on the number of harmful effects attributable to the drug; and the typical response of physicians to LSD-induced anxiety states and the effect of that response as compared to the response made by experienced drug culture participants.

The theory indicates useful lines of research with respect to other common drugs as well. Large numbers of people take tranquilizers, barbiturates and amphetamines. Some frankly take them for "kicks" and are participants in drug-using cultures built around those drugs, while others are respectable middleclass citizens who probably do not participate in any "hip" user culture. Do these "square" users have some shared cultural understandings of their own with respect to use of these drugs? What are the differential effects of the drugs—both on subjective experience and on rates of morbidity associated with drug use—among the two classes of users? How do physicians handle the pathological effects of these drugs, with which they are relatively familiar, as compared to their handling of drugs which are only available illicitly?

The theory may have implications for the study of drugs not ordinarily used recreationally as well. Some drugs used in ordinary medical practice (such as the adrenocortical steroids) are said to carry a risk of provoking psychosis. It may be that this danger arises when the drug produces changes in subjective experience which the user does not anticipate, does not connect with the drug, and thus interprets as signs of insanity. Should the physician confirm this by diagnosing a "drug psychosis," a vicious circle of increasing validation of the diagnosis may ensue. The theory suggests that the physician using such drugs might do well to inquire carefully into the feelings that produce such anxiety reactions, interpret them to the patient as common, transient and essentially harmless side effects, and see whether such action would not control the phenomenon. Drugs that have been incriminated in this fashion would make good subjects for research designed to explore some of the premises of the argument made here.

The sociologist may find most interesting the postulated connection between historical stages in the development of a culture and the nature of individual subjective experience. Similar linkages might be discovered in the study of political and religious movements. For example, at what stages in the development of such movements are individuals likely to experience euphoric and ecstatic feelings? How are these related to shifts in the culture and organization of social relations within the movement? The three-way link between history, culture and social organization, and the person's subjective state may point the way to a better understanding than we now have of the social bases of individual experience.

18

A SYMBOLIC
INTERACTIONIST VIEW
OF ADDICTION

Alfred R. Lindesmith

I SHALL BE CONCERNED in this paper with problems that arise in the search for a general theory concerning addiction to opiate-type drugs. There are, of course, phenomena of different sorts involved in addiction, and they are appropriately dealt with by various specialties. Since much dispute and misunderstanding in this area stems from the multidisciplinary nature of the total problem and a diversity of methodological assumptions, I shall try to state explicitly those assumptions which will be basic in the subsequent discussion. It should be noted that because I will be concerned only with matters that seem relevant to the development of a general theory at the level of social psychology, and because of limitations of space and time, many aspects of addiction will necessarily be slighted or omitted entirely. This in no way implies that these aspects are regarded as of no importance or that they may not be of central importance to someone asking other kinds of questions.

One could, I think, frequently predict in advance what kind of theory of addiction will be proposed by a given investigator from knowledge of his training and intellectual background, for each tends to find in the phenomena confirmation of the general theories of human behavior which he brings with him to the study. Insofar as this is true, it implies that theories of addiction are based upon something other than the facts of addiction. If the data serve only to confirm diverse preexisting convictions, the resulting controversy is likely to be a noisy and futile interdisciplinary squabble not conducive to the convergence of professional opinion, which is essential to scientific progress.

On the assumption that such controversy would be more productive if disputing theorists explicitly stated what their basic methodological assumptions are, I shall state four which are basic to the remarks on the addiction problem made here: (1) Addiction must first of all be defined so that we know what we are talking about and, ideally, so that we can sort all persons into two contrasting categories, addicts and nonaddicts, with a small additional number who are in a state of transition from one category to the other. (2) A definition of addiction as a behavioral phenomenon is not an arbitrary matter which each investigator can make to suit his own tastes, but should rather be the result of an investigative process which specifies what the essential or common aspects of the behavior in fact are. (3) A general theory of addiction must be applicable to all the cases covered by the definition, not merely to some or most of them or, what is worse, merely to those that a given researcher happens to be interested in. (4) An acceptable general theory should be falsifiable; i.e., it should suggest or imply the nature and possible source of the empirical evidence which will definitely discredit or disprove it if it is false.

Of course, it is one thing to affirm these principles and another to apply them in the study of complex human behavior. Nevertheless, when a theorist makes his assumptions explicit, the critic is in a position of knowing whether he should discuss the evidence or concern himself with the theorist's conceptions of scientific method and logic.

DEFINITION OF
ADDICTION

There is actually considerable confusion about the definition of addiction. There are, for example, some who equate it with physical dependence and tolerance. Although this condition is indispensable in the origin of addiction and although it is highly important that it be investigated and explained, addiction as a behavioral phenomenon cannot be defined in terms of it alone if one accepts the previously stated methodological principles. If physical dependence is equated with addiction, no specific unitary form of behavior has been identified; for the definition would extend to lower animals, to infants born of drug-using mothers, and to unconscious patients receiving drugs without their knowledge, and it would not cover addicts who are forced to abstain from using drugs solely because of incarceration or who do so voluntarily.

I recall a discussion with an investigator who held the common view that addiction arises from defects of personality but also insisted that lower animals, even decorticate dogs, that are given morphine become addicts. To maintain both of these views, one would also be logically required to attribute the addiction of the dogs to personality defects. Other writers have concluded, also inappropriately, that, because lower animals and newborn infants can be addicts (as defined by them), addiction has nothing whatever to do with personality, motivations, beliefs, and so on, and is purely a biological matter.

Additional problems are indicated by the various terms applied to persons who have been addicted but are not currently using drugs, either because they are locked up or because they are voluntarily abstaining. The former are ordinarily called addicts, but sometimes they are not. Those who are voluntarily abstaining may be called "former addicts," "nonaddicts," "post-addicts," or simply "addicts who are not using drugs." If a person is declared to be an addict even though he is not using drugs, an adequate behavioral definition must cover the situation and be equally applicable to addicts who are using drugs and to those who are not.

A further problem is that of defining a "cured addict." The World Health Organization has proposed a definition, often cited, which includes the following: "Drug addiction is a state of periodic or chronic intoxication, detrimental to the individual and to society, produced by the repeated consumption of a drug. . . ." Apart from the question of whether it is correct to say that a heroin addict is in a state of intoxication, this definition suggests that if the regular use of an opiate has effects which are not demonstrably detrimental to the individual or the society, such a person would not be an addict. There are many studies which have made the point that there are addicts in whom detrimental effects appear to be absent or minimal and that there are some in whom the effects appear to be beneficial.[6,7,17,18,29,30] Addicts of the latter sort might be former alcoholics, persons with certain types of mental disease, certain sex offenders and violent criminals, and addicted persons receiving drugs medically for the alleviation of pain. It is inappropriate that a scientific definition include a moralistic judgment such as that implied by the word "detrimental."

My inclination is to regard that behavior designated as the "craving" for drugs as the central and defining feature of addiction and to think of the tendency to relapse and of other commonly emphasized features as corollary aspects. From this standpoint a person does not need to be using drugs to be an addict and he might be physically dependent upon them without being addicted. Those who have experimented with the lower animals generally assert that the characteristic craving for drugs in human addicts cannot be induced in lower species.[9]

The most difficult problem posed by this kind of definition is to identify the craving for drugs in the nonusing addict who is voluntarily abstaining or locked up in an institution where drugs are not available. Abstaining addicts frequently assert with evident sincerity their intention never to use drugs again, and they may also deny that they feel a desire to use them. Nevertheless, such persons do relapse. It is commonly believed that, given the appropriate circumstances and temptations, almost anyone who has been "hooked" will resume his habit. This suggests that the impulse to relapse exists in a latent or unconscious form, which the person himself often does not recognize. Another possibility is that the craving of the nonusing addict is partly based upon cognitive factors, i.e., upon knowledge gained from experiencing the drug's effects. The person who has been "hooked" might be compared with one who has had his first sex experience; both have learned things which it will be exceedingly difficult for them ever to forget, even if they do not repeat the experience.

In characterizing the behavior of addicts for the purposes of developing a general theory, it is necessary to avoid taking any particular limited historical aspect as representative of the total picture. For example, during the long history of opium use it was first used orally for thousands of years; later it began to be smoked. Also opium has been used in all social classes and in an extremely wide range of contexts. Morphine addiction dates only from the beginning, and hypodermic addiction from about the middle, of the nineteenth century. Intravenous injection of heroin is exclusively a twentieth-century phenomenon. Allowance must be made for all of these variations. If this is not done, theories are likely to be based on passing contemporary fads. We need to remember that, although hipsters and adolescent delinquents are frequently addicted in our contemporary society, they were not during most of the previous century[12] and are not in most other Western nations. The emphasis on addiction in the underworld needs to be balanced by a consideration of the fact that the most persistent ecological feature of addiction rates in the Western world has been the high prevalence of addiction in the medical profession and its ancillary professions.

THE EFFECTS
OF OPIATES

For one who wishes to learn of the effects of an opiate-type drug as perceived by the user, there are only two primary sources of data: One must either talk with and observe someone who uses it, or one must oneself use the drug. The former method is generally preferred, and the latter carefully avoided, even by those who hold to theories which imply that they would not become addicted. Considering that this leaves the addict as the main source of information, there is an astonishing disregard and even lack of interest in what he has to say. The addict is said to be unreliable, a pathologic liar, and prone to rationalize, and it is therefore assumed permissible for a given writer to attribute effects to the drug which the users deny experiencing.

The assessment of the drug's psychologic and other effects is a matter of central importance to theory, for every theory rests upon some sort of assumption of what the essential effects are. The matter is confused by a number of factors which are peculiar to opiate-type drugs but which are not operative in the case of alcohol or marihuana, or at least not to the same extent. In the first place, the "hopped-up dope fiend" in the throes of uncanny psychologic experiences is a popular stereotype, which, by frequent repetition, has acquired a certain authority. Then, too, the effects of regular doses over a period of time change so that the effects upon the addict are not comparable with those upon the beginner. Effects also vary from person to person; they vary according to social context; and they differ with different methods of administration. Finally, distinctions must be made between impact effects immediately following an injection and subsequent effects, and one must discriminate between those which may be regarded as part of the pharmacology of the situation and those which are psychogenic in origin in the sense that they arise from such factors as the addict's craving, his knowledge of what he is taking, and other similar influences.

Perhaps one of the most interesting features of the effects of drugs is the marked differences at all stages of drug use between the reports of addicts and those of nonaddicts or persons who do not know what they are receiving. It has been observed, for example, that when nonaddicts were given small injections of heroin or placebos without knowing which, those who received the placebos reported somewhat greater pleasurable effects than those who took heroin.[3] Isbell has observed that effects generally perceived as unpleasant by the uninitiated, when the drug is first used, are valued positively by the addict who has learned to regard them as evidence of the potency of the shot.[16] The hospital patient receiving regular morphine injections without being addicted makes reports on the drug's effects which bear little resemblance to those that addicts make and shows, in contrast to the latter, relatively little need for increased doses after a certain minimal level is reached.

In general, one may say that many of the perceived or reported effects of drugs upon addicts are not so much effects of the drug as they are of the user's craving for drugs. Although it is true that the addict craves drugs because he likes the effects, there is also truth in the statement that he likes the effects because he craves the drug. Future research with the use of placebo techniques may well unravel some of these matters which presently seem paradoxical. There is reasonably reliable evidence at hand to indicate, for example, that addicts can be deceived into believing that they are under the influence of drugs when in fact they are not and that they are not under the influence of drugs when in fact they are.[7,25] This assertion does not apply to intravenous injection or to the addict suffering acute withdrawal distress. However, it appears that if the method of intake is changed, say, from intravenous to oral use, and control of the dose is taken away from the user, he is likely to complain that he cannot feel the effects and under certain conditions may reach the conclusion that he is not receiving drugs, and he may then even exhibit withdrawal symptoms.

Shortly after the Second World War it was thought for a time that a new form of heroin addiction which did not involve withdrawal distress had been discovered. What had actually happened was that the drugs were being so heavily diluted that some addicts, without their knowing it, had been virtually taken off drugs by the peddlers and were using primarily sugar of milk flavored with a little quinine. Mr. Harry J. Anslinger has provided an interesting account of a prominent lady of Washington society, a personal friend of his, who was addicted to Demerol and who was successfully taken off drugs by means of a gradual ambulatory withdrawal without her realizing it.[1]

Chopra has reported from India on a device employed by him which involved administering opiates to addicts, who failed to recognize the effects.[7] The device was used to distinguish patients with genuine medical complaints from addicts who came to the hospital faking symptoms in order to be given opiates. Chopra prepared a tonic, called "tonic X," which had opium, disguised in taste and smell, as its essential ingredient. Persons who complained of symptoms for which opiates were customarily given were provided with this tonic, and it was found that the malingering addicts invariably betrayed themselves by denying that they felt any relief.

Some of the difficulties involved in accepting the popular conception that addicts use drugs to obtain an ecstatic sense of euphoria may be illustrated in the statement of an addict published in December, 1917, in *American Medicine*. The author, whose identity was known to the editor and whose good faith was vouched for by him, was a prominent member of the New York Bar. After relating that he had been given morphine for nearly a year by his physician to relieve attacks of gallstones and gallbladder inflammation, the author described his inability to get along without drugs and commented as follows:

> I have since then kept my daily amount of morphine medication at a minimum which permitted me to work and maintain good health and bodily function. The idea which I have heard so often expressed, that addicts tend to increase their daily intake of narcotic, is certainly untrue in my case, and there seems to me no reason nor temptation to do so. . . . As I have never experienced the slightest pleasurable or sensually enjoyable sensations from the administration of morphine, there seems to me no foundation for this prevalent idea of tendency to increase. It may be true of the degenerate who has become addicted, but it certainly is untrue in my case, and must be untrue of the thousands like me. . . ." [4,11,22]

Reports of this sort are not uncommon from persons who do not use the drug intravenously, who are not members of the underworld subculture of users, and who become addicted through therapeutic use. If one also considers that the addicted individual commonly reports upon a great many unpleasant effects associated with addiction, such as those of anxiety, fear, remorse, and guilt, as well as various painful physical effects, the pleasure theory seems wholly inadequate.[24,29]

An additional inconsistency of the pleasure theory is indicated by the fact that marihuana seems greatly superior to opium as a pleasure-producing agent; its pleasures do not fade as do those of opium with continued use; its psychologic effects are described with enthusiasm and hyperbole; its pleasurable effects are not counterbalanced by the extensive evil social and physical consequences which ordinarily bedevil heroin addicts. If pleasure is the key, marhuana should be the prime drug of addiction, far ahead of either opium or alcohol.

It appears that perhaps the only generalization about the effects of an opiate upon addicts that one can make with relatively complete assurance is that this drug, regardless of any other circumstances, does relieve the pains of withdrawal.

If addicts are readily available as subjects, various types of experiments suggest themselves which might help to discriminate between various aspects and phases of the psychologic effects of opiates. For example, drugs and placebos might be administered by oral route, by subcutaneous injection, by intravenous injection, and perhaps by means of suppositories,[28] to groups of addicts under circumstances which would indicate what the possibilities of deceiving the addict are and how his perceptions of effects are altered by knowledge of what he is getting. We might thus be enabled to distinguish more sharply between the essential effects of the drug and those that are peculiar to a specific mode of use. Systematic observations on the perceived effects by nonaddicted hospital patients who receive the drug regularly would also be of great value for comparative purposes.

THE MOTIVES
OF ADDICTS

The motives for using opiate-type drugs which addicts report or which are attributed to them by others are legion, and it is probably impossible to make any simple kind of generalization about them or to find any particular motive or set of motives that can be ascribed to all addicts. The situation is complicated by the fact that the motives for first use characteristically differ from those for continued use to the point of physical dependence, that motives for use after dependence is established are not the same as those at earlier stages, and that motives for relapse have their own characteristics. Writers in this field commonly fail to distinguish between the various stages and often seize upon a single type of motive common at some point in the process among addicts of a particular group or type, project it into all phases, and hail it as the essential motive of all addicts.

The social psychologist, who is committed to the idea that an explanation of the behavior of addicts must be sought in motives, has to contend with the fact that many persons have become addicted without ever themselves taking drugs voluntarily. This still occurs now and then in the course of medical practice, and during the nineteenth century it happened more frequently than now. Few, if any, substances have been used for more purposes in medicine than has opium, which was a prime therapeutic agent for more than 2,000 years. During these centuries there were undoubtedly millions of persons who became addicted as a simple consequence of following the instructions of a physician and many others who became addicted by having the drug administered to them without being consulted or instructed in the matter. It has been suggested that addicts of this sort should, in all fairness to them, not be called addicts (Ref. 2, p. 40), and of course it would be a great advantage to a psychologic theory of addiction if convincing rationalizations could be found for ignoring these cases.

The initial trial of opiates among those who use drugs voluntarily commonly occurs in our society as a result of such motives as the desire to have thrills, to satisfy curiosity, and to do what others are doing; sometimes, no doubt, using opiates is also a gesture of defiance, rebellion, protest, or despair. In other cultures, depending upon the popular beliefs and fads of the time, opium has been used for religious purposes, as an aphrodisiac to prolong sexual pleasure by delaying the orgasm, to restore fertility or cure impotence, to relieve fatigue or the tedium of old age, as a popular remedy for countless diseases, and simply as a matter of social custom. Opium smoking appeared as a passing fad in a relatively elite section of the American underworld during the late nineteenth and early twentieth centuries. Preoccupation with drugs, including heroin, emerged as a fad during this century among persons variously designated as "hipsters," "cool cats," "beats," and so on.[12] Drug-using fads have also appeared in the upper classes, for example, among intellectuals and literati.

Whatever the motives for initial use may be, they tend to change with continued use because the effects of the drug change, but initial motives may also persist until addiction is established. Sometimes, persons who have begun to use drugs will abandon their use before they become addicted. After physical dependence is established, new motives commonly appear; the most important of these are avoidance, postponement, or alleviation of the pain of withdrawal. But again, not all of those who become physically dependent upon drugs become addicts.

The motives attributed to addicts are often thought to be linked with the effects of the drug, although this is not necessarily the case; for the drug may be used to the point of addiction for the sake of an effect which it does not in fact produce as, for example, when it is used to restore fertility or sexual potency. In most theories it is assumed that the motivations of the user are based upon the euphoric effect. Since this effect tends to be greatly reduced or eliminated when physical dependence is established, and is, moreover, heavily counteracted by many dysphoric or unpleasant effects, it is difficult to see how this position can be maintained.

If one considers the variety of social contexts in which opiates have been and are being used, it seems necessary to admit that there are many paths that lead to addiction and that there is no motive or set of motives which can be said to be characteristic of all addicts. Certainly no general motivational theory can be based on a particular group of addicts using drugs in a certain way and in a specific social context without taking into account the multitudinous other patterns that are known.

A new and popular idea in sociologic circles has been developed in recent years from the study of young, urban, delinquent male addicts in this country. It is that addiction and other forms of deviance arise from what is called "anomie." This term is taken to refer to the discrepancy between such culturally indoctrinated goals as that of achieving success and status and the perceived or available means of reaching such goals. The inner conflict or frustration that results is thought to exert pressure upon the individual to resort to some sort of adaptive device to relieve tension. Addiction is conceived of as one such device by which the person escapes his problem by renouncing society's goals as well as the established norms for attaining them. The addict, in short, is said to be a "retreatist," who solves his problems by withdrawing from them into a quasi-private world dominated by the self-contained "kick" of the heroin fix. Cloward and Ohlin have elaborated on this view by suggesting that the persons who are double failures, that is, in both the legitimate and the criminal worlds, are those who tend to become addicts.[8]

Although it is not clear whether Cloward and Ohlin regarded their hypothesis merely as a special theory for some adolescent drug-using gang members in contemporary America or as a general theory of addiction, there is clearly some disposition to regard it as the latter. As such, it is inapplicable to addiction in the medical profession, to the opium smokers of the nineteenth century, and to addiction arising from the popular or medical-therapeutic use of opiates. It also is inapplicable to addicts who are successful criminals, whatever that may mean. It is well known that most addicted thieves in this country, like most nonaddicted thieves, are of the petty variety, who might be called failures. However, there are also numerous exceptional addicted shoplifters, pickpockets, con men, and others who have extraordinary criminal competence. Some of these, it is thought, may owe some of their success to the fact of their addiction, which provides them with extraordinary motivation to practice their skills. In the legitimate world also, highly successful and even eminent persons become addicted, and some of these retain their eminence, their occupations, and their social positions while they are addicts. Although there are admittedly few such cases, their theoretical significance is not diminished by their limited numbers.

The conception of the addict as a "retreatist" is also inaccurate, for the newly addicted individual quickly discovers that the demands of his habit, especially the economic ones, force him to attach more, rather than less, significance to monetary success and put him into an extraordinarily active and abrasive contact with society. De Quincey stated the matter as follows:

> The opium-eater loses none of his moral sensibilities or aspirations; he wishes and longs as earnestly as ever to realize what he believes possible, and feels to be exacted by duty; but his intellectual apprehension of what is possible infinitely outruns his power, not of execution only, but even of power to attempt.[10]

This statement contradicts the anomie theory of addiction, for it affirms as a consequence of addiction what the theory takes as a cause or antecedent.

The fact of illegality is a matter of the greatest importance in determining the nature of the drug problem, the ecology of addiction, and the motives for which drugs are used. The consequences that follow from legal definitions and practices need to be examined in greater depth than has thus far been done. One obvious consequence is to create a synthetic association between addiction and criminality. Another is to create a pattern of availability of drugs which not only makes them accessible to, but almost literally thrusts them upon the attention of, the underworld. The correspondence between addiction in the medical profession and the slums is not to be found in the area of motivation and personality but rather in the availability of narcotics.

THE ADDICTION-PRONE
PERSONALITY

The way in which personality types said to be predisposed to addiction are characterized appears to depend strongly on the nature of the investigator's specific experiences with addicts and upon his intellectual training and orientation. In this respect there has been little material change since 1928, when Terry and Pellens made the following observations:

> The evidence submitted in support of such statements, in practically every instance coming under our notice, has been secured *after* the development of the addiction and was not based on knowledge of the individual's condition *prior* to addiction. . . . It may be said with equal truth, considering the claims of those who state that certain types of individuals comprise the bulk of chronic opium users, that for one reason or another in the writings of many, "types" as generally understood are not considered as such until extraneous circumstances, possibly even the use of the drug itself, have altered the individual or group in question. . . . Wherever the truth may lie, the evidence submitted in support of the statements appearing in this chapter dealing with type predisposition and with the effects of opium on mental and ethical characteristics is, in our opinion, insufficient to warrant the opinions expressed. . . . In general, however, it would appear from the data submitted that this condition is not restricted to any social, economic, mental or other group; that there is no type which may be called the habitual user of opium, but that all types are actually or potentially users (Ref. 27, pp. 514–16).

The direct and indirect consequences of addiction have still not been sorted out, and there is much confusion between the antecedents and consequences of addiction. The legal-system process by which the addict is exposed, arrested, and processed itself has tremendous effects upon personality and motivation and tends to make all addicts look somewhat alike. Investigators are strongly disposed to project the apparent postaddiction similarities of addicts upon the person prior to addiction and have long engaged in what may well be a futile search for the addiction-prone personality type.

In addition to considering the effects of institutionalization upon addicts, one must also consider its effects upon investigators. The institutionalized researcher or observer who is accustomed to handling inmates in an authoritarian setting tends to assign certain types of traits to those over whom he exercises power. He is in a unique position to note the recalcitrance of inmates who do not respond as it is thought they should to the benevolent and well-intentioned programs imposed upon them. By long familiarity with institutional life he sometimes comes to attach little significance to the loss of liberty by others, and he may have difficulty in understanding why addicts seem not to understand or appreciate that they are being locked up for their own good.

There is substantial political and sociologic literature on the effects of power both upon those who govern and those who are governed. A particularly relevant portion of this literature analyzes "total institutions," of which the prison is an example.

Goffman has observed that the staff of such an establishment ". . . tends to evolve what may be thought of as a *theory of human nature*. As an implicit part of institutional perspective, this theory rationalizes the scene, provides a subtle means of maintaining social distance from inmates and a stereotyped view of them, and gives sanction to the treatment accorded them." [14] Staff stereotypes of the inmates are consensually validated in private conversation between staff members and by feedback from indoctrinated inmates and sycophants who have learned the staff vocabulary. There is no better illustration of this point than Marie Nyswander's candid description of the changes in her attitudes toward addicts which occurred when she left Lexington and began dealing with them in private medical practice.[23]

The prison inmate, Goffman observes, feels mortified, humiliated, and threatened by the impersonal routine and petty requirements of institutional life. He is stripped of his autonomy and his possessions, his privacy and identity are violated, and he feels reduced to almost childlike dependence on his captors. As Sykes has remarked, "In a very fundamental sense, a man perpetually locked up in a cage is no longer a man at all; rather, he is a semi-human organism with a number. The identity of the individual, both to himself and to others, is largely compounded of the web of symbolic communications by which he is linked to the external world."[26]

An astonishing variety of terms have been employed in the attempt to characterize the addict, particular types of addicts, and the addiction-prone personality, usually with the assumption that the attribute named has some etiologic significance. From a small segment of the literature the following examples have been gleaned: "alienated," "frustrated," "passive psychopath," "aggressive psychopath," "emotionally unstable," "nomadic," "inebriate," "narcissistic," "dependent," "sociopath," "hedonistic," "childlike," "paranoid," "rebellious," "hostile," "infantile," "neurotic," "over-attached to the mother," "retreatist," "cyclothymic," "constitutionally immoral," "hysterical," "neurasthenic," "hereditarily neuropathic," "weak character and will," "lack of moral sense," "self-indulgent," "introspective," "extroverted," "self-conscious," "motivational immaturity," "pseudo-psychopathic delinquent," and, finally, "essentially normal."[2,27]

It is of interest to observe that in this list opposite traits are sometimes mentioned; that most of the same terms are applied to other groups, such as alcoholics, prisoners, tramps, sex offenders, and thieves; that almost all these descriptions are based on observations of addicts in captivity or on secondhand reports of such observations; that many of the alleged attributes are clearly effects or integral aspects of addiction, rather than antecedents, and that all of them are poorly defined concepts, frequently used simply as expressions of disapproval. The very multiplicity of these characterizations is scientifically embarrassing, and their number is increasing.

The process of evaluating the addict's personality is usually one that involves interaction or a series of transactions between two parties, each of whom inevitably evaluates the other. Just as there tends to be a staff stereotype of inmates, so also are there inmate stereotypes of the staff, and both of these, and the situation which gives rise to them, ought to be known if one wishes to give an objective evaluation. Like inmates, investigators also have personality needs, peculiarities, emotional problems, and other personal attributes which are likely to influence the judgments they make of incarcerated deviants as heavily stigmatized as drug addicts are. That psychodynamic and cultural factors influence evaluations of addicts' personalities is strongly suggested by the persistence with which even tough-minded investigators use appellations which lack any semblance of objective or operational definition. Whenever general intuitive evaluations are replaced by specific objective tests accompanied by the use of adequate control populations, the alleged special attributes of addicts either disappear entirely or are found both among addicts and nonaddicts, with a somewhat greater frequency in one group than in the other.[13]

A GENERAL THEORY
OF ADDICTION

Instead of asking "What are the motives for using drugs?" I have approached the matter in another way by, in effect, rephrasing the question to read, "What is the experience in which the craving for drugs is produced?" The latter question does not inquire into motives and cannot be answered in terms of them. The suggestion which I made in 1947 as an answer to this question was that the characteristic craving of the opiate addict is generated in the repetition of the experience of using drugs to relieve withdrawal distress, provided that this distress is properly understood by the user.[20,21] The essential idea involved was not original with me but may be found in the literature, although without elaboration (Ref. 27, pp. 601–2).

I feel that the strength of this position has increased. The attempt to account for addiction in terms of an addiction-prone personality type or in terms of the euphoric effects of drugs seems more inadequate and confused than ever now that more investigators have entered the field. It seems especially remarkable to me that Wikler, from a very different background and basic orientation, has recently suggested a theory which seems to be very similar in many essential respects to mine.[24] In the study of alcoholism there are also some signs of a significant convergence of interest on withdrawal symptoms as a matter of critical significance.

The position that I have proposed has been misinterpreted in a number of ways. For example, some have interpreted it to mean that a person becomes an addict when he defines himself as such; others, that addiction arises from and consists of the motive of avoiding or alleviating withdrawal distress; and still others, that an individual becomes an addict in the instant of time when he first experiences and understands withdrawal distress. Actually I did not intend to say any of these things.

The argument was that when the experience of withdrawal distress is assimilated and grasped conceptually, the individual thereafter learns to crave the drug and acquires the behavior and attitudes of the addict from the repetition of the experience. No one can be a full-fledged nonaddict in one moment of time and a full-fledged addict in the next. From the repetition of the experience, in what may be called a cognitive-conditioning process, the individual's responses to and attitudes toward the drug are established as a conceptually controlled pattern. The withdrawal distress is indispensable only in the origin of this pattern, not in its continuance. The person does not become an addict because he defines himself as one, but defines himself as an addict because he realizes that he is one. An addict does not relapse because of withdrawal distress but because of the previously established craving, which may be thought of as something like the results of conditioning in the lower animals except that it is conceptually elaborated. It is, I think, of considerable relevance to the position that abstaining addicts when placed in a position that tempts them to relapse, sometimes experience, along with a desire for drugs, some of the actual symptoms of withdrawal, indicating a basic, psychologically primitive linkage between the two phenomena. It is also pertinent to observe that the addict's anticipatory anxiety about having his drugs cut off greatly intensifies his reaction to incipient withdrawal symptoms and by the same token enhances the perceived effects of a shot.

This position has some pronounced theoretical and practical virtues. For example, it offers a ready explanation of the relatively low or absent addictive potential of a number of substances that produce considerable euphoria, such as marihuana and cocaine. By linking addiction with linguistic and conceptual processes found only in socialized human beings, it harmonizes with the fact that most of those who have administered opiate-type drugs to lower animals take the view of Dr. Maurice H. Seevers: "In any [lower] animal that we have ever studied there is no such thing as development of actual desire for continuous repetition of the drug experience."[9] The origin of addiction is attributed not to influences which are present in some instances and absent in others, but to experiences which all addicts undoubtedly have.

From the point of view of verifiability, or falsifiability, as stated at the beginning of this paper, the proposed hypothesis implies that if a randomly selected group of ordinary adults were to receive regular shots of morphine or heroin over a prolonged period of time in accordance with the other conditions specified, all of them would become addicted regardless of personality traits, character, social class, or motives.

The contrary view could conceivably be tested by a similar experiment with a previously identified group composed 50 per cent of psychopaths (or addiction-prone types) and 50 per cent of nonpsychopaths. In this view, the prediction would then presumably be that the psychopaths would become addicted and that the others would not. It is, of course, interesting to note that persons who hold to the addiction-prone-personality theory are generally very careful not to test it on themselves even when they are certain that they do not qualify as the addiction-prone type.

The view proposed by the author emphasizes the wisdom of this sort of caution and may shed some light on famous last words of persons before being addicted, to the effect that they will not become addicts because they are not the type. From this standpoint, addiction is based, not upon the initial effects of opiates, which are experienced by many persons who never become addicted and which diminish or vanish about the time physical dependence is well established, but rather upon effects which appear only after physical dependence is established. If we can agree that simple hedonistic theories which seek to account for human behavior in terms of rational assessment of pain and pleasure are unacceptable today, this also is a point in favor of the theory. The addict's craving, it is implied, is not a rational assessment or choice of any sort, but basically an irrational compulsion arising from the repetition of a sequence of experiences in a process like that which leads to a conditioned response. It is assumed that the principal difference between the consequences of the conditioning process in human beings and lower animals lies in the fact that human beings are capable of conceptual thought and language behavior, and therefore the craving is symbolically elaborated, and responses arising from it are directed or controlled by conceptual processes.

The psychologist D. O. Hebb has suggested that the human hunger for food is comparable with the hunger for opium and that both come to be controlled by conceptual processes. He observes, concerning the hunger for food: "Finally, the development of conceptual processes controlling eating makes possible an association of eating with other conceptual processes."[15]

Following this cue, it may be said that the observed effects of addiction upon personality and character follow from the indirect conceptually mediated effects which addiction has upon the person's conceptions of himself and his status in society. They assuredly cannot be attributed directly to the drug, for in that case the same effects would be found in hospital patients who receive drugs without their knowledge and in persons dying of cancer.

There is a measure of agreement here with the psychoanalytically oriented approach, which also rejects the hedonistic calculus and conceives of the craving as a basically irrational and unconscious compulsion which gets to be symbolically elaborated in very complex ways in the motivations and rationalizations of addicts.[5] There are also, of course, many points of disagreement and dissimilarity, which I will not attempt to discuss.

Finally, it should be remembered that if any given general theory of the origin of the craving for drugs could be conclusively proved, this would by no means answer all questions. Indeed, if one may judge from experience in other fields, the problems would multiply rather than diminish. There are, moreover, many important problems with respect to addiction which, although related, are analytically separate and distinct from those which have been considered here. For example, it is of the greatest importance that we know more than we do about the individual motives and the social environments conducive to the abuse of drugs; a relatively unexplored problem is that of tracing the effects of availability of drugs upon addiction rates and exploring the relationships between control policies, legal definitions, availability, and patterns of use; an area of theoretical interest is the comparison of various forms of addiction; the determination of how addicts are selected in a statistical sense from exposed populations is an important matter. And it would be of the greatest interest to examine and attempt to account for the various public attitudes toward addicts and the narcotics problem, including such matters as changing images of the addict projected by the mass media, the addict as a scapegoat, vested interests in the narcotics problem, and many other similar matters.

REFERENCES

[1] Anslinger, H. J., and Oursler, Will: "The Murderers: The Shocking Story of the Narcotics Gangs," p. 175, Farrar, Straus & Cudahy, Inc., New York, 1961.

[2] Ausubel, D. P.: "Drug Addiction: Physiological, Psychological, and Sociological Aspects," Random House, Inc., New York, 1958.

[3] Beecher, Henry K.: "Measurement of Subjective Responses," p. 321, Oxford University Press, Fair Lawn, N.J., 1959.

[4] Bishop, Ernest S.: "The Narcotic Drug Problem," p. 137, The Macmillan Company, New York, 1921.

[5] Chessick, R. D., The "Pharmacogenic Orgasm" in the Drug Addict, *Arch. Gen. Psychiat.*, 3:545 (1960).

[6] Chopra, R. N.: The Present Position of the Opium Habit in India, *Indian J. Med. Res.*, 16:389 (1928).

[7] Chopra, R. N. and Bose, J. P.: Psychological Aspects of Opium Addiction, *Indian Med. Gaz.*, 66:663 (1931).

[8] Cloward, R. A., and Ohlin, L. E.: "Delinquency and Opportunity: A Theory of Delinquent Gangs," p. 179, The Free Press of Glencoe, New York, 1960.

[9] N.Y. Academy of Medicine, Committee on Public Health Relations: "Conferences on Drug Addiction among Adolescents," p. 123, McGraw-Hill Book Company, New York, 1953.

[10] De Quincey, Thomas: "Confessions of an English Opium-eater," p. 163, Mershon, New York (undated).

[11] Emmerich, Otto: "Die Heilung des chronischen Morphinismus," p. 123, Berlin, 1894.

[12] Finestone, H.: Cats, Kicks and Color, *Social Problems*, 5:2 (1957).

[13] Gerard, D. L., and Kornetsky, C.:

Adolescent Opiate Addiction: A Study of Control and Addict Subject, *Psychiat. Quart.*, 24:457–486 (1955).

[14] Goffman, Erving: "On the Characteristics of Total Institutions: Staff-Inmate Relations," in D. Cressey (ed.), "The Prison," p. 78, Holt, Rinehart and Winston, Inc., New York, 1961.

[15] Hebb, D. O.: "The Organization of Behavior," p. 199, John Wiley & Sons, Inc., New York, 1949.

[16] Isbell, H., and White, W. M.: Clinical Characteristics of Addictions, *Am. J. Med.*, 14:558 (May, 1953).

[17] Kolb, Lawrence: Pleasure and Deterioration from Narcotic Addiction, *Mental Health*, 9:699 (1925).

[18] Kolb, Lawrence: Drug Addiction—A Study of Some Medical Cases, *A.M.A. Arch. Neurol. Psychiat.*, 16:389 (1928).

[19] Kolb, Lawrence: Drug Addiction in Its Relation to Crime, *Mental Hyg.*, 9:74 (1925).

[20] Lindesmith, Alfred R.: "Opiate Addiction," Principia Press of Trinity University, San Antonio, Tex., 1947.

[21] Lindesmith, Alfred R.: Problems and Implications of Drug Addiction and Related Behavior, in "Emerging Problems in Social Psychology," The University of Oklahoma Lectures in Social Psychology, Series III, p. 249, Institute of Group Relations, University of Oklahoma, Norman, Okla., 1956.

[22] Meyers, Fritz: Ueber einge seltener vorkommende Formen von Rauschgiftsucht, *Munchen. Med. Wochschr.*, 80:732 (1933).

[23] Nyswander, Marie: "The Drug Addict as a Patient," p. ix, Grune and Stratton, Inc., New York, 1956.

[24] *Proceedings, White House Conference on Narcotic and Drug Abuse*, Washington, Sept. 27–28, 1962, p. 150.

[25] Report of the Mayor's Committee on Drug Addiction to the Honorable Richard O. Patterson, Jr., Commissioner of Correction, New York City, *Am. J. Psychiat.*, 10:433 (1930).

[26] Sykes, G. M.: "The Society of Captives: A Study of a Maximum Security Prison," p. 6, Princeton University Press, Princeton, N.J., 1958.

[27] Terry, C. E., and Pellens, Mildred: "The Opium Problem," The Committee on Drug Addiction with the Bureau of Social Hygiene, Inc., New York, 1928.

[28] Vaille, C., and Stern, G.: Drug Addiction: Medical and Social Aspects in France, *Bull. Narcotics, U.N. Dep. Social Affairs*, 6(2):10 (1954).

[29] Wikler, A.: "Opiate Addiction: Psychological and Neurophysiological Aspects in Relation to Clinical Problems," Charles C Thomas, Springfield, Ill., 1953.

[30] Wolff, P.: Alcohol and Drug Addiction in Germany, *Brit. J. Inebriety*, 31(4):141 (1933).

19

THEORIES
OF HYPNOSIS

H. J. Eysenck

WHEN WE TURN TO MODERN THEORIES of hypnosis, it cannot be said that we leave the realm of absurdity behind. Some, at least, of the more recent theories of hypnosis are equally implausible as Mesmer's original notions, or Charcot's views. A brief mention of some of the better-known ones may serve to show the reader how very little agreement there is between different authorities.

One of the older and more respectable theories sees in it a modified form of sleep. The very term "hypnosis" shows that originally the sleep-like characteristic of the hypnotic trance suggested an identification of the two states, and Pavlov comes foremost in claiming that sleep and hypnosis are similar, involving a spread of cerebral inhibition in both cases. This theory is almost certainly false. The physiological reaction of the organism under hypnosis is quite different from that which is observed in sleep. Thus, certain reflexes are abolished in sleep, but not under hypnosis. Electroencephalogram recordings, or "brain waves," show different characteristics in the two states. The evidence is very strong in opposing an identification of these two states.

A more acceptable hypothesis would regard hypnosis as a conditioned response. Such a view might in due course be elaborated into a proper theory, but at the moment it fails completely to account for many of the phenomena associated with hypnosis. How, one might ask, could conditioning account for spontaneous post-hypnotic amnesias? While conditioning cannot be com-

From H. J. Eysenck's book *Sense and Nonsense in Psychology*, pp. 64–67, published by Penguin Books 1958. (Text, Chapter 9)

pletely rejected as a likely part of a true theory of hypnosis, certainly by itself it is not sufficient.

Much the same might be said of dissociation as an explanation of hypnotic phenomena. It is well known that parts of the cortex and the central nervous system can be dissociated from the remainder, and many hypnotic phenomena seem to be of this character. However, it will be difficult to account for hypnosis in terms of dissociation because very little is, in fact, known about association, so that we would merely be explaining one unknown by another.

A similar objection might be presented against another view which looks upon hypnosis as an exaggerated form of suggestibility. While, undoubtedly, there is a considerably increased degree of suggestibility in hypnosis, it is idle to seek for an explanatory principle in the laws of suggestibility, because very little is known about suggestibility itself. Again we would merely be attempting to explain one unknown by another.

Among the more esoteric theories is a Freudian one, according to which susceptibility to hypnosis depends on the extent of "transference" formed between the subject and the hypnotist. This "transference" is a special relationship which revives attitudes originally present in the parent–child relationship. Added to this are various erotic components which are supposed to be present in hypnosis, which is considered to be a manifestation of the Oedipus complex, of masochistic tendencies, and so on.

Weirdest of all is a theory which states essentially "that the phenomena of hypnosis result from the subject's motive to behave like a hypnotized person, as defined by the hypnotist, and as understood by the subject." This is perhaps the most question-begging of all, because it leaves unanswered the two crucial questions as to why the subject should want to behave in this fashion, and how he manages to do this. It is all very well to say a person wants to behave like a hypnotized subject, but how does that help him to produce an analgesia to an operation?

Most promising perhaps is a theory of ideo-motor action. There is ample experimental evidence to show that ideas of certain movements are closely related to the execution of these movements. If electrodes and an amplifier are connected to the muscles of the arm, and the subject is told to lie quite still on a couch, but to imagine that he is lifting that arm, then a barrage of nervous impulses is recorded as passing through the nerves and into the muscles which would have been used had the movement, in fact, been executed. Thus, nerve transmission and mental images or ideas are closely related, and, indeed, it appears that the one is never found without the other. Without going into the question of which causes which, the mutual interdependence of mental and physical phenomena does not seem to be in doubt. Under these conditions, the possibility of achieving changes in a person's behaviour through verbal means, as in hypnosis, appears possible. At best, this is only a partial theory and it stands very much in need of considerable amplification. If it could be combined with some such form of inhibition theory as will be discussed in a later chapter, we might here have the beginning of a true theory of hypnosis. At the moment such a theory cannot be said to exist, and all that we can do is to note the experimental facts, which are reasonably well established, and hope that a greater interest in these important discoveries will eventually lead to greater knowledge.

20

BEHAVIOUR
UNDER HYPNOSIS

H. J. Eysenck

THE NEXT PHENOMENON FREQUENTLY OBSERVED is known as that of positive hallucinations. Here the subject will see, hear, and feel the presence of objects which, objectively, are not present at all. Tell him that his fiancée is sitting in the chair opposite and he will greet her, go across and kiss her, and generally behave as if his fiancée were actually there. Tell him that a lion has just come in through the window and he will show all signs of cringing fear, and may rush out of the room in terror.

The converse of positive hallucinations are negative hallucinations, which can also be easily induced. Here the subject fails to see, feel, or hear objects and persons which are, in fact, actually present. Suggest to him that he and the hypnotist are alone in the room and he will pay no attention to other people and behave as if they were not there. Suggest to him that he cannot feel any touch on his skin, or that he cannot hear a certain sound and he will, in fact, behave as if that were true. Positive and negative hallucinations of this kind are relatively easy to produce in susceptible subjects, but the criticism is often made that we may be dealing with a simple desire on the part of the hypnotized person to please the experimenter and that all these manifestations are faked in some way. Alternatively, it is suggested that hypnotized people are in reality in the pay of the hypnotist and merely pretend to go through the hoop in response to favours received. This criticism may sound reasonable to anyone who has not, in actual fact, seen the differ-

From H. J. Eysenck's book *Sense and Nonsense in Psychology*, pp. 36–43, 50–51, published by Penguin Books, 1958. (Text, Chapter 9)

ence in behaviour between a person merely pretending to be hypnotized and a person in a trance. Nor does it account for phenomena such as this. A stage hypnotist had hypnotized a rather pompous, well-dressed young man on the stage, and had got him to take off his trousers and to ride around the stage on a broom-stick. The public were shrieking with laughter at this sight, but when the hypnotist wakened the subject from the trance, the latter took one look at his rather undignified appearance, picked up the broom, and knocked the hypnotist flat. It is difficult to consider this as part of the act!

Probably more convincing is the fact that certain hallucinations can be produced by hypnosis which give rise to acts impossible to imitate in the normal state. Take a glass full of soapy water and suggest to a hypnotized person that it is bubbling champagne. He will drink it down with every sign of enjoyment. This is a very difficult feat to encompass in the normal state. The reader who doubts it might like to carry out the experiment on himself! Similarly, it is possible for a normal person to pretend to feel afraid of the non-existing lion who comes through the window, but he would find it very difficult indeed to produce all the autonomic and physiological signs of fear which are not under voluntary control, and which nevertheless can be shown to be present in the hypnotized person. In general it might be said that while a certain amount of faking undoubtedly does occur in stage performances, it would be very difficult, if not impossible, for such fakes not to be detected in the psychological laboratory.

The unique nature of hypnotic phenomena becomes even more apparent when we turn to another field which has been extensively investigated. In connexion with negative hallucinations I mentioned the possibility of producing anaesthesia, i.e. a failure to feel a touch applied to the skin of the subject. It is similarly possible to produce a complete insensitivity to pain, usually referred to as hypnotic analgesia. For many years this phenomenon has been the subject of doubt and derision, possibly because most of the phenomena described so far might just have been capable of simulation and faking. Too much is known, however, about people's response to pain to leave one in any doubt that if the phenomena described by hypnotists are, in fact, accurate, then we are dealing in hypnosis with something quite beyond the usual.

Let us start with a simple demonstration. The deeply hypnotized subject is told that a needle will be pushed through his hand and that he will not feel any pain whatsoever. He is also told that there will be no bleeding. The hypnotist then pushes a needle through the subject's hand; the latter does not even look at it and goes on talking as if nothing had happened. There is no bleeding, or else very little. Again the reader who believes that hypnotic phenomena can be faked might like to try the experiment on himslf!

The pushing of a needle through the hand is one thing; major operations are quite another. Yet there is no doubt that in literally thousands of cases, major amputations have been carried out under hypnosis without pain, and without the usual accompaniment of shock, and other traumatic physiological indices. Much of the credit for the introduction of hypnosis into this field goes to Elliotson, a young physician at one of London's major hospitals during the middle of the last century, and to Esdaile, a physician working in India. Anaesthetics had not been discovered then, and any kind of operation, particularly a major one, was a very bloody affair, in the true sense of that term. Elliotson's experiments with hypnosis were not well received by his colleagues, who resented his crusading vigour and did not like the odd and unorthodox nature of the method. Esdaile perfected the technique, and finally his claims were investigated by a special commission, which, though incredulous at first, was forced to report that he had in fact succeeded in carrying out major operations without any evidence of pain or shock on the part of the persons operated upon. This caused considerable and acrimonious controversy, but the discovery of anaesthetics around this time caused medical people to sink back with thankfulness into lethargic uninterestedness in hypnosis and similar oddities, and rest content with the more physical type of anaesthetic, such as ether and chloroform, which they felt they could understand more easily. Nowadays hypnosis is very little used in medical treatment for the purpose of the suppression of pain, although it is superior in many ways to the best available anaesthetics. Occasionally promising results are reported in childbirth, and more recently in connexion with the extraction of teeth. Hypnodontics, as this new method is somewhat oddly called, has already produced a large number of reports of bloodless and painless extractions of teeth, and a few years ago a public exhibition was given in the United States in which, before a large group of dentists, two upper bicuspids and one lower bicuspid, all on the right side, were extracted without the use of drugs or chemical anaesthetics. The periosteum was lifted away and the three teeth extracted without the slightest indication of pain, and without bleeding, while the patient remained in a deep trance. Posthypnotically there was no sign of bleeding or recollection of pain.

Another phenomenon which appears spontaneously, and has been remarked on from the earliest days of hypnosis, is that of *rapport*. By this is meant a special relationship obtaining between the hypnotist and his subject, such that the latter takes orders, accepts suggestions, and so on, only from the former and not from anyone else. The Freudian concept of transference, i.e. the existence of a special relation between patient and therapist, is in many ways a watered-down version of the notion of *rapport*. It is quite likely, in fact, that the underlying rationale of these two phenomena, when carefully examined, will be found to be somewhat similar. Although psychoanalysts have always protested against this notion, there seems to be little doubt that suggestion, although not necessarily of a hypnotic kind, plays a very important part in their treatment.

Rapport, once it is established, can be transferred to other people at the command of the hypnotist. He may tell the hypnotized subject, "This is Mr. Smith. I want you to carry out everything he tells you, just as you would carry out everything that I tell you." Such a command establishes *rapport* between the subject and Mr. Smith, and in this way *rapport* can be handed on through a whole series of people. In the absence of such a voluntary transfer, the hypnotized subject would not be at all suggestible to anything Mr. Smith, or anybody else, might say to him; his *rapport* is entirely with the person who carried out the original hypnosis.

Post-hypnotic amnesia, or a complete forgetting of everything that happened under hypnosis, is a very frequent concomitant of the hypnotic trance. It was first encountered in the case of Victor, the young shepherd hypnotized by the Marquis de Puységur, whom we have already mentioned. When he awoke from the hypnosis he had no recollection of anything that happened during that period. Such amnesias are common in deep states of trance, and do not require to be suggested to the subject. They are apparently a spontaneous outgrowth of the deep hypnotic trance. When the trance is less deep it may be necessary for the hypnotist to suggest that the subject should forget everything that happened; such commands are usually obeyed without difficulty, except in the very slightest stages of hypnosis, where they may be ineffective.

There is thus a continuity between the last moment before the subject sinks into the hypnotic trance and the first moment when he is awakened, with a complete amnesia for everything that happened in between. This may be illustrated by an experiment carried out on a rather boastful and arrogant young man who came to the laboratory loudly protesting to everyone within earshot that he did not believe in hypnosis, that he knew nobody could hypnotize him, and that he would soon show the experimenters up for a bunch of incompetent fools. He kept on talking in this fashion while the hypnotic suggestions were repeated to him, which were to the effect that he would fall into a deep sleep when the experimenter knocked on the table with a reflex hammer held in his hand. The young man was just saying, ". . . and furthermore, I don't believe for a minute that anybody with as strong a will-power . . .", when the experimenter rapped on the table. The subject's eyes closed immediately, he stopped talking, and fell into a reasonably deep trance. For slightly over two hours a series of experiments were conducted with him, which showed him to be a very good subject indeed. At the end of that period the suggestion was made to him that he would awake without remembering anything about this hypnotic period. The moment the experimenter again rapped on the table with a reflex hammer he continued talking, saying, ". . . as I can possibly be hypnotized." He was quite incredulous when told of what had happened and only an agitated reference to his watch led him finally to believe that he had actually been hypnotized.

If after awakening the subject we hypnotize him again, then his second hypnotic state is in contact through memory with the first, but whatever happened between the two hypnotic states is not recollected. However, these amnesias can be removed by suggestion. If it is suggested to the subject at the end of the hypnotic trance that he will recall everything that has happened during the trance, there is usually little difficulty in making him conscious of and remember what would normally be unconscious and forgotten.

One of the most striking ways in which post-hypnotic amnesia is found to work is in the case of another hypnotic phenomenon, which has excited considerable interest from the very day of its discovery. This is the phenomenon of post-hypnotic suggestion. If, under hypnosis, the subject is given a suggestion to be carried out at a given time, or after receiving a certain signal, he will carry out this suggestion, although he may at the time not be in a hypnotic trance at all, but may have returned to the waking state. Here is a typical case record to illustrate this. The subject is hypnotized and told that he will be awakened after ten minutes. He is further told that some time after this the hypnotist will blow his nose three times. Upon the receipt of this signal, the subject will get up, go out into the hall, pick up the third umbrella from the left on the rack, go back into the room, and put up the umbrella there. After a little while the subject is then awakened; he talks animatedly, has forgotten all about his experience, and when questioned as to whether he has been asked to do anything, seems astonished at the idea, and certainly cannot recall anything of the kind.

When the experimenter blows his nose three times, the subject becomes vaguely restless and uneasy; finally, he gets up, leaves the room, picks up the designated umbrella, brings it back into the room and puts it up. When questioned as to the reasons for his actions, he cannot, of course, give the true reason because he is unconscious of it. Instead he will make up as good a reason as he can. Thus, he may say, "Well, you know the old superstition about putting up umbrellas in a building. We were talking just now about superstition and I wanted to show you that I was not superstitious myself." Many of these rationalizations are quite remarkable in their ingenuity, and intelligent people in particular can usually find a good reason for doing almost anything that has been suggested to them under hypnosis. What is more, they apparently believe their own rationalizations implicitly. The tendency of human beings to rationalize their actions and to believe in their own rationalizations implicitly is, unfortunately, a phenomenon too widespread and too well known to have escaped the notice of philosophers and psychologists from the very beginning of interest in human actions. What is important in this demonstration is the way in which it becomes possible to control the situation in such a way that the true cause of a person's conduct is known to the experimenter, but not to the person himself. Oddly enough, this very powerful method of investigating the process of rationalization has not been used to any considerable extent for experimental purposes; it has largely remained an amusing demonstration and an after-dinner game.

There is no doubt about the great strength of post-hypnotic suggestion and its capacity to produce action. What apparently happens is that the post-hypnotic suggestion sets up an encapsulated action tendency in the mind which is relatively independent of voluntary control, and powerfully demands action before it can be reintegrated with the remainder of the subject's mind.

In this it very much resembles in miniature the kind of complex so often found in neurotic and otherwise emotionally unstable patients. The cause of this action tendency is unknown to the subject, and even where it is guessed, as in the case of the psychologist just mentioned, this knowledge does not seem capable of counteracting the determining influence of this small "complex." When it is remembered that in the particular case just mentioned this single suggestion triumphed over the strength and will-power of a well-integrated, strong-willed, competent person, who, in fact, had guessed what was happening, it will be realized that hypnosis and hypnotic suggestions are no playthings, but carry with them an almost frightening degree of strength and importance.

In discussing some of the evidence, I have not mentioned the many studies in which patients have been asked to remember certain events which happened at a relatively early stage of their lives, and where later checks revealed that these had actually happened. This type of work is too much open to falsification and all sorts of uncontrolled influences to be of much value. The alleged events which the hypnotized person experiences under regression may have been discussed with him by other people long after they had in fact happened; the memories of the witnesses may themselves be affected by the story told by the subject who is being regressed; also, certain confirmative details may be elaborated by the experimenter to the exclusion of items that had not fitted in. Quite recently, however, this unsatisfactory type of evidence has been transformed into a scientifically useful and quite decisive method of experimentation. The idea is so simple, and so lacking in any technical complexity, that the reader might like to exercise his own ingenuity in deciding how he would solve this particular problem. The patient under hypnotic regression tells of certain events and memories of things that happened many years ago. How can the truthfulness of these memories be checked without relying on subjective memories of other people? The answer to this problem is a very simple one, but any reader who can think out the right answer has shown more scientific inventiveness than hundreds of academic and medical hypnotists who have repeated the same type of invalid and useless investigation time and time again.

The solution essentially consists in finding an objective fact which at the time to which the subject is regressed would be well known to him, but which during the course of his life he would certainly forget. Facts of this kind are the day of the week on which his fourth, or eighth, or tenth birthday fell, or the day of the week on which a certain Christmas celebration fell, and so on. The procedure of testing is a very simple one. The subject is asked on what day of the week, say, his sixth birthday fell. Practically no one succeeds in correctly remembering this far-off event, which took place twenty or more years ago. He is then hypnotized and gradually regressed to this particular day. Now birthdays are of the very greatest importance to children, and they know perfectly well *at that time* what day of the week their birthday is. Consequently, having been regressed to the day, the subject is simply asked what day of the week it is. Correct answers have been obtained for 93 percent of subjects, regressed to the age of ten; 82 per cent of subjects regressed to the age of seven; and 69 per cent of those regressed to the age of four.

Experiments such as those described in some detail above leave little doubt that there is a substantial amount of truth in the hypothesis that age regression does, in fact, take place, and that memories can be recovered which most people would think had been completely lost.

PART IV

SOCIALIZATION
AND INTERACTION

IN THE CHILD'S ACQUISITION OF LANGUAGE from his earliest babblings and simplest vocalizations to the final convergence with adult speech, the progression is from the instrumental use of words, word-sentences, and gestures to the more complicated forms of speech. Ways of speaking are intimately connected with ways of thinking and to the development of self-control and logical thought.

Another consequence of the linguistic socialization of children is that they become implicated in increasingly wider systems of social relationships. Confined at first to the simplest kinds of acts, and acting in relation to the simplest kinds of social relationships, they gradually develop the capacity to participate in complex social structures. To understand those structures and that level of complex participation, social scientists have borrowed from drama the idea of "role." When a child has developed the ability to grasp the role of one other person at a time, he is on the road to becoming a social being. However, before he can participate in organized adult activity the child must be able to conceive his own role from the standpoint of all other participants. Mead's concept of the generalized other applies to the organized roles of participants within any defined situation; it refers not to an actual group of people, but rather to a conception or an interpretation that a person derives from his experiences. He then regulates his behavior in terms of these supposed opinions and attitudes of others. Conscience, morality, and objectivity are generated in this process.

The concept of role has been applied by sociologists to the study of social structures, organizations, groups, and institutions. It was introduced into the tradition of social psychology especially to describe the processes of cooperative behavior and communication. Role carries with it the implication that social life may be viewed as a drama with actors cast in multiple roles, switching from one to another as they enter into different social contexts or encounters with other actors. Roles should be conceived as complex systems of conceptually controlled or guided behavior that are loosely defined by the expectations of others but always somewhat fluid and open, permitting a certain amount of ad libbing or departure from the script. Roles include a sense of identity and a perspective or attitude. Persons are able to take the roles of others by putting themselves in the position of others and imagining how they feel and think. This process of role-taking may sometimes result in acquiring new perspectives and modes of responses. As actors perform in the roles in which they are cast, and as they take into account the roles of others, they tend to be concerned with presenting themselves in such a fashion as to create desired impressions in others. Sometimes coalitions or teams are formed to handle these matters of identity and impression management.

Like role-playing, much social interaction is relatively fluid and transient, although some, such as that which occurs in a court of law or in the prosecution of a criminal, may be more narrowly circumscribed and highly resistant to change. All forms of social interaction, however, are somewhat indeterminate or open-ended, leaving the way open for bargaining, compromise, negotiation, and improvisation. New patterns are constantly in the process of being fashioned as old ones are discarded or modified to meet situations and conditions. Central features of interaction as viewed by social psychologists are the assessments of self and others, continuous reassessment, and the fact that it is a process rather than a fixed or predetermined pattern.

21

PLAY, THE GAME, AND THE GENERALIZED OTHER

George H. Mead

WE WERE SPEAKING of the social conditions under which the self arises as an object. In addition to language we found two illustrations, one in play and the other in the game, and I wish to summarize and expand my account on these points. I have spoken of these from the point of view of children. We can, of course, refer also to the attitudes of more primitive people out of which our civilization has arisen. A striking illustration of play as distinct from the. game is found in the myths and the various plays which primitive people carry out, especially in religious pageants. The pure play attitude which we find in the case of little children may not be found here, since the participants are adults, and undoubtedly the relationship of these play processes to that which they interpret is more or less in the minds of even the most primitive people. In the process of interpretation of such rituals, there is an organization of play which perhaps might be compared to that which is taking place in the kindergarten in dealing with the plays of little children, where these are made into a set that will have a definite structure or relationship. At least something of the same sort is found in the play of primitive people. This type of activity belongs, of course, not to the everyday life of the people in their dealing with the objects about them—there we have a more or less definitely developed self-consciousness—but in their attitudes toward the forces about them, the nature upon which they depend; in their attitude toward this nature which is vague and uncertain, there we have a much more primitive response;

Reprinted from *George Herbert Mead on Social Psychology*, Anselm L. Strauss, ed., pp. 216–228. By permission of The University of Chicago Press. Copyright 1934, 1936, 1956, and 1964 by The University of Chicago Press. (Text, Chapter 11)

and that response finds its expression in taking the role of the other, playing at the expression of their gods and their heroes, going through certain rites which are the representation of what these individuals are supposed to be doing. The process is one which develops, to be sure, into a more or less definite technique and is controlled; and yet we can say that it has arisen out of situations similar to those in which little children play at being a parent, at being a teacher—vague personalities that are about them and which affect them and on which they depend. These are personalities which they take, roles they play, and insofar control the development of their own personality. This outcome is just what the kindergarten works toward. It takes the characters of these various vague beings and gets them into such an organized social relationship to each other that they build the character of the little child.[1] The very introduction of organization from outside supposes a lack of organization at this period in the child's experience. Over against such a situation of the little child and primitive people, we have the game as such.

The fundamental difference between the game and play is that in the latter the child must have the attitude of all the others involved in that game. The attitudes of the other players which the participant assumes organize into a sort of unit, and it is that organization which controls the response of the individual. The illustration used was of a person playing baseball. Each one of his own acts is determined by his assumption of the action of the others who are playing the game. What he does is controlled by his being everyone else on that team, at least insofar as those attitudes affect his own particular response. We get then an "other" which is an organization of the attitudes of those involved in the same process.

The organized community or social group which gives to the individual his unity of self can be called "the generalized other." The attitude of the generalized other is the attitude of the whole community.[2] Thus, for example, in the case of such a social group as a ball team, the team is the generalized other insofar as it enters—as an organized process on social activity—into the experience of any one of the individual members.

[1] "The Relation of Play to Education," *University of Chicago Record,* I (1896–97), 140 ff.

[2] It is possible for inanimate objects, no less than for other human organisms, to form parts of the generalized and organized—the completely socialized—other for any given human individual, insofar as he responds to such objects socially or in a social fashion (by means of the mechanism of thought, the internalized conversation of gestures). Any thing—any object or set of objects, whether animate or inanimate, human or animal, or merely physical—toward which he acts, or to which he responds, socially, is an element in what for him is the generalized other; by taking the attitudes of which toward himself, he becomes conscious of himself as an object or individual, and thus develops a self or personality. Thus, for example, the cult, in its primitive form, is merely the social embodiment of the relation between the given social group or community and its physical environment—an organized social means, adopted by the individual members of that group or community, of entering into social relations with that environment, or (in a sense) of carrying on conversations with it; and in this way that environment becomes part of the total generalized other for each of the individual members of the given social group or community.

If the given human individual is to develop a self in the fullest sense, it is not sufficient for him merely to take the attitudes of other human individuals toward himself and toward one another within the human social process and to bring that social process as a whole into his individual experience merely in these terms. He must also, in the same way that he takes the attitudes of other individuals toward himself and toward one another, take their attitudes toward the various phases or aspects of the common social activity or set of social undertakings in which, as members of an organized society or social group, they are all engaged. He must then, by generalizing these individual attitudes of that organized society or social group itself as a whole, act toward different social projects which at any given time it is carrying out, or toward the various larger phases of the general social process which constitutes the group's life and of which these projects are specific manifestations. Getting these broad activities of any given social whole or organized society within the experiential field of any one of the individuals involved or included in that whole is, in other words, the essential basis and prerequisite of the fullest development of that individual's self—only insofar as he takes the attitudes of the organized social group to which he belongs toward the organized, co-operative social activity or set of such activities in which that group as such is engaged, does he develop a complete self or possess the sort of complete self he has developed. And on the other hand, the complex co-operative processes and activities and institutional functionings of organized human society are also possible only insofar as every individual involved in them or belonging to that society can take the general attitudes of all other such individuals with reference to these processes and activities and institutional functionings and to the organized social whole of experiential relations and interactions thereby constituted—and can direct his own behavior accordingly.

It is in the form of the generalized other that the social process influences the behavior of the individuals involved in it and carrying it on, that is, that the community exercises control over the conduct of its individual members; for it is in this form that the social process or community enters as a determining factor into the individual's thinking. In abstract thought the individual takes the attitude of the generalized other[3] toward himself, without reference

---

[3] We have said that the internal conversation of the individual with himself in terms of words or significant gestures—the conversation which constitutes the process or activity of thinking—is carried on by the individual from the standpoint of the "generalized other." And the more abstract that conversation is, the more abstract thinking happens to be, the further removed is the generalized other from any connection with particular individuals. It is especially in abstract thinking that the conversation involved is carried on by the individual with the generalized other, rather than with any particular individuals. Thus it is, for example, that abstract concepts are concepts stated in terms of the attitudes of the entire social group or community; they are stated on the basis of the individual's consciousness of the attitudes of the generalized other toward them, as a result of his taking these attitudes of the generalized other and then responding to them. And thus it is also that abstract propositions are stated in a form which anyone—any other intelligent individual—will accept.

to its expression in any particular other individuals; and in concrete thought, he takes that attitude insofar as it is expressed in the attitudes toward his behavior of those other individuals with whom he is involved in the given social situation or act. But only by taking the attitude of the generalized other toward himself, in one or another of these ways, can he think at all; for only thus can thinking—or the internalized conversation of gestures which constitutes thinking—occur. And only through the taking by individuals of the attitude or attitudes of the generalized other toward themselves is the existence of a universe of disclosure, as that system of common or social meanings which thinking presupposes at its context, rendered possible.

The self-conscious human individual, then, takes or assumes the organized social attitudes of the given social group or community (or of some one section thereof) to which he belongs, toward the social problems of various kinds which confront that group or community at any given time and which arise in connection with the correspondingly different social projects or organized co-operative enterprises in which that group of community as such is engaged; and as an individual participant in these social projects or co-operative enterprises, he governs his own conduct accordingly. In politics, for example, the individual identifies himself with an entire political party and takes the organized attitudes of that entire party toward the rest of the given social community and toward the problems which confront the party within the given social situation; and he consequently reacts or responds in terms of the organized attitudes of the party as a whole. He thus enters into a special set of social relations with all the other individuals who belong to that political party; and in the same way he enters into various other special sets of social relations, with various other classes of individuals respectively, the individuals of each of these classes being the other members of some one of the particular organized subgroups (determined in socially functional terms) of which he himself is a member within the entire given society or social community. In the most highly developed, organized, and complicated human social communities—those evolved by civilized man—these various socially functional classes or subgroups of individuals to which any given individual belongs (and with the other individual members of which he thus enters into a special set of social relations) are of two kinds. Some of them are concrete social classes or subgroups, such as political parties, clubs, corporations, which are all actually functional social units, in terms of which their individual members are directly related to one another. The others are abstract social classes or subgroups, such as the class of debtors and the class of creditors, in terms of which their individual members are related to one another only more or less indirectly and which only more or less indirectly function as social units, but which afford or represent unlimited possibilties for the widening and ramifying and enriching of the social relations among all the individual members of the given society as an organized and unified whole. The given individual's membership in several of these abstract social classes or subgroups makes possible his entrance into definite social relations (however indirect) with an almost infinite number of other individuals who also belong to or are included within one or another of these abstract social classes or subgroups cutting across functional lines of demarcation which divide different human social communities from one another, and including individual members from several (in some cases from all) such communities. Of these abstract social classes or subgroups of human individuals the one which is most inclusive and extensive is, of course, the one defined by the logical universe of discourse (or system of universally significant symbols) determined by the participation and communicative interaction of individuals; for all such classes or subgroups, it is the one which claims the largest number of individual members and which enables the largest conceivable number of human individuals to enter into some sort of social relation, however indirect or abstract it may be, with one another—a relation arising from the universal functioning of gestures as significant symbols in the general human social process of communication.

I have pointed out, then, that there are two general stages in the full development of the self. At the first of these stages, the individual's self is constituted simply by an organization of the particular attitudes of other individuals toward himself and toward one another in the specific social acts in which he participates with them. But at the second stage in the full development of the individual's self, that self is constituted not only by an organization of these particular individual attitudes, but also by an organization of the social attitudes of the generalized other or the social group as a whole to which he belongs. These social or group attitudes are brought within the individual's field of direct experience and are included as elements in the structure or constitution of his self, in the same way that the attitudes of particular other individuals are; and the individual arrives at them, or succeeds in taking them, by means of further organizing, and then generalizing, the attitudes of particular other individuals in terms of their organized social bearings and implications. So the self reaches its full development by organizing these individual attitudes of others into the organized social or group attitudes, and by thus becoming an individual reflection of the general systematic pattern of social or group behavior in which it and the others are all involved—a pattern which enters as a whole into the individual's experience in terms of these organized group attitudes which, through the mechanism of his central nervous system, he takes toward himself, just as he takes the individual attitudes of others.

The game has a logic, so that such an organization of the self is rendered possible. There is a definite end to be obtained; the actions of the different individuals are all related to each other with reference to that end so that they do not conflict; one is not in conflict with himself in the attitude of another man on the team. If one has the attitude of the person throwing the ball, he can also have the response of catching the ball. The two are related so that they further the purpose of the game itself. They are interrelated in a unitary, organic fashion. There is a definite unity, then, which is introduced into the organization of other selves when we reach such a stage as that of the game, as against the situation of play where there is a simple succession of one role after another, a situation which is, of course, characteristic of the child's own personality. The child is one thing at one time and another at another, and what he is at one moment does not determine what he is at another. That is both the charm of childhood as well as its inadequacy. You cannot count on the child; you cannot assume that all the things he does are going to determine what he will do at any moment. He is not organized into a whole. The child has no definite character, no definite personality.

The game is then an illustration of the situation out of which an organized personality arises. Insofar as the child does take the attitude of the other and allows that attitude of the other to determine the thing he is going to do with reference to a common end, he is becoming an organic member of society. He is taking over the morale of that society and is becoming an essential member of it. He belongs to it insofar as he does allow the attitude of the other that he takes to control his own immediate expression. What is involved here is some sort of an organized process. That which is expressed in terms of the game is, of course, being continually expressed in the social life of the child, but this wider process goes beyond the immediate experience of the child himself. The importance of the game is that it lies entirely inside of the child's own experience, and the importance of our modern type of education is that it is brought as far as possible within this realm. The different attitudes that a child assumes are so organized that they exercise a definite control over his response, as the attitudes in a game control his own immediate response. In the game we get an organized other, a generalized other, which is found in the nature of the child itself, and finds its expression in the immediate experience of the child. And it is that organized activity in the child's own nature controlling the particular response which gives unity, and which builds up his own self.

What goes on in the game goes on in the life of the child all the time. He is continually taking the attitudes of those about him, especially the roles of those who in some sense control him and on whom he depends. He gets the function of the process in an abstract sort of a way at first. It goes over from the play into the game in a real sense. He has to play the game. The morale of the game takes hold of the child more than the larger morale of the whole community. The child passes into the game, and the game expresses a social situation in which he can completely enter; its morale may have a greater hold on him than that of the family to which he belongs or the community in which he lives. There are all sorts of social organizations, some of which are fairly lasting, some temporary, into which the child is entering, and he is playing a sort of social game in them. It is a period in which he likes "to belong," and he gets into organizations which come into existence and pass out of existence. He becomes a something which can function in the organized whole, and thus tends to determine himself in his relationship with the group to which he belongs. That process is one which is a striking stage in the development of the child's morale. It constitutes him a self-conscious member of the community to which he belongs.

Such is the process by which a personality arises. I have spoken of this as a process in which a child takes the role of the other and said that it takes place essentially through the use of language. Language is predominantly based on the vocal gesture by means of which co-operative activities in a community are carried out. Language in its significant sense is that vocal gesture which tends to arouse in the individual the attitude which it arouses in others, and it is this perfecting of the self by the gesture which mediates the social activities that gives rise to the process of taking the role of the other. The latter phrase is a little unfortunate because it suggests an actor's attitude which is actually more sophisticated than that which is involved in our own experience. To this degree it does not correctly describe that which I have in mind. We see the process most definitely in a primitive form in those situations where the child's play takes different roles. Here the very fact that he is ready to pay money, for instance, arouses the attitude of the person who receives money, the very process is calling out in him the corresponding activities of the other person involved. The individual stimulates himself to the response which he is calling out in the other person, and then acts in some degree in response to that situation. In play the child does definitely act the role which he himself has aroused in himself. It is that which gives, as I have said, a definite content in the individual which answers to the stimulus that affects him as it affects somebody else. The content of the other that enters into one personality is the response in the individual which his gesture calls out in the other.

We can illustrate our basic concept by a reference to the notion of property. When we say "This is my property. I shall control it," that affirmation calls out a certain set of responses which must be the same in any community in which property exists. It involves an organized attitude with reference to property which is common to all the members of the community. One must have a definite attitude of control of his own property and respect for the property of others. Those attitudes (as organized sets of responses) must be there on the part of all, so that when one says such a thing he calls out in himself the response of the others. He is calling out the response of what I have called a generalized other. That which makes society possible is such common responses, such organized attitudes, with reference to what we term property, the cults of religion, the process of education, and the relations of the family. Of course, the wider the society, the more definitely universal these objects must be. In any case, there must be a definite set of responses, which we can speak of as abstract and which can belong to a very large group. Property is in itself a very abstract concept. It is that which the individual himself can control and nobody else can control. The attitude is different from that of a dog toward a bone. A dog will fight any other dog trying to take the bone. The dog is not taking the attitude of the other dog. A man who says "This is my property" is taking an attitude of the other person. The man is appealing to his rights because he is able to take the attitude which everybody else in the group has with reference to property, thus arousing in himself the attitude of others.

What makes the organized self is the organization of the attitudes which are common to the group. A person is a personality because he belongs to a community, because he takes over the institutions of that community into his own conduct. He takes its language as a medium by which he gets his personality, and then through a process of taking the different roles that all the others furnish, he comes to get the attitude of the members of the community. Such, in a certain sense, is the structure of a man's personality. There are certain common responses which each individual has toward certain common things, and insofar as those common responses are awakened in the individual when he is affecting other persons, he arouses his own self. The structure, then, on which the self is built is this response which is common to all, for one has to be a member of a community to be a self. Such responses are abstract attitudes, but they constitute just what we term a man's character. They give him what we term his principles, the acknowledged attitudes of all members of the community toward the values of that community. He is putting himself in the place of the generalized other, which represents the organized responses of all the members of the group. It is that which guides conduct controlled by principles, and a person who has such an organized group of responses is a man whom we say has character, in the moral sense.

It is a structure of attitudes, then, which makes a self, as distinct from a group of habits. All of us have, for example, certain groups of habits, such as the particular intonations in speech. This is a set of habits of vocal expression which one has but which one does not know about. The sets of habits which we have of that sort mean nothing to us; we do not hear the intonations of our speech that others hear unless we are paying particular attention to them. The habits of emotional expression which belong to our speech are of the same sort. We may know that we have expressed ourselves in a joyous fashion, but the detailed process is one which does not come back to our conscious selves. There are whole bundles of such habits which do not enter into a conscious self but which help to make up what is termed the unconscious self.

After all, what we mean by self-consciousness is an awakening in ourselves of the group of attitudes which we are arousing in others, especially when it is an important set of responses which go to make up the members of the community. It is unfortunate to fuse or mix up consciousness, as we ordinarily use that term, and self-consciousness. Consciousness, as frequently used, simply has reference to the field of experience, but self-consciousness refers to the ability to call out in ourselves a set of definite responses which belong to the others of the group. Consciousness and self-consciousness are not on the same level. A man alone has, fortunately or unfortunately, access to his own toothache, but that is not what we mean by self-consciousness.

I have so far emphasized what I have called the structures upon which the self is constructed, the framework of the self, as it were. Of course we are not only what is common to all: each one of the selves is different from everyone else; but there has to be such a common structure as I have sketched in order that we may be members of a community at all. We cannot be ourselves unless we are also members in whom there is a community of attitudes which control the attitudes of all. We cannot have rights unless we have common attitudes. That which we have acquired as self-conscious persons makes us members of society and gives us selves. Selves can only exist in definite relationships to other selves. No hard-and-fast line can be drawn between our own selves and the selves of others, since our own selves exist and enter as such into our experience only insofar as the selves of others exist and enter as such into our experience also. The individual possesses a self only in relation to the selves of the other members of his social group; and the structure of his self expresses or reflects the general behavior pattern of this social group to which he belongs, just as does the structure of the self of every other individual belonging to this social group.

22

ROLE-TAKING: PROCESS VERSUS CONFORMITY

Ralph H. Turner

ONLY A CURSORY GLANCE AT SOCIOLOGICAL JOURNALS is necessary to document both the great importance and the divers applications of "role theory" in current thought and research. First gaining currency as G. H. Mead's (1) "taking the role of the other," and adopted by psychologists reflecting Kurt Lewin's Gestalt approach (2), role theory was made to serve rather different purposes by three popular developments. Ralph Linton (3, pp. 113–131) employed the concept "role" to allow for variability within culture; Jacob Moreno (4) made staged "role-playing" the basis of psychodramatic therapy and research; and investigators bent on uncovering strains in organizational functioning chose "role conflict" as their orienting concept.

Simultaneously, several important criticisms have emerged. The charge has been made that the referents for the term "role" are so heterogenous as to defy rigorous study and coherent theory formation. Some critics have minimized the importance of roles, suggesting that they are superficially adopted and abandoned without important implications for the actor's personality (5). Role theory has been repudiated as a system of rigid cultural and mechanical determinism (6, pp. 81–82). Role theory often appears to be entirely negative, to consist of elaborate generalizations about the malfunctioning of roles in role conflict, role strain, and so on, but to lack any theory of how roles function normally. Finally, role theory is sometimes redundant, merely sub-

From *Human Behavior and Social Process* by Arnold Rose, Ed., pp. 22–40. Copyright © 1962 by Houghton Mifflin Company. Reprinted by permission of the publisher, Houghton Mifflin Company. (Text, Chapter 12)

stituting the term "role" for "social norm" or "culture" without introducing any novel dynamic principle.

All of these criticisms have some merit, but we believe that their validity arises from the dominance of the Linton concept of role and the employment of an oversimplified model of role functioning in many current organizational studies. Role-conflict theory should be firmly grounded in a sophisticated conception of normal role-playing and role-taking as processes. Such a conception is found or implied in the earlier Meadian theory. This essay will call attention to some pertinent aspects of the theory in order to show that there is more to it than simply an extension of normative or cultural deterministic theory and that the concept of role does add novel elements to the conception of social interaction.

BASIC ELEMENTS IN ROLE-TAKING

The Role-Making Process

An initial distinction must be made between taking the existence of distinct and identifiable roles as the starting point in role theory, and postulating a tendency to create and modify conceptions of self- and other-roles as the orienting process in interactive behavior. The latter approach has less interest in determining the exact roles in a group and the specific content of each role than in observing the basic tendency for actors to behave *as if* there were roles. Role in the latter sense is a sort of ideal conception which constrains people to render any action situation into more or less explicit collections of interacting roles. But the relation of the actor to the roles which he comfortably assumes may be like that of the naive debater to the set of assumptions from which he confidently assumes that his explicit arguments are deducible, but which he can neither specify nor defend fully when challenged. Roles "exist" in varying degrees of concreteness and consistency, while the individual confidently frames his behavior as if they had unequivocal existence and clarity. The result is that in attempting from time to time to make aspects of the roles explicit he is creating and modifying roles as well as merely bringing them to light; the process is not only role-taking but *role-making*.

Military and bureaucratic behavior had best be viewed not as the ideal-typical case for role theory, but as a distorted instance of the broader class of role-taking phenomena. The formal regulation system restricts the free operation of the role-making process, limiting its repertoire and making role boundaries rigid. As the context approaches one in which behavior is completely prescribed and all misperformance is institutionally punished, the process of role-taking-role-making becomes increasingly an inconsequential part of the interaction that occurs.

Free from formal regulation, the self- and other-role perspective in any situation may occasionally shift. Roles resemble poles on axes, each axis constituting a dimension in space. In factor analysis, an infinite number of placements of the axes will meet equally well the logical requirements of the data. Similarly, from the point of view of the role-making process an actor has an infinite number of definitions of the boundaries between roles which will serve equally well the logical requirements of role-taking. But the placement of any one of these boundaries, whether for a fleeting instant or for a longer period, limits or determines the identification of other roles. It is this tendency to shape the phenomenal world into roles which is the key to role-taking as a core process in interaction.

"Self-Roles" and "Other-Roles"

Within the ideal framework which guides the role-taking process, every role is a way of relating to other-roles in a situation. A role cannot exist without one or more relevant other-roles toward which it is oriented. The role of "father" makes no sense without the role of child; it can be defined as a pattern of behavior only in relation to the pattern of behavior of a child. The role of the compromiser can exist only to the extent that others in a group are playing the role of antagonists. The role of hero is distinguished from the role of the foolhardy only by the role of the actor's real or imaginary audience.

This principle of role reciprocity provides a generalized explanation for changed behavior. A change in one's own role reflects a changed assessment or perception of the role of relevant others. Interaction is always a *tentative* process, a process of continuously testing the conception one has of the role of the other. The response of the other serves to reinforce or to challenge this conception. The product of the testing process is the stabilization or the modification of one's own role.

The idea of role-taking shifts emphasis away from the simple process of enacting a prescribed role to devising a performance on the basis of an imputed other-role. The actor is not the occupant of a position for which there is a neat set of rules—a culture or set of norms—but a person who must act in the perspective supplied in part by his relationship to others whose actions reflect roles that he must identify. Since the role of alter can only be inferred rather than directly known by ego, testing inferences about the role of alter is a continuing element in interaction. Hence the tentative character of the individual's own role definition and performance is never wholly suspended.

Linton's famous statement of status and role probably established the conception of role as a cultural given in contrast to Mead's treatment of role chiefly as the perspective or vantage point of the relevant other. Linton moved the emphasis from taking the role of the other to enacting the role prescribed for the self. In so doing, he disregarded the peculiar conception of interaction which revolves about the improvising character of the "I," the more rigid social categorization of the "me" than of the "I," and the continuing dialectic between "I" and "me" (1).

Roles as Meaningful
Groupings of Behavior

Role-taking and role-making always constitute the grouping of behavior into units. The isolated action becomes a datum for role analysis only when it is interpreted as the manifestation of a configuration. The individual acts as if he were expressing some role through his behavior and may assign a higher degree of reality to the assumed role than to his specific actions. The role becomes the point of reference for placing interpretations on specific actions, for anticipating that one line of action will follow upon another, and for making evaluations of individual actions. For example, the lie which is an expression of the role of friend is an altogether different thing from the same lie taken as a manifestation of the role of confidence man. Different actions may be viewed as the same or equivalent; identical actions may be viewed as quite different: placement of the actions in a role context determines such judgments.

The grouping aspect of role-taking is perhaps most clearly indicated in the judgments people make of the *consistency* of one another's behavior. Such judgments often violate logical criteria for consistency. But the folk basis for these judgments is the subsumability of a person's behavior under a single role. The parent who on one occasion treats his child with gentleness and on another spanks him is unlikely to be adjudged inconsistent because both types of behavior, under appropriate circumstances, are supposed to be reasonable manifestations of the same parental role. A more devastating extension of the judgment of inconsistency is that the behavior doesn't make sense, that it is unintelligible. Behavior is said to make sense when a series of actions is interpretable as indicating that the actor has in mind some role which guides his behavior.

The socially structured world of experience has many dimensions of classification. The role dimension refers to types of actors. It is the nature of the role that it is capable of being enacted by different actors, but remains recognizable in spite of individual idiosyncrasies. While people tend to be given stable classification according to the major roles they play, the specific referent for the term "role" is a type of actor rather than a type of person. Such a distinction allows for the contingency that one individual may adopt even conflicting roles on occasion, and that otherwise quite different people may play the same role.

There is a kind of structure represented in this conception of role—and implied, we believe, in the work of G. H. Mead—that falls between the rigidity of role as a set of prescriptions inherent in a position and Kingsley Davis' view of role as the actual behavior of the occupant of a status (7, pp. 89–91). Role refers to a pattern which can be regarded as the consistent behavior of a single type of actor. The behavior of the occupant of a given status is a unique constellation, its components tied together only by their emanation from a single individual who is oriented to a single status during the period of his action. But the folk judgment of consistency requires that some more general principle be invoked. The principle must either be one which is already recognized in the group or one which is capable of representation to a relevant group. The unique behavior of the occupant of a given position may or may not constitute a role, either to him or to relevant others, depending upon whether a principle is employed in light of which the behavior seems consistent.

A point of view in important respects similar to this one but also in important respects dissimilar is represented in Merton's statement on *role-sets* (8). The occupant of an organizational position is said to have a distinct role for each type of relevant other with whom he interacts in that position. The cluster of roles which he assumes by virtue of occupying the position is his "role-set." The key importance of self-other interaction in role theory is thus acknowledged. But limitation of the concept "role" to a single reciprocity provides less scope for what we regard as the other important feature of the role-taking process, namely, the process of discovering and creating "consistent" wholes out of behavior. The problem of the school teacher-mother which arises out of the need to compromise two roles because of simultaneous involvement in both is in important respects different from that of the school teacher who must devise and enact her role in simultaneous relationship to students, parents, and principal. In the latter instance there is no question of abandoning one relationship, and the essence of the role is devising a pattern which will cope effectively with the different types of relevant others while at the same time meeting some recognizable criteria of consistency. Except in special instances, these are not experienced as separate roles by their enactors or those to whom they are relevant other-roles.

Role-taking as a process of devising and discovering consistent patterns of action which can be identified with types of actors suggests a theorem regarding role-conflict situations which should be worthy of empirical test. Whenever the social structure is such that many individuals characteristically act from the perspective of two given roles simultaneously, there tends to emerge a single role which encompasses the action. The single role may result from a merger process, each role absorbing the other, or from the development and recognition of a third role which is specifically the pattern viewed as consistent when both roles might be applicable. The parent and spouse roles illustrate the former tendency. In popular usage the sharp distinctions are not ordinarily made between parent and spouse behavior that sociologists invoke in the name of logical, as distinct from folk, consistency. The politician role exemplifies the second tendency, providing a distinct perspective from which the individual may act who otherwise would be acting simultaneously as a party functionary and as a government official. What would constitute a role conflict from the latter point of view is susceptible of treatment as a consistent pattern from the point of view of the politician role.

THE CHARACTER OF
ROLES AS UNITS

Two lines of further clarification are required in order to give substance to the view enunciated here. First, the character of the reciprocities among roles must be specified in greater detail. How do self and other interect? How does the role of alter affect that of ego? Second, the character of the grouping principle that creates boundaries between roles requires further exploration. There is an apparent paradox in saying on the one hand that a fixed set of roles does not exist and on the other hand that people make judgments of consistency and inconsistency on the basis of their success in bringing a succession of actions into the sphere of a single role. Since the second area of elaboration concerns the relation of role-taking as process to the kind of investigation which centers on social structure rather than the individual actor, we shall examine it first.

Roles in Organization
and Culture

The normal role-taking process, as we have suggested, is a tentative process in which roles are identified and given content on shifting axes as interaction proceeds. Both the identification of the roles and their content undergo cumulative revision, becoming relatively fixed for a period of time only as they provide a stable framework for interaction. The usual procedures of formal organization lessen the tentative character of interaction, making each functionary's performance less dependent upon his conception of the roles of relevant others, and minimizing the Gestalt-making process by substituting role prescriptions. The effort is normally only partially successful, as indicated by the abundant literature on informal organization within formal structures.

Studies of informal groups suggest that role differentiation develops around the axes of group functioning, such as the axes of securing agreement, acceptance of responsibility, guarding of group norms, etc. (9). Interaction in such a context permits role-taking in its "purest" form to occur. Interaction involving organizational or status roles is more complex, producing a compromise between the role-taking process and the simple conformity behavior demanded by organizational prescriptions.

The manner in which formal designations "cramp" role-taking can perhaps best be seen in relation to the reciprocity of self-other roles. In actual interaction the identification of a role is not merely a function of the behavior of the actor but of the manifested other-role. The role of leader, for example, incorporates a complex of actions which are supposed to be reflections of certain competencies and sentiments. But if the relevant others fail to reciprocate, or if they are already reciprocating to another person in the role of leader, the identical behavior serves to label the actor as "dissenter" and "trouble-maker" rather than "leader." Such labeling by the relevant others eventually forces redefinition on the would-be leader, who must then either continue in the dissenter role or change his behavior. Organizational definitions, however, seek to attach the informal leader-follower roles to specific positions whose occupants can be formally named. Part of the formalization procedure is the specification of ritual forms of behavior by which each participant acknowledges the nature of the reciprocity. The formalization is supposed to keep the officially designated followers adhering to the follower role, even when the leader fails to enact his leader role, and similarly to prohibit erosion of the leader role in case of non-reciprocation.

The effectiveness of such formalization efforts in limiting the normal range of role-taking adjustments is quite varied. The parent may maintain the exemplar role in the face of his child's non-reciprocation, or he may abandon it to enact a role on the axis of his child's pattern of behavior. The corporation official may continue to act with dignity as if his orders were being obeyed, or he may abandon responsibility and adopt a comprehensive pattern attuned to impotency. But the formal role itself, considered apart from the effective incorporation of the informal role, is merely a skeleton consisting of rules which are intended to invoke the appropriate informal roles. The formalized roles are to the full roles as detonators to explosives—merely devices to set them in motion.

The Framework of Role Differentiation

The unity of a role cannot consist simply in the bracketing of a set of specific behaviors, since the same behavior can be indicative of different roles under different circumstances. The unifying element is to be found *in some assignment of purpose or sentiment to the actor*. Various actions by an individual are classified as intentional and unintentional on the basis of a role designation. The administrator, for example, must make decisions which necessarily help some and hurt others. But the hurt done to some is defined as inadvertent insofar as the role is viewed as that of the impartial or responsible administrator. The individual who plays a nurturant, comfort-giving role necessarily establishes a relationship in which he is superordinated to the comfort-receiver, but the superordination is inadvertent. Since the role definition itself directs perception selectively, the superordination or the administrative harm may not be noticed by the actor or by relevant others. Role-taking involves selective perception of the actions of another and a great deal of selective emphasis, organized about some purpose or sentiment attributed to the other.

Not all combinations of behavior are susceptible of being classed into a single role. Since, as we indicated at the start, the role-taker acts as if roles were real and objective entities, there must be criteria by which the actor assures himself that what he has in mind is truly a role. Such verification derives from two sources, the "internal" validation of the interaction itself, and the external validation supplied by what G. H. Mead called "the generalized other."

Internal validation lies in the successful anticipation of the behavior of relevant others within the range necessary for the enactment of one's own role. This in turn depends upon the existence of roles which provide a pattern for interacting with an individual exhibiting the peculiar selection of behavior whose coherency as a role is subject to verification. The internal criterion means that a given constellation of behavior is judged to constitute a role on the basis of its relation to other roles.

The internal criterion can easily suggest that we have let a system of fixed roles in through the back door unless two important observations are made. First, there is not just one role which enables an individual to interact in what is adjudged a consistent way with any given other-role. Roles are often comprehensive alternative ways of dealing with a given other-role. The range of possibilities is further enhanced by the fact that normal interaction is to a large extent limited in intimacy, intensity, and duration, so that only a small segment of each role is activated. We propose as a reasonable hypothesis that the narrower the segment of a role activated the wider the range of other-roles with which it may deal and which may deal with it.

Second, in light of our statement that role-making is a Gestalt-making process, what cannot be conceived as constituting a role when related to a single relevant other-role may be so conceived when viewed as interacting with two or more different other-roles. The total role of the school super-intendent in the study by Gross and associates (10) would not produce the requisite predictability in the responding teacher role, and therefore would have to be treated as incoherent behavior when viewed from its relation to the teacher role alone. But when seen as a way of maximizing predictability simultaneously in the relevant other-roles of school board member, teacher, and parent, the behavior becomes increasingly susceptible of interpretation as the manifestation of a single role. What is inconsistent behavior viewed in relation to only a single type of relevant other is perfectly coherent in relation to a system of others.

The internal criterion insures that there is constant modification of the content of specific roles, occasional rejection of the identification of a role, and sometimes the "discovery" or creation of a new role. Such modification takes place in the continued interplay between the somewhat vague and always incomplete ideal conceptions of roles and the experience of their overt enactment by self and other. Since each interaction is in some respects unique, each interaction incorporates some improvisation on the theme supplied by self-role and other-role. The very act of expressing a role in a novel item of role behavior enables the actor to see the role in a slightly different light. Similarly, the uniqueness in alter's behavior and the unique situation in which alter's behavior must be anticipated or interpreted serve to cast his role slightly differently. Internal testing includes experiencing in varying degrees the sentiments or purposes which provide the role's coherence. Differing degrees of involvement in the role at the time of its enactment, and differing relations vis-à-vis alter, allow the role to be understood in different ways, and each such experience leaves its residual effect upon the self- and other-role conceptions of the participants.

What we have called the *external validation* of a role is based upon ascertaining whether the behavior is judged to constitute a role by others whose judgments are felt to have some claim to correctness or legitimacy. The simplest form of such a criterion is discovery of a name in common use for the role. If the pattern of behavior can be readily assigned a name, it acquires *ipso facto* the exteriority and constraint of Durkheim's "collective representations" (11). Naming does not assure that there will be agreement on the content of the role; it merely insures that people will do their disagreeing as if there were something real about which to disagree.

Major norms and values serve as criteria of role coherency since they are ordinarily applied with the implicit assumption that no person can really both support and disparage any major norm or value. There is probably considerable popular agreement on the existence and character of a role of murderer, which incorporates a much more comprehensive pattern of behavior than just the act of killing or actions which are functionally connected with murder. The role is a more or less imaginary constellation of actions and sentiments and goals which describe an actor whose relation to the major sacred norms of society is consistent in the simplest way—by being comprehensively negative. Because most individuals have no opportunity to test their conception of the role of murderer by internal criteria, such roles remain relatively impervious to the lack of empirical confirmation, and can serve as sufficient other-roles for the highly segmented self-roles which the ordinary citizen has an opportunity to enact in relation to the murderer.

Role validation is also anchored in the membership of recognized groups and the occupancy of formalized positions. People easily form conceptions of the American Legionnaire, the Jew, the Oriental, etc., incorporating the sentiment and goals distinctively ascribed to members of the group. The greater tangibility of formal statuses and organizational positions as compared with informal roles means further that there is a tendency to merge the latter with the former. Informal roles are often named by borrowing from formal statuses with which they are associated, as in references to a "fatherly" role or a "judicious" role.

Finally, external verification includes a sense of what goes together and what does not, based upon experience in seeing given sets of attitudes, goals, and specific actions carried out by the same individuals. The sense derives on the one hand from what has actually been rendered customary by the prevailing social structure and on the other from the example of key individuals whom the individual takes as role models. Some of the divisions of task and sentiment imposed by the culture follow lines which increase efficiency in society, but others arise from accidental circumstances or perpetuate divisions which no longer have functional implications. Acceptance of the role behavior of an individual model as a standard may lead to the inclusion of much otherwise extraneous behavior within a role and to the judgment that kinds of actions which, by other criteria are contradictory, are actually not inconsistent.

Each of the several criteria, both internal and external, must operate in relation to the others. Under conditions of perfect harmony, the various criteria converge to identify the same units as roles and to identify their content similarly. But under the normal loose operation of society various criteria are partially consistent and partially at odds. Since working human motivations do not divide as neatly as society's major norms would have them, there is often a penumbra on the boundaries of those roles which are oriented to the mores when both the external normative and the internal interactive criteria are brought into play. The formal rules which are invoked when roles are named from organizational positions and statuses do not necessarily fit entirely the sentiment which is experienced when the role is played or taken in actual interaction. These discrepancies which arise from the operation of multiple criteria for role units insure that the framework of roles will operate as a hazily conceived ideal framework for behavior rather than as an unequivocal set of formulas. In a sense, role conceptions are creative compromises, and an important phase of role theory should concern itself with how they are achieved.

THE NATURE OF
ROLE INTERACTION

Two facets of the role-taking process have been stressed in this statement, namely, the process of grouping behavior into "consistent" units which correspond to generalizable types of actors, and the process of organizing behavior vis-à-vis relevant others. We have elaborated somewhat the character and bases for the Gestalt-forming aspect of role-taking. There remains for further clarification the nature of relationships between self- and other-roles.

Dynamics of Self
and Other

The customary use of the concept of role in sociological and related literature today depicts the dynamic relationship between roles as primarily *conformity*. There are three key terms in this popular model, namely, *conformity, expectation,* and *approval*. A component of each role is a set of expectations regarding the behavior of individuals in relevant other-roles. When ego takes the role of alter the aspect of alter's role to which he is crucially sensitive is the set of expectations with respect to his (ego's) role. Ego takes the role of alter in order to conform to alter's expectations. Lack of conformity must be explained by erroneous role-taking, or by deficiencies in empathic ability or opportunities to perceive and judge the role of the other. The confirmation that role-taking and role-playing have proceeded correctly according to the conformity principle is the registration of approval.

We suggest that the foregoing model is not in itself incorrect; it is merely of insufficient generality. It describes only one of several ways in which the role-taking and role-playing process may occur, only one of several kinds of dynamic relations which may exist between self- and other-roles. Instead, we propose that the relations between self- and other-roles are interactive in a full sense, the dynamic principles being of several sorts, depending upon the objectives of the role-players and upon the character of their relationships with one another. Furthermore, the enactment of a given role often involves the simultaneous role-taking relationship with several different other-roles, and the dynamic relationship between each self- and other-role may be of a different sort.

In some athletic events such as the game of baseball the roles are highly standardized and the allowance for improvisation is at a minimum, so that the assumption that each role incorporates clear expectations for each other-role is quite valid. But in most situations what the role-player expects from the relevant other on the basis of the latter's role is not likely to be a specific action but some behavior which will be susceptible to interpretation as directed toward the ends associated with the other-role, expressive of the sentiment which dominates the role in question, or as consistent with the values attached to the role. A group torn by internal dissension may turn to someone who it is hoped will enact the role of compromiser. In doing so they have an expectation which identifies the general purpose and sentiment which will guide his actions and some general conception of the kind of behavior which will contribute to the achievement of compromise and which will not. But they do not have any exact notion of what the specific steps will be.

The articulation of behavior between roles may be described better by the term "preparedness" than by the term "expectation." The crucial consideration is that ego's role *prepares* him for a loosely definable *range* of responses from alter on the basis of the latter's role. The potential responses of alter, then, divide into those which are readily interpretable upon the basis of the assumed self- and other-roles and those which seem not to make sense from this vantage point. A response which fell outside of the preparedness range would be one of two kinds. It might be a response which was initially perceived as irrelevant, that is, not interpretable as the expression of any role in the context of the present focus of interaction. Or it might be a response which seemed to indicate a different role from that which had been attributed to alter.

The more or less definite expectations for ego's role which are part of alter's role, the preferences, the conceptions of legitimate and illegitimate behavior, and the evaluations, all directed toward ego's role, are a part but not the whole of alter's role. Role-taking may or may not concentrate on these aspects, and when it does it has been referred to as reflexive role-taking (12). Role-taking is always incomplete, with differential sensitivity to various aspects of the other-role. Only under special circumstances is the sensitization likely to be exclusively to the reflexive aspect. Such sensitization goes along with a conformity relationship, but not necessarily with approval in the simple sense.

The most general purpose associated with sensitization to the reflexive aspects of the other-role is to validate a self-image. The object is to present the self in a fashion which will conform to the relevant other's conception of the role by which the actor seeks to be identified. The role may, however, be one of which the relevant other approves or disapproves or toward which he is neutral. The young "tough" may be unsure that he has sufficiently exemplified the desired self-image until he provokes a vigorous condemnation from the teacher. The individualist may be dissatisfied until he provokes disagreement from a conventional person.

Elsewhere the kinds of dynamic relationship between roles have been discussed under the headings of role standpoint and reflexive versus non-reflexive role-taking (12). But the most general form of self–other relationship is that in which the relationship is a means to the accomplishment of either some shared goal or separate individual goals. Under such circumstances, the role relationship will be pragmatic, the two roles (or the same role enacted by two interacting individuals) being viewed as an efficient division of labor. In role-taking the salient aspects of the other-role will be their instrumental features, and the self-role will be enacted in such a fashion as to combine effectively with the instrumental features of the other-role to accomplish the intended purpose. Conformity to alter's expectations may enter as a partial determinant in this truly interactive relation but principally because it is an adjunct to the efficient accomplishment of the objective. The conformity principle may also come to be dominant because the effects of the role interaction in the promotion of the group goal are not readily apparent, as in a standby military organization or in an educational organization where no real tests of the effectiveness of the educational process are available. But conformity remains a special instance of the more general interactive principle rather than the general principle itself.

The Normative Component
of Role-Taking

Roles are often identified as sets of norms applicable to an actor playing a recognizable part. Since norms are at least partially equatable with expectations, such a conception may convey the same simple conformity formula with which we have just dealt. However, there is an essentially normative element in the concept of role which derives from the fact that a minimum of predictability is the precondition of interaction. This interdependency has been well described by Waller and Hill (13, pp. 328–332) by reference to the "interlocking habit systems" which develop between marriage partners. To the extent to which one member patterns his behavior to fit with the past regularities of behavior in the other, the former's behavior becomes inappropriate when the latter makes unanticipated alterations in his behavior. The inappropriateness invokes indignation against the innovator and the charge that he had no right to alter his behavior. Thus, although no norm originally existed and no explicit commitment had been made, a norm has in fact developed because of the damage which one person's unpredictable behavior does to the other. The prediction is of two sorts, prediction of the role to be played and prediction that behavior will continue to exemplify the same role once it is established in interaction. It is the latter which is most fundamental. The basic normative element in role-taking-and-playing is the requirement that the actor be consistent—that his behavior remain within the confines of a single role. So long as it remains within the role, the other will be generally prepared to cope with the behavior, whether he approves of it or not.

In institutional contexts, the additional normative element that designates a priori what role each individual must play is introduced to insure the required division of labor and to minimize the costs of exploratory role-setting behavior. But the norm of consistency is the more fundamental since it applies to role-taking in both informal and formalized settings, while the norm which assigns roles to persons applies chiefly in the latter.

The norm of consistency is mitigated in operation by an implicit presumption that actors are adhering to the norm. Indications that an actor is from an out-group, special symbols of deviant identity, or glaring evidences of "inconsistency," cause the assumption to be questioned. But in the absence of such cues, the initial presumption that each actor must be adhering to *some* role creates a strong bias in favor of finding a set of interpretations of his behavior which will allow it to be seen as pertaining to a single role. The bias may go as far as the synthesizing of a partially new role for one of the actors. Once the actor's role has been identified, either on the basis of indications of his position, placing oneself in his situation, or bits of his behavior, there is a further presumption that his subsequent behavior represents the same role. The flexibility with which most actions can be interpreted, emphasized, and de-emphasized, affords considerable scope for the role-taker to find confirmation of his preconceptions.

The normative principle of consistency, then, works both in the direction of enforcing a pattern onto behavior and in the direction of allowing a range of actions to be subsumed under a given role. The following hypotheses are suggested. The restricting impact of the consistency norm on behavior tends to be greater under conditions of dominance, whether authoritarian or instrumental, when participants are sensitized to interpret deviations from standard roles as symbolic denials of the dominance–submission relationship. The restricting effect tends to be greater when there is relatively little basis for faith in the role enactor's possession of the appropriate role sentiment. Such faith in turn arises out of prior experience with the other's role performance or out of esteem accorded the other by persons whose judgments are respected.

Many studies of role conflict proceed as if the dynamics of adjustment lie primarily in a choice of which set of expectations to honor in the face of an urgent desire to adhere to two or more incompatible sets. If the view is accepted that conformity is but one type of working adjustment to the other-role, then role conflict should be seen in the light of attempts to establish some kind of working relationship with the roles of relevant others. In its most general sense, role conflict exists when there is no immediately apparent way of simultaneously coping effectively with two different relevant other-roles, whether coping is by conformity to expectation or by some other type of response. The problem of a man whose friend has committed a serious crime need not be primarily or exclusively how to conform to the expectations both of his friend and of the police. The problem is to cope with the roles of each, conformity to expectation being but one of the alternatives before him. The definition of modern woman's problem as primarily how to conform simultaneously to the conflicting expectations of those with traditional and egalitarian views of her role reveals the same limited conception. The problem is more fundamentally how to engage in effective interaction with men, some of whom have modern and some traditional and some mixed conceptions of the masculine role, and with women who may have the same or different conceptions of the feminine role.

SUMMARY
AND IMPLICATIONS

Role theory, originally depicting a tentative and creative interaction process, has come increasingly to be employed as a refinement of conformity theory. In consequence, the theory has become relatively sterile except with respect to the consequences of role conflict and other forms of deviation from the conventional model of role behavior. Role taking, however, suggests a process whereby actors attempt to organize their interaction so that the behavior of each can be viewed as the expression of a consistent orientation which takes its meaning (or consistency) from its character as a way of coping with one or more other actors enacting similarly consistent orientations. Conformity to perceived expectations is but one special way in which an actor's role-playing may be related to the role of relevant others. From this viewpoint, role behavior in formal organizations becomes a working compromise between the formalized role prescriptions and the more flexible operation of the role-taking process. Role conflict is the attempt to devise an orientation from which the actor can cope effectively with multiple other-roles which apparently cannot be dealt with in a "consistent" fashion.

The conception of role relations as fully interactive rather than merely conforming harmonizes with current trends in sociology and anthropology to subordinate normative to functional processes in accounting for societal integration. Emphasis on the binding power of the mores and folkways or on the blind adherence to custom corresponds with a society populated by people playing roles principally as sets of expectations with which they must comply. On the other hand, a functional view emphasizes the interdependence of activities in accounting for cultural persistence and social stability. The interactive consequence of role relationships provides the social-psychological mechanism through which the functional principle of social stability operates.

REFERENCES

[1] Mead, George H. *Mind, Self, and Society,* ed. by Charles W. Morris. Chicago: The University of Chicago Press, 1935.

[2] Newcomb, Theodore. *Social Psychology.* New York: The Dryden Press, 1950.

[3] Linton, Ralph. *The Study of Man.* New York: Appleton-Century Co., 1936.

[4] Moreno, Jacob. *Who Shall Survive?* Washington, D.C.: Nervous and Mental Disease Monograph, N. 58, 1934.

[5] Kluckhohn, Clyde, and Henry A. Murray. "Personality Formation: The Determinants," in Clyde Kluckhohn, Henry A. Murray, and David Schneider (eds.), *Personality in Nature, Society, and Culture.* New York: Alfred A. Knopf, 1953, pp. 53–67.

[6] Allport, Gordon. *Becoming.* New Haven: Yale University Press, 1955.

[7] Davis, Kingsley. *Human Society.* New York: The Macmillan Company, 1948.

[8] Merton, Robert K. "Role Set: Problems in Sociological Theory," *British Journal of Sociology,* Vol. 8 (June 1957), pp. 106–120.

[9] Benne, Kenneth D., and Paul Sheats. "Functional Roles of Group Members," *Journal of Social Issues,* Vol. 4 (May 1948), pp. 41–49.

[10] Gross, Neal, Ward S. Mason, and Alexander W. McEachern, *Explorations in Role Analysis.* New York: John Wiley & Sons, 1958.

[11] Durkheim, Emile. *Sociology and Philosophy.* London: Cohen and West, 1953.

[12] Turner, Ralph H. "Role Taking, Role Standpoint, and Reference Group Behavior," *American Journal of Sociology,* Vol. 61 (January 1956), pp. 316–328.

[13] Waller, Willard, and Reuben Hill. *The Family: A Dynamic Interpretation.* New York: The Dryden Press, 1951.

[14] Bates, Frederick L. "Position, Role, and Status: A Reformulation of Concepts," *Social Forces,* Vol. 34 (May 1956), pp. 313–321.

[15] Blumer, Herbert. "Psychological Import of the Human Group," in Muzafer Sherif and M. O. Wilson (eds.), *Group Relations at the Crossroads.* New York: Harper & Brothers, 1953, pp. 185–202.

[16] Brim, Orville G., Jr., "Family Structure and Sex-Role Learning by Children," *Sociometry,* Vol. 21 (March 1958), pp. 1–18.

[17] Cottrell, Leonard S., Jr. "The Analysis of Situational Fields in Social Psychology," *American Sociological Review,* Vol. 7 (June 1942), pp. 370–382.

[18] Coutu, Walter. *Emergent Human Nature.* New York: Alfred A. Knopf, 1949.

[19] Faris, Ellsworth. *The Nature of Human Nature.* New York: McGraw-Hill Book Company, Inc., 1937.

[20] Faris, Robert E. L. *Social Psychology.* New York: The Ronald Press Company, 1952.

[21] Kirkpatrick, Clifford. "The Measurement of Ethical Consistency in Marriage," *International Journal of Ethics,* Vol. 46 (July 1936), pp. 444–460.

[22] Lindesmith, Alfred R., and Anselm L. Strauss. *Social Psychology.* New York: The Dryden Press, 1956.

[23] Miyamoto, S. Frank, and Sanford M. Dornbusch. "A Test of Interactionist Hypotheses of Self-Conception," *American Journal of Sociology,* Vol. 61 (March 1956), pp. 399–403.

[24] Neiman, Lionel J., and James W.

Hughes. "The Problem of the Concept of Role: A Resurvey of the Litterature," *Social Forces,* Vol. 30 (December 1951), pp. 141–149.

[25] Parsons, Talcott, Robert F. Bales, and others. *Family, Socialization and Interaction Process.* Glencoe, Ill.: The Free Press, 1955.

[26] Sarbin, Theodore R. "Role Theory," in Gardner Lindzey (ed.) *Handbook of Social Psychology,* Vol. I. Reading, Mass.: Addison-Wesley Publishing Company, Inc., 1954, pp. 223–258.

[27] Videbeck, Richard. "Dynamic Properties of the Concept Role," *Midwest Sociologist,* Vol. 20 (May 1958), pp. 104–108.

[28] Videbeck, Richard, and Alan P. Bates. "An Experimental Study of Conformity to Role Expectations," *Sociometry,* Vol. 22 (March 1959), pp. 1–11.

23

NEGOTIATING
A DIVISION OF LABOR
AMONG PROFESSIONALS
IN THE STATE
MENTAL HOSPITAL

Leonard Schatzman

Rue Bucher

THIS PAPER IS CONCERNED with some ways in which psychiatric professionals at state hospitals negotiate the tasks that they perform—that is, how they develop an institutional order that meets the requirements of patient care and treatment, and at the same time approximates their own professional requirements. The influence of professional career, treatment ideology, and institutional requirement will be dealt with primarily as the context within which the negotiation of tasks occurs and order is developed.[1]

THE CONTEXT OF
NEGOTIATION

In recent years, state hospitals have been adding many and varied professionals to their staffs. These professionals bring with them new ideas about

From *Psychiatry* 27 (1964), 266-277. Reprinted by special permission of the authors and The William Alanson White Psychiatric Foundation, Inc. (Text, Chapter 12)

[1] In an earlier paper, the authors and their colleagues sketched the larger problem of negotiated order: Anselm Strauss and others, "The Hospital and Its Negotiated Order," pp. 147–169, in *The Hospital in Modern Society,* edited by Eliot Freidson; New York, Free Press of Glencoe, 1963. For a similar approach by a political scientist, see Norton E. Long, "The Local Community as an Ecology of Games," *Amer. J. Sociology* (1958) 64:251–261. For a similar position, see also Sherman Krupp, *Pattern in Organizational Analysis;* Philadelphia, Chilton, 1961; esp. pp. 172–175, "Organization, As a System of Bargained Transactions."

treatment and care, and the skills with which, hopefully, custodially oriented hospitals can change markedly. However, their coming to the state hospitals often poses a great many problems, centering principally around the allocation of tasks and the coordination of work. These problems emerge for a number of reasons:

(1) The professionals come from different educational institutions and work with varied skills, often on different levels.

(2) They come with different conceptions of both their own professional roles and requirements, and those of their new colleagues.[2]

(3) They come with different conceptions of proper—and improper— treatment and care (including psychotherapeutic, somatotherapeutic, milieu-therapeutic, and eclectic-pragmatic orientations).

(4) The professionals exhibit varying degrees of commitment to their own professional requirements, to the treatment philosophy which they espouse, and to the institution in which they work.

(5) They tend to have different career plans and models, and are located at different stages in their respective careers.[3]

(6) Because of frequent personnel turnover and new additions, at any one time some professionals are arriving, some are preparing to leave, and some have just left—and there is little assurance that specific existing tasks will be carried on by persons from the same profession.

Given this professional and institutional context—and we dare say most psychiatric institutions today exhibit some of these conditions—it is clear that a state of flux and lack of stable structure characterize the state hospitals that are rapidly changing to meet current standards of psychiatric practice.[4]

In the course of a more extensive study recently completed by the authors and other colleagues, we found a state hospital situation which involved all the conditions indicated above. The situation was particularly interesting to us as sociologists since it provided data for research in the processes of inter-professional work and coordination. We shall briefly give some history of the hospital, and tell of the team situations as we found them, and then discuss negotiation among the professional personnel.

---

[2] The conceptual framework for this item relates to one sketched in Rue Bucher and Anselm Strauss, "Professions in Process," *Amer. J. Sociology* (1961) 66:325–334.

[3] For conceptually related literature on careers, see: Everett C. Hughes, *Men and Their Work;* Glencoe, Ill., Free Press, 1958. Howard S. Becker and Anselm L. Strauss, "Careers, Personality, and Adult Socialization," *Amer. J. Sociology* (1956) 62:253–263.

[4] Wallace S. Sayre, a public administrator, has suggested certain features of hospitals in general which mitigate against static structure. Writing in "Principles of Administration," a two-part article in *Hospitals* (1956) Vol. 30, he says: ". . . these stresses between organization and profession are made the more complex by a multiplicity of professions, a multiplicity of values and perspectives not easily reconciled into a harmonious organization. . . ." (January 16; p. 34). "The hospital would seem to be an organizational setting where many semi-autonomous cooperators meet for the purpose of using common services and facilities and to provide services to each other, but in a loosely integrated organizational system." (February 1; p. 50.)

Two years prior to our study, a new superintendent had arrived at the relatively old-style, static, state hospital. As a psychodynamically oriented psychiatrist, he was understandably appalled at the conditions he found there. Given his mandate from the state to bring the hospital up to current psychiatric standards, but confronted with relatively few resources with which to transform a large hospital with well entrenched traditions and their defenders, he chose to introduce modern psychiatry ward by ward, rather than attempt a massive assault upon the traditions. His plan was to attract psychiatrists to the hospital by offering to each a single ward, a professional team, and considerable autonomy and freedom for organizing treatment. Several psychiatrists and other professionals were thereby recruited for the "treatment wards"; a few came from the existing ranks but most from the outside.

When we arrived to study the state hospital, eight treatment wards had been established. Because we had time to study only five of these, we made our selection according to special situations of interest to us. Four of the wards that we selected were the hospital's archetypes of treatment ideology and organization. Three that we did not study were variations of the archetypes. The eighth ward, which had no single recognizable treatment philosophy and no immediately recognizable team structure, proved to be a fortunate choice for sociological inquiry, since it allowed us to observe a situation marked by incoherence in philosophy, professional role confusion, strife, and frustration.

Our data consist of field observations and interviews bearing upon the work and social structures of these five team-run wards. The teams were multidisciplinary, consisting of psychiatrist-chief, physician, nurse, psychologist, social worker, and recreational or occupational therapist. In addition to these professionals, there was at least one psychiatric aide on each team. Almost daily observations for approximately one month at each locale yielded considerable data on the teams and the specific conditions under which teamwork was negotiated and carried out.

All five teams operated under several relatively similar and constant conditions: (1) inadequate physical facilities, (2) patient-staff ratio (a range of 65-85 patients per team), (3) number and types of personnel available for work, (4) a random-rotational system of patient admission to the unit (except for sex; there were two male and three female wards), (5) a wide range of diagnostic types, mostly schizophrenia, (6) institutional mandates to organize a treatment system and to get patients discharged upon improvement. Nevertheless, the wards were different from each other, principally in treatment ideology,[5] organization of treatment, and division of labor among

---

[5] The term "ideology" with respect to professions has had a number of meanings in the literature. In one usage, professional ideology refers to the definition of the field, its subject matter, boundaries, and the sense of mission held by members of a profession. For this meaning of the term, see Howard S. Becker and James W. Carper, "The Elements of Identification with an Occupation," *Amer. Sociol. Review* (1956) 21:289–298. In another usage, ideology refers to a system of beliefs about the nature of the reality

the professionals. In terms of philosophy of treatment predominant on each ward, the team situations as first encountered were as follows:

Ward A

The first ward, whose ideology we named *The Radical Patient-Government System,* would ordinarily be recognized as a variant form of "therapeutic community." The ward's predominant philosophy was that each patient must come to understand himself and take over increasing responsibility for his own welfare and disposition. The principal medium for this process must be the patient peer group—or, more precisely, the transactional network among peers within which patients negotiate their own treatment and management. Thus, patients organized as a government, voted upon matters related to management and treatment, and literally dictated drug usage, passes, and discharges, as well as mutual discipline, ward cleanliness, routines, and the like. The staff members were encouraged to interact with individual patients—but only very briefly—to help each patient interpret his personal action and feeling. Otherwise, staff members were to redirect patients to the larger (patient community) group for matters pertaining to ward life and to mutual disposition. Most generally, the staff was expected to maintain the broader conditions of institutional existence so that this kind of patient system could survive and perform its intended functions.

Ward B

Our second ward was run under what we referred to as *The Representative System.* Here, the philosophy was that patients must be helped to develop insight into their problems, and that help must come from the staff as much as from patients. Thus, a patient "acts out" his primary familiar difficulties with other patients but "works through" his problems in interaction with the staff. Patients were arbitrarily divided into four aggregates, each of which was "represented" by one of four professionals. The representative was regarded as a strong, knowing, and kindly parent who functions to organize both the management and treatment of patients. However, the organization was not an arbitrary imposition by the representative; rather, its shape and direction were products of skillful negotiation between him and the patients.

Thus, a healthy family situation was created in order to provide a proper model for behavior and a context wherein the patient not only negotiates with the "parent" for more or less medication, for passes, and for creature

---

with which the profession is concerned. In this sense, ideology is the set of assumptions and principles guiding the instrumental activity of professionals. For this use of the term, see the work of Daniel J. Levinson and his colleagues, in *The Patient and the Mental Hospital,* edited by Milton Greenblatt, Daniel J. Levinson, and Richard H. Williams; Glencoe, Ill., Free Press, 1957; Chapters 3, 11, and 15. We are using the latter sense of the term in this paper, encompassing the former meaning under the term "professional identity."

comforts, but discovers in the interactional process appropriate communication skills and patterns of emotional expression. Patients also had group meetings supervised by the staff. In these meetings they revealed their personal and mutual concerns, which became the context for direct negotiation with the parent-representative.

Ward C

The third ward was organized under what we called *The Psychotherapeutic Authority System.* The prevalent philosophy followed closely the psychotherapeutic model; etiology, symptomology, and course of mental illness were seen psychodynamically. On the most abstract level, the concept of mental illness seen here was not too different from that found on the previously mentioned wards. However, the treatment ideology was decidely different. Here, the psychiatrist was the principal personage—the expert whose skills are necessary, for proper diagnosis, for psychotherapeutic planning tailored to individual patients, and for psychotherapeutic contact with the patient. The other personnel were expected to care for the patients, carry out specific therapeutic strategies, and, most important, to feed back all intelligence to the chief. Information thus gained was utilized by the chief to restructure therapeutic strategies.

Ward D

The Medical Authority System in this ward was developed and controlled by the one chief who had been recruited from the old hospital structure. On this ward, no single and clear therapeutic ideology existed, except that in contrast to all of the other treatment wards, its orientation tended to be more medical—that is, it made much greater use of electroshock and drugs. In earlier years, the chief had been clearly somatotherapeutic in orientation, and more recently had become eclectic and pragmatic. Nevertheless, in his conversations with us, he revealed strong commitment to a medical-empiricist orientation.

Ward E

This team-ward [organized under] *The Unresolved System* had no single or dominant treatment ideology. The team itself was divided in its purposes and fragmented in structure. The psychiatrist-chief held an orientation similar to that of the chief on Ward C: He "saw" patients, developed programs for each of them, and expected his staff to follow his suggestions and report to him on patient progress. This organization of treatment was carried on quite independently (except for discharge planning), and was separate from the activities of the physician, whose orientation was somatic and whose most pressing concerns were patient census and disposition, patient control, and progress reports. The psychologist and social worker were intent upon pur-

suing milieutherapeutic interests in the form of small and large group thera-
pies. The nurse was the main work-link for all the personnel by virtue of her
ubiquitous presence and her willingness to follow the orders or requests of
all her colleagues. Only two types of ward activity looked like total team
action: (1) thrice-weekly patient-group meetings with the psychiatrist, physician, and psychologist rotating leadership (with the other two leaders absent
from each meeting by mutual agreement); and (2) weekly team meetings,
which were largely monologues by the psychiatrist (if present) or the
physician.

We hasten to make two distinct points about these descriptions. First, they
are representations of ward ideology and structure covering only a relatively
short span of time. The total organization of treatment upon each ward
seemed never fully to crystallize. Rather, it appeared relatively stable only
from time to time during the tenure of each chief. Second, we focused mainly
upon predominant ideology, in part to separate it from professional considerations that will be highlighted in subsequent discussion. However, it should
be clearly understood that in a psychiatric setting, treatment ideology largely
defines both what treatment should be and what it should not be, thereby
suggesting what tasks should be done and what tasks should be forbidden
as antitherapeutic. Ideology may also imply the prerequisite skills for these
tasks, but leave the field open for contests concerning who can lay claim to
essential and ancillary tasks and who should be forbidden their performance.

For each ward, the organization of treatment tended to reflect not only
the professional and ideological orientations of the chief, but also those of
the team members. Except for the Ward D chief, all the chiefs were relatively young psychiatrists trained in the tradition of psychodynamic, one-
to-one therapy. While they came with ideological predispositions, they had
little or no experience with state hospitals, and had only the vaguest notions
of how to implement their therapeutic ideals in such an environment. Therefore, they had to feel their way in organizing treatment programs and, perhaps most importantly, each (including the chief of Ward D) had to learn
how to deal with a "prefabricated" team. Thus, although formal responsibility and authority were vested in the chief, in practice each had to come
to terms with his team by negotiating with its members concerning methods
of treatment and assignment of tasks.

Negotiation among team members was accentuated by the relative fluidity
of team composition. Various members, including some chiefs, came and
went during the teams' existence. Because professionals did not arrive simultaneously on the scene, the conditions for ideological and power struggle
were kept alive. When a new psychologist, for example, was assigned to a
ward, bringing his own ideological predispositions and aspirations, he was
not necessarily content to take over the precise functions of the preceding
psychologist. The arrival of a new team member tended rather to initiate a
new round of ideological soundings, of instructions and arguments, and of
negotiations over the assignment of tasks. The total organization of treat-

ment and the division of labor underwent intermittent amendment. As an organization of treatment (consistent with an ideology) was being forged upon each ward, the team members simultaneously were laying claims to given tasks; when, for whatever reason, the ideology was altered, changes in the division of labor were to be anticipated.

Much of what we have noted about the team histories and special problems is an abstraction from the sum total of our observations. When we first began looking around, not only at who did what, but how this or that task came to be done by a given person, we quickly realized that thinking in terms of "social roles," "role expectations," and the like, would not take us very far toward understanding this situation. Role analysis requires rather considerable consensus among participants about social roles and a greater measure of role stability than was apparent here. Actions that were performed in terms of expectations accompanying professional roles were no more striking or prevalent than those performed without such expectations or those unperformed despite expectations. Simple reference to departures from traditional expectations provided no clues to specific processes of role change, and no explanation for what we were seeing. Nor could we call this situation a condition of "social disorganization," since no reasonably stable organization had existed in the first place. We thought it most fruitful to view observed events within a framework of evolving social forms, whose details and rules were collectively vague and uncertain (though, often enough, unilaterally clear), and for which few proven models existed. Moreover, we saw that existent models of treatment or team organization were frequently contested. Some professionals were unfamiliar with certain models (community therapy, for example); others lacked sympathy for or were opposed to particular types (electroshock or small-group therapy); and others saw some models as inappropriate to state hospitals (one-to-one psychotherapy). While discussing or arguing the merits of treatment forms, the professionals were also making various claims to "essential" roles, aspiring to new ones, dumping old ones, and forcing each other to assume unwanted roles. Since this is what we saw most clearly, we regarded as important the search for emergent work and team patterns. In short, we came to assume that we were witnessing a field of negotiation and that the outcomes of negotiative action actually were divisions of professional labor.

THE ARTICULATION
OF CLAIMS

Having discussed the context within which negotiations occurred, we turn now to a description of how claims, and the grounds for them, were articulated. In the articulation process, some claims were made vocal and clear, while others were left tacit and implicit. However, almost any task undertaken or sought by a professional was subject to review and denial. Even tasks backed by law and institutional authority were called into question. Ostensibly, tacit claims were easily and frequently awakened as shifts in ideology or social structure set off the alarm. Moreover, even claims that had been won earlier were not insured against loss. The nature of the claim and the extent to which its achievement required explication was determined by the profession involved, the predominant ideology, and the ward's immediate division of labor. Aggressiveness in claiming reflected serious opposition to the claim itself or to the claimant, as well as the strength of the claimant's requirements.

When listening to the claims being made, we found the arguments and negotiation revolving around a number of grounds. We were attracted to the matter of grounds or logic partly because of the frequency with which they had to be articulated, and partly because of the frequency with which they failed to impress the claimant's colleagues. The grounds selected for the rhetoric depended a great deal upon the profession of the claimant as well as upon the nature of the claims itself. For example, one might expect the physicians to argue on the basis of legality (including certification), appointed authority (institutional authorization), or tradition—and some physicians did just this. We also heard reference to formal education (including degrees), to prior experience with the task in question, to current need or expediency, and to a desire or wish to perform a task (or "try it").

One other supposed qualification, that of "knowledge," bears special mention. Since the conditions for claiming were so fertile, and since claiming invited argumentation, the more articulate professionals were in an advantageous position. They were able to "demonstrate" their knowledge (and, by inference, their abilities) in team meetings on the ward and at hospital staff meetings. They could thereby "prove" the quality of their prior experience, their formal education, and their ability to interpret patient behavior or needs. In an atmosphere where formal status, titles, and authority were not generally held sacred or inviolate the person who "knew" what he was talking about could more easily make his claims stick.

The rhetorical grounds which we have listed do not cover all the logical possibilities; nor are they mutually exclusive. Moreover, the explicit arguments did not preclude those held tacitly. A professional who explicitly argued on grounds of license and tradition may have been implicitly claiming the utility of his formal education. Certainly, the "needs of the patients" often served as implicit grounds. Since rhetoric is usually directed at some special audience or audiences, claimants were often forced to weigh what they would actually articulate and what they would keep implicit. For example, on Wards A and B, where a sort of philosophical equalitarianism reigned, it was wise not to argue on the grounds of appointed authority, and to leave this rationale implicit.

This suggests that arguments or grounds have "takers" and "no takers"— that is, that grounds must be shifted depending upon the professional, the claim, and the audience. For example, the psychologist of Ward E was persuaded to accept the social worker's claim that he should conduct small-group therapy on the grounds of prior experience, but the physician was not persuaded. The latter tended to accept only grounds of legality, appointed authority, or tradition for any professional task. As this particular argument progressed, the social worker shifted his argument, basing his claim on knowledge by demonstrating a conceptual grasp of group dynamics. But the physician, who neither understood nor appreciated group dynamics, was "no taker," and the social worker's claim was not honored. On Ward B the vocal claim of the nurse that she should conduct group therapy was honored on the same grounds as it was argued: knowledge and expediency. But honoring was possible because the team's dominant ideology conferred special status upon the nurse as a representative of an aggregate of patients. Thus, the context within which claims were asserted and the rhetoric used made claims or grounds acceptable and reasonable, or unacceptable and unreasonable—or even ridiculous.

Not all acquired tasks were gained through claiming; some were preferred to and others were forced upon particular professionals. Implicitly, at least, those who did the proferring or forcing were claiming their right to do so. Nevertheless, the team's dominant treatment ideology and current division of labor often suggested that one member of the team undertake some specific task. If the task was relatively desirable and seemed appropriate for one of the professionals, it was offered. If the task was undesirable but necessary, it was more likely to be forced upon a professional. In such cases, someone —or a coalition—had to decide what was necessary and for whom it was appropriate. As an example of a transfer of a desirable task, when the psychologist of Ward B fell behind in "mental status examinations" of patients, he offered to teach the nurse to do them, and to share that work with her; she was pleased to accept. In contrast, the nurse of Ward E was forced to help make beds, a task which she abhorred. In both instances, a conception of tasks appropriate to psychiatric nursing was introduced by non-nursing personnel.

Not all tasks were performed or developed in the context of claims and negotiation. Many areas of work attracted little attention, making it possible for a professional to do things that others were not interested in, or failed to see as particularly important. To some extent, the same held true for the shedding or curtailing of tasks. But again, the situation—mainly ideological —determined what in the total array of possible activities was essential and what was not. And the professional situation—the division of labor on any one team—determined whether any specific act could freely be developed or whether it constituted an invasion of another professional's territory. Thus, both ideology and interprofessional agreements made certain acts permissible or not permissible. The complexity of the above points can be illustrated by the following: The psychiatrist-chief of Ward B was not permitted by his team to do psychotherapy, since (1) he was not a "representative," and (2) psychotherapy could not (ideologically) be given to one patient unless all patients were given psychotherapy. On Ward D, any professional could engage in psychotherapy—that is, one-to-one engagement, with treatment intended—with any patient; even the aide could if she wished. Thus, on one ward, psychotherapy was a closed area, not even subject to claims; on another ward, psychotherapy was an open area, with no claiming or negotiative process necessary.

THE NEGOTIATION
OF CLAIMS [6]

We turn our attention now to how the professionals attempted to adjust their special interests to the reality of their situations. What was real was the presence of other professionals who were also intent upon fostering their own interests, which might be informal and personal, formal and professional, or intellectual and ideological. For each professional, the fostering of interests meant getting to do what was important—because he was trained to do the task, because his professional integrity required doing it, because it was something that had to be done and no one else was doing it, because he wanted to do it, and so on. This also meant holding on to important things he was already doing, or dropping unimportant and degrading tasks. The negotiations that we have selected for discussion consist mainly of those that best lend themselves to generalization. [7]

The Representative System on Ward B provided the most opportunity for free and open negotiation of claims, with probably the best chances for successfully realizing them. On the other end of the continuum from open negotiation and success was the Unresolved System on Ward E. Neither system seemed to have a greater number of negotiative acts than the other; negotiation simply took different forms and affected the participants differently. On Ward B, negotiation tended to be rhetorical. Professionals stated their claims openly, arguing the appropriate grounds and mustering allies for the inevitable team vote. On any issue which affected professional status interests, alignments developed "naturally." However, claimants could appeal to neutrals or to opponents on other than status grounds—ideological grounds, for example. This was quite feasible because tasks and responsibility were shared among the representatives rather than divided, and because an equalitarian philosophy mitigated against the strength of status distinctions. Also, behind the rhetorical negotiation and corralling of allies, was a unique

[6] For those interested in concrete details of negotiation in industry, an excellent reference is Melville Dalton, *Men Who Manage;* New York, Wiley, 1959. For negotiation in tuberculosis hospitals, see Julius Roth, *Timetables;* Indianapolis, Bobbs-Merrill, 1963.
[7] Certain other features of negotiation and its consequences in psychiatric hospitals are explored in the authors' forthcoming book (see footnote 1), especially in the chapters titled "Professionals and Their Organization of Work" and "Negotiated Order and the Coordination of Work."

system which conferred upon one's colleague what one was claiming for oneself: An actual or potential opponent was not being asked to give up a task, but to confer the right to do what he himself was doing. For example, the physician was reluctant to allow the social worker to recommend types and amounts of drugs, but he himself could lay claim to dealing with patients' relatives and the larger community. Each professional could freely use another as a consultant. In practice, the physician was still the physician to all the ward's patients. He had but to concede to the other professionals their right (through openly negotiated in-group agreement) to the "first decision" on management and treatment; the physician did not lose his claim to instruct and advise, or argue the case before the entire team for a "second decision."

The Representative System itself evolved out of a series of rhetorical negotiations starting with the nurse's efforts to force her colleagues (principally the social worker and psychologist) to do in fact what they were implicitly claiming—show an interest in ward affairs and have concern for patients. The nurse argued on grounds of expediency ("I can't keep track of them by myself") and ideology or knowledge ("treatment starts with contact and understanding"). The ensuing discussion led to a plan to divide all patients into manageable aggregates, at first solely for the purpose of improving the surveillance of patients. This nurse thereby successfully disclaimed the sole responsibility for surveillance and at the same time engineered the consent of three other professionals into an equal partnership. From surveillance to management and finally to treatment, the sharing of tasks became increasingly pronounced. As the professionals continued to give and get, team meetings became the principal means for one professional's control over the other, and for mutual instruction which reinforced an evolving equalitarian philosophy and the sharing of labor.

What transpired was also due, in part, to the roles played by personnel who were "nonrepresentatives." Although the psychiatrist-chief was partial to milieutherapy, he was not doctrinaire, and he was far less concerned with the form treatment was to take than with establishing team consensus. Very early, he made his claims to intellectual leadership and to teaching rather than to directing psychiatric treatment. In these roles, he was honored by all except the social worker, who was ideologically committed to the ideas prevailing on Ward A, and who attempted—at first with only partial success —to establish himself, on grounds of knowledge, as the ideologist of the team. However, existing alliances temporarily prevented the social worker from successfully negotiating his claim to lead the team into a new treatment form. The chief allied himself with the nurse because she was leading the team toward a sharing of labor, thereby achieving consensus based upon similar work rather than upon traditional statuses and a division of tasks by profession. The nonpsychiatrically trained physician also allied himself with the nurse because she was a "medical" person and because she accepted his preferred role of teacher of psychodynamics. The OT and RT, who neither claimed nor were offered positions as representatives, recognized the nurse as the daily operations leader and voted with her on major issues.

A few days after our withdrawal from the ward, however, the social worker succeeded in persuading the team (principally the nurse) to convert to the patient government system. He was able to bring about this change largely through negotiation with the nurse, with the help of others from Ward A (patient government). The use of allies from another ward was common, particularly by professionals whose claims were persistently blocked. The operations on Ward E comprise another illustration of such maneuvering.

On Ward E, the context for the negotiation of claims was markedly different, so team members necessarily attempted to engineer consent to their claims in different ways. There were alliances, but these were mostly collusive in character. Not only were claims difficult to realize, they were even difficult to articulate. Nevertheless, as persons with strong professional, ideological, or institutional commitments, the personnel persisted in claiming and in attempting to realize their claims. Whereas the professionals of Ward B sought alliances within the team structure, those of Ward E went far afield in search of forces to bring to bear upon those who would not negotiate— going even to the hospital superintendent. They also went elsewhere to satisfy claims directly—for example, they did psychotherapy on another ward, or engaged in part-time work outside the hospital itself.

Just prior to our period of observation, Ward E had no psychiatrist-chief, but he was promised and awaited. In the meantime, the ward was headed by a physician who antedated the team system itself. The physician's authorized control over the patients and the personnel backed up his oft articulated claim to operational leadership, but this was a forced claim since ideological leadership belonged to the psychologist. The physician was willing to negotiate with nobody except the psychologist, to whom he preferred a kind of lieutenancy plus freedom to develop a treatment program. The physician needed a working colleague ("I needed help, and he was the only one around who knew anything"), at least until the psychiatrist arrived. He regarded the nurse and social worker as "young novices," incapable of intelligent and professional initiative—therefore, unworthy of the privilege of negotiation. The psychologist refused the lieutenancy but was forced into a position as team consultant. He himself "didn't want to get involved" and found part-time work as a therapist outside the hospital.

The claim of the social worker to the right to conduct small group therapy was denied by the physician, as was the nurse's claim to a medical colleagueship. The social worker sought to make the psychologist an ally, but the latter refused; the nurse preferred him the role of teacher, but he refused to give his time. He withheld his own major claims until the arrival of the psychiatrist. Thus, negotiation within the team came to a virtual standstill, and most claims remained pending. The stage was set for a full round of negotiation: The physician wanted responsibility and operational leadership to pass to another "responsible" person; the psychologist wanted an "intellectual" colleague; the nurse wanted someone to teach her psychodynamics; and the social worker wanted an ally to help mitigate the physician's "arbitrary power." Both nurse and social worker were intent upon performing tasks for which they had very real and imposing models, mainly on Wards A and B.

The psychiatrist who arrived was relatively young and quite inexperienced in state hospital psychiatry. His initial intentions were to observe and to learn the ongoing system, and then begin to assume operational leadership. The physician quickly sized him up as a "boy" and grimly held onto operational leadership. While the others saw the psychiatrist in different ways, all waited for the inevitable contest over the chieftainship. While waiting, the psychologist, social worker, and nurse met frequently to find ways of helping the psychiatrist to "usurp" the real power. In the meantime the social worker made a private claim to the psychiatrist that he should be allowed to conduct small group therapy, and was granted the right to do so. The physician did not prevent the social worker from organizing a "discharge planning group," but instead discharged or transferred, within days, some of the patients selected for a few weeks of group planning. In this way, he disclaimed the implicit claim of the psychiatrist that he could honor a claim that the physician would not honor.

Another private agreement was negotiated between the nurse and psychologist, a mutual exchange whereby the psychologist taught the nurse diagnostic techniques in exchange for her sharing some of his responsibility in this task. Much earlier, the psychologist and the physician had agreed to share responsibility for this work. The adjustment of claims on the basis of private negotiation continued until the psychiatrist was able to effect his major claim. He did this by simple assertion and action, but not until he had secured leverage from the alliance within the team, and explicit assurance from the institution's administration that his claim to the chieftainship was indeed honored and authorized. Thus, in contrast to the early negotiation on Ward B, professional personnel on this team attempted to effect some of their claims by secret alliances, private agreements, and a search for power and claim satisfaction outside the ward.

The reader may argue that both Wards B and E were somewhat unusual: In the former, personnel were freely sharing and exchanging tasks beyond what might be expected; in the latter no one was able to satisfy his professional requirements. But what situations existed on the other wards, and what kinds of negotiation were characteristic there? On Ward A, all the major claims of the social worker and psychologist were realized. These two, under the operational and ideological leadership of the psychiatrist-chief, had established the milieutherapeutic revolution on the ward, had together developed its basic design, and were in a position to dictate tasks for the physician and nurse. Theoretically, the team formulated and implemented ward policy democratically, but in practice the three milieutherapists refused to negotiate except within the framework they had established. The physician and nurse were forced to share unfamiliar and, for them, undesirable tasks. Whereas the blocking of open negotiation on Ward E hopefully seemed temporary, that on Ward A seemed endless. Quitting the team was one way of handling this situation, and several nurses had earlier used this route in search of professional satisfaction. It was also possible to negotiate with other teams for a transfer. In this way, an earlier Ward A nurse who had found the situation there "intolerable," was able to privately negotiate with the chief of Ward D for a transfer to D, where she could satisfy all her major claims. The physician and nurse on Ward A remained for the duration of our observation, but fought those who persisted in denying their claims.

On Wards C and D, the nurses and physicians had privately and satisfactorily negotiated their claims with their chiefs or willingly accepted the tasks proferred by them. Although ideologically poles apart, both chiefs had similar perspectives on the allocation of tasks: Both wanted and achieved a division of labor generally along traditional lines, according to occupation. In this endeavor, they were aided by their physicians and nurses, but opposed by their psychologists and social workers. Actually, on Ward D there was no social worker: One had recently quit the ward because the chief and his team (except for the psychologist) would not accept an aspiring psychiatric social worker as opposed to a traditional one. A succession of social workers had served on Ward D prior to our observations, each being granted no room for negotiation. The chief, himself, finally assumed some of the traditional social work tasks (principally contacting relatives of patients) and ". . . gave up on social workers."

An interesting set of similarities in personal-professional circumstances confronted both the psychologist of Ward D and the social worker of Ward C, with some similar consequences for negotiative patterns. Both were relatively older than colleagues in their own professions and had been educated to older career models. In the ideological and organizational ferment of this hospital, they were learning new ideas and ways, but yet were not as doctrinaire and bold in bargaining as the others. Each attempted to negotiate for "second careers" but seemed more willing than their colleagues to settle for less. The Ward C social worker attempted, without negotiating, to function as a free agent in psychotherapeutic experiments. The chief intervened, but rather than restrict this kind of professional action entirely, proferred carefully supervised tasks closely related to individual therapy. This arrangement was entirely consistent with the chief's treatment ideology and views on professional work. The psychologist of Ward D negotiated privately with his chief for freedom to treat patients both in groups and individually, bolstering his claim by pointing to distinctive treatment programs being conducted by the nurse and the OT. The chief honored the psychologist's claims but insisted on close supervision, which the psychologist accepted. The psychologist of Ward C developed a number of time-consuming commitments in other areas of the hospital to escape his chief's supervision and forcing of tasks, thereby following a pattern of disengagement—a main or ancillary pattern characteristic of nearly every professional who was unsuccessful in negotiating his major claims.

Thus, participation in these teams had different consequences for the professionals in terms of their immediate claims and career aspirations. Several outcomes were possible: Aspirations could be fulfilled, thwarted, or turned in new directions. The claims were either made upon traditional and time-honored tasks, or upon functions that represented emergent or newly conceived tasks for the respective professions. The negotiation of tasks by the social workers and psychologists tended to run parallel; on the other hand, that of nurses and physicians was linked. Furthermore, on wards where the aspirations of social workers and psychologists were facilitated, those of the nurses and physicians were either thwarted (as on A) or turned in new directions (as on B); the opposite occurred on wards where the aspirations of nurses and physicians were satisfied. Except for Ward E, these differential effects obtained generally. They can be accounted for as a product of (1) the team ideology which developed upon the wards, (2) the division of labor suggested or dictated by the ideology, and (3) the professional identifications and aspirations of the team members.

IMPLICATIONS

Since World War II many older institutions have been quite visibly, and dramatically, affected by new ideas and technologies. In addition, wholly new institutions have arisen as if impatient with the rates of change in the older ones. Increasingly, institutional order is being negotiated rather than "given." The negotiations and their context, as portrayed above, are much in evidence in many psychiatric institutions throughout the country. Since our study (1958-1962), we have had the opportunity to carry on observations in other settings, including private and county hospitals and day care centers. The persons and particulars may be different, but the negotiative processes as sketched here are much in evidence and very pertinent to the division or sharing of professional labor and to the treatment of patients in all these institutions.

The introduction of new ideas and technologies foretells a reshuffling of tasks among the personnel in existing systems, and foretells new opportunities for creating, negotiating, and realizing professional claims. The failure of some of the professionals in our study to negotiate their claims successfully suggests that some settings are quicker than others in responding to newer professional models and missions. Negotiations are most intense and persistent when new ideas are offered in a context of institutional expansion and experimentation, and when they appear to spell "progress." Undoubtedly, some professionals in psychiatric settings will have a stake in continuing to espouse traditional organization. But the new ways provide others with real or imagined possibilities for new tasks, and provide both the rationale for new claims and the ideas with which to devalue existing ideas and task structures. If a new way has any validity, it will, in time, provide its own justification, however outlandish it may appear at first to those whose interests it seems to threaten.

As professional schools expand and proliferate, increasing numbers of psychiatric professionals enter old and new work settings. They come increasingly with upgraded education, and with newer professional work models and missions, as well as with newer treatment ideologies. They tend to be more articulate and insistent about their claims. Undoubtedly, they meet with variable success in negotiating their claims. In any case, the modern scene, we predict, will offer more negotiation among professionals, particularly as working situations become increasingly complex and interprofessional in structure.

24

DEVIANCE DISAVOWAL: THE MANAGEMENT OF STRAINED INTERACTION BY THE VISIBLY HANDICAPPED[1]

Fred Davis

A RECURRING ISSUE IN SOCIAL RELATIONS is the refusal of those who are viewed as deviant[2] to concur in the verdict. Or, if in some sense it can be said that they do concur, they usually place a very different interpretation on the fact or allegation than do their judges. In our society this is especially true of deviance which results from ascription (e.g., the Negro) as against that which partakes to some significant degree of election (e.g., the homosexual). And, while it may be conjectured that ultimately neither the Negro

From *Social Problems* 9 (Fall 1961), 120–132. Reprinted by permission of the author and the Society for the Study of Social Problems. (Text, Chapter 13)

[1] The study from which this paper derives was supported by a grant from the Association for the Aid of Crippled Children. I am indebted to Stephen A. Richardson and David Klein of the Association for their help and advice. I also wish to thank Frances C. Macgregor, Cornell Medical Center, New York, for having so generously made available to me case materials from her research files on persons with facial disfigurements. See Frances C. Macgregor et al., *Facial Deformities and Plastic Surgery: A Psychosocial Study,* Springfield, Ill.: Charles C Thomas, 1953.
[2] Following Lemert, as used here the term deviant (or deviance) refers 1) to a person's deviation from prevalent or valued norms, 2) to which the community-at-large reacts negatively or punitively, 3) so as to then lead the person to define his situation largely in terms of this reaction. All three conditions must be fulfilled for it to be said that deviance exists (secondary deviation, in Lemert's definition). In this sense the Negro, the career woman, the criminal, the Communist, the physically handicapped, the mentally ill, the homosexual, to mention but a few, are all deviants, albeit in different ways and with markedly different consequences for their life careers. Edwin M. Lemert, *Social Pathology,* New York: McGraw-Hill, 1951, 75–77.

nor the homosexual would be cast in a deviant role were it not for society's devaluation of these attributes in the first place, barring such a hypothetical contingency it remains the more persuasive argument in a democracy to be able to claim that the social injury from which one suffers was in no way self-inflicted.

In these pages I wish to discuss another kind of non self-inflicted social injury, the visible physical handicap. My aim though is not to survey and describe the many hardships of the visibly handicapped,[3] but to analyze certain facets of their coping behavior as it relates to the generalized imputations of deviance they elicit from society, imputations which many of them feel it necessary to resist and reject.

There are, of course, many areas in which such imputations bear heavily upon them: employment, friendship, courtship, sex, travel, recreation, residence, education. But the area I treat here is enmeshed to some extent in all of these without being as categorically specific as any. I refer to situations of sociability, and more specifically to that genre of everyday intercourse which has the characteristics of being: 1) face-to-face, 2) prolonged enough to permit more than a fleeting glimpse or exchange, but not so prolonged that close familiarity immediately ensues, 3) intimate to the extent that the parties must pay more than perfunctory attention to one another, but not so intimate that the customary social graces can be dispensed with, and 4) ritualized to the extent that all know in general what to expect, but not so ritualized as to preclude spontaneity and the slightly novel turn of events. A party or other social affair, a business introduction, getting to know a person at work, meeting neighbors, dealing with a salesman, conversing with a fellow passenger, staying at a resort hotel—these are but a few of the everyday social situations which fall within this portion of the spectrum of sociability, a range of involvement which can also be thought of as the zone of first impressions.

In interviews I conducted with a small number of very articulate and socially skilled informants who were visibly handicapped[4] I inquired into their handling of the imputation that they were not "normal, like everyone else." This imputation usually expresses itself in a pronounced stickiness of interactional flow and in the embarrassment of the normal by which he conveys the all too obvious message that he is having difficulty in relating to the handicapped person[5] as he would to "just an ordinary man or woman." Frequently

[3] Comprehensive and excellent reviews are to be found in R. G. Barker et al., *Adjustment to Physical Handicap and Illness: A Survey of the Social Psychology of Physique and Disability,* New York: Soc. Sci. Res. Council, 1953, Bulletin 55, 2nd ed. and Beatrice A. Wright, *Physical Disability, A Psychological Approach,* New York: Harper, 1960.

[4] Six were orthopedically handicapped, three blind and two facially disfigured. Additional detailed biographical and clinical materials were secured on one blind and four facially disfigured persons, making for a total of sixteen records.

[5] Throughout this paper, whether or not the term "handicap" or "handicapped" is joined by the qualifier "visible," it should be read in this way. Unfortunately, it will not be possible to discuss here that which sociologically distinguishes the situation of the visibly handicapped from that of persons whose physical handicaps are not visible or

he will make *faux pas,* slips of the tongue, revealing gestures and inadvertent remarks which overtly betray this attitude and place the handicapped person in an even more delicate situation.[6] The triggering of such a chain of interpersonal incidents is more likely with new persons than with those with whom the handicapped have well-established and continuing relations. Hence, the focus here on more or less sociable occasions, it being these in which interactional discomfort is felt most acutely and coping behavior is brought into relief most sharply.

Because the visibly handicapped do not comprise a distinct minority group or subculture, the imputations of generalized deviance that they elicit from many normals are more nearly genuine interactional emergents than conventionalized sequelae to intergroup stereotyping as, for example, might obtain between a Negro and white. A sociable encounter between a visibly handicapped person and a normal is usually more subject to ambiguity and experimentation in role postures than would be the case where the parties perceived by each other primarily in terms of member group characteristics. The visibly handicapped person must with each new acquaintance explore the *possibilities* of a relationship. As a rule there is no ready-made symbolic shorthand (e.g., "a Southerner can't treat a Negro as a social equal," "the Irish are anti-Semitic," "working class people think intellectuals are effeminate") for anticipating the quality and degree of acceptance to be accorded him. The exchange must be struck before its dangers and potentialities can be seen and before appropriate corrective maneuvers can be fed into the interaction.[7]

THE HANDICAP AS
THREAT TO SOCIABLE
INTERACTION

Before discussing how the visibly handicapped cope with difficult interaction, it is appropriate to first consider the general nature of the threat posed to the interactional situation *per se* as a result of their being perceived routinely (if not necessarily according to some prevalent stereotype) as "different," "odd," "estranged from the common run of humanity," etc.; in short, other than normal. (Achieving ease and naturalness of interaction with normals serves naturally as an important index to the handicapped person of the ex-

---

readily apparent, and how both differ from what is termed the "sick role." These are, though, important distinctions whose analysis might illuminate key questions in the study of deviance.

[6] In the sections that follow the discussion draws heavily on the framework of dramaturgic analysis developed by Erving Goffman. See especially his "Alienation from Interaction," *Human Relations,* 10 (1957), 47–60; "Embarrassment and Social Organization," *American Journal of Sociology,* 62 (November, 1956), 264–71; *Presentation of Self in Everyday Life,* New York: Doubleday and Co., Inc., 1959.

[7] Cf. Anselm Strauss, *Mirrors and Masks,* Glencoe, Ill.: Free Press, 1959, 31–43.

tent to which his preferred definition of self—i.e., that of someone who is merely different physically but not socially deviant—has been accepted. Symbolically, as long as the interaction remains stiff, strained or otherwise mired in inhibition, he has good reason to believe that he is in effect being denied the status of social normalcy he aspires to or regards as his due.) The threat posed by the handicap to sociability is, at minimum, fourfold: its tendency to become an exclusive focal point of the interaction, its potential for inundating expressive boundaries, its discordance with other attributes of the person and, finally, its ambiguity as a predicator of joint activity. These are not discrete entities in themselves as much as varying contextual emergents which, depending on the particular situation, serve singly or in combination to strain the framework of normative rules and assumptions in which sociability develops. Let us briefly consider each in turn.

A Focal Point
of Interaction

The rules of sociable interaction stipulate a certain generality and diffuseness in the attentions that parties are expected to direct to each other. Even if only superficially, one is expected to remain oriented to the whole person and to avoid the expression of a precipitous or fixed concern with any single attribute of his, however noteworthy or laudable it may be.[8] When meeting someone with a visible handicap, a number of perceptual and interpretative responses occur which make adherence to this rule tenuous for many. First, there is the matter of visibility as such. By definition, the visibly handicapped person cannot control his appearance sufficiently so that its striking particularity will not call a certain amount of concentrated attention to itself.[9] Second, the normal, while having his attention so narrowly channeled, is immediately constrained by the requirements of sociability to act as if he were oriented to the totality of the other rather than to that which is uppermost in his awareness, i.e., the handicap. Although the art of sociability may be said to thrive on a certain playful discrepancy between felt and expressed interests, it is perhaps equally true that when these are too discrepant strain and tension begin to undermine the interaction. (Conversely, when not discrepant enough, flatness and boredom frequently ensue.)[10] Whether the handicap is overtly and tactlessly responded to as such or, as is more commonly the case, no explicit reference is made to it, the underlying condition of heightened, nar-

---

[8] Kurt H. Wolff, ed., *The Sociology of Georg Simmel*, Glencoe, Ill.: Free Press, 1950, 45–46.

[9] Cf. R. K. White, B. A. Wright and T. Dembo, "Studies in Adjustment to Visible Injuries," *Journal of Abnormal and Social Psychology*, 43 (1948), 13–28.

[10] In a forthcoming paper, "Fun in Games: An Analysis of the Dynamics of Social Interaction," Goffman discusses the relationship between spontaneous involvement in interaction and the manner in which "external attributes"—those which in a formal sense are not situationally relevant—are permitted to penetrate the situation's boundaries.

rowed, awareness causes the interaction to be articulated too exclusively in terms of it. This, as my informants described it, is usually accompanied by one or more of the familiar signs of discomfort and stickiness: the guarded references, the common everyday words suddenly made taboo, the fixed stare elsewhere, the artificial levity, the compulsive loquaciousness, the awkward solemnity.[11]

Second-order interactional elaborations of the underlying impedance are also not uncommon. Thus, for example, the normal may take great pains to disguise his awareness, an exertion that is usually so effortful and transparent that the handicapped person is then enjoined to disguise his awareness of the normal's disguise. In turn, the normal sensing the disguise erected in response to his disguise . . . and so forth. But unlike the infinitely multiplying reflections of an object located between opposing mirrors, this process cannot sustain itself for long without the pretense of unawareness collapsing, as witness the following report by a young woman:

> I get suspicious when somebody says, "Let's go for a uh, ah [imitates confused and halting speech] push with me down the hall," or something like that. This to me is suspicious because it means that they're aware, really aware, that there's a wheelchair here, and that this is probably uppermost with them. . . . A lot of people in trying to show you that they don't care that you're in a chair will do crazy things. Oh, there's one person I know who constantly kicks my chair, as if to say "I don't care that you're in a wheelchair. I don't even know that it's there." But that is just an indication that he *really* knows it's there."

Inundating Potential

The expressive requirements of sociability are such that rather strict limits obtain with respect to the types and amount of emotional display that are deemed appropriate. Even such fitting expressions as gaiety and laughter can, we know, reach excess and lessen satisfaction with the occasion. For many normals, the problem of sustaining sociable relations with someone who is visibly handicapped is not wholly that of the discrepancy of the inner feeling evoked, e.g., pity, fear, repugnance, avoidance. As with much else in sociability, a mere discrepancy of the actor's inner state with the social expectation need not result in a disturbance of interaction. In this instance it is specifically the marked dissonance of such emotions with those outward expressions deemed *most* salient for the occasion (e.g., pleasure, identification, warm interest) that seems to result frequently in an inundation and enfeeblement of the expressive controls of the individual. With some persons, the felt intrusion, of this kind of situationally inappropriate emotion is so swift and overwhelming as to approximate a state of shock, leaving them expressively naked, so to speak. A pointed incident is told by a young blind girl:

> One night when I was going to visit a friend two of the people from my office put me into a taxi. I could tell that at first the taxi driver didn't know I was blind

---

[11] Cf. Goffman on "other-consciousness" as a type of faulty interaction. "Alienation from Interaction," *op. cit.*

because for a while there he was quite a conversationalist. Then he asked me what these sticks were for [a collapsible cane]. I told him it was a cane, and then he got so different. . . . He didn't talk about the same things that he did at first. Before this happened he joked and said, "Oh, you're a very quiet person. I don't like quiet people, they think too much." And he probably wouldn't have said that to me had he known I was blind because he'd be afraid of hurting my feelings. He didn't say anything like that afterwards.

The visibly handicapped are of course aware of this potential for inundating *Heading* the expressive boundaries of situations and many take precautions to minimize such occurrences as much as possible. Thus, an interior decorator with a facial deformity would when admitted to a client's house by the maid station himself whenever he could so that the client's entrance would find him in a distantly direct line of vision from her. This, he stated, gave the client an opportunity to compose herself, as she might not be able to were she to come upon him at short range.

Contradiction of Attributes

Even when the inundating potential is well contained by the parties and the normal proves fully capable of responding in a more differentiated fashion to the variety of attributes presented by the handicapped person (e.g., his occupational identity, clothes, speech, intelligence, interests, etc.), there is frequently felt to be an unsettling discordance between these and the handicap. Sociable interaction is made more difficult as a result because many normals can only resolve the seeming incongruence by assimilating or subsuming (often in a patronizing or condescending way) the other attributes to that of the handicap, a phenomenon which in analogous connections has been well described by Hughes.[12] Thus, one informant, a strikingly attractive girl, reports that she frequently elicits from new acquaintances the comment, "How strange that someone so pretty should be in a wheelchair." Another informant, a professional worker for a government agency, tells of the fashionable female client who after having inquired on how long the informant had been in her job remarked, "How nice that you have something to do." Because the art of sociability deigns this kind of reductionism of the person, expressions of this type, even when much less blatant, almost invariably cast a pall on the interaction and embarrass the recovery of smooth social posture. The general threat inherent in the perceived discordance of personal attributes is given pointed expression by still another informant, a paraplegic of upper middle class background who comments on the attitude of many persons in his class:

Now, where this affects them, where this brace and a crutch would affect them, is if they are going someplace or if they are doing something, they feel that, first, you would call attention and, second—you wouldn't believe this but it's true; I'll use the cruelest words I can—no cripple could possibly be in their social stratum.

[12] Everett C. Hughes, *Men and their work*, Glencoe, Ill.: Free Press, 1958, 102–06.

Ambiguous Predicator

Finally, to the extent to which sociability is furthered by the free and spontaneous initiation of joint activity (e.g., dancing, games, going out to eat; in short, "doing things") there is frequently considerable ambiguity as regards the ability of the handicapped person to so participate and as regards the propriety of efforts which seek to ascertain whether he wants to. For the normal who has had limited experience with the handicapped it is by no means always clear whether, for example, a blind person can be included in a theater party or a crippled person in a bowling game. Even if not able to engage in the projected activity as such, will he want to come along mainly for the sake of company? How may his preferences be gauged without, on the one hand, appearing to "make a thing" out of the proposal or, on the other, conveying the impression that his needs and limitations are not being sufficiently considered? Should he refuse, is it genuine or is he merely offering his hosts a polite, though half-hearted, out? And, for each enigma thus posed for the normal, a counter-enigma is posed for the handicapped person. Do they really want him? Are they merely being polite? In spite of the open invitation, will his acceptance and presence lessen somehow their enjoyment of the activity? It is easy to see how a profusion of anticipatory ambiguities of this kind can strain the operative assumptions underlying sociable relations.

PROCESS OF DEVIANCE DISAVOWAL AND NORMALIZATION

The above features then, may be said to comprise the threat that a visible handicap poses to the framework of rules and assumptions that guide sociability. We may now ask how socially adept handicapped persons cope with it so as to either keep it at bay, dissipate it or lessen its impact upon the interaction. In answering this question we will not consider those broad personality adjustments of the person (e.g., aggression, denial, compensation, dissociation, etc.) which at a level once removed, so to speak, can be thought of as adaptive or maladaptive for, among other things, sociability. Nor, at the other extreme, is it possible in the allotted space to review the tremendous variety of specific approaches, ploys and stratagems that the visibly handicapped employ in social situations. Instead, the analysis will attempt to delineate in transactional terms the stages through which a sociable relationship with a normal typically passes, assuming, of course, that the confrontation takes place and that both parties possess sufficient social skill to sustain a more than momentary engagement.

For present purposes we shall designate these stages as: 1) fictional acceptance, 2) the facilitation of reciprocal role-taking around a normalized projection of self and 3) the institutionalization in the relationship of a definition of self that is normal in its moral dimension, however qualified it may be with respect to its situational contexts. As we shall indicate, the unfolding of these stages comprises what may be thought of as a process of deviance disavowel of normalization,[13] depending on whether one views the process from the vantage point of the "deviant" actor or his alters.[14]

Fictional Acceptance

In Western society the overture phases of a sociable encounter are to a pronounced degree regulated by highly elastic fictions of equality and normalcy. In meeting those with whom we are neither close nor familiar, manners dictate that we refrain from remarking on or otherwise reacting too obviously to those aspects of their persons which in the privacy of our thoughts betoken important differences between ourselves. In America at least, these fictions tend to encompass sometimes marked divergencies in social status as well as a great variety of expressive styles; and, it is perhaps the extreme flexibility of such fictions in our culture rather than, as is mistakenly assumed by many foreign observers, their absence that accounts for the seeming lack of punctiliousness in American manners. The point is nicely illustrated in the following news item:

NUDE TAKES A STROLL IN MIAMI

MIAMI, Fla., Nov. 13, (UPI)—A shapely brunette slowed traffic to a snail's pace here yesterday with a 20-minute nude stroll through downtown Miami. . . .

"The first thing I knew something was wrong," said Biscayne Bay bridgetender E. E. Currey, who was working at his post about one block away, "was when I saw traffic was going unusually slow."

Currey said he looked out and called police. They told him to stop the woman, he said.

Currey said he walked out of his little bridge house, approached the woman nervously, and asked, "Say, girl, are you lost?"

"Yes," she replied. "I'm looking for my hotel."

Currey offered help and asked, "Say, did you lose your clothes?"

"No," he said the woman replied, "Why?"

Currey said that he had to step away for a moment to raise the bridge for a ship and the woman walked away. . . .[15]

Unlike earlier societies and some present day ones in which a visible handicap automatically relegates the person to a caste-like, inferior, status like

---

[13] As used here the term "normalization" denotes a process whereby alter for whatever reason comes to view as normal and morally acceptable that which initially strikes him as odd, unnatural, "crazy," deviant, etc., irrespective of whether his perception was in the first instance reasonable, accurate or justifiable. Cf. Charlotte G. Schwartz, "Perspectives on Deviance—Wives' Definitions of their Husbands' Mental Illness," *Psychiatry*, 20 (August, 1957), 275–91.

[14] Because of the paper's focus on the visibly handicapped person, in what follows his interactional work is highlighted to the relative glossing over of that of the normal. Actually, the work of normalization calls for perhaps as much empathic expenditure as that of deviance disavowal and is, obviously, fully as essential for repairing the interactional breach occasioned by the encounter.

[15] *San Francisco Chronicle,* November 14, 1960.

that of mendicant, clown or thief—or more rarely to an elevated one like that of oracle or healer—in our society the visibly handicapped are customarily accorded, save by children,[16] the surface acceptance that democratic manners guarantee to nearly all. But, as regards sociability, this proves a mixed blessing for many. Although the polite fictions do afford certain entree rights, as fictions they can too easily come to serve as substitutes for "the real thing" in the minds of their perpetrators. The interaction is kept starved at a bare subsistence level of sociability. As with the poor relation at the wedding party, so the reception given the handicapped person in many social situations: sufficient that he is here, he should not expect to dance with the bride.

At this stage of the encounter, the interactional problem confronting the visibly handicapped person is the delicate one of not permitting his identity to be circumscribed by the fiction while at the same time playing along with it and showing appropriate regard for its social legitimacy. For, as transparent and confining as the fiction is, it frequently is the only basis upon which the contact can develop into something more genuinely sociable. In those instances in which the normal fails or refuses to render even so small a gesture toward normalizing the situation, there exists almost no basis for the handicapped person to successfully disavow his deviance.[17] The following occurrence related by a young female informant is an apt, if somewhat extreme, illustration:

> I was visiting my girl friend's house and I was sitting in the lobby waiting for her when this woman comes out of her apartment and starts asking me questions. She just walked right up. I didn't know her from Adam, I never saw her before in my life. "Gee, what do you have? How long have you been that way? Oh gee, that's terrible." And so I answered her questions, but I got very annoyed and wanted to say, "Lady, mind your own business."

[16] The blunt questions and stares of small children are typically of the "Emperor's Clothes" variety. "Mister, why is your face like that?" "Lady, what are you riding around in that for? Can't you walk?" Nearly all my informants spoke of how unnerving such incidents were for them, particularly when other adults were present. None the less, some claimed to value the child's forthrightness a good deal more than they did the genteel hypocrisy of many adults.

[17] On the other side of the coin there are of course some handicapped persons who are equally given to undermining sociable relations by intentionally flaunting the handicap so that the fiction becomes extremely difficult to sustain, An equivalent of the "bad nigger" type described by Strong, such persons were (as in Strong's study) regarded with a mixture of admiration and censure by a number of my informants. Admiration, because the cruel stripping away of pretenses and forcing of issues was thought morally refreshing, especially since, as the informants themselves recognized, many normals refuse to grant anything more than fictional acceptance while at the same time imagining themselves ennobled for having made the small sacrifice. Censure, because of the conviction that such behavior could hardly improve matters in the long run and would make acceptance even more difficult for other handicapped persons who later came into contact with a normal who had received such treatment. Cf. Samuel M. Strong, "Negro–White Relations as Reflected in Social Types," *American Journal of Sociology,* 52 (July, 1946), p. 24.

"Breaking Through":
Facilitating Normalized
Role-Taking

In moving beyond fictional acceptance what takes place essentially is a re-definitional process in which the handicapped person projects images, attitudes and concepts of self which encourage the normal to identify with him (i.e., "take his role") in terms other than those associated with imputations of deviance.[18] Coincidentally, in broadening the area of minor verbal involvements, this also functions to drain away some of the stifling burden of unspoken awareness that, as we have seen, so taxes ease of interaction. The normal is cued into a large repertoire of appropriate responses, and even when making what he, perhaps mistakenly, regards as an inappropriate response (for example, catching himself in the use of such a word as cripple or blind) the handicapped person can by his response relieve him of his embarrassment. One young informant insightfully termed the process "breaking through":

> The first reaction a normal individual or good-legger has is, "Oh gee, there's a fellow in a wheelchair," or "there's a fellow with a brace." And they don't say, "Oh gee, there is so-and-so, he's handsome" or "he's intelligent," or "he's a boor," or what have you. And then as the relationship develops they don't see the handicap. It doesn't exist any more. And that's the point that you as a handicapped individual become sensitive to. You know after talking with someone for awhile when they don't see the handicap any more. That's when you've broken through.

What this process signifies from a social psychological standpoint is that as the handicapped person expands the interactional nexus he simultaneously disavows the deviancy latent in his status; concurrently, to the degree to which the normal is led to reciprocally assume the redefining (and perhaps unanticipated) self-attitudes proffered by the handicapped person, he comes to normalize (i.e., view as more like himself) those aspects of the other which at first connoted deviance for him. (Sometimes, as we shall see, the normal's normalizing is so complete that it is unwittingly applied to situations in which the handicapped person cannot possibly function "normally" due to sheer physical limitations.) These dynamics might also be termed a process of identification. The term is immaterial, except that in "identifying" or "taking the role of the other" much more is implicated sociologically than a mere subjective congruence of responses. The fashioning of shared perspectives also implies a progressively more binding legitimation of the altered self-representations enacted in the encounter; that is, having once normalized his perception of the handicapped person, it becomes increasingly more compromising—self-discrediting, as it were—for the normal to revert to treating him as a deviant again.

---

[18] George H. Mead, *Mind, Self and Society,* Chicago: University of Chicago Press, 1934. See also the discussion on interaction in Strauss, *op. cit.,* 44–88.

The ways in which the visibly handicapped person can go about disavowing deviance are, as we have stated, many and varied. These range from relatively straightforward conversational offerings in which he alludes in passing to his involvement in a normal round of activities, to such forms of indirection as interjecting taboo or privatized references by way of letting the normal know that he does not take offense at the latter's uneasiness or regard it as a fixed obstacle toward achieving rapport. In the above quote, for example, the informant speaks of "good-leggers," an in-group term from his rehabilitation hospital days, which along with "dirty normals" he sometimes uses with new acquaintances "because it has a humorous connotation . . . and lots of times it puts people at their ease."[19]

Still other approaches to disavowing deviance and bridging fictional acceptance include: an especially attentive and sympathetic stance with respect to topics introduced by the normal, showing oneself to be a comic, wit or other kind of gifted participant, and, for some, utilizing the normalization potential inherent in being seen in the company of a highly presentable normal companion.[20] These, and others too numerous to mention, are not of course invariably or equally successful in all cases; neither are such resources equally available to all handicapped persons, nor are the handicapped equally adept at exploiting them. As a class of corrective strategies however, they have the common aim of overcoming the interactional barrier that lies between narrow fictional acceptance and more spontaneous forms of relatedness.

Inextricably tied in with the manner of approach are considerations of setting, activity and social category of participants, certain constellations of which are generally regarded as favorable for successful deviance disavowal and normalization while others are thought unfavorable. Again, the ruling contingenices appear to be the extent to which the situation is seen as containing elements in it which: 1) contextually reduce the threat posed by the visible handicap to the rules and assumptions of the particular sociable occasion, and 2) afford the handicapped person opportunities for "breaking through" beyond fictional acceptance.

The relevance of one or both of these is apparent in the following social situations and settings about which my informants expressed considerable agreement as regards their preferences, aversions and inner reactions. To begin with, mention might again be made of the interactional rule violations frequently experienced at the hands of small children. Many of the informants were quite open in stating that a small child at a social occasion caused them

---

[19] Parallel instances can easily be cited from minority group relations as, for example, when a Jew in conversation with a non-Jew might introduce a Yiddish phrase by way of suggesting that the other's covert identification of him as a Jew need not inhibit the interaction unduly. In some situations this serves as a subtle means of declaring, "O.K., I know what's bothering you. Now that I've said it, let's forget about it and move on to something else."

[20] Alan G. Gowman, "Blindness and the Role of the Companion," *Social Problems,* 4 (July, 1956).

much uneasiness and cramped their style because they were concerned with how, with other adults present, they would handle some barefaced question from the child. Another category of persons with whom many claimed to have difficulty is the elderly. Here the problem was felt to be the tendency of old people to indulge in patronizing sympathy, an attitude which peculiarly resists re-definition because of the fulsome virtue it attributes to itself. In another context several of the informants laid great stress on the importance of maintaining a calm exterior whenever the physical setting unavoidably exposed them to considerable bodily awkwardness. (At the same time, of course, they spoke of the wisdom of avoiding, whenever possible, such occasions altogether.) Their attitude was that to expressively reflect gracelessness and a loss of control would result in further interactional obstacles toward assimilating the handicapped person to a normal status.

> It makes me uncomfortable to watch anyone struggling, so I try to do what I must as inconspicuously as possible. In new situations or in strange places, even though I may be very anxious, I will maintain a deadly calm. For example, if people have to lift the chair and I'm scared that they are going to do it wrong, I remain perfectly calm and am very direct in the instructions I give.

As a final example, there is the unanimity with which the informants expressed a strong preference for the small, as against the large or semipublic social gathering. Not only do they believe that, as one handicapped person among the non-handicapped, they stand out more at large social gatherings, but also that in the anonymity which numbers further there resides a heightened structural tendency for normals to practice avoidance relations with them. The easy assumption on such occasions is that "some other good soul" will take responsibility for socializing with the handicapped person. Even in the case of the handicapped person who is forward and quite prepared to take the initiative in talking to others, the organization and ecology of the large social gathering is usually such as to frustrate his attempts to achieve a natural, non-deviant, place for himself in the group. As one young man, a paraplegic, explained:

> The large social gathering presents a special problem. It's a matter of repetition. When you're in a very large group of people whom you don't know, you don't have an opportunity of talking to three, four or five at a time. Maybe you'll talk to one or two usually. After you've gone through a whole basic breakdown in making a relationship with one—after all, it's only a cocktail party—to do it again, and again, it's wearing and it's no good. You don't get the opportunity to really develop something.

Institutionalization of the Normalized Relationship

In "breaking through" many of the handicapped are confronted by a delicate paradox, particularly in those of their relationships which continue beyond the immediate occasion. Having disavowed deviance and induced the other to respond to him as he would to a normal, the problem then becomes one of sustaining the normalized definition in the face of the many small amendments and qualifications that must frequently be made to it. The person confined to a wheelchair, for example, must brief a new acquaintance on what to do and how to help when they come to stairs, doorways, vehicle entrances, etc. Further briefings and rehearsals may be required for social obstructions as well: for example, how to act in an encounter with—to cite some typical situations at random—an overly helpful person, a waitress who communicates to the handicapped person only through his companion, a person who stares in morbid fascination.[21]

Generally, such amendments and special considerations are as much as possible underplayed in the early stages of the relationship because, as in the case of much minority group protest, the fundamental demand of the handicapped is that they first be granted an irreducibly equal and normal status, it being only then regarded as fitting and safe to admit to certain incidental incapacities, limitations and needs. At some point however, the latter must be broached if the relationship to the normal is to endure in viable form. But to integrate effectively a major claim to "normalcy" with numerous minor waivers of the same claim is a tricky feat and one which exposes the relationship to the many situational and psychic hazards of apparent duplicity: the tension of transferring the special arrangements and understandings worked out between the two to situations and settings in which everyone else is "behaving normally"; the sometimes lurking suspicion of the one that it is only guilt or pity that cements the relationship, of the other that the infirmity is being used exploitatively, and of on-lookers that there is something "neurotic" and "unhealthy" about it all.[22]

From my informants' descriptions it appears that this third, "normal, but . . ." stage of the relationship, if it endures, is institutionalized mainly in either one of two ways. In the first, the normal normalizes his perceptions to such an extent as to suppress his effective awareness of many of the areas in which the handicapped person's behavior unavoidably deviates from the normal standard. In this connection several of the informants complained that a recurring problem they have with close friends is that the latter frequently overlook the fact of the handicap and the restrictions it imposes on them. The friends thoughtlessly make arrangements and involve them in activities in which they, the handicapped, cannot participate conveniently or comfortably.

---

21 *Ibid.*

22 The rhetoric of race relations reflects almost identical rationalizations and "insights" which are meant among other things to serve as cautions for would-be transgressors. "Personally I have nothing against Negroes [the handicapped], but it would be bad for my reputation if I were seen socializing with them." "She acts nice now, but with the first argument she'll call you a dirty Jew [good-for-nothing cripple]." "Regardless of how sympathetic you are toward Negroes [the disabled], the way society feels about them you'd have to be a masochist to marry one."

The other major direction in which the relationship is sometimes institutionalized is for the normal to surrender some of his normalcy by joining the handicapped person in a marginal, half-alienated, half-tolerant, outsider's orientation to "the Philistine world of normals."[23] Gowman[24] nicely describes the tenor and style of this relationship and its possibilities for sharply disabusing normals of their stereotyped approaches to the handicapped. *Épater le bourgeois* behavior is often prominently associated with it, as is a certain strictly in-group license to lampoon and mock the handicap in a way which would be regarded as highly offensive were it to come from an uninitiated normal. Thus, a blind girl relates how a sighted friend sometimes chides her by calling her "a silly blink." A paraplegic tells of the old friend who tries to revive his flagging spirits by telling him not to act "like a helpless cripple." Unlike that based on over-normalization, the peculiar strength of this relationship is perhaps its very capacity to give expressive scope to the negative reality of the larger world of which it is inescapably a part while simultaneously removing itself from a primary identification with it.

IMPLICATIONS

Two, more general, implications seem worth drawing from this analysis.[25]

First, in studies which trace the process wherein an actor who deviates comes to be increasingly defined as a deviant (e.g., the pre-mental patient, the pre-alcoholic, the pre-juvenile delinquent), unusual prominence is given to the normalizing behavior of those close to him (spouse, parents, friends, etc.). The picture that emerges is one of these persons assuming nearly the whole burden—by rationalizing, denying and overlooking his offensive acts—of attempting to re-establish a socially acceptable relationship with him. He is depicted typically as compulsively wedded to his deviance and incapable or uninterested in making restitutive efforts of his own. Finally, following some critical act of his, normalization fails *in toto* and community agencies are called in to relieve the primary group of its unmanageable burden.

There is much about this picture that is doubtlessly true and consonant with the ascertainable facts as we later come to learn of them from family, friends, police, courts and social agencies. We may question, however, whether it is a wholly balanced picture and whether, given the situational biases of these informational sources, all of the relevant facts have had an equal chance to surface. The perspective developed here suggests that it may be useful to consider whether, and to what extent, the deviator himself is not also engaged, albeit ineffectively, in somehow trying to sustain a normal definition of his

[23] Students of race relations will recognize in this a phenomenon closely akin to "inverse passing" as when a white becomes closely identified with Negroes and passes into a Negro subculture.

[24] Gowman, *op. cit.*

[25] I am indebted to Sheldon Messinger for his valuable comments in these connections.

person. Were research to indicate that such is the case, we might then ask what it is about his reparative efforts and the situations in which they occur that, as contrasted with the subjects of this study, so often lead to failure and an exacerbation of the troublesome behavior. (We probably will never know, except inferentially by gross extrapolation, of the possibly many cases in which some such interactive process succeeds in favorably resolving the deviating behavior.) In other words, as against the simplistic model of a compulsive deviant and a futile normalizer we would propose one in which it is postulated that both are likely to become engaged in making corrective interactional efforts toward healing the breach. And, when such efforts fail, as they frequently do, it is as important in accounting for the failure to weigh the interactional dynamics and situational contexts of these efforts as it is the nature of the deviant acts and the actor.

Second, we would note that the interactional problems of the visibly handicapped are not so dissimilar from those which all of us confront, if only now and then and to a lesser degree. We too on occasion find ourselves in situations in which some uncamouflageable attribute of ours jars the activity and the expectations of our company. We too, if we wish to sustain—and, as is typically the case, our company wishes us to sustain—a fitting and valued representation of ourselves, will tacitly begin to explore with them ways of redressing, insulating and separating the discrepant attribute from ourselves.[26] Our predicament though is much less charged with awareness, more easily set to rights, than that of the visibly handicapped person and his company. But it is precisely this exaggeration of a common interactional predicament that affords us an added insight into the prerequisites and unwitting assumptions of sociable behavior in general. Put differently, it can be said that our understanding of a mechanism is often crude and incomplete until it breaks down and we try to repair it. Breakdown and repair of interaction is what many of the visibly handicapped experience constantly in their lives. In studying this with them we are also studying much about ourselves of which we were heretofore unaware.

---

[26] Goffman, "Embarrassment and Social Organization," *op. cit.*

25

ON FACE-WORK:
AN ANALYSIS
OF RITUAL ELEMENTS
IN SOCIAL INTERACTION

Erving Goffman

EVERY PERSON LIVES IN A WORLD of social encounters, involving him either in face-to-face or mediated contact with other participants. In each of these contacts, he tends to act out what is someimes called a *line*—that is, a pattern of verbal and nonverbal acts by which he expresses his view of the situation and through this his evaluation of the participants, especially himself. Regardless of whether a person intends to take a line, he will find that he has done so in effect. The other participants will assume that he has more or less willfullly taken a stand, so that if he is to deal with their response to him he must take into consideration the impression they have possibly formed of him.

The term *face* may be defined as the positive social value a person effectively claims for himself by the line others assume he has taken during a particular contact.[1] Face is an image of self delineated in terms of approved social attributes—albeit an image that others may share, as when a person

From *Psychiatry* 18 (1955) 213–231. Reprinted by special permission of the author and The William Alanson White Psychiatric Foundation, Inc. (Text, Chapter 13)

[1] For discussions of the Chinese conception of face, see the following: Hsien Chin Hu, "The Chinese Concept of 'Face,'" *Amer. Anthropologist* (1944) n.s. 46:45–64. Martin C. Yang, *A Chinese Village;* New York, Columbia Univ. Press, 1945; pp. 167–72. J. Macgowan, *Men and Manners of Modern China;* London, Unwin, 1912; pp. 301–12. Arthur H. Smith, *Chinese Characteristics;* New York, Fleming H. Revell Co., 1894; pp. 16–18. For a comment on the American Indian conception of face, see Marcel Mauss, *The Gift* (Ian Cunnison, tr.); London, Cohen & West, 1954; p. 38.

makes a good showing for his profession or religion by making a good showing for himself.

A person tends to experience an immediate emotional response to the face which a contact with others allows him; he cathects his face; his "feelings" become attached to it. If the encounter sustains an image of him that he has long taken for granted, he probably will have few feelings about the matter. If events establish a face for him that is better than he might have expected, he is likely to "feel good"; if his ordinary expectations are not fulfilled, one expects that he will "feel bad" or "feel hurt." In general, a person's attachment to a particular face, coupled with the ease with which disconfirming information can be conveyed by himself and others, provides one reason why he finds that participation in any contact with others is a commitment. A person will also have feelings about the face sustained for the other participants, and while these feelings may differ in quantity and direction from those he has for his own face, they constitute an involvement in the face of others that is as immediate and spontaneous as the involvement he has in his own face. One's own face and the face of others are constructs of the same order; it is the rules of the group and the definition of the situation which determine how much feeling one is to have for face and how this feeling is to be distributed among the faces involved.

A person may be said to *have,* or *be in,* or *maintain* face when the line he effectively takes presents an image of him that is internally consistent, that is supported by judgments and evidence conveyed by other participants, and that is confirmed by evidence conveyed through impersonal agencies in the situation. At such times the person's face clearly is something that is not lodged in or on his body, but rather something that is diffusely located in the flow of events in the encounter and becomes manifest only when these events are read and interpreted for the appraisals expressed in them.

The line maintained by and for a person during contact with others tends to be of a legitimate institutionalized kind. During a contact of a particular type, an interactant of known or visible attributes can expect to be sustained in a particular face and can feel that it is morally proper that this should be so. Given his attributes and the conventionalized nature of the encounter, he will find a small choice of lines will be open to him and a small choice of faces will be waiting for him. Further, on the basis of a few known attributes, he is given the responsibility of possessing a vast number of others. His coparticipants are not likely to be conscious of the character of many of these attributes until he acts perceptibly in such a way as to discredit his possession of them; then everyone becomes conscious of these attributes and assumes that he willfully gave a false impression of possessing them.

Thus while concern for face focuses the attention of the person on the current activity, he must, to maintain face in this activity, take into consideration his place in the social world beyond it. A person who can maintain face in the current situation is someone who abstained from certain actions in the past that would have been difficult to face up to later. In addition, he fears loss of face now partly because the others may take this as a sign that consideration for his feelings need not be shown in the future. There is nevertheless a limitation to this interdependence between the current situation and the wider social world: an encounter with people whom he will not have dealings with again leaves him free to take a high line that the future will discredit, or free to suffer humiliations that would make future dealings with them an embarrassing thing to have to face.

A person may be said to *be in wrong face* when information is brought forth in some way about his social worth which cannot be integrated, even with effort, into the line that is being sustained for him. A person may be said to *be out of face* when he participates in a contact with others without having ready a line of the kind participants in such situations are expected to take. The intent of many pranks is to lead a person into showing a wrong face or no face, but there will also be serious occasions, of course, when he will find himself expressively out of touch with the situation.

When a person senses that he is in face, he typically responds with feelings of confidence and assurance. Firm in the line he is taking, he feels that he can hold his head up and openly present himself to others. He feels some security and some relief—as he also can when the others feel he is in wrong face but successfully hide these feelings from him.

When a person is in wrong face or out of face, expressive events are being contributed to the encounter which cannot be readily woven into the expressive fabric of the occasion. Should he sense that he is in wrong face or out of face, he is likely to feel ashamed and inferior because of what has happened to the activity on his account and because of what may happen to his reputation as a participant. Further, he may feel bad because he had relied upon the encounter to support an image of self to which he has become emotionally attached and which he now finds threatened. Felt lack of judgmental support from the encounter may take him aback, confuse him, and momentarily incapacitate him as an interactant. His manner and bearing may falter, collapse, and crumble. He may become embarrassed and chagrined; he may become shamefaced. The feeling, whether warranted or not, that he is perceived in a flustered state by others, and that he is presenting no usable line, may add further injuries to his feelings, just as his change from being in wrong face or out of face to being shamefaced can add further disorder to the expressive organization of the situation. Following common usage, I shall employ the term *poise* to refer to the capacity to suppress and conceal any tendency to become shamefaced during encounters with others.

In our Anglo-American society, as in some others, the phrase "to lose face" seems to mean to be in wrong face, to be out of face, or to be shamefaced. The phrase "to save one's face" appears to refer to the process by which the person sustains an impression for others that he has not lost face. Following Chinese usage, one can say that "to give face" is to arrange for another to take a better line than he might otherwise have been able to take,[2]

---

[2] Smith, *op. cit.*, p. 17.

the other thereby gets face given him, this being one way in which he can gain face.

As an aspect of the social code of any social circle, one may expect to find an understanding as to how far a person should go to save his face. Once he takes on a self-image expressed through face he will be expected to live up to it. In different ways in different societies he will be required to show self-respect, abjuring certain actions because they are above or beneath him, while forcing himself to perform others even though they cost him dearly. By entering a situation in which he is given a face to maintain, a person takes on the responsibility of standing guard over the flow of events as they pass before him. He must ensure that a particular *expressive order* is sustained—an order which regulates the flow of events, large or small, so that anything that appears to be expressed by them will be consistent with his face. When a person manifests these compunctions primarily from duty to himself, one speaks in our society of pride; when he does so because of duty to wider social units, and receives support from these units in doing so, one speaks of honor. When these compunctions have to do with postural things, with expressive events derived from the way in which the person handles his body, his emotions, and the things with which he has physical contact, one speaks of dignity, this being an aspect of expressive control that is always praised and never studied. In any case, while his social face can be his most personal possession and the center of his security and pleasure, it is only on loan to him from society; it will be withdrawn unless he conducts himself in a way that is worthy of it. Approved attributes and their relation to face make of every man his own jailer; this is a fundamental social constraint even though each man may like his cell.

Just as the member of any group is expected to have self-respect, so also he is expected to sustain a standard of considerateness; he is expected to go to certain lengths to save the feelings and the face of others present, and he is expected to do this willingly and spontaneously because of emotional identification with the others and with their feelings.[3] In consequence, he is disinclined to witness the defacement of others.[4] The person who can witness another's humiliation and unfeelingly retain a cool countenance himself is said

---

[3] Of course, the more power and prestige the others have, the more a person is likely to show consideration for their feelings, as H. E. Dale suggests in *The Higher Civil Service of Great Britain* (Oxford, Oxford Univ. Press, 1941), p. 126n. "The doctrine of 'feelings' was expounded to me many years ago by a very eminent civil servant with a pretty taste in cynicism. He explained that the importance of feelings varies in close correspondence with the importance of the person who feels. If the public interest requires that a junior clerk should be removed from his post, no regard need be paid to his feelings; if it is a case of an Assistant Secretary, they must be carefully considered, within reason; if it is a Permanent Secretary, his feelings are a principal element in the situation, and only imperative public interest can override their requirements."

[4] Salesmen, especially street "stemmers," know that if they take a line that will be discredited unless the reluctant customer buys, the customer may be trapped by considerateness and buy in order to save the face of the salesman and prevent what would ordinarily result in a scene.

in our society to be "heartless," just as he who can unfeelingly participate in his own defacement is thought to be "shameless."

The combined effect of the rule of self-respect and the rule of considerateness is that the person tends to conduct himself during an encounter so as to maintain both his own face and the face of the other participants. This means that the line taken by each participant is usually allowed to prevail, and each participant is allowed to carry off the role he appears to have chosen for' himself. A state where everyone temporarily accepts everyone else's line is established.[5] This kind of mutual acceptance seems to be a basic structural feature of interaction, especially the interaction of face-to-face talk. It is typically a "working" acceptance, not a "real" one, since it tends to be based not on agreement of candidly expressed heartfelt evaluations, but upon a willingness to give temporary lip service to judgments with which the participants do not really agree.

The mutual acceptance of lines has an important conservative effect upon encounters. Once the person initially presents a line, he and the others tend to build their later responses upon it, and in a sense become stuck with it. Should the person radically alter his line, or should it become discredited, then confusion results, for the participants will have prepared and committed themselves for actions that are now unsuitable.

Ordinarily, maintenance of face is a condition of interaction, not its objective. Usual objectives, such as gaining face for oneself, giving free expression to one's true beliefs, introducing depreciating information about the others, or solving problems and performing tasks, are typically pursued in such a way as to be consistent with the maintenance of face. To study face-saving is to study the traffic rules of social interaction; one learns about the code the person adheres to in his movement across the paths and designs of others, but not where he is going, or why he wants to get there. One does not even learn why he is ready to follow the code, for a large number of different motives can equally lead him to do so. He may want to save his own face because of his emotional attachment to the image of self which it expresses, because of his pride or honor, because of the power his presumed status allows him to exert over the other participants, and so on. He may want to save the others' face because of his emotional attachment to an image of

---

[5] Surface agreement in the assessment of social worth does not, of course, imply equality; the evaluation consensually sustained of one participant may be quite different from the one consensually sustained of another. Such agreement is also compatible with expression of differences of opinion between two participants, provided each of the disputants shows "respect" for the other, guiding the expression of disagreement so that it will convey an evaluation of the other that the other will be willing to convey about himself. Extreme cases are provided by wars, duels, and barroom fights, when these are of a gentlemanly kind, for they can be conducted under consensual auspices, with each protagonist guiding his action according to the rules of the game, thereby making it possible for his action to be interpreted as an expression of a fair player openly in combat with a fair opponent. In fact, the rules and etiquette of any game can be analyzed as a means by which the image of a fair player can be expressed, just as the image of a fair player can be analyzed as a means by which the rules and etiquette of a game are sustained.

them, or because he feels that his coparticipants have a moral right to this protection, or because he wants to avoid the hostility that may be directed toward him if they lose their face. He may feel that an assumption has been made that he is the sort of person who shows compassion and sympathy toward others, so that to retain his own face, he may feel obliged to be considerate of the line taken by the other participants.

By *face-work* I mean to designate the actions taken by a person to make whatever he is doing consistent with face. Face-work serves to counteract "incidents"—that is, events whose effective symbolic implications threaten face. Thus poise is one important type of face-work, for through poise the person controls his embarrassment and hence the embarrassment that he and others might have over his embarrassment. Whether or not the full consequences of face-saving actions are known to the person who employs them, they often become habitual and standardized practices; they are like traditional plays in a game or traditional steps in a dance. Each person, subculture, and society seems to have its own characteristic repertoire of face-saving practices. It is to this repertoire that people partly refer when they ask what a person or culture is "really" like. And yet the particular set of practices stressed by particular persons or groups seems to be drawn from a single logically coherent framework of possible practices. It is as if face, by its very nature, can be saved only in a certain number of ways, and as if each social grouping must make its selections from this single matrix of possibilities.

The members of every social circle may be expected to have some knowledge of face-work and some experience in its use. In our society, this kind of capacity is sometimes called tact, *savoir-faire,* diplomacy, or social skill. Variation in social skill pertains more to the efficacy of face-work than to the frequency of its application, for almost all acts involving others are modified, prescriptively or proscriptively, by considerations of face.

If a person is to employ his repertoire of face-saving practices, obviously he must first become aware of the interpretations that others may have placed upon his acts and the interpretations that he ought perhaps to place upon theirs. In other words, he must exercise perceptiveness.[6] But even if he is properly alive to symbolically conveyed judgments and is socially skilled, he must yet be willing to exercise his perceptiveness and his skill; he must, in short, be prideful and considerate. Admittedly, of course, the possession of perceptiveness and social skill so often leads to their application that in our society terms such as politeness or tact fail to distinguish between the inclination to exercise such capacities and the capacities themselves.

---

[6] Presumably social skill and perceptiveness will be high in groups whose members frequently act as representatives of wider social units such as lineages or nations, for the player here is gambling with a face to which the feelings of many persons are attached. Similarly, one might expect social skill to be well developed among those of high station and those with whom they have dealings, for the more face an interactant has, the greater the number of events that may be inconsistent with it, and hence the greater the need for social skill to forestall or counteract these inconsistencies.

I have already said that the person will have two points of view—a defensive orientation toward saving his own face and a protective orientation toward saving the others' face. Some practices will be primarily defensive and others primarily protective, although in general one may expect these two perspectives to be taken at the same time. In trying to save the face of others, the person must choose a tack that will not lead to loss of his own; in trying to save his own face, he must consider the loss of face that his action may entail for others.

In many societies there is a tendency to distinguish three levels of responsibility which a person may have for a threat to face that his actions have created. First, he may appear to have acted innocently; his offense seems to be unintended and unwitting, and those who perceive his act can feel that he would have attempted to avoid it had he foreseen its offensive consequences. In our society one calls such threats to face *faux pas, gaffes,* boners, or bricks. Secondly, the offending person may appear to have acted maliciously and spitefully, with the intention of causing open insult. Thirdly, there are incidental offenses; these arise as an unplanned but sometimes anticipated by-product of action—action which the offender performs in spite of its offensive consequences, although not out of spite. From the point of view of a particular participant, these three types of threat can be introduced by the participant himself against his own face, by himself against the face of the others, by the others against their own face, or by the others against himself. Thus the person may find himself in many different relations to a threat to face. If he is to handle himself and others well in all contingencies, he will have to have a repertoire of face-saving practices for each of these possible relations to threat.

THE BASIC KINDS
OF FACE-WORK

The Avoidance Process

The surest way for a person to prevent threats to his face is to avoid contacts in which these threats are likely to occur. In all societies one can observe this in the avoidance relationship [7] and in the tendency for certain delicate transactions to be conducted by go-betweens. [8] Similarly, in many societies,

[7] In our own society an illustration of avoidance is found in the middle- and upper-class Negro who avoids certain face-to-face contacts with whites in order to protect the self-evaluation projected by his clothes and manner. See, for example, Charles Johnson, *Patterns of Negro Segregation;* New York, Harper, 1943; ch. 13. The function of avoidance in maintaining the kinship system in small preliterate societies might be taken as a particular illustration of the same general theme.

[8] An illustration is given by K. S. Latourette, *The Chinese: Their History and Culture* (New York, Macmillan, 1942): "A neighbor or a group of neighbors may tender their good offices in adjusting a quarrel in which each antagonist would be sacrificing his face by taking the first step in approaching the other. The wise intermediary can effect the reconciliation while preserving the dignity of both" (Vol. 2: p. 211).

members know the value of voluntarily making a gracious withdrawal before an anticipated threat to face has had a chance to occur.[9]

Once the person does chance an encounter, other kinds of avoidance practices come into play. As defensive measures, he keeps off topics and away from activities which would lead to the expression of information that is inconsistent with the line he is maintaining. At opportune moments he will change the topic of conversation or the direction of activity. He will often present initially a front of diffidence and composure, suppressing any show of feeling until he has found out what kind of line the others will be ready to support for him. Any claims regarding self may be made with belittling modesty, with strong qualifications, or with a note of unseriousness; by hedging in these ways he will have prepared a self for himself that will not be discredited by exposure, personal failure, or the unanticipated acts of others. And if he does not hedge his claims about self, he will at least attempt to be realistic about them, knowing that otherwise events may discredit him and make him lose face.

Certain protective maneuvers are as common as these defensive ones. The person shows respect and politeness, making sure to extend to others any ceremonial treatment which might be their due. He employs discretion; he leaves unstated facts which might implicitly or explicitly contradict and embarrass the positive claims made by others.[10] He employs circumlocutions and deceptions, phrasing his replies with careful ambiguity so that the others' face is preserved even if their welfare is not.[11] He employs courtesies, making slight modifications of his demands on or appraisals of the others so that

[9] In an unpublished paper Harold Garfinkel has suggested that when the person finds that he has lost face in a conversational encounter, he may feel a desire to disappear or "drop through the floor," and that this may involve a wish not only to conceal loss of face but also to return magically to a point in time when it would have been possible to save face by avoiding the encounter.

[10] When the person knows the others well, he will know what issues ought not to be raised and what situations the others ought not to be placed in, and he will be free to introduce matters at will in all other areas. When the others are strangers to him, he will often reverse the formula, restricting himself to specific areas he knows are safe. On these occasions, as Simmel suggests, ". . . discretion consists by no means only in the respect for the secret of the other, for his specific will to conceal this or that from us, but in staying away from the knowledge of all that the other does not expressly reveal to us." See *The Sociology of Georg Simmel* (Kurt H. Wolff, tr. and ed.); Glencoe, Ill., Free Press, 1950; pp. 320–21.

[11] The western traveler used to complain that the Chinese could never be trusted to say what they meant but always said what they felt their Western listener wanted to hear. The Chinese used to complain that the Westerner was brusque, boorish, and unmannered. In terms of Chinese standards, presumably, the conduct of a Westerner is so gauche that he creates an emergency, forcing the Asian to forgo any kind of direct reply in order to rush in with a remark that might rescue the Westerner from the compromising position in which he had placed himself. (Smith, *op. cit.*, ch. 8, "The Talent for Indirection.") This is an instance of the important group of misunderstandings which arise during interaction between persons who come from groups with different ritual standards.

they will be able to define the situation as one in which their self-respect is not threatened. In making a belittling demand upon the others, or in imputing uncomplimentary attributes to them, he may employ a joking manner, allowing them to take the line that they are good sports, able to relax from their ordinary standards of pride and honor. And before engaging in a potentially offensive act, he may provide explanations as to why the others ought not to be affronted by it. For example, if he knows that it will be necessary to withdraw from the encounter before it has terminated, he may tell the others in advance that it is necessary for him to leave, so that they will have faces that are prepared for it. But neutralizing the potentially offensive act need not be done verbally; he may wait for a propitious moment or natural break —for example, in conversation, a momentary lull when no one speaker can be affronted—and then leave, in this way using the context instead of his words as a guarantee of inoffensiveness. /

When a person fails to prevent an incident, he can still attempt to maintain the fiction that no threat to face has occurred. The most blatant example of this is found where the person acts as if an event which contains a threatening expression has not occurred at all. He may apply this studied nonobservance to his own acts—as when he does not by any outward sign admit that his stomach is rumbling—or to the acts of others, as when he does not "see" that another has stumbled.[12] Social life in mental hospitals owes much to this process; patients employ it in regard to their own pecularities, and visitors employ it, often with tenuous desperation, in regard to patients. In general, tactful blindness of this kind is applied only to events which, if perceived at all, could be perceived and interpreted only as threats to face.

A more important, less spectacular kind of tactful overlooking is practiced when a person openly acknowledges an incident as an event that has occurred, but not as an event that contains a threatening expression. If he is not the one who is responsible for the incident, then his blindness will have to be supported by his forbearance; if he is the doer of the threatening deed, then his blindness will have to be supported by his willingness to seek a way of dealing with the matter which leaves him dangerously dependent upon the cooperative forbearance of the others.

Another kind of avoidance occurs when a person loses control of his expressions during an encounter. At such times he may try not so much to overlook the incident as to hide or conceal his activity in some way, thus making it possible for the others to avoid some of the difficulties created by a participant who has not maintained face. Correspondingly, when a person is caught out of face because he had not expected to be thrust into interaction, or because strong feelings have disrupted his expressive mask, the others may protectively turn away from him or his activity for a moment, to give him time to assemble himself.

---

[12] A pretty example of this is found in parade-ground etiquette which may oblige those in a parade to treat anyone who faints as if he were not present at all.

The Corrective Process

When the participants in an undertaking or encounter fail to prevent the occurrence of an event that is expressively incompatible with the judgments of social worth that are being maintained, and when the event is of the kind that is difficult to overlook, then the participants are likely to give it accredited status as an incident—to ratify it as a threat that deserves direct official attention—and to proceed to try to correct for its effects. At this point one or more participants find themselves in an established state of ritual disequilibrium or disgrace, and an attempt must be made to re-establish a satisfactory ritual state for them. I use the term *ritual* because I am dealing with acts through whose symbolic component the actor shows how worthy he is of respect or how worthy he feels others are of it. The imagery of equilibrium is apt here because the length and intensity of the corrective effort is nicely adapted to the persistence and intensity of the threat.[13] One's face, then, is a sacred thing, and the expressive order required to sustain it is therefore a ritual one.

The sequence of acts set in motion by an acknowledged threat to face, and terminating in the re-establishment of ritual equilibrium, I shall call an *interchange*.[14] Defining a message or move as everything conveyed by an actor during a turn at taking action, one can say that an interchange will involve two or more moves and two or more participants. Obvious examples in our society may be found in the sequence of "Excuse me" and "Certainly," and in the exchange of presents or visits. The interchange seems to be a basic concrete unit of social activity and provides one natural empirical way to study interaction of all kinds. Face-saving practices can be usefully classified according to their position in the natural sequence of moves which comprise this unit. Aside from the event which introduces the need for a corrective interchange, four classic moves seem to be involved.

There is, first, the challenge, by which participants take on the responsibility of calling attention to the misconduct; by implication they suggest that the threatened claims are to stand firm and that the threatening event itself will have to be brought back into line.

The second move consists of the offering, whereby a participant, typically

---

[13] This kind of imagery is one that social anthropologists seem to find naturally fitting. Note, for example, the implications of the following statement by Margaret Mead in her "Kinship in the Admiralty Islands" (*Anthropological Papers of the American Museum of Natural History*, 34:183–358): "If a husband beats his wife, custom demands that she leave him and go to her brother, real or officiating, and remain a length of time commensurate with the degree of her offended dignity" (p. 274).

[14] The notion of interchange is drawn in part from Eliot D. Chapple, "Measuring Human Relations," *Genetic Psychol. Monographs* (1940) 22:3–147, especially pp. 26–30, and from A. B. Horsfall and C. A. Arensberg, "Teamwork and Productivity in a Shoe Factory," *Human Organization* (1949) 8:13–25, especially p. 19. For further material on the interchange as a unit see E. Goffman, "Communication Conduct in an Island Community," unpublished Ph.D. dissertation, Department of Sociology, University of Chicago, 1953, especially chs. 12 and 13, pp. 165–95.

the offender, is given a chance to correct for the offense and re-establish the expressive order. Some classic ways of making this move are available. On the one hand, an attempt can be made to show that what admittedly appeared to be a threatening expression is really a meaningless event, or an unintentional act, or a joke not meant to be taken seriously, or an unavoidable, "understandable" product of extenuating circumstances. On the other hand, the meaning of the event may be granted and effort concentrated on the creator of it. Information may be provided to show that the creator was under the influence of something and not himself, or that he was under the command of somebody else and not acting for himself. When a person claims that an act was meant in jest, he may go on and claim that the self that seemed to lie behind the act was also projected as a joke. When a person suddenly finds that he has demonstrably failed in capacities that the others assumed him to have and to claim for himself—such as the capacity to spell, to perform minor tasks, to talk without malapropisms, and so on—he may quickly add, in a serious or unserious way, that he claims these incapacities as part of his self. The meaning of the threatening incident thus stands, but it can now be incorporated smoothly into the flow of expressive events.

As a supplement to or substitute for the strategy of redefining the offensive act or himself, the offender can follow two other procedures: he can provide compensations to the injured—when it is not his own face that he has threatened; or he can provide punishment, penance, and expiation for himself. These are important moves or phases in the ritual interchange. Even though the offender may fail to prove his innocence, he can suggest through these means that he is now a renewed person, a person who has paid for his sin against the expressive order and is once more to be trusted in the judgmental scene. Further, he can show that he does not treat the feelings of the others lightly, and that if their feelings have been injured by him, however innocently, he is prepared to pay a price for his action. Thus he assures the others that they can accept his explanations without this acceptance constituting a sign of weakness and a lack of pride on their part. Also, by his treatment of himself, by his self-castigation, he shows that he is clearly aware of the kind of crime he would have committed had the incident been what it first appeared to be, and that he knows the kind of punishment that ought to be accorded to one who would commit such a crime. The suspected person thus shows that he is thoroughly capable of taking the role of the others toward his own activity, that he can still be used as a responsible participant in the ritual process, and that the rules of conduct which he appears to have broken are still sacred, real, and unweakened. An offensive act may arouse anxiety about the ritual code; the offender allays this anxiety by showing that both the code and he as an upholder of it are still in working order.

After the challenge and the offering have been made, the third move can occur: the persons to whom the offering is made can accept it as a satisfactory means of re-establishing the expressive order and the faces supported by this order. Only then can the offender cease the major part of his ritual offering.

In the terminal move of the interchange, the forgiven person conveys a sign of gratitude to those who have given him the indulgence of forgiveness.

The phases of the corrective process—challenge, offering, acceptance, and thanks—provide a model for interpersonal ritual behavior, but a model that may be departed from in significant ways. For example, the offended parties may give the offender a chance to initiate the offering on his own before a challenge is made and before they ratify the offense as an incident. This is a common courtesy, extended on the assumption that the recipient will introduce a self-challenge. Further, when the offended persons accept the corrective offering, the offender may suspect that this has been grudgingly done from tact, and so he may volunteer additional corrective offerings, not allowing the matter to rest until he has received a second or third acceptance of his repeated apology. Or the offended persons may tactfully take over the role of the offender and volunteer excuses for him that will, perforce, be acceptable to the offended persons.

An important departure from the standard corrective cycle occurs when a challenged offender patently refuses to heed the warning and continues with his offending behavior, instead of setting the activity to rights. This move shifts the play back to the challengers. If they countenance the refusal to meet their demands, then it will be plain that their challenge was a bluff and that the bluff has been called. This is an untenable position; a face for themselves cannot be derived from it, and they are left to bluster. To avoid this fate, some classic moves are open to them. For instance, they can resort to tactless, violent retaliation, destroying either themselves or the person who had refused to heed their warning. Or they can withdraw from the undertaking in a visible huff—righteously indignant, outraged, but confident of ultimate vindication. Both tacks provide a way of denying the offender his status as an interactant, and hence denying the reality of the offensive judgment he has made. Both strategies are ways of salvaging face, but for all concerned the costs are usually high. It is partly to forestall such scenes that an offender is usually quick to offer apologies; he does not want the affronted persons to trap themselves into the obligation to resort to desperate measures.

It is plain that emotions play a part in these cycles of response, as when anguish is expressed because of what one has done to another's face, or anger because of what has been done to one's own. I want to stress that these emotions function as moves, and fit so precisely into the logic of the ritual game that it would seem difficult to understand them without it.[15] In fact, spontaneously expressed feelings are likely to fit into the formal pattern of the ritual interchange more elegantly than consciously designed ones.

---

[15] Even when a child demands something and is refused, he is likely to cry and sulk not as an irrational expression of frustration but as a ritual move, conveying that he already has a face to lose and that its loss is not to be permitted lightly. Sympathetic parents may even allow for such display, seeing in these crude strategies the beginnings of a social self.

MAKING POINTS:
THE AGGRESSIVE USE
OF FACE-WORK

Every face-saving practice which is allowed to neutralize a particular threat opens up the possibility that the threat will be willfully introduced for what can be safely gained by it. If a person knows that his modesty will be answered by others' praise of him, he can fish for compliments. If his own appraisal of self will be checked against incidental events, then he can arrange for favorable incidental events to appear. If others are prepared to overlook an affront to them and act forbearantly, or to accept apologies, then he can rely on this as a basis for safely offending them. He can attempt by sudden withdrawal to force the others into a ritually unsatisfactory state, leaving them to flounder in an interchange that cannot readily be completed. Finally, at some expense to himself, he can arrange for the others to hurt his feelings, thus forcing them to feel guilt, remorse, and sustained ritual disequilibrium.[16]

When a person treats face-work not as something he need be prepared to perform, but rather as something that others can be counted on to perform or to accept, then an encounter or an undertaking becomes less a scene of mutual considerateness than an arena in which a contest or match is held. The purpose of the game is to preserve everyone's line from an inexcusable contradiction, while scoring as many points as possible against one's adversaries and making as many gains as possible for oneself. An audience to the struggle is almost a necessity. The general method is for the person to introduce favorable facts about himself and unfavorable facts about the others in such a way that the only reply the others will be able to think up will be one that terminates the interchange in a grumble, a meager excuse, a face-saving I-can-take-a-joke laugh, or an empty stereotyped comeback of the "Oh yeah?" or "That's what you think" variety. The losers in such cases will have to cut their losses, tacitly grant the loss of a point, and attempt to do better in the next interchange. Points made by allusion to social class status are sometimes called snubs; those made by allusions to moral respectability are sometimes called digs; in either case one deals with a capacity at what is sometimes called "bitchiness."

In aggressive interchanges the winner not only succeeds in introducing information favorable to himself and unfavorable to the others, but also demonstrates that as interactant he can handle himself better than his adversaries. Evidence of this capacity is often more important than all the other

---

[16] The strategy of maneuvering another into a position where he cannot right the harm he has done is very commonly employed but nowhere with such devotion to the ritual model of conduct as in revengeful suicide. See, for example, M. D. W. Jeffreys, "Samsonic Suicide, or Suicide of Revenge Among Africans," *African Studies* (1952) 11: 118–22.

information the person conveys in the interchange, so that the introduction of a "crack" in verbal interaction tends to imply that the initiator is better at footwork than those who must suffer his remarks. However, if they succeed in making a successful parry of the thrust and then a successful riposte, the instigator of the play must not only face the disparagement with which the others have answered him but also accept the fact that his assumption of superiority in footwork has proven false. He is made to look foolish; he loses face. Hence it is always a gamble to "make a remark." The tables can be turned and the aggressor can lose more than he could have gained had his move won the point. Successful ripostes or comebacks in our society are sometimes called squelches or toppers; theoretically it would be possible for a squelch to be squelched, a topper to be topped, and a riposte to be parried with a counterriposte, but except in staged interchanges this third level of successful action seems rare.[17]

THE CHOICE OF
APPROPRIATE FACE-WORK

When an incident occurs, the person whose face is threatened may attempt to reinstate the ritual order by means of one kind of strategy, while the other participants may desire or expect a practice of a different type to be employed. When, for example, a minor mishap occurs, momentarily revealing a person in wrong face or out of face, the others are often more willing and able to act blind to the discrepancy than is the threatened person himself. Often they would prefer him to exercise poise,[18] while he feels that he cannot afford to overlook what has happened to his face and so becomes apologetic and shamefaced, if he is the creator of the incident, or destructively assertive, if

[17] In board and card games the player regularly takes into consideration the possible responses of his adversaries to a play that he is about to make, and even considers the possibility that his adversaries will know that he is taking such precautions. Conversational play is by comparison surprisingly impulsive; people regularly make remarks about others present without carefully designing their remarks to prevent successful comeback. Similarly, while feinting and sandbagging are theoretical possibilities during talk, they seem to be little exploited.

[18] Folklore imputes a great deal of poise to the upper classes. If there is truth in this belief it may lie in the fact that the upper-class person tends to find himself in encounters in which he outranks the other participants in ways additional to class. The ranking participant is often somewhat independent of the good opinion of the others and finds it practical to be arrogant, sticking to a face regardless of whether the encounter supports it. On the other hand, those who are in the power of a fellow-participant tend to be very much concerned with the valuation he makes of them or witnesses being made of them, and so find it difficult to maintain a slightly wrong face without becoming embarrassed and apologetic. It may be added that people who lack awareness of the symbolism in minor events may keep cool in difficult situations, showing poise that they do not really possess.

the others are responsible for it.[19] Yet on the other hand, a person may manifest poise when the others feel that he ought to have broken down into embarrassed apology—that he is taking undue advantage of their helpfulness by his attempts to brazen it out. Sometimes a person may himself be undecided as to which practice to employ, leaving the others in the embarrassing position of not knowing which tack they are going to have to follow. Thus when a person makes a slight *gaffe,* he and the others may become embarrassed not because of inability to handle such difficulties, but because for a moment no one knows whether the offender is going to act blind to the incident, or give it joking recognition, or employ some other face-saving practice.

COOPERATION IN
FACE-WORK

When a face has been threatened, face-work must be done, but whether this is intiated and primarily carried through by the person whose face is threatened, or by the offender, or by a mere witness,[20] is often of secondary importance. Lack of effort on the part of one person induces compensatory effort from others; a contribution by one person relieves the others of the task. In fact, there are many minor incidents in which the offender and the offended simultaneously attempt to initiate an apology.[21] Resolution of the situation to everyone's apparent satisfaction is the first requirement; correct apportionment of blame is typically a secondary consideration. Hence terms such as tact and *savoir-faire* fail to distinguish whether it is the person's own face that his diplomacy saves or the face of the others. Similarly, terms such as *gaffe* and *faux pas* fail to specify whether it is the actor's own face he has

[19] Thus, in our society, when a person feels that others expect him to measure up to approved standards of cleanliness, tidiness, fairness, hospitality, generosity, affluence, and so on, or when he sees himself as someone who ought to maintain such standards, he may burden an encounter with extended apologies for his failings, while all along the other participants do not care about the standard, or do not believe the person is really lacking in it, or are convinced that he is lacking in it and see the apology itself as a vain effort at self-elevation.

[20] Thus one function of seconds in actual duels, as well as in figurative ones, is to provide an excuse for not fighting that both contestants can afford to accept.

[21] See, for instance, Jackson Toby, "Some Variables in Role Conflict Analysis" [*Social Forces* (1952) 30:323–37]: "With adults there is less likelihood for essentially trival issues to produce conflict. The automatic apology of two strangers who accidentally collide on a busy street illustrates the integrative function of etiquette. In effect, each of the parties to the collision says, 'I don't know whether I am responsible for this situation, but *if* I am, you have a right to be angry with me, a right that I pray you will not exercise.' By defining the situation as one in which both parties must abase themselves, society enables each to keep his self-respect. Each may feel in his heart of hearts, 'Why can't that stupid ass watch where he's going?' But overtly *each plays the role of the guilty party* whether he feels he has been miscast or not" (p. 325).

threatened or the face of other participants. And it is understandable that if one person finds he is powerless to save his own face, the others seem especially bound to protect him. For example, in polite society, a handshake that perhaps should not have been extended becomes one that cannot be declined. Thus one accounts for the *noblesse oblige* through which those of high status are expected to curb their power of embarrassing their lessers,[22] as well as the fact that the handicapped often accept courtesies that they can manage better without.

Since each participant in an undertaking is concerned, albeit for differing reasons, with saving his own face and the face of the others, then tacit cooperation will naturally arise so that the participants together can attain their shared but differently motivated objectives.

One common type of tacit cooperation in face-saving is the tact exerted in regard to face-work itself. The person not only defends his own face and protects the face of the others, but also acts so as to make it possible and even easy for the others to employ face-work for themselves and him. He helps them to help themselves and him. Social etiquette, for example, warns men against asking for New Year's Eve dates too early in the season, lest the girl find it difficult to provide a gentle excuse for refusing. This second-order tact can be further illustrated by the widespread practice of negative-attribute etiquette. The person who has an unapparent negatively valued attribute often finds it expedient to begin an encounter with an unobtrusive admission of his failing, especially with persons who are uninformed about him. The others are thus warned in advance against making disparaging remarks about his kind of person and are saved from the contradiction of acting in a friendly fashion to a person toward whom they are unwittingly being hostile. This strategy also prevents the others from automatically mak-

---

[22] Regardless of the person's relative social position, in one sense he has power over the other participants and they must rely upon his considerateness. When the others act toward him in some way, they presume upon a social relationship to him, since one of the things expressed by interaction is the relationship of the interactants. Thus they compromise themselves, for they place him in a position to discredit the claims they express as to his attitude toward them. Hence in response to claimed social relationships every person, of high estate or low, will be expected to exercise *noblese oblige* and refrain from exploiting the compromised position of the others.

Since social relationships are defined partly in terms of voluntary mutual aid, refusal of a request for assistance becomes a delicate matter, potentially destructive of the asker's face. Chester Holcombe, *The Real Chinaman* (New York, Dodd, Mead, 1895) provides a Chinese instance: "Much of the falsehood to which the Chinese as a nation are said to be addicted is a result of the demands of etiquette. A plain frank 'no' is the height of discourtesy. Refusal or denial of any sort must be softened and toned down into an expression of regretted inability. Unwillingness to grant a favor is never shown. In place of it there is seen a chastened feeling of sorrow that unavoidable but quite imaginary circumstances render it wholly impossible. Centuries of practice in this form of evasion have made the Chinese matchlessly fertile in the invention and development of excuses. It is rare, indeed, that one is caught at a loss for a bit of artfully embroidered fiction with which to hide an unwelcome truth" (pp. 274–75).

ing assumptions about him which place him in a false position and saves him from painful forbearance or embarrassing remonstrances.

Tact in regard to face-work often relies for its operation on a tacit agreement to do business through the language of hint—the language of innuendo, ambiguities, well-placed pauses, carefully worded jokes, and so on.[23] The rule regarding this unofficial kind of communication is that the sender ought not to act as if he had officially conveyed the message he has hinted at, while the recipients have the right and the obligation to act as if they have not officially received the message contained in the hint. Hinted communication, then, is deniable communication; it need not be faced up to. It provides a means by which the person can be warned that his current line or the current situation is leading to loss of face, without this warning itself becoming an incident.

Another form of tacit cooperation, and one that seems to be much used in many societies, is reciprocal self-denial. Often the person does not have a clear idea of what would be a just or acceptable apportionment of judgments during the occasion, and so he voluntarily deprives or depreciates himself while indulging and complimenting the others, in both cases carrying the judgments safely past what is likely to be just. The favorable judgments about himself he allows to come from the others; the unfavorable judgments of himself are his own contributions. This "after you, Alphonse" technique works, of course, because in depriving himself he can reliably anticipate that the others will compliment or indulge him. Whatever allocation of favors is eventually established, all participants are first given a chance to show that they are not bound or constrained by their own desires and expectations, that they have a properly modest view of themselves, and that they can be counted upon to support the ritual code. Negative bargaining, through which each participant tries to make the terms of trade more favorable to the other side, is another instance; as a form of exchange perhaps it is more widespread than the economist's kind.

A person's performance of face-work, extended by his tacit agreement to help others perform theirs, represents his willingness to abide by the ground rules of social interaction. Here is the hallmark of his socialization as an interactant. If he and the others were not socialized in this way, interaction in most societies and most situations would be a much more hazardous thing for feelings and faces. The person would find it impractical to be oriented to symbolically conveyed appraisals of social worth, or to be possessed of feelings—that is, it would be impractical for him to be a ritually delicate object. And as I shall suggest, if the person were not a ritually delicate object, occasions of talk could not be organized in the way they usually are. It is no wonder that trouble is caused by a person who cannot be relied upon to play the face-saving game.

[23] Useful comments on some of the structural roles played by unofficial communication can be found in a discussion of irony and banter in Tom Burns, "Friends, Enemies, and the Polite Fiction," *Amer. Sociol. Rev.,* (1943) 18:654–62.

FACE AND
SOCIAL RELATIONSHIPS

When a person begins a mediated or immediate encounter, he already stands in some kind of social relationship to the others concerned, and expects to stand in a given relationship to them after the particular encounter ends. This, of course, is one of the ways in which social contacts are geared into the wider society. Much of the activity occurring during an encounter can be understood as an effort on everyone's part to get through the occasion and all the unanticipated and unintentional events that can cast participants in an undesirable light, without disrupting the relationships of the participants. And if relationships are in the process of change, the object will be to bring the encounter to a satisfactory close without altering the expected course of development. This perspective nicely accounts, for example, for the little ceremonies of greeting and farewell which occur when people begin a conversational encounter or depart from one. Greetings provide a way of showing that a relationship is still what it was at the termination of the previous coparticipation, and, typically, that this relationship involves sufficient suppression of hostility for the participants temporarily to drop their guards and talk. Farewells sum up the effect of the encounter upon the relationship and show what the participants may expect of one another when they next meet. The enthusiasm of greetings compensates for the weakening of the relationship caused by the absence just terminated, while the enthusiasm of farewells compensates the relationship for the harm that is about to be done to it by separation.[24]

It seems to be a characteristic obligation of many social relationships that each of the members guarantees to support a given face for the other members in given situations. To prevent disruption of these relationships, it is therefore necessary for each member to avoid destroying the others' face. At the same time, it is often the person's social relationship with others that leads him to participate in certain encounters with them, where incidentally he will be dependent upon them for supporting his face. Furthermore, in many relationships, the members come to share a face, so that in the presence of third parties an improper act on the part of one member becomes a source

[24] Greetings, of course, serve to clarify and fix the roles that the participants will take during the occasion of talk and to commit participants to these roles, while farewells provide a way of unambiguously terminating the encounter. Greetings and farewells may also be used to state, and apologize for, extenuating circumstances—in the case of greetings for circumstances that have kept the participants from interacting until now, and in the case of farewells for circumstances that prevent the participants from continuing their display of solidarity. These apologies allow the impression to be maintained that the participants are more warmly related socially than may be the case. This positive stress, in turn, assures that they will act more ready to enter into contacts than they perhaps really feel inclined to do, thus guaranteeing that diffuse channels for potential communication will be kept open in the society.

of acute embarrassment to the other members. A social relationship, then, can be seen as a way in which the person is more than ordinarily forced to trust his self-image and face to the tact and good conduct of others.

THE NATURE OF
THE RITUAL ORDER

The ritual order seems to be organized basically on accommodative lines, so that the imagery used in thinking about other types of social order is not quite suitable for it. For the other types of social order a kind of schoolboy model seems to be employed: if a person wishes to sustain a particular image of himself and trust his feelings to it, he must work hard for the credits that will buy this self-enhancement for him; should he try to obtain ends by improper means, by cheating or theft, he will be punished, disqualified from the race, or at least made to start all over again from the beginning. This is the imagery of a hard, dull game. In fact, society and the individual join in one that is easier on both of them, yet one that has dangers of its own.

Whatever his position in society, the person insulates himself by blind-nesses, half-truths, illusions, and rationalizations. He makes an "adjustment" by convincing himself, with the tactful support of his intimate circle, that he is what he wants to be and that he would not do to gain his ends what the others have done to gain theirs. And as for society, if the person is willing to be subject to informal social control—if he is willing to find out from hints and glances and tactful cues what his place is, and keep it—then there will be no objection to his furnishing this place at his own discretion, with all the comfort, elegance, and nobility that his wit can muster for him. To protect this shelter he does not have to work hard, or join a group, or compete with anybody; he need only be careful about the expressed judgments he places himself in a position to witness. Some situations and acts and persons will have to be avoided; others, less threatening, must not be pressed too far. Social life is an uncluttered, orderly thing because the person voluntarily stays away from the places and topics and times where he is not wanted and where he might be disparaged for going. He co-operates to save his face, finding that there is much to be gained from venturing nothing.

Facts are of the schoolboy's world—they can be altered by diligent effort but they cannot be avoided. But what the person protects and defends and invests his feelings in is an idea about himself, and ideas are vulnerable not to facts and things but to communications. Communications belong to a less punitive scheme than do facts, for communications can be by-passed, with-drawn from, disbelieved, conveniently misunderstood, and tactfully conveyed. And even should the person misbehave and break the truce he has made with society, punishment need not be the consequence. If the offense is one that the offended persons can let go by without losing too much face, then they are likely to act forbearantly, telling themselves that they will get even with the offender in another way at another time, even though such an occasion may never arise and might not be exploited if it did. If the offense is great, the offended persons may withdraw from the encounter, or from future similar ones, allowing their withdrawal to be reinforced by the awe they may feel toward someone who breaks the ritual code. Or they may have the offender withdrawn, so that no further communication can occur. But since the offender can salvage a good deal of face from such operations, withdrawal is often not so much an informal punishment for an offense as it is merely a means of terminating it. Perhaps the main principle of the ritual order is not justice but face, and what any offender receives is not what he deserves but what will sustain for the moment the line to which he has committed himself, and through this the line to which he has committed the interaction.

Throughout this paper it has been implied that underneath their differences in culture, people everywhere are the same. If persons have a universal human nature, they themselves are not to be looked to for an explanation of it. One must look rather to the fact that societies everywhere, if they are to be so-cieties, must mobilize their members as self-regulating participants in social encounters. One way of mobilizing the individual for this purpose is through ritual; he is taught to be perceptive, to have feelings attached to self and a self expressed through face, to have pride, honor, and dignity, to have considerateness, to have tact and a certain amount of poise. These are some of the elements of behavior which must be built into a person if practical use is to be made of him as an interactant, and it is these elements that are referred to in part when one speaks of universal human nature.

Universal human nature is not a very human thing. By acquiring it, the person becomes a kind of construct, built up not from inner psychic pro-pensities but from moral rules that are impressed upon him from without. These rules, when followed, determine the evaluation he will make of him-self and of his fellow-participants in the encounter, the distribution of his feelings, and the kinds of practices he will employ to maintain a specified and obligatory kind of ritual equilibrium. The general capacity to be bound by moral rules may well belong to the individual, but the particular set of rules which transforms him into a human being derives from requirements established in the ritual organization of social encounters. And if a particular person or group or society seems to have a unique character all its own, it is because its standard set of human-nature elements is pitched and combined in a particular way. Instead of much pride, there may be little. Instead of abiding by the rules, there may be much effort to break them safely. But if an encounter or undertaking is to be sustained as a viable system of inter-action organized on ritual principles, then these variations must be held within certain bounds and nicely counterbalanced by corresponding modifica-tions in some of the other rules and understandings. Similarly, the human nature of a particular set of persons may be specially designed for the special kind of undertakings in which they participate, but still each of these persons must have within him something of the balance of characteristics required of a usable participant in any ritually organized system of social activity.

26
CLOSED AWARENESS

Barney G. Glaser

Anselm L. Strauss

IN AMERICAN HOSPITALS, frequently the patient does not recognize his impending death even though the hospital personnel have the information. This situation can be described as a "closed awareness" context. Providing the physician decides to keep the patient from realizing, or even seriously suspecting, what his true status is, the problem is to *maintain* the context as a closed one. With a genuinely comatose patient, the staff members naturally need not guard against disclosure of his terminal condition. As an interactant, the comatose person is what Goffman has called a "non-person."[1] Two nurses caring for him can speak in his presence without fear that, overhearing them, he will suspect or understand what they are saying about him. Neither they nor the physicians need to engage in tactics to protect him from any dread knowledge. And of course with terminal babies, no precautions against disclosure are needed either. But with conscious patients, care must be taken not to disclose the staff's secret.

Reprinted from *Awareness of Dying* (Chicago: Aldine Publishing Company, 1965), pp. 29–46; copyright © 1965 by Barney G. Glaser and Anselm L. Strauss. (Text, Chapter 13)

[1] Erving Goffman, *The Presentation of Self in Everyday Life* (Edinburgh, Scotland: University of Edinburgh, 1956), pp. 95–96.

CONTRIBUTING
STRUCTURAL CONDITIONS

There are at least five important structural conditions which contribute to the existence and maintenance of the closed awareness context.[2] First, most patients are not especially experienced at recognizing the signs of impending death. Of course, a patient who has been in an auto accident and is injured terribly, although still conscious, may recognize how close death is. He may also recognize it if he is himself a physician or a nurse, or if as a chronic hospitalized patient he has encountered fatal signs in dying comrades.[3] But most Americans have not had such opportunities to witness rehearsals for their own deaths.

A second structural condition is that American physicians ordinarily do not tell patients outright that death is probable or inevitable. As a number of studies have shown, physicians find medical justifications for not disclosing dying status to their patients.[4] For instance, Dr. Donald Oken has recently demonstrated that a chief reason offered is "clinical experience."[5] The physician states from "clinical experience," that when one announces terminality to a patient, he is likely to "go to pieces"; one must therefore carefully judge whether or not to tell after sizing up the individual patient. In actual fact, Oken notes, the clinical experience is not genuinely grounded experience, but a species of personal mythology. Generally the experience consists of one or two unfortunate incidents—or even incidents recounted by colleagues— and this effectively cuts off further clinical experimentation to discover the possible range of consequences of disclosure.

Among several articles of faith in professional ideology which support not disclosing terminality, is the belief that patients really do not wish to know whether they are dying. If they did, then they would find out anyhow, so there is no sense telling them directly. Presumably some patients do not wish to know their fates, but there is no really good evidence that *all* wish to remain in blissful ignorance or that these patients will find out while in the hospital. And there is some good evidence that they do wish to know.[6] Quite possibly

---

[2] *Cf.* Barney Glaser and Anselm Strauss, "Awareness Contexts and Social Interaction," *American Sociological Review,* 29 (October, 1964), pp. 669–679.

[3] Renée Fox, *Experiment Perilous* (New York: Free Press of Glencoe, 1959).

[4] Herman Feifel, "Death" in Norman L. Farberow, *Taboo Topics* (New York: Atherton Press, 1963), p. 17.

[5] Donald Oken, "What to Tell Cancer Patients: A Study of Medical Attitudes," *Journal of the American Medical Association,* 175 (April 1, 1961), pp. 1120–28. See the bibliography cited in his paper for further studies on physician's tendency not to announce terminality. See also our further discussion in Chapter 8 of physicians' announcements.

[6] Eighty-two percent of Feifel's sample of sixty patients wanted to be informed about their condition.

also, physicians, like other Americans, shy away from the embarrassment and brutality of making direct reference to another person about his impending death. They also undoubtedly would rather avoid the scene that an announcement of impending death is likely to precipitate.

A third structural condition is that families also tend to guard the secret. Family members sometimes may reveal it, but in our own study we never witnessed deliberate disclosure by a family member. One psychiatrist told us, however, that he had disagreed with his father's physician about the wisdom of not telling his father, and so had made the disclosure himself. (Family members, of course, usually confirm what the physician has already announced.) An interesting contrast is the usual practice in Asian countries, where the extended kin gather around the hospital death bed, two or more days before death is expected, openly indicating to the patient that they are there to keep him company during his passage out of life.

A fourth structural condition is related both to the organization of hospitals and to the commitments of personnel who work within them. Our hospitals are admirably arranged, both by accident and by design, to hide medical information from patients. Records are kept out of reach. Staff is skilled at withholding information. Medical talk about patients generally occurs in far-removed places, and if it occurs nearby it is couched in medical jargon. Staff members are trained to discuss with patients only the surface aspects of their illnesses, and, as we shall see, they are accustomed to acting collusively around patients so as not to disclose medical secrets.

A fifth structural condition, perhaps somewhat less apparent, is that ordinarily the patient has no allies who reveal or help him discover the staff's knowledge of his impending death. Not only his family but other patients withhold that information, if they know. When a patient wants less distressing information, he may readily find allies among the other patients; but when he lies dying, the other patients follow ordinary rules of tact, keeping their knowledge to themselves or at least away from the doomed person. There may be exceptional incidents: the parents of a dying teenager told neighbors about his condition, and these neighbors told their son who in turn spilled out this information to the patient himself. Among adults, such failures of secrecy ordinarily do not occur.

While together these structural conditions contribute to the occurrence and maintenance of the closed awareness context, a change in any one condition may precipitate a change to another type of context. For example, the physician may decide to tell the patient—which leads to an "open awareness" context; or a patient begins to suspect something amiss because he begins to learn some of the indicators relevant to increasingly grave illness—which leads to a "suspicion awareness" context. In a later section of this chapter we shall discuss how changing structural conditions may transform the closed awareness context.

THE PATIENT'S
FICTIONAL BIOGRAPHY

A newly hospitalized patient has some basic questions about his condition. He wants to know, if he does not know already, just how ill he is, and whether he is going to get better or worse, *how* much better or worse, and how quickly he will progress or retrogress. In short, he ordinarily is passionately concerned with his own sick status—he wishes to know what may usefully be referred to as his "future biography."

The patient who is dying but who has not yet discovered or been told of his terminality faces a peculiar problem in getting an accurate assessment of his condition from the medical and nursing personnel. Can he trust the doctor, can he trust the nurses and aides, to yield him a true account of his story?[7] Or will their account be tinged by deceit and perhaps thoroughly false? A false account is a real possibility, although the patient may not recognize it as such. So trust is important in his transactions with the staff members.

Developing trust is also basic in the staff's transactions with the patient. To keep the patient unaware of his terminality, the staff members must construct a *fictional* future biography, for him, and they must sustain his belief in that biography by getting and keeping his trust.

What is involved in winning the patient's "trust?" First, consider a child who is old enough to know about death but still too young to doubt that his elders will properly care for him during his illness. The essence of his relations with adults is that he takes their actions at face value. What they are doing to him, and what they make him do is, as they explain, to make him get better. With children of this age, hospital personnel need not be so concerned about betraying their own behind-the-scenes knowledge. Such suspicions as the child may have will be more "I don't trust them to help me" rather than "I don't trust them because they are not telling me the truth about my condition." Consequently, personnel on pediatric wards report no great danger of unwarily letting their younger patients know they are dying. Indeed, they report that less control of one's face in a child's presence is needed, as he is not so apt to draw conclusions from an expression.

With adults the matter of trust in physicians and nurses is rather more complicated. Trust does not arise automatically; it must either be part of the

[7] Research in hospitals where psychotherapy is practiced indicates the patients collectively develop a philosophy that one must have faith in one's doctor. *Cf.* William Caudill *et al.,* "Social Structure and the Interaction Process on a Psychiatric Ward," *American Journal of Psychiatry,* 22 (1952), pp. 314–334; also Anselm Strauss *et al., Psychiatric Ideologies and Institutions* (New York: Free Press of Glencoe, 1964), pp. 271–273. But compare with the frequent distrust of doctors found in TB hospitals: Julius Roth, *Timetables* (Indianapolis: Bobbs-Merrill, 1963).

history of a particular relationship or it must be earned. Furthermore, once earned it must be maintained. The importance of keeping trust can be seen in the dilemma of an unaware patient who has long placed trust in a particular physician, but whose suspicions have now been aroused by some incident or remark. Can the man still be trusted in this new domain, trusted not only to "pull me through my illness" but "to tell me the worst?" In general, the physician and others must not arouse any suspicion by their words and actions that they are concealing knowledge about terminality. They must not even seem to fail in giving honest answers to any questions that might touch upon terminality. When staff members succeed in acting convincingly, the patient accepts their account of his future biography as accurate, or at least as accurate as they know how to make it.

ASSESSMENT MANAGEMENT

To sustain the unaware patient's belief in their version of his future biography, the staff members must control his assessments of those events and cues which might lead him to suspect or gain knowledge of his terminality. Their attempts at managing his assessments involve them in a silent game played to and around him; during which they project themselves to him as people who are trying to help him get better, or at least to keep him from getting worse. They must be sufficiently committed to this game, and sufficiently skilled at it, not to give it away. Their advantage is that they can collaborate as a team, sometimes a very experienced one, against an opponent who, as noted earlier, has ordinarily not much experience in discovering or correctly interpreting signs of impending death, and who is usually without allies.

Though the staff's explanations of his condition initially may seem convincing to the unaware patient, and though he may greatly trust the staff, he may begin to see and hear things that arouse his suspicions about his condition. Inevitably he wonders about, and requires explanation for, a host of events: Why is he given certain treatments or exposed to certain tests and procedures? Why is he moved from one room to another? Why has one more physician dropped into his room to examine him? Why is he not getting better more quickly? He wants answers to questions stimulated by various events even when he does not in the slightest suspect their true significance.

The staff members usually hasten to give him reasonable interpretations of those events. Frequently they even offer interpretations before he requests them, because they calculate he may otherwise secretly suspect the real meanings of those events. Their interpretations may be intentionally incorrect or only partly correct—if they feel that a correct one will potentially or actually reveal terminality to the patient. Thus, many of their interpretations are meant to mislead him. Of course a correct interpretation is offered when the staff member judges it will neither disclose nor arouse suspicions of terminality.

A patient near death, for instance, may be moved to a special space or room, but is informed that this move is only to permit more intensive care. A patient may even be sent home to die on request of his family, but his discharge from the hospital is explained in quite other terms. Occasionally the physician will give a patient an incorrect or incomplete diagnosis to explain his symptoms—as in one instance when a patient was discovered, through a diagnostic operation, to have incurable cancer of the pancreas but was sent home with a diagnosis of diabetes and given instructions in the use of insulin. If the patient believes that he has taken a turn for the worse, or at least is not improving, staff members are ready with reasonable answers that are meant to mislead him. At the very least, certain of his symptoms must be explained away, discounted, as signifying something much less alarming than they appear to him. Sometimes the physician warns him of anticipated symptoms, discounting them in advance. The physician and the nurses may also go out of their way continually to reassure him that things will turn out "all right," and indeed are "coming along fine." They will fabricate, hint at, or suggest favorable progress. Nurses especially compare the patient's condition, and his progress, with that of other patients they have known (including themselves), thus suggesting reasons for optimism. If the patient asks the nurses "Am I going to die?" as occasionally patients do without even real suspicion, they refer him to his physician for an answer ("Have you asked your physician?"), or change the subject without answering the question, or turn it aside with a stock answer (for instance, "We all have to go sometime"). When a patient asks the same question of the physician, the latter may simply lie.

The staff members also use tactics intended to encourage the patient to make his own interpretations inaccurately optimistic. They will comment favorably on his daily appearance, hoping he will interpret their comments optimistically. Some comments are downright misrepresentations and others are ambiguous enough to be misread easily. Staff members will attempt to establish a mood consonant less with terminality than with "things are not so bad even if not yet better." They also practice a sleight of hand, like magicians, drawing the patient's attention away from a dangerous cue by focusing his attention on an innocent one. They raise false scents, sometimes displaying elaborate interest in the symptoms he himself brings up for consideration. The physician may even put on diagnostic dramas for him, sending him for irrelevant tests. A certain amount of conversation with him about his imminent, or eventual, return home may occur; and his own reading of physical and temporal cues that represent progress to him may be supported. There is also what one might call a "sociability shield," or conversation that circumvents disclosure; during this conversation, personnel carry on as if the entire situation were quite normal. With such interactional devices, the staff simultaneously projects their own trustworthy medical identities, conveying to the patient that he is not expected to die.

In addition to all these devices, other techniques reduce cues that might arouse the patient's suspicion. Space is carefully managed, so that talk about him occurs away from his presence. If a nurse believes her involvement with, or sadness about, the patient might give the secret away, she may move quickly outside his visual range. She may even request an assignment away from him. Possibly revealing cues are also reduced by decreasing the time spent with the patient. Personnel who fear that they may unwittingly disclose something may remain with the patient very little, or choose to work on his body rather than talk much with him. They may keep tabs on his physical condition by popping in and out of his room, but thereby keep conversation at a minimum. Sometimes, when the patient is extremely close to death but there is nothing much to be done for him, staff members tend to go no farther than the doorway. If the patient becomes genuinely comatose, nurses or aides can again circulate freely in the patient's room.

The disclosing cues are minimized most subtly by reducing the range of expression and topic. The face can be managed so as to minimize the dangerous cues it conveys; hence the conventionally bland or cheerful faces of nurse and physician. A less obvious mode of minimizing such cues is to censor and select conversational topics. Staff members, for instance, steer conversation away from potentially revealing subjects and toward safer ones. They may talk, especially, about the relatively straightforward meanings of procedures being used on the patient's body, providing those meanings are not revealing.

One aspect of talk that personnel are cautious about is its present-future orientation. When a patient is defined as certain to die within a few days, nurses tend to focus their conversation with him on the immediate present, discussing such matters as current doses of medication for pain relief or other topics relevant to his comfort. But if they do not anticipate death for some time, then they will extend the temporal range implied in their talk. One nurse thus said, before leaving for a weekend, "See you next week." Another told a patient that he would need another X ray in two weeks. Similarly, they talk about blood tests to be done next week, or about the family's impending visit. One young nurse told us that she used to chat with a young patient about his future dates and parties, but that after discovering his certain and imminent death, she unwittingly cut out all references to the distant future. It is not easy to carry on a future-oriented conversation without revealing one's knowledge that the conversation is, in some sense, fraudulent, especially if the speaker is relatively inexperienced.

Staff members, again especially if they are inexperienced, must also guard against displaying those of their private reactions to him and to his impending death as might rouse the patient's suspicions of his terminality. For instance, young nurses are sometimes affected by terminal patients of their own age whose deaths become standing reminders of their own potential death. ("I found . . . that the patients who concerned me most when they died were women of my own age. . . .") Identification of this kind is quite common, and makes more difficult the staff members' control of their behavioral cues.

Their reactions to the patient's "social loss"[8] can also be revealing. In our society, certain values are highly esteemed—among them youth, beauty, integrity, talent, and parental and marital responsibility—and when a terminal patient strikingly embodies such values, staff members tend to react to the potential or actual loss to his family or to society. But such reactions must not be allowed to intrude into the fictionalized future biography that is directly and indirectly proffered to the patient. Since personnel tend to share a common attribution of social value, that intrusion is quite possible unless they keep tight control over their reactions. Although the staff's control is not always fully conscious, it is no less real.

Finally, because the patient is usually in contact with many staff members during each day, his suspicions of terminality may be aroused if they do not give consistent answers to his questions or if their behavior yields him inconsistent cues. So they must strive for consistency. But if he queries any inconsistency, then the staff members must offer him reasonable interpretations to explain away the "apparent" inconsistency.

FROM CLOSED TO OTHER
AWARENESS CONTEXTS

Inherently, this closed awareness context tends toward instability, as the patient moves either to suspicion or full awareness of his terminality. The principal reasons for the instability of closed awareness require only brief notation, as they have already been adumbrated. First, any breakdown in the structural conditions that make for the closed awareness context may lead to its disappearance.[9] Those conditions include the physician's decision not to tell the patient, the family's supporting agreement, and the tactful silence of other patients. For example, such a break occurs repeatedly at one Veterans Administration hospital we studied, where patients who are eventually judged to be hopelessly terminal are sometimes asked whether they would care to become research subjects and receive medication that might prolong their lives.

Some unanticipated disclosures or tip-offs, stemming from organizational conditions, can also occur. The staff members who work in emergency rooms in hospitals need to be especially careful in controlling their facial surprises or immediately compassionate distress when suddenly confronted by obviously

[8] Barney Glaser and Anselm Strauss, "The Social Loss of Dying Patients," *American Journal of Nursing* (June 1964), pp. 119–121.

[9] The Catholic practice of giving the sacrament requires calling in a priest prior to possible death, and this may function as an announcement to the dying patient. But non-Catholics probably need to be told that this is done only to insure that the patient does not die without the sacrament. If he recovers, whether to live for many years or merely days, then he may receive the sacrament once or perhaps several times again.

dying patients, often the battered victims of accidents caused by others' care-lessness. Staff members' control in these instances is not always successful. On other hospital services, rotation of nursing staff may bring the patient into contact with new persons who do not always know of his terminality or who have not been coached properly in the history of how the staff has conducted itself in the presence of this patient. Even the daily shift carries hidden dangers. For instance, the doctor may inform the day shift that his patient is dying, but unless specific measures are taken to transmit this information to the night shift, the patient may be cared for by personnel not sufficiently alert to the dangers of unwitting disclosure. This danger is especially grave when the patient is worried about certain new symptoms.

New symptoms understandably are likely to perplex and alarm the patient; and the longer his retrogressive course, the more difficult it becomes to give him plausible explanations, though a very complicated misrepresentational drama can be played for his benefit. Even so, it becomes somewhat more difficult to retain the patient's trust over a long time. When a patient's physical symptoms become compelling, sometimes he can force nurses into almost an open admission of the truth. Not to hint at, or tacitly admit to, the truth would be to risk losing his trust altogether. So it is not unknown for the staff to "snow a patient under" with drugs as he nears death, partly to reduce his suffering (and perhaps their own) and partly to reduce the likelihood that finally he will correctly read the fateful signs. Indeed, sometimes a race with time occurs, there being some question whether the patient will die, or at least become comatose, before he becomes suspicious or aware of his terminality.

Another threat to closed awareness, closely linked with retrogressive physical symptoms, is that some treatments make little sense to a patient who does not recognize that he is dying. Just as many polio patients will not take full advantage of rehabilitation programs because they do not anticipate being cured, so a terminal patient may refuse a medicine, a machine, an awkward position or an inconvenient diet.[10] To accomplish her task, the nurse may have to hint at the extreme seriousness of her patient's condition, hoping that he will get the point just long enough for her to complete the procedure. But if this tactic works, it may then also stimulate an attempt by the patient to discover what is really happening to him. The staff then must redouble its assessment management. For instance, the nurse who alarmed him must immediately assure him that he has interpreted her words incorrectly—but she may not be wholly or at all successful. The physician can also have problems when explaining to his patient why he must undergo certain additional treatments, tests and operations, or why he needs to return to the hospital "for a while."

At times, moreover, a patient may be unable to cope with his immensely deteriorating physical condition unless nurses interpret that condition and

---

[10] *Cf.* Fred Davis, "Uncertainty in Medical Prognosis," *American Journal of Sociology,* 66 (July 1960), p. 45.

its symptoms to him. To do this, nurses may feel forced to talk of his dying. Not to disclose at this desperate point can torture and isolate the patient, which runs counter to a central value of nursing care, namely to make the patient as comfortable as possible. Similarly, the physician's inaccessibility may force nurses to disclose the truth in order to do something immediately for, or with the patient.

The danger that staff members will give the show away by relaxing their usual tight control also increases as the patient nears death, especially when the dying takes place slowly. For instance, concerned personnel will continually pause at the patient's door, popping their heads into his room to see how he is—or if he is still alive. Sometimes a patient very close to death will be given more privileges because of simple compassion for him (like permitting him to eat previously denied favorite foods or to take an automobile ride or even to return home permanently); occasionally this can cue him into suspicion awareness. The staff will also sometimes relax their guard when they believe the patient is too far gone (physically dazed, comatose, or senile) to understand what would otherwise be revealing cues or downright disclosing conversations—but he may be sentient enough to understand.

This last set of conditions brings us to the question of whether, and how, personnel actually may engineer a change of the closed awareness context. For instance, a physician may drop hints to the patient that he is dying, giving the information gradually, and hoping that eventually the patient will comprehend the finality of his medical condition. Nurses have so often confided to us that they hoped certain patients were really aware of impending death that we can be sure they have signaled, however ambiguously, to such patients, especially when the latter are well beloved and the nurses can see no good reason why they should not be prepared for death even though the physicians choose not to tell. The true situation can be deliberately conveyed to a patient by facial expression, by carefully oblique phrasing of words, or merely by failure to reassure him about his symptoms and prognosis. And of course the family members may occasionally signal or hint at the dreadful truth. Indeed, when the family actually knows the truth, the hazards to maintaining closed awareness probably are much increased, if only because kin are more strongly tempted to signal the truth.

CONSEQUENCES OF
CLOSED AWARENESS

So many discrete consequences seem to flow from this closed awareness context that we must restrict our attention to a few of its consequences for the patient, his family, the hospital personnel, and the hospital itself. We shall return to this discussion of interactional consequences in later chapters; here we shall merely initiate it.

We can approach the consequences of closed awareness by touching on a contrasting situation. In her book *Experiment Perilous,* Renée Fox has described a small research hospital whose patients recognized their own inevitable terminality because that was why they were research patients.[11] Death was an open and everyday occurrence. Patients could talk familiarly to each other, about their respective fatal conditions, as well as to the staff members. Various consequences seemed to flow from this generally *open* situation, including the following: Patients could give each other support; and the staff could support patients. Patients could even raise the flagging spirits of the staff! From their deathbeds, they could thank the physicians for their unstinting efforts and wish them luck in solving their research problems in time to save other patients. They could close their lives with proper rituals, such as letter writing and praying. They could review their lives and plan realistically for their families' futures. All these various possibilities, available to aware patients in the open awareness situation, are of course not available to unaware patients in the closed awareness situation.

When patients are kept unaware of their terminality, then other consequences emerge. Since the unaware patient believes he will recover, he acts on that supposition. He may often be extremely cooperative with physicians and nurses because he believes faithful following of their orders will return him to good health. He talks and think as if his period of illness is only an interruption of normal life. Thus he may convert his sick room into a temporary workplace, writing his unfinished book, telephoning his business partners, and in other ways carrying on his work somewhat "as usual." He carries on his family life and friendship relations, also, with only the interruption necessitated by temporary illness. And of course, he can plan, if plans are called for, as if life stretched away before him. Since, in reality, it does not, other consequences may attend his acting as though it did. He may work less feverishly on his unfinished book than if he knew time was short, and so fail to finish it. He may set plans into operation that make little sense because he will soon be dead, and the plans will have to be undone after his death. Also, the unaware patient may unwittingly shorten his life because he does not realize that special care is necessary to extend it. Thus he may not understand the necessity for certain treatments and refuse them. Unaware cardiac patients, as another instance, may even destroy themselves by insisting upon undue activity.

A word or two should be said about the next of kin. It is commonly recognized that it is in some ways easier for the family to face a patient who does not know of his terminality, especially if he is the kind of person who is likely to die "gracelessly." And if an unaware person is suddenly stricken and dies, sometimes his family is grateful that "he died without knowing." On the other hand, when the kin must participate in the non-disclosure drama, especially if it lasts very long, the experience can be very painful. What is more, family members suffer sometimes because they cannot express their grief

[11] Renée Fox, *op. cit.*

openly to the dying person; this is especially true of husbands and wives who are accustomed to sharing their private lives. Other consequences for the family of a patient who dies without awareness are poignantly suggested in the following anecdote: The dying man's wife had been informed by the doctor, and had shared this information with friends, whose daughter told the patient's young son. The son developed a strong distrust for the doctor, and felt in a way disinherited by his father since they had not discussed the responsibilities that would fall to him in the future (nor could they). The father, of course, could do nothing to ameliorate this situation because he did not know that he was going to die; and so, this closed awareness situation was, perhaps unnecessarily, made more painful and difficult for the family members.

We have already indicated in detail what difficulties the closed awareness context creates for the hospital staff, especially for the nurses. Nurses may sometimes actually be relieved when the patient talks openly about his demise and they no longer have to guard against disclosure. By contrast, the closed context instituted by the physician permits him to avoid the potentially distressing scene that may follow an announcement to his patient, but subjects nurses to strain, for they must spend the most time with the unaware patient, guarding constantly against disclosure. The attending physician visits the patient briefly and intermittently, sometimes rarely.

On the other hand, under certain conditions, nurses prefer the closed context. Some do not care to talk about death with a patient, especially a patient who does not accept it with fortitude. An unaware person is sometimes easier to handle anyway, for precisely the reason that he has not "given up," or is not taking death "badly" or "hard." (At one county hospital where we observed both nurses and interns, it was remarkable how little strain they experienced in their frequent contact with extremely ill, but unaware, terminal patients.) Nonetheless, as we shall show later in more details, the closed awareness situation prevents staff members from enjoying certain advantages that accompany a patient's resigned—or joyous—meeting with death.

As for the hospital itself, the important consequences of closed awareness derive mainly from the consequences for the staff. Unaware patients who die quickly tend to do so without fuss, so the hospital's routine work is delayed less. On the other hand, as one can readily imagine, a patient who moves explosively and resentfully from an unaware to a highly suspicious or fully aware state is relatively disruptive. But these are only transitory consequences; the long-run consequences are most important.

The most crucial institutional consequence has already been mentioned: because American physicians choose not to tell most patients about terminality, the burden of dealing with unaware patients falls squarely and persistently upon the nursing personnel. Quite literally, if subtly, this considerable burden is built into the organization of the hospital services that deal with terminal patients. Another social structural condition intrinsic to the functioning of American hospitals also increases the nurse's burden. We refer to the nursing staff's commitment to work relatively closely with and around patients. Again, this structural condition can be better appreciated if one thinks of the contrast in Asian hospitals, where the family clusters thickly and persistently around the dying patient. A corollary of this familial clustering is that the nursing personnel can remain at a relatively great emotional distance from, and spend relatively little time with, the patient. The enormously high patient-to-personnel ratio increases the probability of great distance and little contact. Although American nurses are sometimes criticized for a propensity to anchor themselves at the nurses' station, they do spend more time with fewer patients, including those who are dying unaware.

Finally, we must ask about the consequences of closed awareness for continued interaction with the patient. Perhaps little need be said about this aspect of the closed awareness context. It should be abundantly clear that closed awareness can change smoothly and easily, or explosively and brutally, into another type of awareness context, depending on how the closed awareness was managed, and on the conditions under which the terminal patient discovered what the staff members were doing to or for him. At the most painful extreme, he can feel betrayed; the happiest outcome is that he feels grateful for their protection and genuine sensibility.

27

MASS COMMUNICATION AND PARA-SOCIAL INTERACTION: OBSERVATIONS ON INTIMACY AT A DISTANCE

Donald Horton

R. Richard Wohl

ONE OF THE STRIKING CHARACTERISTICS of the new mass media—radio, television, and the movies—is that they give the illusion of face-to-face relationship with the performer. The conditions of response to the performer are analogous to those in a primary group. The most remote and illustrious men are met *as if* they were in the circle of one's peers; the same is true of a character in a story who comes to life in these media in an especially vivid and arresting way. We propose to call this seeming face-to-face relationship between spectator and performer a *para-social relationship*.

In television, especially, the image which is presented makes available nuances of appearance and gesture to which ordinary social perception is attentive and to which interaction is cued. Sometimes the "actor"—whether he is playing himself or performing in a fictional role—is seen engaged with others; but often he faces the spectator, uses the mode of direct address, talks as if he were conversing personally and privately. The audience, for its part, responds with something more than mere running observation; it is, as it were, subtly insinuated into the program's action and internal social relationships and, by dint of this kind of staging, is ambiguously transformed

From *Psychiatry*, 9 (1956), 215–229. Reprinted by permission of The William Alanson White Psychiatric Foundation, Inc. (Text, Chapter 13)

into a group which observes and participates in the show by turns. The more the performer seems to adjust his performance to the supposed response of the audience, the more the audience tends to make the response anticipated. This simulacrum of conversational give and take may be called *para-social interaction*.

Para-social relations may be governed by little or no sense of obligation, effort, or responsibility on the part of the spectator. He is free to withdraw at any moment. If he remains involved, these para-social relations provide a framework within which much may be added by fantasy. But these are differences of degree, not of kind, from what may be termed the ortho-social. The crucial difference in experience obviously lies in the lack of effective reciprocity, and this the audience cannot normally conceal from itself. To be sure, the audience is free to choose among the relationships offered, but it cannot create new ones. The interaction, characteristically, is one-sided, non-dialectical, controlled by the performer, and not susceptible of mutual development. There are, of course, ways in which the spectators can make their feelings known to the performers and the technicians who design the programs, but these lie outside the para-social interaction itself. Whoever finds the experience unsatisfying has only the option to withdraw.

What we have said so far forcibly recalls the theatre as an ambiguous meeting ground on which real people play out the roles of fictional characters. For a brief interval, the fictional takes precedence over the actual, as the actor becomes identified with the fictional role in the magic of the theatre. This glamorous confusion of identities is temporary: the worlds of fact and fiction meet only for the moment. And the actor, when he takes his bows at the end of the performance, crosses back over the threshold into the matter-of-fact world.

Radio and television, however—and in what follows we shall speak primarily of television—are hospitable to both these worlds in continuous interplay. They are alternately public platforms and theatres, extending the para-social relationship now to leading people of the world of affairs, now to fictional characters, sometimes even to puppets anthropomorphically transformed into "personalities," and, finally, to theatrical stars who appear in their capacities as real celebrities. But of particular interest is the creation by these media of a new type of performer: quiz-masters, announcers, "interviewers" in a new "show-business" world—in brief, a special category of "personalities" whose existence is a function of the media themselves. These "personalities," usually, are not prominent in any of the social spheres beyond the media.[1] They exist for their audiences only in the para-social relation. Lacking an appropriate name for these performers, we shall call them *personae*.

---

[1] They may move out into positions of leadership in the world at large as they become famous and influential. Frank Sinatra, for example, has become known as a "youth leader." Conversely, figures from the political world, to choose another example, may become media "personalities" when they appear regularly. Fiorello LaGuardia, the late Mayor of New York, is one such case.

THE ROLE OF
THE PERSONA

The persona is the typical and indigenous figure of the social scene presented by radio and television. To say that he is familiar and intimate is to use pale and feeble language for the pervasiveness and closeness with which multitudes feel his presence. The spectacular fact about such personae is that they can claim and achieve an intimacy with what are literally crowds of strangers, and this intimacy, even if it is an imitation and a shadow of what is ordinarily meant by that word, is extremely influential with, and satisfying for, the great numbers who willingly receive it and share in it. They "know" such a persona in somewhat the same way they know their chosen friends: through direct observation and interpretation of his appearance, his gestures and voice, his conversation and conduct in a variety of situations. Indeed, those who make up his audience are invited, by designed informality, to make precisely these evaluations—to consider that they are involved in a face-to-face exchange rather than in passive observation. When the television camera pans down on a performer, the illusion is strong that he is enhancing the presumed intimacy by literally coming closer. But the persona's image, while partial, contrived, and penetrated by illusion, is no fantasy or dream; his performance is an objectively perceptible action in which the viewer is implicated imaginatively, but which he does not imagine.

The persona offers, above all, a continuing relationship. His appearance is a regular and dependable event, to be counted on, planned for, and integrated into the routines of daily life. His devotees "live with him" and share the small episodes of his public life—and to some extent even of his private life away from the show. Indeed, their continued association with him acquires a history, and the accumulation of shared past experiences gives additional meaning to the present performance. This bond is symbolized by allusions that lack meaning for the casual observer and appear occult to the outsider. In time, the devotee—the "fan"—comes to believe that he "knows" the persona more intimately and profoundly than others do; that he "understands" his character and appreciates his values and motives.[2] Such an accumulation of knowledge and intensification of loyalty, however, appears to be a kind of growth without development, for the one-sided nature of the connection precludes a progressive and mutual reformulation of its values and aims.[3]

The persona may be considered by his audience as a friend, counselor, com-

---

[2] Merton's discussion of the attitude toward Kate Smith of her adherents exemplifies, with much circumstantial detail, what we have said above. See Robert K. Merton, Marjorie Fiske, and Alberta Curtis, *Mass Persuasion; The Social Psychology of a War Bond Drive;* New York, Harper, 1946; especially Chapter 6.

[3] There does remain the possibility that over the course of his professional life the persona, responding to influences from his audience, may develop new conceptions of himself and his role.

forter, and model; but, unlike real associates, he has the peculiar virtue of being standardized according to the "formula" for his character and performance which he and his managers have worked out and embodied in an appropriate "production format." Thus his character and pattern of action remain basically unchanged in a world of otherwise disturbing change. The persona is ordinarily predictable, and gives his adherents no unpleasant surprises. In their association with him there are no problems of understanding or empathy too great to be solved. Typically, there are no challenges to a spectator's self—to his ability to take the reciprocal part in the performance that is assigned to him—that cannot be met comfortably. This reliable sameness is only approximated, and then only in the short run, by the figures of fiction. On television, Groucho is always sharp; Godfrey is always warmhearted.

THE BOND
OF INTIMACY

It is an unvarying characteristic of these "personality" programs that the greatest pains are taken by the persona to create an illusion of intimacy. We call it an illusion because the relationship between the persona and any member of his audience is inevitably one-sided, and reciprocity between the two can only be suggested. There are several principal strategies for achieving this illusion of intimacy.

Most characteristic is the attempt of the persona to duplicate the gestures, conversational style, and milieu of an informal face-to-face gathering. This accounts, in great measure, for the casualness with which even the formalities of program scheduling are treated. The spectator is encouraged to gain the impression that what is taking place on the program gains a momentum of its own in the very process of being enacted. Thus Steve Allen is always pointing out to his audience that "we never know what is going to happen on this show." In addition, the persona tries to maintain a flow of small talk which gives the impression that he is responding to and sustaining the contributions of an invisible interlocutor. Dave Garroway, who has mastered this style to perfection, has described how he stumbled on the device in his early days in radio.

> Most talk on the radio in those days was formal and usually a little stiff. But I just rambled along, saying whatever came into my mind. I was introspective. I tried to pretend that I was chatting with a friend over a highball late in the evening. . . . Then—and later—I consciously tried to talk to the listener as an individual, to make each listener feel that he knew me and I knew him. It seemed to work pretty well then and later. I know that strangers often stop me on the street today, call me Dave and seem to feel that we are old friends who know all about each other.[4]

[4] Dave Garroway as told to Joe Alex Morris, "I Lead a Goofy Life," *The Saturday Evening Post*, February 11, 1956; p. 62.

In addition to creating an appropriate tone and patter, the persona tries as far as possible to eradicate, or at least to blur, the line which divides him and his show, as a formal performance, from the audience both in the studio and at home. The most usual way of achieving this ambiguity is for the persona to treat his supporting cast as a group of close intimates. Thus all the members of the cast will be addressed by their first names, or by special nicknames, to emphasize intimacy. They very quickly develop, or have imputed to them, stylized character traits which, as members of the supporting cast, they will indulge in and exploit regularly in program after program. The member of the audience, therefore, not only accumulates an historical picture of "the kinds of people they really are," but tends to believe that this fellowship includes him by extension. As a matter of fact, all members of the program who are visible to the audience will be drawn into this by-play to suggest this ramification of intimacy.

Furthermore, the persona may try to step out of the particular format of his show and literally blend with the audience. Most usually, the persona leaves the stage and mingles with the studio audience in a question-and-answer exchange. In some few cases, and particularly on the Steve Allen show, this device has been carried a step further. Thus Allen has managed to blend even with the home audience by the maneuver of training a television camera on the street outside the studio and, in effect, suspending his own show and converting all the world outside into a stage. Allen, his supporting cast, and the audience, both at home and in the studio, watch together what transpires on the street—the persona and his spectators symbolically united as one big audience. In this way, Allen erases for the moment the line which separates persona and spectator.

In addition to the management of relationships between the persona and performers, and between him and his audience, the technical devices of the media themselves are exploited to create illusions of intimacy.

> For example [Dave Garroway explains in this connection], we developed the "subjective-camera" idea, which was simply making the camera be the eyes of the audience. In one scene the camera—that's you, the viewer—approached the door of a dentist's office, saw a sign that the dentist was out to lunch, sat down nervously in the waiting room. The dentist returned and beckoned to the camera, which went in and sat in the big chair. "Open wide," the dentist said, poking a huge, wicked-looking drill at the camera. There was a roar as the drill was turned on, sparks flew and the camera vibrated and the viewers got a magnified version of sitting in the dentist's chair—except that it didn't hurt.[5]

All these devices are indulged in not only to lure the attention of the audience, and to create the easy impression that there is a kind of participation open to them in the program itself, but also to highlight the chief values stressed in such "personality" shows. These are sociability, easy affability, friendship, and close contact—briefly, all the values associated with free

[5] Reference footnote 4; p. 64.

access to and easy participation in pleasant social interaction in primary groups. Because the relationship between persona and audience is one-sided and cannot be developed mutually, very nearly the whole burden of creating a plausible imitation of intimacy is thrown on the persona and on the show of which he is the pivot. If he is successful in initiating an intimacy which his audience can believe in, then the audience may help him maintain it by fan mail and by the various other kinds of support which can be provided indirectly to buttress his actions.

THE ROLE
OF THE AUDIENCE

At one extreme, the "personality" program is like a drama in having a cast of characters, which includes the persona, his professional supporting cast, nonprofessional contestants and interviewees, and the studio audience. At the other extreme, the persona addresses his entire performance to the home audience with undisturbed intimacy. In the dramatic type of program, the participation of the spectator involves, we presume, the same taking of successive roles and deeper empathic involvements in the leading roles which occurs in any observed social interaction.[6] It is possible that the spectator's "collaborative expectancy"[7] may assume the more profound form of identification with one or more of the performers. But such identification can hardly be more than intermittent. The "personality" program, unlike the theatrical drama, does not demand or even permit the esthetic illusion—that loss of situational reference and self-consciousness in which the audience not only accepts the symbol as reality, but fully assimilates the symbolic role. The persona and his staff maintain the para-social relationship, continually referring to and addressing the home audience as a third party to the program; and such references remind the spectator of his own independent identity. The only illusion maintained is that of directness and immediacy of participation.

When the persona appears alone, in apparent face-to-face interaction with the home viewer, the latter is still more likely to maintain his own identity without interruption, for he is called upon to make appropriate responses which are complementary to those of the persona. This "answering" role is, to a degree, voluntary and independent. In it, the spectator retains control over the content of his participation rather than surrendering control through identification with others, as he does when absorbed in watching a drama or movie.

This independence is relative, however, in a twofold sense: First, it is rela-

---

[6] See, for instance: George H. Mead, *Mind, Self and Society;* Chicago, Univ. of Chicago Press, 1934. Walter Coutu, *Emergent Human Nature;* New York, Knopf, 1949. Rosalind Dymond, "Personality and Empathy," *J. Consulting Psychol.* (1950) 14:343–350.

[7] Burke uses this expression to describe an attitude evoked by formal rhetorical devices, but it seems equally appropriate here. See Kenneth Burke, *A Rhetoric of Motives;* New York, Prentice-Hall, 1950; p. 58.

tive in the profound sense that the very act of entering into any interaction with another involves *some* adaptation to the other's perspectives, if communication is to be achieved at all. And, second, in the present case, it is relative because the role of the persona is enacted in such a way, or is of such a character, that an *appropriate* answering role is specified by implication and suggestion. The persona's performance, therefore, is open-ended, calling for a rather specific answering role to give it closure.[8]

The general outlines of the appropriate audience role are perceived intuitively from familiarity with the common cultural patterns on which the role of the persona is constructed. These roles are chiefly derived from the primary relations of friendship and the family, characterized by intimacy, sympathy, and sociability. The audience is expected to accept the situation defined by the program format as credible, and to concede as "natural" the rules and conventions governing the actions performed and the values realized. It should play the role of the loved one to the persona's lover; the admiring dependent to his father-surrogate; the earnest citizen to his fearless opponent of political evils. It is expected to benefit by his wisdom, reflect on his advice, sympathize with him in his difficulties, forgive his mistakes, buy the products that he recommends, and keep his sponsor informed of the esteem in which he is held.

Other attitudes than compliance in the assigned role are, of course, possible. One may reject, take an analytical stance, perhaps even find a cynical amusement in refusing the offered gambit and playing some other role not implied in the script, or view the proceedings with detached curiosity or hostility. But such attitudes as these are, usually, for the one-time viewer. The faithful audience is one that can accept the gambit offered; and the functions of the program for this audience are served not by the mere perception of it, but by the role-enactment that completes it.

THE COACHING
OF AUDIENCE ATTITUDES

Just how the situation should be defined by the audience, what to expect of the persona, what attitudes to take toward him, what to "do" as a participant in the program, is not left entirely to the common experience and intuitions of the audience. Numerous devices are used in a deliberate "coaching of attitudes," to use Kenneth Burke's phrase.[9] The typical program format calls for a studio audience to provide a situation of face-to-face interaction for the persona, and exemplifies to the home audience an enthusiastic and "correct" response. The more interaction occurs, the more clearly is demonstrated the kind of man the persona is, the values to be shared in association with him, and the kind of support to give him. A similar model of appropriate

---

[8] This is in contrast to the closed system of the drama, in which all the roles are predetermined in their mutual relations.

[9] Kenneth Burke, *Attitudes Toward History, Vol. 1;* New York, New Republic Publishing Co., 1937; see, for instance, p. 104.

response may be supplied by the professional assistants who, though technically performers, act in a subordinate and deferential reciprocal relation toward the persona. The audience is schooled in correct responses to the persona by a variety of other means as well. Other personae may be invited as guests, for example, who play up to the host in exemplary fashion; or persons drawn from the audience may be maneuvered into fulfilling this function. And, in a more direct and literal fashion, reading excerpts from fan-mail may serve the purpose.

Beyond the coaching of specific attitudes toward personae, a general propaganda on their behalf flows from the performers themselves, their press agents, and the mass communication industry. Its major theme is that the performer should be loved and admired. Every attempt possible is made to strengthen the illusion of reciprocity and rapport in order to offset the inherent impersonality of the media themselves. The jargon of show business teems with special terms for the mysterious ingredients of such rapport: ideally, a performer should have "heart," should be "sincere";[10] his performance should be "real" and "warm."[11] The publicity compaigns built around successful performers continually emphasize the sympathetic image which, it is hoped, the audience is perceiving and developing.[12]

The audience, in its turn, is expected to contribute to the illusion by believing in it, and by rewarding the persona's "sincerity" with "loyalty." The audience is entreated to assume a sense of personal obligation to the performer, to help him in his struggle for "success" if he is "on the way up," or to maintain his success if he has already won it. "Success" in show business is itself a theme which is prominently exploited in this kind of propaganda. It

[10] See Merton's acute analysis of the audience's demand for "sincerity" as a reassurance against manipulation. Reference footnote 2; pp. 142–146.

[11] These attributes have been strikingly discussed by Mervyn LeRoy, a Hollywood director, in a recent book. Although he refers specifically to the motion-picture star, similar notions are common in other branches of show business. "What draws you to certain people?" he asks. "I have said before that you can't be a really fine actress or actor without heart. You also have to possess the ability to project that heart, that feeling and emotion. The sympathy in your eyes will show. The audience has to feel sorry for the person on the screen. If there aren't moments when, rightly or wrongly, he moves the audience to sympathy, there's an actor who will never be big box-office." Mervyn LeRoy and Alyce Canfield, *It Takes More Than Talent;* New York, Knopf, 1953; p. 114.

[12] Once an actor has succeeded in establishing a good relationship with his audience in a particular kind of dramatic role, he may be "typed" in that role. Stereotyping in the motion-picture industry is often rooted in the belief that sustained rapport with the audience can be achieved by repeating past success. (This principle is usually criticized as detrimental to the talent of the actor, but it is a *sine qua non* for the persona whose professional sucess depends upon creating and sustaining a plausible and unchanging identity.) Sometimes, indeed, the Hollywood performer will actually take his name from a successful role; this is one of the principles on which Warner Brothers Studios selects the names of some of its actors. For instance, Donna Lee Hickey was renamed Mae Wynn after a character she portrayed, with great distinction, in *The Caine Mutiny.* See "Names of Hollywood Actors," *Names* (1955) 3:116.

forms the basis of many movies; it appears often in the patter of the leading comedians and in the exhortations of MC's; it dominates the so-called amateur hours and talent shows; and it is subject to frequent comment in interviews with "show people."[13]

CONDITIONS OF ACCEPTANCE
OF THE PARA-SOCIAL ROLE
BY THE AUDIENCE

The acceptance by the audience of the role offered by the program involves acceptance of the explicit and implicit terms which define the situation and the action to be carried out in the program. Unless the spectator understands these terms, the role performances of the participants are meaningless to him; and unless he accepts them, he cannot "enter into" the performance himself. But beyond this, the spectator must be able to play the part demanded of him; and this raises the question of the compatibility between his normal self—as a system of role-patterns and self-conceptions with their implicated norms and values—and the kind of self postulated by the program schema and the actions of the persona. In short, one may conjecture that the probability of rejection of the proffered role will be greater the less closely the spectator "fits" the role prescription.

To accept the gambit without the necessary personality "qualifications" is to invite increasing dissatisfaction and alienation—which the student of the media can overcome only by a deliberate, imaginative effort to take the postulated role. The persona himself takes the role of his projected audience in the interpretation of his own actions, often with the aid of cues provided by a studio audience. He builds his performance on a cumulative structure of assumptions about their response, and so postulates—more or less consciously—the complex of attitudes to which his own actions are adapted. A spectator who fails to make the anticipated responses will find himself further and further removed from the base-line of common understanding.[14] One

---

[13] The "loyalty" which is demanded of the audience is not necessarily passive or confined only to patronizing the persona's performance. Its active demonstration is called for in charity appeals, "marathons," and "telethons"; and, of course, it is expected to be freely transferable to the products advertised by the performer. Its most active form is represented by the organization of fan clubs with programs of activities and membership obligations, which give a continuing testimony of loyalty.

[14] Comedians on radio and television frequently chide their audience if they do not laugh at the appropriate places, or if their response is held to be inadequate. The comedian tells the audience that if they don't respond promptly, he won't wait, whereupon the audience usually provides the demanded laugh. Sometimes the chiding is more oblique, as when the comedian interrupts his performance to announce that he will fire the writer of the unsuccessful joke. Again, the admonition to respond correctly is itself treated as a joke and is followed by a laugh.

would expect the "error" to be cumulative, and eventually to be carried, perhaps, to the point at which the spectator is forced to resign in confusion, disgust, anger, or boredom. If a significant portion of the audience fails in this way, the persona's "error in role-taking"[15] has to be corrected with the aid of audience research, "program doctors," and other aids. But, obviously, the intended adjustment is to some average or typical spectator, and cannot take too much account of deviants.

The simplest example of such a failure to fulfill the role prescription would be the case of an intellectual discussion in which the audience is presumed to have certain basic knowledge and the ability to follow the development of the argument. Those who cannot meet these requirements find the discussion progressively less comprehensible. A similar progressive alienation probably occurs when children attempt to follow an adult program or movie. One observes them absorbed in the opening scenes, but gradually losing interest as the developing action leaves them behind. Another such situation might be found in the growing confusion and restiveness of some audiences watching foreign movies or "high-brow" drama. Such resistance is also manifested when some members of an audience are asked to take the opposite-sex role— the woman's perspective is rejected more commonly by men than vice versa —or when audiences refuse to accept empathically the roles of outcasts or those of racial or cultural minorities whom they consider inferior.[16]

It should be observed that merely witnessing a program is not evidence that a spectator has played the required part. Having made the initial commitment, he may "string along" with it at a low level of empathy but reject it retrospectively. The experience does not end with the program itself. On the contrary, it may be only after it has ended that it is submitted to intellectual analysis and integrated into, or rejected by, the self; this occurs especially in those discussions which the spectator may undertake with other people in which favorable or unfavorable consensual interpretations and judgments are arrived at. It is important to enter a qualification at this point. The suspension of immediate judgment is probably more complete in the viewing of the dramatic program, where there is an esthetic illusion to be accepted, than in the more self-conscious viewing of "personality" programs.

---

[15] Coutu, reference footnote 6; p. 294.
[16] See, for example, W. Lloyd Warner and William E. Henry, "The Radio Day Time Serial: A Symbolic Analysis," *Genetic Psychol. Monographs* (1948) 37:3–71, the study of a daytime radio serial program in which it is shown that upper-middle-class women tend to reject identification with lower-middle-class women represented in the drama. Yet some people are willing to take unfamiliar roles. This appears to be especially characteristic of the intellectual whose distinction is not so much that he has cosmopolitan tastes and knowledge, but that he has the capacity to transcend the limits of his own culture in his identifications. Remarkably little is known about how this ability is developed.

VALUES OF THE
PARA-SOCIAL ROLE
FOR THE AUDIENCE

What para-social roles are acceptable to the spectator and what benefits their enactment has for him would seem to be related to the systems of patterned roles and social situations in which he is involved in his everyday life. The values of a para-social role may be related, for example, to the demands being made upon the spectator for achievement in certain statuses. Such demands, to pursue this instance further, may be manifested in the expectations of others, or they may be self-demands, with the concomitant emergence of more or less satisfactory self-conceptions. The enactment of a para-social role may therefore constitute an exploration and development of new role possibilities, as in the experimental phases of actual, or aspired to, social mobility.[17] It may offer a recapitulation of roles no longer played—roles which, perhaps, are no longer possible. The audience is diversified in terms of life-stages, as well as by other social and cultural characteristics; thus, what for youth may be the anticipatory enactment of roles to be assumed in the future may be, for older persons, a reliving and re-evaluation of the actual or imagined past.

The enacted role may be an idealized version of an everyday performance—a "successful" para-social approximation of an ideal pattern, not often, perhaps never, achieved in real life. Here the contribution of the persona may be to hold up a magic mirror to his followers, playing his reciprocal part more skillfully and ideally than do the partners of the real world. So Liberace, for example, outdoes the ordinary husband in gentle understanding, or Nancy Berg outdoes the ordinary wife in amorous complaisance. Thus, the spectator may be enabled to play his part suavely and completely in imagination as he is unable to do in actuality.

If we have emphasized the opportunities offered for playing a vicarious or actual role, it is because we regard this as the key operation in the spectator's activity, and the chief avenue of the program's meaning for him. This is not to overlook the fact that every social role is reciprocal to the social roles of others, and that it is as important to learn to understand, to decipher, and to anticipate their conduct as it is to manage one's own. The function of the mass media, and of the programs we have been discussing, is also the exemplification of the patterns of conduct one needs to understand and cope with in

---

[17] Most students of the mass media occupy a cultural level somewhat above that of the most popular programs and personalities of the media, and necessarily look down upon them. But it should not be forgotten that for many millions indulgence in these media is a matter of looking up. Is it not also possible that some of the media permit a welcome regression, for some, from the higher cultural standards of their present status? This may be one explanation of the vogue of detective stories and science fiction among intellectuals, and might also explain the escape downward from middle-class standards in the literature of "low life" generally.

others as well as of those patterns which one must apply to one's self. Thus the spectator is instructed variously in the behaviors of the opposite sex, of people of higher and lower status, of people in particular occupations and professions. In a quantitative sense, by reason of the sheer volume of such instruction, this may be the most important aspect of the para-social experience, if only because each person's roles are relatively few, while those of the others in his social worlds are very numerous. In this culture, it is evident that to be prepared to meet all the exigencies of a changing social situation, no matter how limited it may be, could—and often does—require a great stream of plays and stories, advice columns and social how-to-do-it books. What, after all, is soap opera but an interminable exploration of the contingencies to be met with in "home life?"[18]

In addition to the possibilities we have already mentioned, the media present opportunities for the playing of roles to which the spectator has—or feels he has—a legitimate claim, but for which he finds no opportunity in his social environment. This function of the para-social then can properly be called compensatory, inasmuch as it provides the socially and psychologically isolated with a chance to enjoy the elixir of sociability. The "personality" program—in contrast to the drama—is especially designed to provide occasion for good-natured joking and teasing, praising and admiring, gossiping and telling anecdotes, in which the values of friendship and intimacy are stressed.

It is typical of the "personality" programs that ordinary people are shown being treated, for the moment, as persons of consequence. In the interviews of nonprofessional contestants, the subject may be praised for having children—whether few or many does not matter; he may be flattered on his youthful appearance; and he is likely to be honored the more—with applause from the studio audience—the longer he has been "successfully" married. There is even applause, and a consequent heightening of ceremony and importance for the person being interviewed, at mention of the town he lives in. In all this, the values realized for the subject are those of a harmonious, successful participation in one's appointed place in the social order. The subject is represented as someone secure in the affections and respect of others, and he probably senses the experience as a gratifying reassurance of social solidarity and self-confidence. For the audience, in the studio and at home, it is a model of appropriate role performance—as husband, wife, mother, as "attractive" middle age, "remarkably youthful" old age, and the like. It is,

---

[18] It is frequently charged that the media's description of this side of life is partial, shallow, and often false. It would be easier and more profitable to evaluate these criticisms if they were formulated in terms of role-theory. From the viewpoint of any given role it would be interesting to know how well the media take account of the values and expectations of the role-reciprocators. What range of legitimate variations in role performance is acknowledged? How much attention is given to the problems arising from changing roles, and how creatively are these problems handled? These are only a few of the many similar questions which at once come to mind.

furthermore, a demonstration of the fundamental generosity and good will of all concerned, including, of course, the commercial sponsor.[19] But unlike a similar exemplification of happy sociability in a play or a novel, the television or radio program is real; that is to say, it is enveloped in the continuing reassurances and gratifications of objective responses. For instance there may be telephone calls to "outside" contestants, the receipt and acknowledgement of requests from the home audience, and so on. Almost every member of the home audience is left with the comfortable feeling that he too, if he wished, could appropriately take part in this healing ceremony.

EXTREME
PARA-SOCIABILITY

For the great majority of the audience, the para-social is complementary to normal social life. It provides a social milieu in which the everyday assumptions and understandings of primary group interaction and sociability are demonstrated and reaffirmed. The "personality" program, however, is peculiarly favorable to the formation of compensatory attachments by the socially isolated, the socially inept, the aged and invalid, the timid and rejected. The persona himself is readily available as an object of love—especially when he succeeds in cultivating the recommended quality of "heart." Nothing could be more reasonable or natural than that people who are isolated and lonely should seek sociability and love wherever they think they can find it. It is only when the para-social relationship becomes a substitute for autonomous social participation, when it proceeds in absolute defiance of objective reality, that it can be regarded as pathological.[20]

The existence of a marginal segment of the lonely in American society has been recognized by the mass media themselves, and from time to time specially designed offerings have been addressed to this minority.[21] In these pro-

[19] There is a close analogy here with one type of newspaper human-interest story which records extreme instances of role-achievement and their rewards. Such stories detail cases of extreme longevity, marriages of especially long duration, large numbers of children; deeds of heroism—role performance under "impossible" conditions; extraordinary luck, prizes, and so on.

[20] Dave Garroway, after making the point that he has many "devout" admirers, goes on to say that "some of them . . . were a bit too devout." He tells the story of one lady "from a Western state" who "arrived in Chicago [where he was then broadcasting], registered at a big hotel as Mrs. Dave Garroway, opened several charge accounts in my name and established a joint bank account in which she deposited a large sum of money. Some months later she took a taxi to my hotel and informed the desk clerk she was moving in. He called a detective agency that we had engaged to check up on her, and they persuaded her to return home. Since then there have been others, but none so persistent." Reference footnote 4; p. 62.

[21] This group presumably includes those for whom "Lonely Hearts" and "Pen Pal" clubs operate.

grams, the maximum illusion of a personal, intimate relationship has been attempted. They represent the extreme development of the para-social, appealing to the most isolated, and illustrate, in an exaggerated way, the principles we believe to apply through the whole range of "personality" programs. The programs which fall in this extreme category promise not only escape from an unsatisfactory and drab reality, but try to prop up the sagging self-esteem of their unhappy audience by the most blatant reassurances. Evidently on the presumption that the maximum of loneliness is the lack of a sexual partner, these programs tend to be addressed to one sex or the other, and to endow the persona with an erotic suggestiveness.[22]

Such seems to have been the purpose and import of *The Lonesome Gal,* a short radio program which achieved such popularity in 1951 that it was broadcast in ninety different cities. Within a relatively short time, the program spread from Hollywood, where it had originated, across the country to New York, where it was heard each evening at 11:15.[23]

The outline of the program was simplicity itself. After a preliminary flourish of music, and an identifying announcement, the main and only character was ushered in the presence of the audience. She was exactly as represented, apparently a lonesome girl, but without a name or a history. Her entire performance consisted of an unbroken monologue unembarrassed by plot, climax, or denouement. On the continuum of para-social action, this is the very opposite of self-contained drama; it is, in fact, nothing but the reciprocal of the spectator's own para-social role. The Lonesome Gal simply spoke in a throaty, unctuous voice whose suggestive sexiness belied the seeming modesty of her words.[24]

From the first, the Lonesome Gal took a strongly intimate line, almost as if she were addressing a lover in the utter privacy of some hidden rendezvous:

> Darling, you look so tired, and a little put out about something this evening. . . .
> You are worried, I feel it. Lover, you need rest . . . rest and someone who understands you. Come, lie down on the couch, relax, I want to stroke your hair gently . . . I am with you now, always with you. You are never alone, you must never forget that you mean everything to me, that I live only for you, your Lonesome Gal.

[22] While the examples which follow are of female personae addressing themselves to male audiences, it should be noted that for a time there was also a program on television featuring *The Continental,* who acted the part of a debonair foreigner and whose performance consisted of murmuring endearing remarks to an invisible female audience. He wore evening clothes and cut a figure in full conformity with the American stereotype of a sauve European lover.

[23] This program apparently evoked no very great amount of comment or criticism in the American press, and we are indebted to an article in a German illustrated weekly for details about the show, and for the verbatim quotations from the Lonesome Gal's monologue which we have retranslated into English. See "Ich bin bei dir, Liebling . . . ," *Weltbild* (Munich), March 1, 1952; p. 12.

[24] This is in piquant contrast to the popular singers, the modesty of whose voice and mien is often belied by the sexiness of the words in the songs they sing.

At some time in the course of each program, the Lonesome Gal specifically assured her listeners that these endearments were not being addressed to the hale and handsome, the clever and the well-poised, but to the shy, the withdrawn—the lonely men who had always dreamed, in their inmost reveries, of finding a lonesome girl to comfort them.

The world is literally full of such lonesome girls, she urged; like herself, they were all seeking love and companionship. Fate was unkind, however, and they were disappointed and left in unrequited loneliness, with no one to console them. On the radio, the voice was everybody's Lonesome Gal:

> Don't you see, darling, that I am only one of millions of lonely girls. I belong to him who spends his Sundays in museums, who strolls in Central Park looking sadly at the lovers there. But I am more fortunate than any of these lovers, because I have you. Do you know that I am always thinking about you? . . . You need someone to worry about you, who will look after your health, you need me. I share your hopes and your disappointments. I, your Lonesome Gal, your girl, to whom you so often feel drawn in the big city where so many are lonely. . . .

The Lonesome Gal was inundated with thousands of letters tendering proposals of marriage, the writers respectfully assuring her that she was indeed the woman for whom they had been vainly searching all their lives.

As a character in a radio program, the Lonesome Gal had certain advantages in the cultivation of para-social attachments over television offerings of a similar tenor. She was literally an unseen presence, and each of her listeners could, in his mind's eye, picture her as his fancy dictated. She could, by an act of imagination, be almost any age or any size, have any background.

Not so Miss Nancy Berg, who began to appear last year in a five-minute television spot called *Count Sheep*.[25] She is seen at 1 A. M. each weekday. After an announcement card has flashed to warn the audience that she is about to appear, and a commercial has been read, the stage is entirely given over to Miss Berg. She emerges in a lavishly decorated bedroom clad in a peignoir, or negligee, minces around the room, stretches, yawns, jumps into bed, and then wriggles out again for a final romp with her· French poodle. Then she crawls under the covers, cuddles up for the night, and composes herself for sleep. The camera pans down for an enormous close-up, and the microphones catch Miss Berg whispering a sleepy "Good-night." From out of the distance soft music fades in, and the last thing the viewers see is a cartoon of sheep jumping over a fence. The program is over.

There is a little more to the program than this. Each early morning, Miss Berg is provided with a special bit of dialogue or business which, brief though it is, delights her audience afresh:

> Once, she put her finger through a pizza pie, put the pie on a record player and what came out was Dean Martin singing "That's Amore." She has read, with ex-

[25] The details relating to this show are based on Gilbert Millstein, "Tired of it All?" *The New York Times Magazine*, September 18, 1955; p. 44. See also "Beddy-Bye," *Time*, August 15, 1955; p. 45.

pression, from "Romeo and Juliet," "Of Time and the River," and her fan mail. She has eaten grapes off a toy ferris-wheel and held an imaginary telephone conversation with someone who, she revealed when it was all over, had the wrong number.[26]

Sometimes she regales her viewers with a personal detail. For instance, she has explained that the dog which appears on the show is her own. Its name is "Phaedeaux," she disclosed coyly, pronounced "Fido."

It takes between twenty and twenty-six people, aside from Miss Berg herself, to put this show on the air; and all of them seem to be rather bemused by the success she is enjoying. Her manager, who professes himself happily baffled by the whole thing, tried to discover some of the reasons for this success in a recent interview when he was questioned about the purpose of the show:

> Purpose? The purpose was, Number 1, to get a sponsor; Number 2, to give people a chance to look at a beautiful girl at 1 o'clock in the morning; Number 3, to do some off-beat stuff. I think this girl's going to be a big star, and this was a way to get attention for her. We sure got it. She's a showman, being slightly on the screwball side, but there's a hell of a brain there. She just doesn't touch things—she caresses things. Sometimes, she doesn't say anything out loud, maybe she's thinking what you're thinking.[27]

The central fact in this explanation seems to be the one which touches on Miss Berg's ability to suggest to her audience that she is privy to, and might share, their inmost thoughts. This is precisely the impression that the Lonesome Gal attempted to create, more directly and more conversationally, in her monologue. Both programs were geared to fostering and maintaining the illusion of intimacy which we mentioned earlier in our discussion. The sexiness of both these programs must, we think, be read in this light. They are seductive in more than the ordinary sense. Sexual suggestiveness is used probably because it is one of the most obvious cues to a supposed intimacy— a catalytic for prompt sociability.

Such roles as Miss Berg and the Lonesome Gal portray require a strict adherence to a standardized portrayal of their "personalities." Their actual personalities, and the details of their backgrounds, are not allowed to become sharply focused and differentiated, for each specification of particular detail might alienate some part of the audience, or might interefere with rapport. Thus, Miss Berg, despite the apparent intimacy of her show—the audience is invited into her bedroom—refuses to disclose her "dimensions," although this is a piece of standard information freely available about movie beauties.

The Lonesome Gal was even more strict regarding personal details. Only once did she appear in a public performance away from her radio show. On that occasion she wore a black mask over her face, and was introduced to her "live" audience on the same mysteriously anonymous terms as she met her radio audience. Rumor, however, was not idle, and one may safely pre-

---

[26] *The New York Times Magazine,* reference footnote 25.
[27] *The New York Times Magazine,* reference footnote 25.

sume that these rumors ran current to provide her with a diffuse glamour of a kind which her audience would think appropriate. It was said that she lived in Hollywood, but that she originally came from Texas, a state which, in popular folklore, enjoys a lively reputation for improbabilities and extravagances. Whispers also had it that French and Indian blood coursed in her veins, a combination all too likely to suggest wildness and passion to the stereotypes of her listeners. For the rest, nothing was known of her, and no further details were apparently ever permitted.

THE IMAGE
AS ARTIFACT

The encouragment of, not to say demand for, a sense of intimacy with the persona and an appreciation of him as a "real" person is in contradiction to the fact that the image he presents is to some extent a construct—a façade—which bears little resemblance to his private character. The puritanical conventions of the contemporary media make this façade a decidedly namby-pamby one. With few exceptions, the popular figures of radio and television are, or give the appearance of being, paragons of middle-class virtue with decently modest intellectual capacities. Since some of them are really very intelligent and all of them are, like the rest of us, strong and weak, good and bad, the façade is maintained only by concealing discrepancies between the public image and the private life.

The standard technique is not to make the private life an absolute secret—for the interest of the audience cannot be ignored—but to create an acceptable façade of private life as well, a more or less contrived private image of the life behind the contrived public image. This is the work of the press agent, the publicity man, and the fan magazine. How successfully they have done their work is perhaps indicated by the current vogue of magazines devoted to the "dirt" behind the façade.[28]

Public preoccupation with the private lives of stars and personae is not self-explanatory. Sheer appreciation and understanding of their performances as actors, singers, or entertainers does not depend upon information about them as persons. And undoubtedly many members of the audience do enjoy them without knowing or caring to know about their homes, children, sports cars, or favorite foods, or keeping track of the ins and outs of their marriages and divorces. It has often been said that the Hollywood stars—and their slightly less glamorous colleagues of radio and television—are modern "heroes" in whom are embodied popular cultural values, and that the interest in them is a form of hero-worship and vicarious experience through iden-

---

[28] Such magazines as *Uncensored* and *Confidential* (which bears the subtitle, "Tells the Facts and Names the Names") enjoy enormous circulations, and may be thought of as the very opposite of the fan magazine. They claim to "expose" the person behind the persona.

tification. Both of these interpretations may be true; we would emphasize, however, a third motive—the confirmation and enrichment of the para-social relation with them. It may be precisely because this is basically an illusion that such an effort is required to confirm it. It seems likely that those to whom para-social relationships are important must constantly strive to overcome the inherent limitations of these relationships, either by elaborating the image of the other, or by attempting to transcend the illusion by making some kind of actual contact with him.

Given the prolonged intimacy of para-social relations with the persona, accompanied by the assurance that beyond the illusion there is a real person, it is not surprising that many members of the audience become dissatisfied and attempt to establish actual contact with him. Under exactly what conditions people are motivated to write to the performer, or to go further and attempt to meet him—to draw from him a personal response—we do not know. The fan phenomenon has been studied to some extent,[29] but fan clubs and fan demonstrations are likely to be group affairs, motivated as much by the values of collective participation with others as by devotion to the persona himself. There are obvious social rewards for the trophies of contact with the famous or notorious—from autographs to handkerchiefs dipped in the dead bandit's blood—which invite toward their possessor some shadow of the attitudes of awe or admiration originally directed to their source. One would suppose that contact with, and recognition by, the persona transfers some of his prestige and influence to the active fan. And most often such attempts to reach closer to the persona are limited to letters and to visits. But in the extreme case, the social rewards of mingling with the mighty are foregone for the satisfaction of some deeply private purpose. The follower is actually "in love" with the persona, and demands real reciprocity which the para-social relation cannot provide.

A case in point is provided in the "advice" column of a newspaper.[30] The writer, Miss A, has "fallen in love" with a television star, and has begun to rearrange and reorder her life to conform to her devotion to this man whom she has never actually met. It is significant, incidentally, that the man is a local performer—the probability of actually meeting him must seem greater than would be the case if he were a New York or Hollywood figure. The border between Miss A's fantasies and reality is being steadily encroached upon by the important affective investment she has made in this relationship. Her letter speaks for itself:

> It has taken me two weeks to get the nerve to write this letter. I have fallen head over heels in love with a local television star. We've never met and I've seen him only on the TV screen and in a play. This is not a 16-year-old infatuation, for I am 23, a college graduate and I know the score. For the last two months I have

[29] M. F. Thorp, *America at the Movies;* New Haven, Yale Univ. Press, 1939. S. Stansfeld Sargent, *Social Psychology;* New York, Ronald Press, 1950. K. P. Berliant, "The Nature and Emergence of Fan Behavior" (unpublished M.A. Thesis, Univ. of Chicago).
[30] Ann Landers, "Your Problems," *Chicago Sun-Times,* October 25, 1955; p. 36.

stopped dating because all men seem childish by comparison. Nothing interests me. I can't sleep and my modeling job bores me. Please give me some advice.

The writer of this letter would seem to be not one of the lonely ones, but rather a victim of the "magic mirror" in which she sees a man who plays the role reciprocal to hers so "ideally" that all the men she actually knows "seem childish by comparison." Yet this is not the image of a fictional hero; it is a "real" man. It is interesting that the newspaper columnist, in replying, chooses to attack on this point—not ridiculing the possibility of a meeting with the star, but denying the reality of the image:

> I don't know what you learned in college, but you are flunking the course of common sense. You have fallen for a piece of celluloid as unreal as a picture on the wall. The personality you are goofy about on the TV screen is a hoked-up character, and any similarity between him and the real man is purely miraculous.

This case is revealing, however, not only because it attests to the vigor with which a para-social relationship may become endowed, but also because it demonstrates how narrow the line often is between the more ordinary forms of social interaction and those which characterize relations with the persona. In an extreme case, such as that of Miss A, her attachment to the persona has greatly invaded her everyday life—so much so that, without control, it will warp or destroy her relations with the opposite sex. But the extreme character of this response should not obscure the fact that ordinarily para-social relations do "play back," as it were, into the daily lives of many. The man who reports to his friend the wise thing that Godfrey said, who carefully plans not to make another engagement at the time his favorite is on, is responding similarly, albeit to a different and milder degree. Para-social interaction, as we have said, is analogous to and in many ways resembles social interaction in ordinary primary groups.

The new mass media are obviously distinguished by their ability to confront a member of the audience with an apparently intimate, face-to-face association with a performer. Nowhere does this feature of their technological resources seem more forcefully or more directly displayed than in the "personality" program. In these programs a new kind of performer, the persona, is featured whose main attribute seems to be his ability to cultivate and maintain his suggested intimacy. As he appears before his audience, in program after program, he carries on recurrent social transactions with his adherents; he sustains what we have called para-social interaction. These adherents, as members of his audience, play a psychologically active role which, under some conditions, but by no means invariably, passes over into the more formal, overt, and expressive activities of fan behavior.

As an implicit response to the performance of the persona, this para-social interaction is guided and to some extent controlled by him. The chief basis of this guidance and control, however, lies in the imputation to the spectator of a kind of role complementary to that of the persona himself. This imputed complementary role is social in character, and is some variant of the role or roles normally played in the spectator's primary social groups. It is defined, demonstrated, and inculcated by numerous devices of radio and television showmanship. When it has been learned, the persona is assured that the entire transaction between himself and the audience—of which his performance is only one phase—is being properly completed by the unseen audience.

Seen from this standpoint, it seems to follow that there is no such discontinuity between everyday and para-social experience as is suggested by the common practice, among observers of these media, of using the analogy of fantasy or dream in the interpretation of programs which are essentially dramatic in character. The relationship of the devotee to the persona is, we suggest, experienced as of the same order as, and related to, the network of actual social relations. This, we believe, is even more the case when the persona becomes a common object to the members of the primary groups in which the spectator carries on his everyday life. As a matter of fact, it seems profitable to consider the interaction with the persona as a phase of the role-enactments of the spectator's daily life.

Our observations, in this paper, however, are intended to be no more than suggestions for further work. It seems to us that it would be a most rewarding approach to such phenomena if one could, from the viewpoint of an interactional social psychology, learn in detail how these para-social interactions are integrated into the matrix of usual social activity.

In this connection, it is relevant to remark that there is a tradition—now of relatively long standing—that spectators, whether at sports events or television programs, are relatively passive. This assertion enjoys the status of an accredited hypothesis, but it is, after all, no more than a hypothesis. If it is taken literally and uncritically, it may divert the student's attention from what is actually transpiring in the audience. We believe that some such mode of analysis as we suggest here attunes the student of the mass media to hints *within the program itself* of cues to, and demands being made on, the audience for particular responses. From such an analytical vantage point the field of observation, so to speak, is widened and the observer is able to see more that is relevant to the exchange between performer and audience.

In essence, therefore, we would like to expand and capitalize on the truism that the persona and the "personality" programs are part of the lives of millions of people, by asking how both are assimilated, and by trying to discover what effects these responses have on the attitudes and actions of the audiences who are so devoted to and absorbed in this side of American culture.

28

IDENTITY CRISIS
AND SOCIAL CHANGE

Louis C. Schaw

SIMON JOSE ANTONIO DE LA SANTISIMA Trinidad de Bolivar y Palacios was born in Caracas, Venezuela, on July 24, 1783, and was the man who by progressive degrees became Simon Bolivar, simply "Bolivar," and finally "The Liberator": the sacred and martyred hero of the South American Continent. This was the man who, in the twelve years between the ages of 29 and 41 (1812–1824), led an armed revolt that liberated from Spain the whole of what is today Central America, Colombia, Venezuela, Ecuador, Bolivia, Peru, and contributed to the independence of Mexico, Chile, Paraguay, Uruguay, and Portuguese Brazil. When Bolivar liberated Spanish-America, he closed an important phase of a process which had started 305 years earlier with the first conquest of the mainland by Cortez.

In 1492, when Columbus discovered the continent, Spain had just re-emerged from eight centuries of Arab domination. In that year, with the fall of Granada, Spain ended the geographical phase of its own reconquest, and within three months decreed the expulsion of Jews and the creation of the Inquisition. This institution aimed at the social, political, and religious conquest of the people as the means of creating a national hegemony.

We should view the involvement of Spain in America as the growth of a unitary system which still remains today a whole, from the point of view of social development and institutions. America's discovery, conquest, and colonization may have diverted the Spanish world both from a centripetal national

From *The Bonds of Work* (San Francisco: Jossey-Bass, Inc., 1968). (Text, Chapter 16)

focus and from the powerful forces that had started the transformation of the European community just at that time.

In addition to the casting out of the Jews and Arabs into exile, Spain, for over 300 years, will export to America numberless men and women. During this extended period of time, Spanish society may have spent forces that could have contributed to the reshaping of Spain itself.

The ecological conditions of the frontier contributed to underlining the centrifugality of the Spanish system; the tendency of parts in the feudal association to disperse when free from the carefully balanced cohesion of family duties, religious beliefs, mutual defense, and balance of power.

This colonial process brought about an imperfect reproduction of Spanish society, but one that in the main features was a restatement of existing conditions in the mother country. Distance and the ambiguities of new conditions made this replica imperfect in one essential respect: if true cohesiveness was lacking and just beginning to emerge in Spain, it almost completely failed to take place in America. If these conditions made for some occasional laxity, it also impelled Spain to impose more drastically in the colonies the main instruments for social cohesiveness.

For 300 years the social and political entities that developed in Latin America related to each other, if at all, through the Spanish central government. In the Iberian peninsula the feudal components had the advantage of co-existing within a geographical unit. In America the colonies took form as relatively small pockets of population isolated by a trackless distance. In this respect, the population patterns in America before the discovery made an important contribution to the development of the new societies. Except for very rare cases, the pattern of conquest and colonization followed the pattern of ethnographic distribution among the native population—mostly along the coastline, with few attempts to incorporate the interior of the country. Only the narrower section of the continent, the Mexican Isthmus and the very northernmost fringe of the southern continent, were spanned.

The longest and thinnest line of continuity ran along the western coast of South America from Peru to Ecuador, following the Incan artery of footpaths, then northward into the valley of the Magdalena River in Western Colombia. At this point the narrow connecting line turned east across the lower but formidable fan of the Andes in their northern tip, to the shores of Colombia in the Atlantic, and then through difficult country to the coastal regions of Venezuela, where it ended. This thin, long line of precarious linkage was to become the backbone along which Bolivar moved to liberate the units strung along its length. Bolivar eventually unified a brief Federation-Empire, the first and last move towards unification of the continental societies.

This was an empire that, for reasons of his own, Bolivar refused to rule; one which he then bitterly accused of thanklessness, and which, in the end, he belittled as not worthy of being governed—certainly not by him.

To trace the roots of this hero's vocation, it may be necessary to search in the area of traditional values as they are embodied in the tradition from which Bolivar emerged.

A dominant sanctioned image of man, the ideal of earthly ambition in feudal Spain had been the knight errant—an idealized image of aggressive physical vigor and spatial motility, controlled only by the equally boundless demands of honor in the search for unearthly love.

The possibility that in the knightly quest one could arrange things so as to carve for oneself at least an "insula," a fief, was a fact of life beyond the legend which Sancho Panza constantly suggested to that most unearthly of Spanish knights: Don Quijote de La Mancha. (Unamuno, 1964.)

In this work Cervantes was reminding his readers of the very earthly possibilities in the most unearthly concerns of the knightly quest. He makes Sancho speak in moderate terms about small fiefs, to underline the very real fact that the major chunks of loot—kingdoms, dukedoms, principalities— were not exactly up for grabs. (If I may, like Cervantes, lapse into the vernacular.) Cervantes codified the birth of the Spanish language in portraying the struggle between a world of developing norms and its conflict with established views of the essential attributes of persons. Social criteria were in danger of making much too earthly and banal man's preferred view of ambition.

Here in emerging Spain values and structural givens converge: a social group facing a situation of having available within itself, without being able to absorb them, a large number of ambitious and well-endowed individuals, had created a meaningful set of symbols that sanctioned ambition while it channelized it through an elaborate system of postponements. In this way the system attempted to handle the question of social mobility and spatial motility among a growing number of potentially entrepreneurial individuals. Later on this item of value-structure had specific relevance to the Bolivars in America. . . .

Ideologically and morally, Don Quijote is an ambitious-unambitious man, a man beset with doubts as to the foundations of himself. He is a knight who often goes mad with a strange sort of sad malady, a madness punctuated with recurrent, blinding lucidity. And all along he is a knight in the endless quest of some ineffable validating essence, a goal that cannot accept any earthly compromise, on principles. The ideology worked as a unifying principle as long as that tragic self-consciousness did not awaken compromising doubts, and as long as there obtained meaningful structural supports that made sense of this special identity segment. . . .

In writing *Don Quijote,* Cervantes could just as easily have been sketching an outline of Bolivar as a man and as a symbol. Don Quijote's and Spain's doubts are at the core of Bolivar's own character.—In compromised and compromising action; in compulsive doubt; in sadistic action and in unearthly love for his honor; in external motility that externalized inner stress; in his undoing what he painfully doubted he ever wanted to do; in the vigor of his

sword and in his lucid speech; in martyrdom, and in the final vilification of
the people that he purported to love, Bolivar acts in a large scale the painful
issues of the doubting, aim-inhibited knight. Trying to escape his doubts, he
remakes himself as he contributes to the clarification of an emerging group
identity. In speaking and acting for his people, for their past and for their
future, he further commits them to his phrasing of the solution: the endless
search for honorable self-definitions. . . .

I came, wrapped in the mantle of Iris, from where the mighty Orinoco pays its
tribute to the god of the waters. I had visited the enchanted springs of the Amazon
and I wished to climb the watchtower of the world. I sought the footsteps of La
Condamine, of Humboldt; boldly I followed them; nothing could hold me back.

I reached the glacial regions, where the air was so thin that I could scarcely breathe.
Never before had human foot trodden the diamond crown placed by the Eternal
Father on the lofty brow of the King of the Andes. "Wrapped in this mantle," I
exclaimed, "which has served as my banner, I have traversed the infernal regions,
crossed rivers and seas, climbed the shoulders of the Andes. Under the feet of
Colombia, the Earth has flattened itself, and Time himself has been unable to check
the march of Liberty. the goddess of war has been humbled by the light of dawn—
wherefore, then, should I not be able to trample upon the white hairs of Chimborazo,
giant of the earth? Why not? I will."

Impelled by a spirit of violence hitherto unknown to me, that appeared to me divine,
I left behind the footsteps of Humboldt and set out to climb beyond the eternal
belt of cloud shrouding Chimborazo. As if driven forward by this unknown spirit
within me, I reached the summit, and, as I touched with my head the pinnacle of
the firmament and saw at my feet a yawning abyss, I fainted.

Feverish delirium engulfed my mind, I felt as if inflamed by a strange, supernatural
fire. The God of Colombia had taken possession of me.

Suddenly Time stood before me—in the shape of a venerable old man, bearing the
weight of all the centuries, frowning, bent, bald, wrinkled, a scythe in his hand.

"I am the Father of the Centuries! I am the Guardian of fame and the secrets of
life. My Mother was Eternity; the limits of my Empire is Infinity. For me there is
no tomb, because I am more powerful than Death. I gaze upon the Past, the Future,
and through my hands goes the Present. Why think vain thoughts, you of the human
race, whether you be young or old, sunk in obscurity or cast in heroic mold?"

"Think you that this universe of yours is anything, that to fight your way to eminence
on an atom of creation is to raise yourselves? Think you that the infinitesimal moments you call centuries can serve for measuring my secrets? Think you that the whole
truth has been vouchsafed to you? Think you, in your madness, that your actions
have any value in my eyes? All about you is less than a dot in presence of the
Infinite, who is my brother."

Filled with terror, I replied: "Surely, oh Time! the miserable mortal who has climbed
thus high must perish! All men have I surpassed in good fortune, for I have raised
myself above all. The earth lies at my feet; I touch Eternity; beneath me I feel the
throbbing of Hell; beside me I contemplate radiant planets, sums of infinite dimensions. I gaze upon the realms of space which inclose matter; I decipher, on your
brow, the history of the past and the thoughts of Destiny."

"Man!" spoke Time to me. "Observe! Learn! Preserve before your mind what you
have seen, trace for your fellow men the picture of the physical universe, of the
moral universe. Hide not the secrets which Heaven has revealed to you! Speak the
Truth to mankind!"

The phantom disappeared. Speechless, stupefied, unconscious, I lay for a long time stretched out upon the enormous diamond which served me for a couch. Finally, the ringing voice of Colombia summoned me. I returned to life! Rising to my feet, I opened with my fingers my heavy eyelids, became a man once more, wrote down what I had heard and seen in my Delirium!

The Chimborazo is a particularly stately peak in the Andes, just south of the equator, rising 20,700 feet from the coastal plain. In January of 1824, Bolivar and his army were in this vicinity. The strategic importance of this situation was very great. The provinces to the north had been liberated and unified under his command. Two years of battles were still to come, but for all general purposes the fight was over. It surely seemed to be over for Bolivar. [The reason was that Bolivar had a vision—"a delirium"—on this mountain peak.] The delirium mentions time, space, and gods, but from his geographical position his army was also towering over Lima, the seat of the most powerful Viceroy in the continent. Lima held great symbolic importance through its association with the Incan empire and the deeds of Pizarro.

These and other elements combined for making of the place and the time a climactic event, but beyond these facts it seems that Bolivar's own inner perception of the moment phrased it as the supreme triumph, and the ultimate surrender—the fulfillment of his vocation. For him his job was done. No subsequent event could again mobilize this inner sense of euphoria. Bolivar saw the rest of the campaign as mere details. He himself did not lead the Revolutionary Army at the battle of Ayacucho. . . .

The moment in which total triumph is contemplated is explored by Bolivar as a very special form of the present. The triumph is a present in which a sudden discontinuity takes place between an infinite past and an infinite future. This present is phrased as a moment which is at the same time an eternity; a moment of both death and rebirth. . . .

From that date on, Bolivar was overcome with a malaise, physical and psychological, which seemed to be something like a relapse into the sickness of mourning and despair that preceded his taking of vows as a liberator. But to make sense of the details of his decline it is necessary to describe the nature of the war which Bolivar had led to this point.

In four months Bolivar was back on the mainland from Jamaica. Now, starting from secondary military command, and through a series of initial failures, and by going on his own (in open defiance of orders), Bolivar develops very swiftly the techniques that will carry him to his goal. At this point he literally steals the loyalist revolution, makes it his own, and transforms it into a war to the death to any Spaniard not born in America, whether Loyalist, Bonapartist, or indifferent. The revolution is now, in fact, a cruel and bloody civil war, a war that systematically destroys any semblance of social and political unity that the colonies may have had under Spanish rule. In this task Bolivar finds numberless cooperators, individuals who, like one of his particularly bloodthirsty generals, so hates the Spaniards that he vows to kill all in sight and then, in sadistic exuberance, promises to kill himself if necessary to insure that all remnants of the hated blood are finally destroyed. But it is also a war which still lasts today, and which in Colombia has become an endemic condition.

In the midst of this new revolution, Bolivar's talents develop with such rapidity that they appear to have been on the ready all along; speed, terror, propaganda, sheer military genius, and a burning sense of purpose become the main components of his chosen work career.

What we have seen in Bolivar as the essential personal requirement for motility now emerges as an important contribution to his chosen work. The distances involved in the campaigns were tremendous. With speed and daring unknown since the Conquistadores, he leads ragged, barefoot bands through rain forests and over high mountain passes deep in eternal snows to surprise an enemy who never guessed he was anywhere near, and certainly not behind them. Bolivar's is also the first and last voice that is heard and heeded all over the continent.

Proclamations, harangues, constitutions, presidential addresses, diatribes, oracular pronouncements, and above all a monumental flow of correspondence become a major aspect of Bolivar's leadership. The word is for him a basic tool in his chosen work; what he did not set down in writing, his various Boswells compiled and annotated. The sheer volume of his recorded words is overwhelming.

It is difficult to apprehend the man and his mission through this forest of verbiage; but the recurrent clarity of his utterances can be as disturbingly opaque as the rest. Self-contradictory and often enigmatic, his speech is nevertheless an act of self-encounter in which we can see Bolivar being impelled to say what he means, but just as often discovering what he means to say, in the act of saying it.

When we consider the manner in which Bolivar's sense of purpose, his sense of inner and outer cohesiveness, and the development of his talents converged in the forceful pursuit of goals associated with aggressive means, it is even more striking that he should feel so vulnerable in triumph.

Although January of 1824 is a climactic point for Bolivar, there is evidence that he had premonitions of his difficulties as he approached the culmination of his achievement in the world. A few months before the appearance of the Delirium, he wrote:

> The higher I rise, the wider the pit opens at my feet. (July 21, 1823)

From this time dates his growing vertigo; then, closer in time to the revelation of the Chimborazo, he reports himself sick with urinary distress, gastric colic, vomiting, and depression, and adds:

> . . . Furthermore I am now possessed by frequent fits of madness even when I am feeling well, so that I lose my reason completely, without feeling the slightest pain or bodily sickness. This country with its Soroche (mountain sickness) just makes these attacks come on more often when I have to climb and cross the high sierras. (January 7, 1824)

Two weeks later he states the issue and his solution more clearly yet:

> Till today I have fought for liberty. From now on I will fight for my glory even though it may be at the expense of everyone else: And my glory consists in not commanding anymore. (January 23, 1824)

Towards the end of that fateful year success and panic is followed by angry withdrawal; he is ready to resolve the issue in seeking martyrdom:

> No matter how sad our death it is bound to be happier than our life. (November 10, 1824)

. . . From here on the denouement is swift. His powers, his talents, and his will (even to live) desert him just as rapidly as they had come to be his when the right moment had arrived for him to act and to speak.

Bolivar's own words tell the history of the next six years. Nothing much changes in the plan, except his determination to suffer and to escape. The following quotations from the correspondence of these years express it best:

> To command disgusts me as much as I love glory, and Glory springs not from commanding but from exercising great virtues. (April 7, 1826)
>
> I could trample everything underfoot but I don't want to enter history as a tyrant. (April 20, 1827)
>
> What matters that I should die so that a whole people may live. (December, 1827)
>
> No one is big with impunity, no one can escape on rising, the biting envy of others. (June, 1828)
>
> I doubt that they have the right to demand of me that I should expire on the cross; I should say more, if it were only the cross I would bear it with patience as the last of my agonies. Jesus Christ endured 33 years of this mortal life: mine already reaches 46. (September 3, 1829)
>
> If they insist in putting me again in command, they can be sure that I will not accept, although this act may result in the ruin of the Republic. My honor and my glory demand this solemn and absolute disengagement so that the world may see that there are men in Colombia who reject supreme power and prefer glory to ambition. (December 12, 1829)

Just as he says, he was being asked to rule. But he demurred and demanded so many conditions that in the end one of his many resignations is accepted. He dies shortly after the National Assembly fails for the first time to re-elect him. On his deathbed he manages to say:

> If my death contributes to end all factions and to consolidate the union, I shall go down to the grave in peace. . . . Yes, to the grave; that is where my countrymen send me. . . . But I forgive them. (December 17, 1830)

This would have been enough, but not for Bolivar. In a letter written on November 9, 1830, he leaves an open testament to his followers in the form of a private letter to a friend. In it he probably allows himself to tell another part of the truth:

> You know that I have held power for twenty years, and I have drawn but a few sure conclusions:

1. America is ungovernable by us.
2. To serve a revolution is to plow the sea.
3. The only thing that one can do in America is emigrate.
4. This country will infallibly fall into the hands of an unbridled crowd of petty tyrants almost too small to notice and of all colors and races.
5. Devoured by all the crimes and extinguished by ferocity, we shall be disdained by the Europeans, who will not deign to conquer us.
6. If it were possible for a part of the world to fall back to primitive chaos, America would.

With this jeremiad, Bolivar expresses the final evaluation of his work—it all had been in vain, or worse—in anger and in despair he rejects the people he had worked with, and for whom he believed he had toiled. But even here as he seeks to escape from them, to dissociate his life from their fate, he stubbornly insists that his dying life can still be a meaningful job. To achieve this he reaches into some primeval social past for a meaningful social role and offers himself as the sacrificial lamb. . . .

But the other aspect of this solution that is central to Bolivar's character is the assumption that the struggle is essentially an external one, and open only to two polar solutions: either the successful externalization of inner dictates or the inner surrender to being internally possessed by external powers. As a Mystic-Warrior, Bolivar integrates both extreme solutions between the taking of his vows and the peak of his success. Here we can see how a man, driven by whatever private motives, had reached into the storehouse of traditional formulas in an attempt to make sense to himself and to others. Apparently he made great sense to his people, and no doubt provided a meaningful formula for them. This version of an integrating and validating process was a new and forceful restatement of tried and true traditional patterns for living, which as Bolivar demonstrated could give meaning to the relationship between private and collective experiences.

This contribution to the propagation and consolidation of meaningful formulations must be seen as an essential part of Bolivar's work. Paradoxically it may have represented the culmination of the Spanish conquest, since the socio-psychological transformation that Bolivar mediated established the claim of the conquered people to live by the values and in the pattern of the European ancestral society; no longer simply within the formal arrangements and in lesser replicas of European institutions, but now committed to their spirit as a part of themselves; in this most important sense, as equals.

We have underlined Bolivar's inner struggle as it climaxes at his moment of triumph. The tension mounts as he realizes that there is nothing left external to fight. He had led a war that successfully destroyed the existing authority and now Bolivar was the supreme lawgiver. It seems that now he no longer has an external enemy to counterbalance his other and polar commitment to inner surrender. It is to this inner surrender that he withdraws. The letters quoted from the correspondence of 1826 to 1827 portray this resolution of the issue. To find a clue to these utterances we must listen to the Spanish mystics as they spoke of their rapture and joy in passionate piety. There are also indications that the withdrawal was energized by something akin to a fear for the consequences of his deed, or a fear of retributive justice. ("The higher I rise, the wider the pit opens at my feet.")

It would be possible to attempt following the intricacies of this man's inner experience through the complexities of its workings, but it may suffice for our purpose to state that whatever their content and dynamics, they had found focus in a drama between archetype like father, mother, country, God, heroes, beauty that Bolivar selected from the iconography of his tradition. And that this drama was about the acceptable conditions under which he was to be controlled. This drama provided a main link between the man and his followers. But if the problem for Bolivar had reverted to an inner issue, the problem for his followers had also changed in a related way.

Free from the Spanish government, the ex-colonies faced the problem of the conditions under which they were to govern each other and themselves. Until then they had been unified like Bolivar (like Spain itself had been) in the task of casting out external dominance. This labor having been accomplished, they now faced each other without the presence of outsiders. In fact they were now in almost the identical position that the mother country had been since the fall of Granada. The problem was now an internal one, so to speak, and neither the Spanish experience nor Bolivar's program for total solutions on the issue of authority had any useful relevance. Cervantes had described the communal burden and the individual tragedy of a state of affairs when men continued to insist in being what their ideal ancestors had been, and therefore became painfully inappropriate to the present. The formulation still holds true three centuries later.

29

THOUGHT REFORM: PSYCHOLOGICAL STEPS IN DEATH AND REBIRTH

Robert Lifton

THERE IS A BASIC SIMILARITY in what both Dr. Vincent and Father Luca experienced during Communist imprisonment. Although they were held in separate prisons far removed from each other, and although they differed very much in their responses to reform, they were both subjected to the same general sequence of psychological pressures. This sequence was essentially the same despite the fact that these men were very different from each other, with different personal and professional life styles. Nor was this thought reform pattern common to just these two: it was experienced by all twenty-five of the Westerners whom I interviewed.

The common pattern becomes especially important in evaluating the stories these Westerners told me. Each was attempting to describe, in most instances as accurately as possible, the details of an ordeal from which he had just emerged. But what each reported was also inevitably influenced by his immediate life situation—his psychological transition between the two worlds, his personal struggles for both integrity and integration, his feelings about succoring and threatening colleagues and strangers in Hong Kong, his view of me as an American, a physician, a psychiatrist, and a person. All of these circumstances could affect his account, and especially its emotional tone. Therefore, both during the interviews and in the later study of my notes, I had to sift out what was most characteristic and most consistent, to eval-

Reprinted from *Thought Reform and the Psychology of Totalism,* by Robert Jay Lifton, M.D., pp. 64–85, by permission of W. W. Norton & Company, Inc. and Victor Gollancz, Ltd. Copyright © 1961 by Robert Jay Lifton. (Text, Chapter 16)

uate this information in terms of my understanding of the people supplying it, and then to piece together a composite analysis of the process itself.

Both Dr. Vincent and Father Luca took part in an agonizing drama of death and rebirth. In each case, it was made clear that the "reactionary spy" who entered the prison must perish, and that in his place must arise a "new man," resurrected in the Communist mold. Indeed, Dr. Vincent still used the phrase, "To die and be reborn"—words which he had heard more than once during his imprisonment.

Neither of these men had himself initiated the drama; indeed, at first both had resisted it, and tried to remain quite outside of it. But their environment did not permit any sidestepping: they were forced to participate, drawn into the forces around them until they themselves began to feel the need to confess and to reform. *This penetration by the psychological forces of the environment into the inner emotions of the individual person is perhaps the outstanding psychiatric fact of thought reform.* The milieu brings to bear upon the prisoner a series of overwhelming pressures, at the same time allowing only a very limited set of alternatives for adapting to them. In the interplay between person and environment, a sequence of steps or operations—of combinations of manipulation and response—takes place. All of these steps revolve about two policies and two demands: the fluctuation between assault and leniency, and the requirements of confession and re-education. The physical and emotional assaults bring about the symbolic death; leniency and the developing confession are the bridge between death and rebirth; the re-education process, along with the final confession, create the rebirth experience.

Death and rebirth, even when symbolic, affect one's entire being, but especially that part related to loyalties and beliefs, to the sense of being a specific person and at the same time being related to and part of groups of other people—or in other words, to one's sense of inner identity. In the broadest terms, everything that happened to these prisoners is related to this matter. Since everyone differs from everyone else in his identity, each prisoner experienced thought reform differently, nor did anyone respond completely to all these steps; at the same time, the experiences had such magnitude that they affected every prisoner in some measure, no matter what his background and character.

THE ASSAULT
UPON IDENTITY

From the beginning, Dr. Vincent was told he was not really a doctor, that all of what he considered himself to be was merely a cloak under which he hid what he really was. And Father Luca was told the same thing, especially about the area which he held most precious—his religion. Backing up this assertion were all of the physical and emotional assaults of early imprisonment: the confusing but incriminating interrogations, the humiliating "struggles," the painful and constricting chains, and the more direct physical brutality. Dr. Vincent and Father Luca each began to lose his bearings on who and what he was, and where he stood in relationship to his fellows. Each felt his sense of self become amorphous and impotent and fall more and more under the control of its would-be remolders. Each was at one point willing to say (and to *be*) whatever his captors demanded.

Each was reduced to something not fully human and yet not quite animal, no longer the adult and yet not quite the child; instead, an adult human was placed in the position of an infant or a sub-human animal, helplessly being manipulated by larger and stronger "adults" or "trainers." Placed in this regressive stance, each felt himself deprived of the power, mastery, and selfhood of adult existence.

In both, an intense struggle began between the adult man and the child-animal which had been created, a struggle against regression and dehumanization. But each attempt on the part of the prisoner to reassert his adult human identity and to express his own will ("I am not a spy. I am a doctor"; or "This must be a mistake. I am a priest, I am telling the truth") was considered a show of resistance and of "insincerity," and called forth new assaults.

Not every prisoner was treated as severely as were Dr. Vincent and Father Luca, but each experienced similar external assaults leading to some form of inner surrender—a surrender of personal autonomy. This assault upon autonomy and identity even extended to the level of consciousness, so that men began to exist on a level which was neither sleep nor wakefulness, but rather an in-between hypnogogic state. In this state they were not only more readily influenced, but they were also susceptible to destructive and aggressive impulses arising from within themselves.

This undermining of identity is the stroke through which the prisoner "dies to the world," the prerequisite for all that follows.

THE ESTABLISHMENT
OF GUILT

Dr. Vincent and Father Luca found themselves unanimously condemned by an "infallible" environment. The message of guilt which they received was both existential (you *are* guilty!) and psychologically demanding (you must learn to *feel* guilty!). As this individual guilt potential was tapped, both men had no choice but to experience—first unconsciously and then consciously—a sense of evil. Both became so permeated by the atmosphere of guilt that external criminal accusations became merged with subjective feelings of sinfulness—of having done wrong. Feelings of resentment, which in such a situation could have been a source of strength, were shortlived; they gave way to the gradual feeling that the punishment was deserved, that more was to be expected.

In making their early false confessions, Dr. Vincent and Father Luca were beginning to accept the guilty role of the criminal. Gradually, a voice within them was made to say, ever more loudly: "It is my sinfulness, and not their injustice, which causes me to suffer—although I do not yet know the full measure of my guilt."

At this point their guilt was still diffuse, a vague and yet pervasive set of feelings which we may call a free-floating sense of guilt. Another prisoner expressed this clearly:

> What they tried to impress on you is a complex of guilt. The complex I had was that I was guilty. . . . I was a criminal—that was my feeling, day and night.

THE SELF-BETRAYAL

The series of denunciations of friends and colleagues which both Dr. Vincent and Father Luca were required to make had special significance. Not only did making these accusations increase their feelings of guilt and shame, it put them in the position of subverting the structures of their own lives. They were, in effect, being made to renounce the people, the organizations, and the standards of behavior which had formed the matrix of their previous existence. They were being forced to betray—not so much their friends and colleagues, as a vital core of themselves.

This self-betrayal was extended through the pressures to "accept help" and in turn "help" others. Within the bizarre morality of the prison environment, the prisoner finds himself—almost without realizing it—violating many of his most sacred personal ethics and behavioral standards. The degree of violation is expanded, very early in the game, through the mechanism of shared betrayal, as another priest described:

> The cell chief kept asking information about Church activities. He wanted me to denounce others, and I didn't want to do this. . . . A Chinese Father was transferred into the cell, and he said to me, "You cannot help it. You must make some denunciations. The things which the Communists know about any of your Church activities you must come out with." . . . Much later I was put in another cell to bring a French priest to confession. He had been stubborn, and had been in solitary for a few months. He was very fearful and looked like a wild animal. . . . I took care of him, washed his clothes for him, helped him to rest. I advised him that what they might know he might as well confess.

Although there is a continuing tension between holding on and letting go, some degree of self-betrayal is quickly seen as a way to survival. But the more of one's self one is led to betray, the greater is one's involvement with his captors; for by these means they make contact with whatever similar tendencies already exist within the prisoner himself—with the doubts, antagonisms, and ambivalences which each of us carries beneath the surface of his loyalties. This bond of betrayal between prisoner and environment may develop to the point where it seems to him to be all he has to grasp; turning back becomes ever more difficult.

THE BREAKING POINT:
TOTAL CONFLICT
AND THE BASIC FEAR

Before long, Father Luca and Dr. Vincent found themselves at an absolute impasse with their environment. Each was looked upon not only as an enemy, but also as a man completely out of step. They were aware of being in painful disagreement with alleged truths about their past, and yet at this point they were unclear about what these "truths" were.

At the same time, they had been impressed with the inflexibility of their milieu. The government, being infallible, would not give way; it was the "stubborn criminal" who had to "change." Their situation was like that of a man taken suddenly from his ordinary routine and placed in a hospital for the criminally insane, where he is accused of a horrendous but vague crime which he is expected to recognize and confess; where his assertion of innocence is viewed as a symptom of his disease, as a paranoid delusion; and where every other inmate-patient is wholly dedicated to the task of pressuring him into a confession and a "cure." The sense of total reversal is like that of Alice after falling down the rabbit hole; but the weirdness of the experience is more that of a Kafka hero.

The prisoner's dilemma leads him to a state of antagonistic estrangement. He is not totally estranged from the environment, because even antagonism is a form of contact; but he is totally cut off from the essential succor of affectionate communication and relatedness, without which he cannot survive. And at the same time, his increasing self-betrayal, sense of guilt, and his loss of identity all join to estrange him from himself—or at least from the self which he has known. He can contemplate the future with only hopelessness and dread. Literally and emotionally, there seems to be no escape from this hermetically-sealed antagonism.

As the assaults continue, and as they are turned inward, he begins to experience one of the most primitive and painful emotions known to man, the fear of total annihilation. This basic fear—considered by some the inherited forerunner of all human anxiety—becomes the final focus for all of the prison pressures. It is fed by every threat and accusation from without, as well as by all of the destructive emotions stimulated within. The fear is compounded by the horrifying realization that the environment seems to be making it come true. Dr. Vincent did not only fear annihilation; he actually felt himself to *be* annihilated. It was this confirmation of a primitive fear which led him to hope for relief through quick death.

This is the point at which physical and mental integration break down.

Some prisoners may be brought by their severe anxiety and depression to the point of suicidal preoccupations and attempts:

> They scolded me in a nasty way. I had the feeling that everyone was cross with me and despised me. I thought, why do they despise me? What have I done? . . . I was eating very little. . . . I refused to eat or drink. . . . I felt very much down. I felt there was no chance for me. . . . It was so utterly hopeless. For six weeks I did nothing but think how I might kill myself.

Others experience the delusions and hallucinations usually associated with psychosis:

> I heard investigations taking place below, and one day I heard my name called. I listened while Chinese were indoctrinated to testify how I had been gathering information on troop movements. . . . The next day I recognized the voice of my Chinese accountant who was told that I had confessed everything and therefore his confession better agree with mine. . . . Once I heard the guards saying in a social conversation with a German that they would soften me up by locking me in a cage which used to be used by the KMT. . . . I was near going nuts.

Such symptoms are clear evidence of the loss of the capacity to cope with one's environment. At the same time, they represent—as do any psychiatric symptoms—protective efforts, attempts on the part of the human organism to ward off something perceived as an even greater danger: in these cases, the anticipation of total annihilation.

Many of Father Luca's transient delusions represented just such a combination of breakdown and restitution. His imagining (and believing) that his consul was visiting the prison, or that he was once more among his fellow Christians, were evidence he had lost the ability to discriminate between the real and the unreal. But in experiencing these same delusions, the content of which reinforced his fantasies of rescue, Father Luca was clinging tenaciously to his own life force, and at the same time warding off his basic fear.

No prisoner, whatever his defenses, ever completely overcame this fear of annihilation. It remained with each in greater or lesser degree throughout imprisonment, and in some cases for a long time afterward. It was a constant inner reminder of the terrible predicament he might again be forced to face should he further displease his captors.

At this point, the prisoner's immediate prospects appear to be physical illness, psychosis, or death. If his death is to remain symbolic—and psychic damage kept from progressing beyond the reversible stage—some form of desperately needed relief must be supplied.

LENIENCY
AND OPPORTUNITY

A sudden change in official attitude—the institution of leniency—supplies this relief. The unexpected show of kindness, usually occurring just when the prisoner is reaching his breaking point, breaks the impasse between him and the environment. He is permitted—even shown how—to achieve some degree of harmony with his outer world.

"Leniency" does not mean that the milieu budges from any of its demands, or even from its standards of reality. It simply lets up on its pressures sufficiently for the prisoner to absorb its principles and adapt himself to them. When Dr. Vincent, after two months of imprisonment, suddenly encountered friendliness and consideration in place of chains and struggles, there was no cessation of the pressure for confession. In fact, the effect of leniency was to spur him on to greater confession efforts. He was able to make these efforts because his leniency was accompanied by guidance; he had a chance to learn and act upon what was expected of him. Father Luca had no such good fortune. He, too, after one month, was given a respite: the removal of chains and handcuffs and the opportunity to sleep; but his was the unusual experience of leniency without guidance. He was willing to comply (his false confession was, among other things, a profound expression of compliance); but he was unable to find the desired approach. In his case, therefore, a new impasse was created, which resulted in a brutal interruption of his leniency.

The timing and the setting of leniency can be extremely dramatic, as it was for another priest.

> It was Christmas Day. I was brought to see the judge. For the first time I found the room full of sunlight. There was no guard and there were no secretaries. There were only the kind faces of the judges offering me cigarettes and tea. It was a conversation more than a questioning. My mother could not have been much more good and kind than the judge was. He said to me, "The treatment you have received here is really too bad. Maybe you are unable to stand it. As a foreigner and a priest, you must be used to good food and better hygienic standards. So just make a confession. But make it really good, so we can be satisfied. Then we will close your trial and finish your case."

In other cases, leniency was utilized to confront the prisoner with a threatening life-or-death alternative. It might include a new "good" interrogator who replaces or alternates with the "bad" one:

> An inspector had talked to me nastily and I collapsed. Soon after, a nicer inspector came to visit me. He was worried—very friendly to me—and asked me if I had heart disease. . . . He said, "Your health is not good; you must have a better room." He called on me again and said, "We must get your case settled now. The government is interested in you. All you must do is change your mind. There are only two ways for you to go: one way leads to life, and the other to death. If you want the road that leads to life, you must take our way. You must reform yourself and re-educate yourself." I said, "That sounds very good." I felt light of heart and told the other cellmates about it. They said, "That's good. Write your confession about how wrong your old political ideas were, and how willing you are to change your mind—and then you will be released."

This threat also was clear in the experience of another prisoner who had been transferred to a hospital after an attempt at suicide:

> At first they told me that I had tried to kill myself because I had a bad conscience. . . . But the doctor seemed very kind. . . . Then an official came to see

me and he spoke to me in a very friendly voice: "The government doesn't want to kill you. It wants to reform you. We don't want to punish you at all, we just want to re-educate you." . . . It was my first glimmer of hope. I felt finally there might be a way out. I wasn't feeling so hopelessly alone any more. The official had actually shown some human quality.

Apparent in all these examples is the immense stimulus which leniency provides for the prisoner's reform effort. Total annihilation is no longer all he can visualize. He has been offered rest, kindness, and a glimpse of the Promised Land of renewed identity and acceptance—even freedom; annihilation is now something he can avoid, and in fact *must* avoid at all costs.

The psychological decompression of his environment serves to win him over to the reform camp, especially to that part of the reform camp which is working on him. In other words, he becomes motivated to help the officials achieve what they are trying to do to him. He becomes, as did Dr. Vincent, their grateful partner in his own reform.

THE COMPULSION
TO CONFESS

Long before any suggestion of leniency, Father Luca and Dr. Vincent had perceived the dominant message of their milieu: only those who confess can survive. Indeed, everything in the way of assaults and leniency—all pressures of breakdown and promised restitution—served to reinforce this message. In such a climate, the two men had no choice but to join in the universal compulsion to confess. Their first expression of this compulsion was the early elaboration of false "crimes." Even when a prisoner was aware that his confession was "wild"—as was Dr. Vincent—he had begun to submit to the confession requirement, and to behave *as if* he were a criminal. This was even more true, and the guilt even more profound, for those who, like Father Luca, came to believe in their own falsehoods.

These first confessions are preliminary (although prison officials do not necessarily mean them to be such) to the main manifestation of the compulsion to confess—the *total* soul purge. Both Dr. Vincent and Father Luca, when their false confessions were rejected, hit upon the expedient of simply confessing everything, with special emphasis on what might be considered most sinful. In doing so, they moved beyond mere playing of the criminal role. They were beginning to accept as valid parts of themselves the two basic identities of thought reform.

The first of these is the identity of the repentant sinner. The prisoner in effect says: "I must locate this evil part of me, this mental abscess, and excise it from my very being, lest it remain to cause me more harm." This leads directly to the second identity—that of the receptive criminal, the man who is, at whatever level of consciousness, not only beginning to concur in the environment's legal and moral judgment of him, but also to commit himself to acquiring the beliefs, values, and identities officially considered desirable. The acceptance of these two identities led both Dr. Vincent and Father Luca to express the idea that one had to get rid of old thoughts and emotions in order to make room for the new ones. Precisely this compulsion to reveal everything provides the continuity between breakdown and restitution, between confession and reform.

The compulsion to confess is not static; it continually gathers momentum, and provokes an increasing sense of submission—as described by another priest:

> After a while one wants to talk . . . they press you, so you feel you must say something. Once you start you are deceived: you are at the top of the tree and you go down. . . . If you say the first word, there is always something more: *"Lao shih"* —No, no, be a good boy! Say the truth!—,*"t'an pai"*—Confess!—are constantly repeated every two minutes. I felt myself wanting to say more to make him shut his mouth, he was so insisting. . . . It made me weak; it made me want to give in.

Equally important, as both Dr. Vincent and Father Luca discovered, is the "creative" participation which each prisoner develops in his confession process. His inner fantasies must always make contact with the demands from without. To be sure, these fantasies are painstakingly and selectively molded by officials and cellmates. But they are never entirely divorced from the man who produces them. This means that a good deal of the energy involved in the confession comes from within the prisoner himself. His compulsion to confess dedicates him to the task of continuously carving out and refilling his own inner void—under the active supervision and broad moral guidance of his captors.

THE CHANNELLING
OF GUILT

Once the compulsion to confess is operating, the prisoner is ready to learn a more precise formula—thought reform's conceptual framework for his expression of guilt and repentance. By adopting the "people's standpoint," he channels nonspecific feelings of guilt into a paranoid, pseudo-logical system. His sense of evil, formerly vague and free-floating, is now made to do specific work for reform. He takes this step, as Vincent so clearly described, by learning to see evidence of personal evil and destructiveness in specific past actions. What was most prosaic, or even generous, must now be viewed as "criminal."

This reinterpretation of events, as absurd as it may sound, has a strong impact because it stimulates forces within the prisoner himself which support the contentions of his environment. He has, like everyone else, struggled with feelings of curiosity, hostility, and vindictiveness not acceptable for public display, but retained as part of his own secret world. Now the awareness of these feelings within himself, and especially of the secretiveness which accompanies them, makes him feel like the "spy" he is accused of being. It is a relatively easy step for him to associate this image of himself as a conspirator with the past events under consideration. Indeed, in making a casual comment about approaching Communist armies, one part of him might really have hoped that this information would reach and benefit the other side; and even if this were not true, it becomes fairly easy for him to imagine that it had been.

Since the people's standpoint is an ultimate statement of bias, its acceptance also involves a basic negative commitment. The prisoner joins in condemning himself less for what he has *done* than for what he has *been:* as a Westerner—and therefore an "imperialist"—he is guilty. For him, this is the real significance of the people's standpoint, and its use of news, information, and intelligence is merely a method of implementing its prejudgment.

The more the prisoner submits to these black-and-white judgments, the more he surrenders all that is subtle or qualified—as another missionary described:

> At first I was always making this distinction: as far as my conscience is concerned, it is no sin, but from their point of view it is a crime. I knew that the judgment would be standing on their point of view. . . . The same action was seen by me and them from a completely different morality—seen through a different window. They are looking through from the outside in, me from the inside out. . . . They said the government is infallible, so what it discovered cannot be untrue. That puts me in a bad position. I said, "I admit the government is infallible." They took my words like rubber. . . . Later I asked the government for a lenient sentence. I could not say that they were unjust, as I was standing on their point of view.

As the prisoner accepts this "higher" group morality, its most harsh judgments make common cause with the most tyrannical parts of his own conscience; through this joining of forces, he is changed from a man who merely feels guilty into one who feels guilty about exactly those actions which the environment considers criminal.

RE-EDUCATION:
LOGICAL DISHONORING

While Father Luca and Dr. Vincent, in a general sense, began their re-education the moment they were imprisoned, its formal inception occurred with the stress upon group study (*hsüeh hsi*) just after the institution of leniency. Both men found that it was not Communist doctrine per se which mattered, but rather the use of Communist doctrine and its reasoning techniques to broaden their own self-exposure.

It was no longer enough to admit guilt, to feel guilty, or even to recognize specific guilty actions. The prisoner had to extend his self-condemnation to every aspect of his being, and learn to see his life as a series of shameful and evil acts—shameful and evil not only in their possible opposition to Communism, but also because they violated his own cherished ideals.

With Father Luca, this desecration of identity took the form of convincing him that he and his missionary colleagues had been "un-Christian" in their conduct in China. Personal dishonoring of this kind was applied to both priests and laymen. It is illustrated in the following exchange between another priest and his prison instructor:

Instructor:	"Do you believe man should serve others?"
Priest:	"Yes, of course I do."
Instructor:	"Are you familiar with the Biblical saying, 'I come on earth to serve, not to be served'?"
Priest:	"Yes, as a priest it is my creed."
Instructor:	"Did you have a servant in your mission?"
Priest:	"Yes, I did."
Instructor:	"Who made your bed in the morning and swept the floor?"
Priest:	"My servant did this."
Instructor:	"You did not live up to your doctrine very well, did you, Father?"

This same priest explained the process of logical dishonoring in Marxist terminology and with a good deal of psychological insight:

> They believe that in each person there is a thesis—his positive element, work, or creed; and an antithesis—his weakness which works against this. The thesis in my case was the Catholic and my missionary work. My antithesis was anything which worked against this due to my personal shortcomings. The Communists attempted to wear down my thesis and encouraged the development of my antithesis. By making the antithesis stronger and the thesis weaker, they seek to have the antithesis replace the thesis as the dominant force in the individual.

The antithesis of which the priest speaks is his negative identity—that part of him which he has been constantly warned never to become. A priest's negative identity is likely to include such elements as the selfish man, the sinner, the proud man, the insincere man, and the unvigilant man. As the reformers encourage a prisoner's negative identity to enlarge and luxuriate, the prisoner becomes ready to doubt the more affirmative self-image (diligent priest, considerate healer, tolerant teacher) which he had previously looked upon as his true identity. He finds an ever-expanding part of himself falling into dishonor in his own eyes.

At this point the prisoner faces the most dangerous part of thought reform. He experiences guilt and shame much more profound and much more threatening to his inner integrity than any experienced in relation to previous psychological steps. He is confronted with his human limitations, with the contrast between what he is and what he would be. His emotion may be called true or genuine guilt, or true shame—or existential guilt—to distinguish it from the less profound and more synthetic forms of inner experience. He undergoes a self-exposure which is on the border of guilt and shame. Under attack is the deepest meaning of his entire life, the morality of his relationship to mankind. The one-sided exploitation of existential guilt is thought reform's trump card, and perhaps its most important source of emotional influence over its participants. Revolving around it are issues most decisive to thought reform's outcome.

Why call this process *logical* dishonoring? Surely it is not logical to have one's identity so disparaged—unless one sees this disparagement as a small but necessary part of a greater system of events. And this is precisely the kind of systematic rationale which the Communists—through their ideology —supply. A prisoner's inconsistencies and evildoings are related to historical forces, political happenings, and economic trends. Thus, his acceptance of his negative identity and the learning of Communist doctrine become inseparable, one completely dependent upon the other. The realignment of affirmation and negation within one's identity requires an endless repetition, a continuous application of self to the doctrine—and indeed, this is the essence of re-education. The prisoner must, like a man under special psychological treatment, analyze the causes of his deficiencies, work through his resistances (or "thought problems") until he thinks and feels in terms of the doctrinal truths to which all of life is reduced. In the process, he may be guided by a particular "instructor" (sometimes referred to as "analyst" or "case analyst") who has special charge of his case, keeps all personal records, and conducts many individual interviews with him. The prisoner's psychological strengths and weaknesses become well known to his personal instructor, then to other officials as well, and are effectively utilized in the undermining process.

What we have said so far of "re-education" hardly lives up to the name: we have talked more of breakdown than of remaking. In actuality, the remaking is also well under way. Even during the earlier stages of identity assault and compulsion to confess, the prisoner experiences stirrings of restitution. The buildup of his negative identity, along with his developing acceptance of Communist doctrine, provide the first contours of something new. He continues, during the years of imprisonment, to loudly proclaim his own demise; but as his re-education proceeds, he finds himself first announcing, and then experiencing, the refashioned identity which is emerging. His sense of nakedness and vulnerability nourishes the growth of the "new man."

PROGRESS
AND HARMONY

The prisoner's new self requires emotional nutriment if it is to continue to develop. This nutriment is supplied by the prisoner's achieving a sense of harmony with his no-longer-strange surroundings. Harmony is partly a matter of gradual adaptation, as both Dr. Vincent and Father Luca made clear. Adaptation in turn is contingent upon progress in reform; and only when this progress has been demonstrated does the prisoner begin to receive the recognition and acceptance which is so precious in such an environment.

Then, as Dr. Vincent described, the prisoner can experience the deep satisfactions of solving all problems; of group intimacy in living, working, and suffering; of surrendering himself to an all-powerful force, and sharing its strength; of laying himself bare in the catharsis of personal confession; of sharing the moral righteousness of a great crusade of mass redemption.

Toward the end of their imprisonment, both Dr. Vincent and Father Luca were living under quite comfortable circumstances. The improvement in their physical surroundings was important enough; the atmosphere of frankness and of being met halfway was exhilarating. Both had regained the status of being human. Talks with judges were man-to-man encounters between people who understood each other and considered one another's feelings. Indeed, Father Luca felt free enough to voice doubts and criticisms; and although he did this partially as a tactic, he was at the same time accepting therapeutic assistance from his captors.

To appreciate the emotional appeal of harmony, one must—as the prisoner invariably does—contrast it with the basic fear and estrangement of the earlier phases of imprisonment. Instead of antagonism and total conflict, he feels in step with a milieu which appreciates him. Identified as a "progressive," he is permitted (and grasps at) a more direct form of self-expression. To be sure, he is still partly the actor; but performance and life have moved closer together, and he is not acting as much as he thinks he is. As he achieves a more intimate communication with his reformers, his entire experience takes on a much greater feeling of reality. Officials in turn show a beginning willingness to accept the prisoner as he is—by no means perfect in his reform, but at least more genuine in his partial reform.

FINAL CONFESSION:
THE SUMMING UP

In this atmosphere of harmony and reality, the prisoner is ready to make a conclusive statement of what he is and what he has been. The confession has long been developing, of course, but it is likely to take its final shape only after he has achieved sufficient "progress" to produce and believe in a "correct" version.

In Father Luca's case—which is especially illustrative for the entire confession process—the two short paragraphs of his final confession seem almost anticlimactic after the millions of self-accusatory words he had already poured out. Yet this briefest of confessions was both a symbol and a summation of all that had gone before. For the officials, it was *the* confession, the statement for the record. For Father Luca, it was the last of an arduous series of confession identities. To understand this, we must review the sequence of his confession responses and his existential involvements, since any confession, whether true or false, contains an interpretation of one's present and past relationship to the world.

Luca's first confession statement (so unacceptable as a confession that it might better be called his pre-confession statement) was his defiance. In claiming that his arrest was either a mistake or a consequence of his faith, he was clinging to the identity of the priest with integrity. But as he began to surrender more and more of this part of himself, and became lost in the labyrinth of his own false confessions, he took on two additional identities: the secret conspirator and the "novelist," or creative confabulator. His belief in his own falsehoods indicated both the degree to which his identity had broken down and the strength of the image created within him of this con-spiratorial self. When he consented to speak about his clerical colleagues, and give details about Catholic groups, he was assuming the imposed identity of the betrayer, and especially the self-betrayer. Then, when the "novel" was abandoned, and he began for the first time to confess *everything*—to lay before his reformers all that came to his mind—he became the ignorant supplicant, groping for acceptance. Next, in organizing specific points in an acceptably self-damning fashion, he was simultaneously the repentant sinner (he could be repentant because he knew better what his sins were) and the relatively advanced confessor (one who had learned the techniques of his environment). In the two paragraphs of his final confession—in which he referred to his "espionage" relationship with another priest, and to his "illegal" church activities—he took on (although hardly completely) the final identity of the "confirmed" criminal.

The reformers thus ended precisely where they had begun. From the beginning they had labelled Luca a criminal; and these two "crimes" were clearly the ones they had originally selected for him to "recognize." Why, then, did they put everyone to so much trouble?

They did so because confession is as much a part of re-education as re-education is of confession. The officials demanded that their accusations become the prisoner's *self*-accusations, and that the confession be made with inner conviction. They required that he present himself in the evil image they had constructed for him—and their reasons for requiring this, as we shall later discuss, are by no means completely rational.

Father Luca's sequence of confession was neither unique nor accidental; the sequence was essentially the same for Dr. Vincent also, and for almost all other prisoners. There is first the attempt at accuracy, then the wild confession, then the return to real events in distorted focus, and finally, the brief "criminal" confession. Since the development of the wild confession usually occurs during the first few days or weeks (Father Luca's lasted for an exceptionally long time), the main trend is a shift from the imaginary to the concrete. Although fantasy and falsehood are by no means eliminated, this shift does give the prisoner the sense that he is moving in the direction of truth. His confession changes from an uncontrolled dream-like (or night-marish) vision to a more responsible reinterpretation of his own life. Thus he becomes more "engaged" in the confession process, more closely bound to his own words. At the same time, the effect of his wild confession has not been entirely lost upon him; he is apt to retain feelings of guilt over it, as if he had really done the things he described.

While each step in the confession is the result of changes in the strength and tone of the environmental pressures, the prisoner experiences many of his responses as personal discoveries. Both Luca and Vincent, in shifting from falsehood to exaggeration, thought they had hit upon a useful and ingenious technique; only later did each realize that the officials' manipulations had made this reaction inevitable. Each step in the confession, then, is a means of adaptation; and it is also, for both prisoner and reformer, a compromise: he wishes to say less, and they demand more.

In this confession sequence, there is a good deal of structuring and planning on the part of prison officials. But they too can be victimized by their impulses, and by the contagious paranoid tones of the environment; their confusion over what is true and what is false—so evident in their treatment of Father Luca—can add to this general emotional turmoil.

The confession thus embodies demand and response, molded creativity, adaptation, compromise, working through, and a good deal of confusion on all sides. Its final version is the prisoner's subjective perception of the environment's message, guided by his reformers, but also including his own guilty re-evaluation of his past actions. Its beginnings in real events, the "logic" of its distortions, and its documented flavor may make it quite believable—both to the outside world and to its creator as well.

REBIRTH

Just before his release Dr. Vincent became once more the physician and teacher, and at the same time he became the advanced and sympathetic student of Chinese Communism. At the end, reformers made it clear he should combine these two aspects of himself. He was expected to bring the scientific and technical emphasis of his profession to his study of Communism, and to carry over a "progressive" approach (pedagogical shortcuts geared to the needs of "the people") to his medical teaching.

The same principle was applied to Father Luca. Toward the end of his imprisonment he was more and more recognized as a priest with the right to hold his religious views, even if the officials would not go so far as to allow him to practice his religion—an enemy ideology—in the prison. Simultaneously he reached a stage of maximum participation in the Communist movement. This combination is best symbolized in his assuming the role of the reformer, working on a Chinese Catholic priest to bring him to confession. The foreign European missionary who had helped to train Chinese colleagues was once more taking the role of the spiritual mentor, but this time under the imposed sponsorship of the Chinese Communist movement which now encompassed them both.

They did not cease to be priest or physician; rather each became a priest or physician sympathetic to, or at least in a working relationship with, Chinese Communism. Although much of their former identities had been dishonored during imprisonment, they had suffered only a temporary, controlled, and partial "death." If anything like a whole man is to walk out of prison, a good deal of the prisoner's old self will have to be resurrected. This resurrection, however, can be permitted only when the imposed thought reform elements are strong enough to dominate the new combination. For it is just this confluence of identities—the bringing together of evil criminal, repentant sinner, student of Communist doctrine, and the man originally imprisoned —which constitutes the rebirth. Heralded by all of the identity shifts of previous steps, this confluence is likely to occur only after prolonged re-education. And since even the prison identities must be carved out of the prisoner's own emotions (albeit with a powerful knife), rebirth means a basic modification, but not a total replacement, of the former self.

It is a modification strong enough, as in the case of Dr. Vincent, to create a profound change in the prisoner's view of the world, and in his personal relationship to the world. He reinterprets his thought and behavior, shifts his values, recodes his sense of reality. The Communist world, formerly considered aggressive and totalitarian, is now seen as peace-loving and democratic. He identifies with his captors, and is happy in his faith.

RELEASE:
TRANSITION AND LIMBO

At this point, the prisoner is ready for release, although the actual timing of a Westerner's release has been determined more by international political considerations than by his progress in reform. In recent cases, a public trial, replete with prosecuting and defense attorneys, has formalized both the conviction and the rebirth. Before an outside audience, the prisoner once more admits his crimes and expresses his new point of view, while the defense attorney makes a plea for additional "leniency." More frequently, the prisoner is simply read his charge and sentence while still within the prison, as happened to both Vincent and Luca. On rare occasions, a Westerner is sentenced to serve additional time in a new setting (considered a true prison) where he undergoes "reform by labor," a procedure of much less emotional involvement. Whether publicly or privately sentenced, the great majority of Western prisoners have been immediately expelled from China.

But release and expulsion, as Vincent in particular discovered, do not put an end to one's troubles. Instead they thrust the Westerner into an environment which immediately questions all that has been so painstakingly built up during the years of imprisonment; and they precipitate a new identity crisis just as severe as the one experienced during incarceration. Although this crisis occurs outside the thought reform milieu, it must be regarded as the final "step" in reform; it cannot be separated from what has gone before.

The presence of this post-release identity crisis in virtually all of my Western subjects during the time of our interviews was what enabled them to describe so vividly the identity conflicts of their thought reform experiences.

Upon arriving in Hong Kong, Dr. Vincent discovered that what he had become in prison was of absolutely no use to him in his new milieu. Alone with his emotions, he found himself in a devastating predicament: he had internalized enough of his prison environment to feel a severe distrust of the non-Communist world, but was sufficiently receptive to the evidence around him to be highly suspicious of the Communist point of view as well. The security he had known during the latter part of imprisonment suddenly vanished, and his identity was shaken to its foundations. Should he still be the "Communist physician" of his rebirth and seek employment through a European Communist party? or should he return to his freelance medical work in underdeveloped countries? In his personal limbo he was unable to feel "safe" (or whole) in either world; instead he felt deceived by both.

He longed nostalgically for the relatively simple, ordered, and meaningful prison experience, now glorified in his memory. He could relinquish this longing only as he began to be able to trust his new environment; this trust in turn depended upon the capacity to trust himself. Once more he underwent a painful identity shift, encompassing what he had been before, what he had become in prison, and what he was in the process of becoming after release.

Father Luca experienced a similar crisis, in some ways attenuated by his immediate welcome into the motherly embrace of the Church. He knew clearly that he was still the dedicated Catholic priest (although it was not easy for him to give up being a "Chinese" Catholic priest). But he retained profound doubts about his own integrity, and especially about the morality of his missionary work. The dishonoring had struck deep chords in him, and had stirred strong anxieties. His problem was not so much whether or not to continue being a Catholic priest—he could conceive of no alternative to this—but rather one of regaining respect for the clerical missionary life to which he was committed.

Nor were Dr. Vincent and Father Luca alone in these conflicts; immediately following release, all prisoners experienced profound struggles about their integrity, their ability to trust, and their search for wholeness. None escaped the personal crisis of this transitional period any more than he could avoid involvement in the other steps; but each man's crisis was his own.

PART V

DEVIANCE

ADULTS AS WELL AS CHILDREN are subjected to socialization processes as they move from one position to another, joining new groups and organizations and assuming new roles. The frames of reference, and the standards and values that we use to evaluate others and ourselves, are derived from groups. Membership in a group is a symbolic matter, connected less with formal or physical inclusion than with how the individual communicates with others and how he thinks. Reference groups are those that are significant positive or negative influences upon a person regardless of whether he actually belongs to them. The broad comprehensive outlooks or perspectives developed by some groups are known as ideologies. Political and occupational ideologies are examples. Alienation consists of the absence of profound and satisfactory group commitments and loyalties.

The behavior of individuals in complex dynamic societies may be disrupted by a variety of pressures arising within the society, or by crises, whether collective or individual. Bodily injuries, disease, natural disasters, and social disasters such as wars or crippling deflations are among the many sources of strain and pressure on individuals. Other sources of individual maladaption are to be found in role conflict and role ambiguity. Adaptive devices for dealing with potentially disorganizing experiences and situations generally involve ways of reorganizing behavior, and the utilizing of collectively devised strategies. The end product may be viewed as considerably better or worse by those who have gone through these processes, as well as by contemporary or later observers and critics.

Deviant behavior is not identical with disorganized or maladapted behavior. People and behavior are inherently neither deviant nor non-deviant, but come to be labeled one way or another by virtue of the reactions of others. These later reactions cover the entire range from strong approval to violent disapproval. Negative reactions to disliked persons and acts may, on the one hand, result in the application of formal control measures such as prosecution and imprisonment or, on the other, be expressed informally through gossip, rebukes, or simple avoidance. Social psychologists have interested themselves in the ways in which behavior comes to be labeled as deviant, in the effects that this has on the deviant and his group, and in the symbolic devices used to counteract or neutralize it. Measures designed to reduce or control deviance sometimes have the opposite of the intended effect: deviance is then amplified and the deviants are increasingly alienated from the wider society. Some forms of deviant behavior are governed by norms and values of sub-groups within the broader society. Other forms do not have direct group support, but are engaged in by persons as individuals rather than as group members. Deviance, then, is a complex and pervasive phenomenon and occurs throughout the whole range of human relationships.

30

DEVIANCE
AND DEVIANCE
AMPLIFICATION

Leslie T. Wilkins

INFORMATION MODIFIES
DEFINITIONS OF DEVIANCE

THE EXPERIENCE WHICH FORMS the basis for classification of usual and unusual events is obtained in different ways and its content will differ. Experience is coded and stored as information, this the mind retrieves from the store
as and when required. In the retrieval process the information may become
distorted owing to its interaction with other information stored at earlier
periods. Some discussion of the ways in which information influences classifications of deviance is necessary in presenting the general theory.

It would appear that information may be classified for the current purpose
according to three types of consideration:

(a) content
(b) amount
(c) channel

By "channel" is meant the different means of receiving information, particularly the difference between directly and indirectly received information. Some
information may be regarded as trivial because of its content, or it may have
no impact because the amount was small or the channel through which the

From Leslie T. Wilkins, *Social Deviance: Social Policy, Action and Research*, pp. 59–65,
90–92, © 1964. Reprinted by permission of Prentice-Hall, Inc., Englewood Cliffs, N.J.,
and Tavistock Publications, Ltd., London. (Text, Chapter 17)

information was received regarded as unreliable. What is regarded as trivial will relate to the perception of the culture in which the observer lives as much as to the degree of unusualness.

As an example of the trivial, but perhaps also unusual, the following might suffice. If I am unaccustomed to going without wearing a jacket, I will perceive a person so eating as acting "abnormally." According to my interpretation of the action in relation to the culture and my status within the culture I may take a different seat at the restaurant, go to a different restaurant, or demand that the person be arrested! In general the dimension of "unusualness" and the dimension of triviality will be negatively correlated. It is difficult to think of something that would be defined by every person as a trivial deviation from normality but that, at the same time, is an extremely rarely observed deviation. If an event or an act committed by any person is *sufficiently* rare, the rare nature of the event would normally be taken to imply lack of triviality. If I have never seen a thing in my life before, and it is very different from anything else I have even seen, I am not likely to regard the matter as trivial unless I have other information to confirm the triviality.

A shopkeeper who notes that 2 percent of his annual turnover seems to disappear in unaccountable ways may perceive this as normal, although he may know that it is due to shoplifting and staff pilfering. Depending upon his experience of variation about the 2 percent, he may define 3 percent loss as abnormal and take action which could result in an increase in the number of reported crimes, and perhaps also of arrested criminals.

It will be obvious that the hypothetical shopkeeper would adjust his behaviour and his definitions if he had further information regarding his expected losses. If, for example, he knew that the majority of stores in his particular chain experienced, say, only 1 percent unaccountable loss, he would begin to consider ways and means of reducing his losses (2 percent) to around the average or adjusted perception of "normal" figures for his company. If he had other information enabling him to point to other "abnormalities" in his district or type of trade, it might be possible that the two abnormalities would be perceived to cancel out to a total situation representing "normality."

As another example of the influence of information on the perception of normality, consider the following experience of the author. Rather late one Saturday evening he was returning to his home from central London. He joined a bus queue, which seemed to him to consist of some six or seven tough and probably delinquent gang members. He inferred this from the way they stood, and particularly from the manner of their dress. They had not spoken. His knowledge of the delinquent sub-culture did not relieve him of certain feelings of anxiety, or at least of a defensive attitude towards the members of the group. However, immediately they spoke he was able completely to modify his perception of "abnormality" or deviance of the group— they spoke in French. From his knowledge of the habitual dress of French youth on holiday in England, he was able to fit this apparently "deviant" behaviour and dress symbolism into a "normal" or expected context. It would seem, therefore, that we may claim that what is defined as deviant is determined by our subjective experience of "non-deviant" or "normal," but that our experience and the resulting classifications can be changed by certain types of information. It would appear that information acts upon our expectations through our storage system and modifies the classifications which provide the basis for our prediction of behaviour.

The amount of information may influence the base against which events are considered with regard to their unusualness. The more odd experiences I may have, the less odd they will seem to be. The quantity of information available to an individual may increase his tolerance because it may increase the range of his experience of all forms of behaviour, or it may decrease his tolerance because his experience has been limited to more of the same kinds of observation. The shopkeeper may, for example, be tolerant of a loss of 2 percent if he has information that only two or three other stores in his chain have a lower rate, but he may be less tolerant if he has information only from those with the lower rates; in the latter case his information is not only less but also biased. Increase in tolerance of events which would otherwise be defined as deviant is not a direct function of increased knowledge.

In recent years technological advance has mainly resulted in speedier communications between places in different parts of the world; highways, railways, and air travel have increased the range of communications both between nationalities and cultures and between different sub-cultures within the same nation. The shopkeeper of the 2 percent loss store can no longer be unaware of the loss rate of other stores. The behaviour of people living in groups in what were once far-away mountains is now observable by tourists, administrators, and social agencies. In times gone by, deviant groups were able to establish their own cultures with reference only to their own sets of norms. Except perhaps for the intrusion of an occasional itinerant anthropologist they were left without contact with the norms of other societies. There have been numerous cultures where the total definitions of normality were out of accord with existing Western values. It was not until the increase in transportation and the increased speed of movement brought these communities into contact with other communities having different concepts of normality that their deviance was defined. The definition of "deviance" was, of course, provided by the more powerful forces.

TYPES OF INFORMATION

Let us refer again to the analogy of bridges. In total, the experience of bridges possessed by the population in 1600 would be much smaller than the experience of bridges possessed by the population today. The base of experience to which any new bridge could be referred for comparison by persons living in 1600 would be a sample of a much smaller (n) than would be the case now. The increase in speed of transport has increased the sample of bridges

available to the population. The individual who travels widely will personally travel over and *directly* experience a large number of bridges in addition
to those he may read about in the press. But the increase in travel may not be
expected to increase his direct experience of crime. This is an example of a
general point. The experience people have of *things* has tended to increase
rapidly—things have to be extremely unusual to occasion surprise today.
But the base of experience of *people* available by which we may be able to
assess *people* may have diminished. In the village community were included
all kinds of people, but the modern housing development tends to be limited
in both class structure and age. There are communities where hardly an elderly
person can be seen on the streets, and there are zones where children do not
play in the public places. In the small local communities the farmer and the
labourer and even the slave in feudal times were in direct contact with each
other. Today more selective living is possible. The middle and upper classes
do not necessarily *have* to know how the working classes live. There is no
need even to give them their orders directly. Intermediary communications
systems have been established so that the direct contact which was essential
in earlier times is not now required.

The telephone makes it possible to talk to people without personally seeing
them; the fact that even the lowest social classes can now be expected to read
means that they may be sent letters and forms to complete. The administration
may ask them whether they have a bathroom or not without seeing (and smell-
ing) for itself. The insane, the criminal, and the deviant can now be isolated
from society so that the normal members of the culture do not gain any experience of the non-normal. The unpleasant smell of the bathroomless homes
contaminates a different sector of the town from that where the authorities
concerned are likely to live. Even a world authority in criminology may not
necessarily ever meet a criminal in order to become informed or to keep up
to date.

In earlier times the young and the old were continuously in touch with
each other; youth was aware of the problems of age, and age was aware of
the problems of youth. The village was aware of the problems of mental deficiency—each village had its village idiot who was part of the total culture.
Everybody knew "Jack" who stood at the corner of the cross-roads and
drooled. The newcomer to the village might feel threatened by Jack's behaviour, but immediately he spoke with a member of the village culture he
would be assured, "Oh! Jack's all right, he's just a little weak in the head—he
was dropped on it when a baby." Thus, apart from indirect experience derived
from newspapers and other mass media, our modern culture has led to the
isolation (and alienation) of deviant groups. The nature of the information
obtained from direct experience and that obtained from mass media differs
in both quality and type. The sample of experience obtained in the village
contains different information, covers a wider range, and is of a different order
from information indirectly obtained in the urban environment.

In urban societies the isolation of deviants has become institutionalized.

Even the direct experience of one social class by visits for "charitable purposes" has been reduced so that the paid social worker, quietly and decently, away from the normal citizen, is charged with the pacification of Jack, and the society has lost its direct information about and feeling for the problems of mental deficiency. The wealthy have moved from the downtown areas and have lost their direct experience of the problems of the idle youth, and so on. This is not merely a replacement of face-to-face communication and the information derived from such situations by other means, but a quantitative and qualitative change in the nature of the information. Clues may be picked up in face-to-face communication covering many dimensions and the information related to the situations which occur in a wide variety of ways. In a real sense members of the urban culture have suffered a *loss of information*, even though Jack may now be better cared for than previously. If it were possible for the urban culture to receive the *same type and quantity* of information regarding deviants as is obtained in the village, it might be possible for the urban cultures to accept a greater range of deviance. But, as will be noted later, the difference between rural and urban communication systems (face-to-face as compared with mass media and the like) necessarily involves also a difference in the type and the quantity of information received.

No value judgements are made here: we merely wish to bring out the point that information is a factor to be considered in explanations of definitions of deviance, and of societies' reactions to it. Value systems come into this discussion when we consider the mechanisms which people have constructed to insulate themselves from information—the ways in which societies' defects and shortcomings may be hidden because the deviants can be isolated and information regarding them rejected and distorted.

If the information individuals within a social system receive about the workings and expectations of the system is biased, they will be robbed of reinforcement of their definitions of normality. The effect of propaganda has been well documented in this regard. The individual's store of information, which serves as the reference for individual definitions of normal and abnormal behaviour, is today easily derived from the mass media. The larger units of society do not provide a set of information sufficiently varied for the individual to rely upon his own direct experience except within some limited range of activities. The average middle-class citizen living in the urban environment may be supposed to have information from his own experience, plus the information he derives from newspapers that is defined by their editors as "newsworthy." The concept of newsworthiness was, as noted earlier, related to the concept of unusualness and to terms involving $x\sigma$. The model used to describe deviant behaviour may perhaps be used to describe the differences between the nature of "news" and the nature of information derived directly by experience. The region of overlap, where the individual has both direct experience of events and the experience of reading the news presentation of the same event, provides a check on the validity of the press comment and a base-line for the integration of the two types of information into a coherent "experience" information set against which further events may be matched. Where there is no common ground between the two types of information intake, there may be a tendency to sum them simply together, ignoring the difference.

THE GENERAL MODEL

It is now possible to take the general postulates put forward individually in the preceding pages and to attempt to relate them together into a complex theory. The following postulates have been stated:

1. People tend to behave with respect to situations and things as they perceive them to be.

2. Distinctions between what is legitimate and what is illegitimate are made culturally.

3. Legitimate and illegitimate opportunities can be distinguished, and the *balance* between the two types of opportunity presents an important variable.

4. If the balance between legitimate and illegitimate opportunities remains constant, the amount of crime will tend to vary according to the total number of opportunities. Hence it follows that the disturbance of the balance will modify the crime rate, if the rate is considered in relation to the opportunity structure.

5. Since perceptions influence behaviour, the definitions(perceptions) of the culture have an influence upon the members of the culture and the subcultures as perceived and defined by the culture itself.

6. Human decision-making skill (information processing) is influenced not only by the nature of the information, but by the "channel" through which it is received.

7. Information which is perceived as irrelevant (orthogonal) to the dimension of action is treated as no information.

8. Systems in which information regarding the functioning of the system is fed back into the system present different characteristics from systems where such feedback information is lacking or is minimal.

9. People do not play "expected values," thus actual odds do not explain behaviour; even perceived expected values may not provide a sufficient basis for prediction of behaviour since small probabilities are not treated in terms of pay-off maximization.

10. Norms are set for the culture, but different sections of a culture will experience greater or lesser difficulties in achieving success within the norms.

The above set of postulates cannot be related together in any simple unidirectional cause → effect model. The model proposed may be described as a deviation-amplifying system. The type of model proposed is well stated by

Magoroh Maruyama (1962). As he says, "The law of causality may now be revised to state A SMALL INITIAL DEVIATION WHICH IS WITHIN THE RANGE OF HIGH PROBABILITY MAY DEVELOP INTO A DEVIATION OF A VERY LOW PROBABILITY or (more precisely) into a deviation which is very improbable within the framework of probabilistic unidirectional causality." Models based on deviation-amplifying systems have been found to be necessary to explain economic behaviour, and it is not surprising, nor does it represent a high degree of originality, to propose similar models for other forms of satisfaction-seeking human behaviour.

The implications of the deviation-amplifying system are far-reaching; as Maruyama says, "these models are not in keeping with the sacred law of causality in the classical philosophy (which) stated that similar conditions produce similar effects." It is now possible to demonstrate that in some cases similar conditions may result in dissimilar products.

Applying the general dynamic model and the postulates stated above to the particular problem of crime, the following system may be proposed:

(a) Certain types of information, in relation to certain systems, lead to more acts being defined as deviant (the x in $x\sigma$ is given a reduced value).

(b) The individuals involved in the acts so defined are "cut off" from the values of the parent system by the very process of definition.

(c) The defining act provides an information set for the individuals concerned and they begin to perceive themselves as deviant. (Perhaps the main way in which any person gets to know what sort of person he is is through feedback from other persons.)

(d) The action taken by society and the resulting self-perception of the individuals defined as deviant, lead to the isolation and alienation of the specified individuals.

(e) This provides the first part of a deviation-amplifying system. The definition of society leads to the development of the self-perception as "deviant" on the part of the "outliers" (outlaws), and it is hardly to be expected that people who are excluded by a system will continue to regard themselves as part of it.

(f) The deviant groups will tend to develop their own values which may run counter to the values of the parent system, the system which defined them as "outliers."

(g) The increased deviance demonstrated by the deviant groups (resulting from the deviation-amplifying effect of the self-perception, which in turn may have derived from the defining acts of society) results in more forceful action by the conforming groups against the nonconformists.

(h) Thus information about the behaviour of the nonconformists (i.e. as (f) above) received by the conforming groups leads to more acts being defined as deviant, or to more stringent action against the "outliers";

and thus the whole system (a)–(g) can itself continue round and round again in an amplifying circuit.

31

THE DRAMATIZATION
OF EVIL

Frank Tannenbaum

THE CRIMINOLOGICAL THEORIST has tended to set off the criminal from the
rest of the population in terms that would make the difference qualitative.[1]
These attitudes have something of absolutism, and their imputation to the
man of the physical or psychological deficiency that shows how he is distinguished from his fellows has something of the definiteness and inevitableness
of the theories of damnation and predestination. The impact of the idea of
"law" in the physical sciences has in this branch of the social sciences led
to a crude assumption of definiteness, separateness, difference, in terms so
absolute as to be final. The imputation of physical or psychic abnormality
has this crude "scientific" basis, that it derives from measurement, testing,
calculation. It permits the use of statistical tables and mathematical formulae.
The fact that the qualities measured are intangible, the traits examined may
be irrelevant, has not prevented the process from finding wide acceptance
and considerable acclaim, and in some instances even legislative sanction.

The issue here, however, is not the adequacy of the method but rather the
fact that all through criminological theory has run the notion of good and
bad in the older days and "normal" and "abnormal" in the current period.
In each period the criminal has been set off from his fellows. This was indicated by Professor Root when he said: "None is so repentant a sinner as to
share the blame with the criminal. If we can localize the blame in the indi-

From Frank Tannenbaum, *Crime and the Community* (New York: Ginn and Co.,
1938), pp. 7–11, 17–20. By permission of Columbia University Press. (Text, Chapter 17)

[1] The environmentalist school does not fall within this classification.

vidual we can exact vengeance with precision and satisfaction. . . ."[2] The underlying causes may be deeper than that: they may lie in the inability to accept deviation from the "normal." The projection of the idea of normal or good is merely the passing of a moral judgment upon our own habits and way of life. The deviate who is a communist, a pacifist, a crank, a criminal, challenges our scheme of habits, institutions, and values. And unless we exclude him and set him apart from the group, the whole structure of our orderly life goes to pieces. It is not that we do not wish to be identified with him: we cannot be identified with him and keep our own world from being shattered about us. The question of values is fundamental. Just because we appreciate the habits, ways, and institutions by which we live, we seem driven to defame and annihilate those activities and individuals whose behavior challenges and repudiates all we live by. Under these circumstances the theories of the criminologists are understandable. They are imputed an evil nature to the evil-doer, whatever the terms upon which that nature was postulated—possession by the devil, deliberate evil-doing, physical stigmata, intellectual inferiority, emotional instability, poor inheritance, glandular unbalance. In each case we had a good explanation for the "unsocial" behavior of the individual, and it left unchallenged our institutional set-up, both theoretic and practical.

THE MEANING OF BEHAVIOR

In each case these theories rest upon the individual criminal, almost as if he were living in a vacuum and his nature were full-blown from the beginning. Even the mildest of the current theories assumes that the criminal is an unsocial creature because he cannot "adjust" to society. Parsons represents this view when he says that the findings "seem to indicate that the bulk of crime is committed by persons who are unable to adjust themselves to society with a sufficient degree of success to meet the requirements of the law." The facts seem to point to just the opposite conclusion. The criminal is a social human being, he is adjusted, he is not necessarily any of the things that have been imputed to him. Instead of being unadjusted he may be quite adjusted to his group, and instead of being "unsocial" he may show all of the characteristics we identify as social in members of other groups. The New York Crime Commission says, "He is adjusted to his own social group and violently objects to any social therapy that would make him maladjusted to it."[3]

Crime is a maladjustment that arises out of the conflict between a group and the community at large. The issue involved is not whether an individual is maladjusted to society, but the fact that his adjustment to a special group

[2] William T. Root, Jr., *A Psychological and Educational Survey of 1916 Prisoners in the Western Penitentiary of Pennsylvania*, p. 10, 1927.

[3] State of New York. Report of the Crime Commission, 1930. Legislative Document (1930) No. 98, p. 243.

makes him maladjusted to the large society because the group he fits into is at war with society.

The difficulty with the older theory is that it assumed that crime was largely an individual matter and could be dealt with when the individual was dealt with. Instead, most delinquencies are committed in groups; most criminals live in, operate with, and are supported by groups. We must face the question of how that group grew up into a conflict group and of how the individual became adjusted to that group rather than to some other group in society. The study of the individual in terms of his special physical or psychical idiosyncrasies would have as much bearing on the question why he became a member of a criminal group as it would on the question why he joined the Ku Klux Klan, was a member of a lynching bee, joined the I. W. W., became a member of the Communist or Socialist party, joined the Seventh Day Adventists or the Catholic Church, took to vegetarianism, or became a loyal Republican. The point is that a person's peculiar physical or psychic characteristics may have little bearing on the group with which he is in adjustment.

The question is not how a criminal is distinguished in his nature from a non-criminal, but how he happened to be drawn into a criminal group and why that criminal group developed that peculiar position of conflict with the rest of society. The important facts, therefore, are to be sought in his behavior history.

Criminal behavior originates as part of the random movement of children in a world of adults, a world with attitudes and organized institutions that stamp and define the activities of the little children. The career of the criminal is a selective process of growth within that environment, and the adult criminal is the product and summation of a series of continued activities and experience. The adult criminal is usually the delinquent child grown up.

The delinquent child is all too frequently "the truant of yesterday."[4] The truant is the school child who found extra-curricular activities more appealing and less burdensome than curricular ones. The step from the child who is a behavior problem in school to the truant is a natural one; so, too, is the step from truancy to delinquency, and that from delinquency to crime. In the growth of his career is to be found the important agency of the gang. But "the majority of gangs develop from the spontaneous play-group."[5]

The play group becomes a gang through coming into conflict with some element in the environment. . . . "The beginning of the gang came when the group developed an enmity toward two Greeks who owned a fruit store on the opposite corner. The boys began to steal fruit on a small scale."[6]

But even after the gang has been formed, in its early stages its activities are not necessarily delinquent, and delinquent and nondelinquent activities may have the same meaning for the children. "We would gather wood together,

---

[4] State of New York. Report of the Crime Commission, 1927. Legislative Document (1927) No. 94, p. 285.

[5] Frederic M. Thrasher, *The Gang*, p. 29. Chicago, 1927.

[6] Thrasher, op. cit., p. 29.

go swimming, or rob the Jews on Twelfth Street."[7] The conflict may arise from play. "We did all kinds of dirty tricks for fun. We'd see a sign 'Please keep the street clean,' but we'd tear it down and say, 'We don't feel like keeping it clean.' " Or the jokes may be other ways of annoying people. "Their greatest fun consists in playing tag on porches and having people chase them."[8] Or it may be more serious annoyance: "such as throwing stones at windows of homes and ridiculing persons in the street who are known as 'odd characters.' "[9] Even a murder may arise out of the ordinary by-play of two gangs of young boys in rivalry.

Once the gang has been developed, it becomes a serious competitor with other institutions as a controlling factor in the boy's life. The importance of the gang lies in its being the only social world of the boy's own age and, in a sense, of his own creation. All other agencies belong to elders; the gang belongs to the boy. Whether he is a leader or just one of the pack, whether his assigned rank has been won by force or ingenuity or represents a lack of superior force or ingenuity, once that rank is established the child accepts it and abides by the rules for changing it.

Children are peculiarly sensitive to suggestion.

> It is known that young people and people in general have little resistance to suggestion, that fashions of thought and fashions of dress spread rapidly through conversation and imitation, and that any form of behavior may be normalized through conversation and participation of numbers.[10]

In the boy's gang, conversation, gossip, approval, participation, and repetition will make any kind of behavior whatsoever normal.

The gang is important, because the reaction of others is the source of the greater part of the individual's conduct. Conduct is learned in the sense that it is a response to a situation made by other people. The smile, the frown, approval and disapproval, praise and condemnation, companionship, affection, dislike, instruments, opportunities, denial of opportunities, are all elements at hand for the individual and are the source of his behavior. It is not essential that the whole world approve; it is essential that the limited world to which the individual is attached approve. What other people think is the more important because what they think will express itself in what they do and in what they say; and in what they do or say, in the way they look, in the sound of their voices, in the physical posture that they assume, the individual finds the stimuli that call out those particular attitudes that will bring the needed and desired approval from his immediate face-to-face companionship. It is here that we must look for the origin of criminal behavior. It is here, largely, that the roots of conduct difficulties are to be found. What one learns to do,

---

[7] Ibid., p. 36.

[8] New York Crime Commission, 1927 Report, p. 371.

[9] Ibid., p. 370.

[10] William I. Thomas and Dorothy S. Thomas, *The Child in America,* p. 164. New York, 1928.

one does if it is approved by the world in which one lives. That world is the very limited world which approves of the conduct one has learned to seek approval for. The group, once it becomes conscious of itself as an entity, tends to feed and fortify itself in terms of its own values. The contrast with the rest of the world merely strengthens the group, and war merely enhances its resistance.

A MATTER OF DEFINITION

In the conflict between the young delinquent and the community there develop two opposing definitions of the situation. In the beginning the definition of the situation by the young delinquent may be in the form of play, adventure, excitement, interest, mischief, fun. Breaking windows, annoying people, running around porches, climbing over roofs, stealing from pushcarts, playing truant—all are items of play, adventure, excitement. To the community, however, these activities may and often do take on the form of a nuisance, evil, delinquency, with the demand for control, admonition, chastisement, punishment, police court, truant school. This conflict over the situation is one that arises out of a divergence of values. As the problem develops, the situation gradually becomes redefined. The attitude of the community hardens definitely into a demand for suppression. There is a gradual shift from the definition of the specific acts as evil to a definition of the individual as evil, so that all his acts come to be looked upon with suspicion. In the process of identification his companions, hang-outs, play, speech, income, all his conduct, the personality itself, become subject to scrutiny and question. From the community's point of view, the individual who used to do bad and mischievous things has now become a bad and unredeemable human being. From the individual's point of view there has taken place a similar change. He has gone slowly from a sense of grievance and injustice, of being unduly mistreated and punished, to a recognition that the definition of him as a human being is different from that of other boys in his neighborhood, his school, street, community. This recognition on his part becomes a process of self-identification and integration with the group which shares his activities. It becomes, in part, a process of rationalization; in part, a simple response to a specialized type of stimulus. The young delinquent becomes bad because he is defined as bad and because he is not believed if he is good. There is a persistent demand for consistency in character. The community cannot deal with people whom it cannot define. Reputation is this sort of public definition. Once it is established, then unconsciously all agencies combine to maintain this definition even when they apparently and consciously attempt to deny their own implicit judgment.

Early in his career, then, the incipient professional criminal develops an attitude of antagonism to the regulated orderly life that he is required to lead.

This attitude is hardened and crystallized by opposition. The conflict becomes a clash of wills. And experience too often has proved that threats, punishments, beatings, commitments to institutions, abuse and defamation of one sort or another, are of no avail. Punishment breaks down against the child's stubbornness. What has happened is that the child has been defined as an "incorrigible" both by his contacts and by himself, and an attempt at a direct breaking down of will generally fails.

The child meets the situation in the only way he can, by defiance and escape—physical escape if possible, or emotional escape by derision, anger, contempt, hatred, disgust, tantrums, destructiveness, and physical violence. The response of the child is just as intelligent and intelligible as that of the schools, of the authorities. They have taken a simple problem, the lack of fitness of an institution to a particular child's needs, and have made a moral issue out of it with values outside the child's ken. It takes on the form of war between two wills, and the longer the war lasts, the more certainly does the child become incorrigible. The child will not yield because he cannot yield—his nature requires other channels for pleasant growth; the school system or society will not yield because it does not see the issues involved as between the incompatibility of an institution and a child's needs, sometimes physical needs, and will instead attempt to twist the child's nature to the institution with that consequent distortion of the child which makes an unsocial career inevitable. The verbalization of the conflict in terms of evil, delinquency, incorrigibility, badness, arrest, force, punishment, stupidity, lack of intelligence, truancy, criminality, gives the innocent divergence of the child from the straight road a meaning that it did not have in the beginning and makes its continuance in these same terms by so much the more inevitable.

The only important fact, when the issue arises of the boy's inability to acquire the specific habits which organized institutions attempt to impose upon him, is that this conflict becomes the occasion for him to acquire another series of habits, interests, and attitudes as a substitute. These habits become as effective in motivating and guiding conduct as would have been those which the orderly routine social institutions attempted to impose had they been acquired.

This conflict gives the gang its hold, because the gang provides escape, security, pleasure, and peace. The gang also gives room for the motor activity which plays a large role in a child's life. The attempt to break up the gang by force merely strengthens it. The arrest of the children has consequences undreamed-of, for several reasons.

First, only some of the children are caught though all may be equally guilty. There is a great deal more delinquency practiced and committed by the young groups than comes to the attention of the police. The boy arrested, therefore, is singled out in specialized treatment. This boy, no more guilty than the other members of his group, discovers a world of which he knew little. His arrest suddenly precipitates a series of institutions, attitudes, and experiences which the other children do not share. For this boy there suddenly appear the police, the patrol wagon, the police station, the other delinquents and criminals found in the police lock-ups, the court with all its agencies such as bailiffs, clerks, bondsmen, lawyers, probation officers. There are bars, cells, handcuffs, criminals. He is questioned, examined, tested, investigated. His history is gone into, his family is brought into court. Witnesses make their appearance. The boy, no different from the rest of his gang, suddenly becomes the center of a major drama in which all sorts of unexpected characters play important roles. And what is it all about? about the accustomed things his gang has done and has been doing for a long time. In this entirely new world he is made conscious of himself as a different human being than he was before his arrest. He becomes classified as a thief, perhaps, and the entire world about him has suddenly become a different place for him and will remain different for the rest of his life.

THE DRAMATIZATION OF EVIL

The first dramatization of the "evil" which separtes the child out of his group for specialized treatment plays a greater role in making the criminal than perhaps any other experience. It cannot be too often emphasized that for the child the whole situation has become different. He now lives in a different world. He has been tagged. A new and hitherto non-existent environment has been precipitated out for him.

The process of making the criminal, therefore, is a process of tagging, defining, identifying, segregating, describing, emphasizing, making conscious and self-conscious; it becomes a way of stimulating, suggesting, emphasizing, and evoking the very traits that are complained of. If the theory of relation of response to stimulus has any meaning, the entire process of dealing with the young delinquent is mischievous in so far as it identifies him to himself or to the environment as a delinquent person.

The person becomes the thing he is described as being. Nor does it seem to matter whether the valuation is made by those who would punish or by those who would reform. In either case the emphasis is upon the conduct that is disapproved of. The parents or the policeman, the older brother or the court, the probation officer or the juvenile institution, in so far as they rest upon the thing complained of, rest upon a false ground. Their very enthusiasm defeats their aim. The harder they work to reform the evil, the greater the evil grows under their hands. The persistent suggestion, with whatever good intentions, works mischief, because it leads to bringing out the bad behavior that it would suppress. The way out is through a refusal to dramatize the evil. The less said about it the better. The more said about something else, still better.

The hard-drinker who keeps thinking of not drinking is doing what he can to initiate the acts which lead to drinking. He is starting with the stimulus to his habit. To succeed he must find some positive interest or line of action which will inhibit the drinking series and which by instituting another course of action will bring him to his desired end.[11]

The dramatization of the evil therefore tends to precipitate the conflict situation which was first created through some innocent maladjustment. The child's isolation forces him into companionship with other children similarly defined, and the gang becomes his means of escape, his security. The life of the gang gives it special mores, and the attack by the community upon these mores merely overemphasizes the conflict already in existence, and makes it the source of a new series of experiences that lead directly to a criminal career.

In dealing with the delinquent, the criminal, therefore, the important thing to remember is that we are dealing with a human being who is responding normally to the demands, stimuli, approval, expectancy, of the group with whom he is associated. We are dealing not with an individual but with a group.

[11] John Dewey, *Human Nature and Conduct,* p. 35. New York, 1922.

711323